St. Helena Library
1492 Library Lane
St. Helena, CA 94574
(707) 963-5244

A Gift From
ST. HELENA PUBLIC LIBRARY
FRIENDS&FOUNDATION

Alta California

FROM SAN DIEGO TO SAN FRANCISCO,
A JOURNEY ON FOOT TO REDISCOVER
THE GOLDEN STATE

NICK NEELY

COUNTERPOINT
Berkeley, California

Alta California

Portions of this book derive from the original research of Professor Alan K. Brown in his translation of Padre Juan Crespí's diaries, *A Description of Distant Roads: Original Journals of the First Expedition into California, 1769–1770*, published by San Diego State University Press, 2001. We are grateful to SDSU Press for the right to incorporate this research.

Library of Congress Cataloging-in-Publication Data
Names: Neely, Nick, author.
Title: Alta California : from San Diego to San Francisco, a journey on foot to rediscover the Golden State / Nick Neely.
Description: Berkeley, California : Counterpoint, 2019.
Identifiers: LCCN 2019018408 | ISBN 9781640091658
Subjects: LCSH: Neely, Nick—Travels—California. | California—Description and travel. | Portolá's Expedition, Calif., 1769–1770.
Classification: LCC F866.2 .N44 2019 | DDC 917.9404—dc23
LC record available at https://lccn.loc.gov/2019018408

Jacket design by Sarah Brody
Book design by Jordan Koluch
Maps by Colin Webber

COUNTERPOINT
2560 Ninth Street, Suite 318
Berkeley, CA 94710
www.counterpointpress.com

Printed in the United States of America
Distributed by Publishers Group West

10 9 8 7 6 5 4 3 2 1

For California

CONTENTS

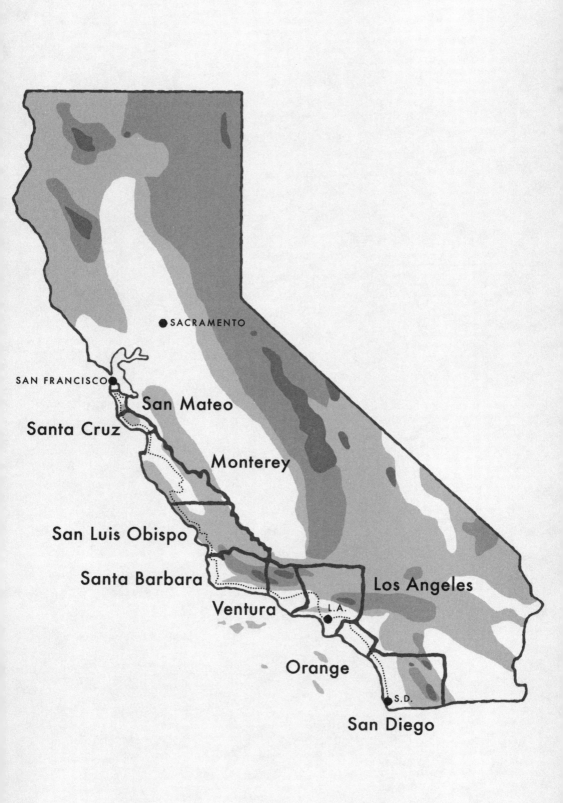

SACRAMENTO

SAN FRANCISCO

San Mateo

Santa Cruz

Monterey

San Luis Obispo

Santa Barbara

Los Angeles

Ventura

L.A.

Orange

S.D.

San Diego

PROLOGUE

AS DARKNESS FELL, I FOUND myself sitting on the bluffs above the Pacific in Gaviota, a community west of Santa Barbara that is more actually a lonely State Park on one of the remotest parts of the California coast. All day I had waited nervously in the campground, sometimes idly cracking walnuts I had gathered—weeks back in Los Angeles, in sight of a nodding pump jack—with granite beach stones on a picnic table, just as a sea otter smashes clams on its belly with a rock. With my grimy fingernails, I teased the antlered nuts from the shells and onto my tongue, usually with a few salty grains of sand. For real fuel, in late afternoon I Jetboiled pasta and squash and poured a can of bland tomato sauce over the steaming tangle. Finally, as dusk approached, I hoisted my pack, which was laden with four liters of water, and scrambled up an eroded slope to the bluff top, where I settled low into the long dry grass like a deer, using my heavy pack as a backrest. The ocean below rolled onto Gaviota Beach, forever, the breakers a drumbeat that fed the rising movement in the sea cave of my chest: I was preparing, in just a few minutes, to walk twenty miles in the dark, without a flashlight, on the Union Pacific railroad tracks. These rails would take me through the exclusive Hollister and Cojo-Jalama Ranches, the vast private holdings that surround Point Conception, where Southern California is said to turn to Northern. I had been denied permission to cross these lands and it was impossible to walk on the beach because of the tides and the rugged point. But I wasn't willing to detour.

This was six weeks, or about halfway, into my journey on foot from San Diego to San Francisco to retrace the first overland Spanish expedition through California. I had already walked through the suburbs of San Diego, inland through Orange County and Los Angeles, then through the sweltering San Fernando Valley and over a high pass to the Santa Clara River Valley, and at last back to the refrigerated coast and its strawberries. I had been stalked by a mountain lion, nearly run over by cars, and escorted out of a neighborhood near Ventura because I wasn't welcome there and was perceived as a threat. I had watched male tarantulas the size of my palm cross an empty road at dusk in search of females, and a colony of endangered terns feed their ruffled fledglings writhing silver baitfish. Most nights I had slept in my two-pound solo tent in the vacant threads of suburbia—dry creek beds are an urban trekker's friend—but tonight I wouldn't sleep. I would walk with the coyotes. The Hollister Ranch, a famous and contentiously off-limits surfing stretch, was scattered with the homes of the rich and famous, and thus private security patrolled its roads.

In 1769, Captain Gaspar de Portolá led a band of Spaniards up this coast. Sometimes called the "Sacred Expedition," from July 14 to November 6, his party of about sixty-three men went north from San Diego on foot and by horse, with over fifty mules shouldering chests of supplies, until finally they crested a low coastal mountain range and saw—"discovered"—an unknown "arm of sea": San Francisco Bay. It was ringed with smoke rising from numerous Ohlone and Miwok villages. In the 1760s, three hundred thousand natives lived in what's now California, sixty thousand of them along the coast. Now the San Francisco Bay alone supports a metropolis of over 7 million. I had grown up there, in a town called Portola Valley. The expedition had traveled south toward my neighborhood, unwittingly plodding above the San Andreas Fault to what today is the heart of Silicon Valley. There the buffcoat soldiers gathered acorns to nourish their famished bodies. By then they were surviving on gifts from the natives or else a single griddle cake of flour a day. We know these details because several members of the expedition kept journals: Portolá (his is quite terse), an engineer named Miguel Costansó, and especially Juan Crespí, the Franciscan friar who was asked to be the expedition's official diarist.

The expedition had set off in search of a fabled harbor described in 1602 as "the best port that could be desired" by the Spanish explorer Sebastián Vizcaíno. A month's voyage north of San Diego, his three ships sailed into a grand bay with a dune shore that made a long curve to the north. It held immense potential, in Vizcaíno's estimation, and he described it glowingly. He named it in honor of his patron, another Gaspar—Gaspar de Zúñiga y Acevedo, the Count of Monte Rey and Viceroy of New Spain—and Monterey Bay became the legend that the Portolá expedition would pursue 167 years later. It was thought that Monterey Bay could resupply Spanish galleons returning to Mexico on the mid-latitude westerlies after trading in the Philippines for fabrics, beeswax, chinaware, silk stockings, and more, though in fact that trade already was waning with the rise of factories in Europe. Simultaneously, it would be an outpost against Russian fur traders trickling down the north coast. But the Portolá expedition was further tasked with scouting sites for possible Catholic missions, which would convert the godless natives and help claim and hold the territory. Portolá was provided with some of the official account from Vizcaíno's voyage, not its entirety, and he didn't have the resulting map, which was kept under lock and key by Spain until the nineteenth century—all of which, along with Vizcaíno's exaggerations, would cause the expedition a massive headache. They would have trouble identifying Monterey Bay and would have to journey back to San Diego, regroup, and then a few months later, in April of 1770, make the trek all over again to finally establish California's second presidio and mission in Monterey. Padre Juan Crespí accompanied Portolá on that return expedition, too, and he lived out the rest of his life in Monterey and Carmel, which became the headquarters of Alta California.

In his journals, Juan Crespí consistently reports on the number of people in the villages they daily encountered, which seemed an anthropological pursuit to me until I remembered he was counting souls. He traveled to New Spain in 1749, twenty years before the march into Alta California, with a small wave of Franciscans from Mallorca. They were led by the zealous padre Junípero Serra, lately canonized by Pope Francis but not without controversy, considering the harsh and abusive means of Serra's colonial miracles. They called each other *condiscípulos* or "fellow students" of the humble teachings of Saint Francis of Assisi and, above all, the word of Christ. "Adios, adios, adios," Crespí wrote, as if to Europe, in a parting letter. A port official jotted down the only known physical description of him as he boarded an armed merchant ship for the Americas: "a middling tall person with black hair and blue eyes, pale-skinned." He was known by his *condiscípulos* as The Blessed or The Mystic, which suggests their fondness for Crespí and their mild irritation with his "dove-like candor," as another padre put it, or a degree of naivete. Apparently Crespí's memory also left something to be desired—he had to read sermons aloud that everyone else knew by heart. But these characteristics would bear the fruit of his California journal: he wrote truly to remember. As the Portolá expedition's official chronicler, it was also his job. He had been specifically charged by the Visitor General of New Spain with recording "the good, the bad, and even the indifferent."

Yet much of the expedition's journey is left to the imagination. Many exciting details are found in Crespí's journals—grizzly bears, earthquakes, and other close encounters—but when I first read them, at times I wanted to reach through the page, grab Crespí softly by his gray wool frock, and beg, "Padre, tell us more." Show us early California. What else could have been written about this coastline, and what still could be written? I began to wonder what it would be like to walk north on Portolá and Crespí's path a quarter millennium later, with the benefit of both fresh eyes and hindsight. This was the path of California.

I had always wanted to undertake a long trek, more specifically to hike the Pacific Crest Trail. Now, if ever, was the time for such a journey. I was thirty-one years old, still fit and fairly unencumbered, but soon, I hoped, I would be on the way to fatherhood and a steady career. In recent years, however, the PCT has become something of a highway: a well-trodden, well-publicized route done at cruising speed; trees and more trees, alpine stretches, clear streams to ford, self-mailed packages to look forward to at remote post offices. It would be fresher and livelier, I realized, to hike an apparition of a trail, a non-trail, one pieced together through both cities and "preserved" spaces, to risk crossing private property, to eat at Burger King *and* cook on an ultralight camp stove, and to walk someone else's itinerary and pace. Coastal California is also home to more species of flora and fauna than any other region of its size in North America, and it hosts more than a quarter of all plants found north of Mexico, not least giant redwoods. Crespí thought they looked like enormous votive candles.

Furthermore, though taking to the woods or desert, to the backcountry, is an elemental and important experience—one that has nurtured me deeply—it is also an escape from our reality and layers of history. In "wilderness areas," signs of former human habitation have been scrubbed to preserve the myth of an untouched, more "authentic" landscape, and this fiction encourages us to overlook and neglect where we actually live. I thought that plodding through our cities and suburbs on a forgotten, but foundational, transect would be the best way to truly see what's become of what we call California, to discover its wild and feral interstices, to immerse myself in the ceaseless detail of landscape, and to confront our past and present head on. Time, I have come to believe, is the one true wilderness.

The Portolá expedition is the seminal moment in California's history. From this long walk, the state that we know and love today—or sometimes love to begrudge—unfolded. The expedition named many of the coast's cities, both official religious names such as Los Angeles, Santa Barbara, and Santa Cruz, and lay monikers dreamt up by the soldiers like Carpinteria, Los Osos, and Gaviota (where they managed to shoot a gull, *una gaviota*). Yet its influence and symbolism is greater. In the expedition's assessment of each valley's agricultural potential is the kernel of the state's vast plantations, of its becoming "the Breadbasket of the World"; and in the coercion of California's natives to work those mission fields a few years later, which arguably was slavery, we can see a parallel to the wildly lopsided power relations that still exist today between growers and immigrant labor. In the expedition's focus on scarce water sources is a glimpse of the state's water controversies and extensive, expensive infrastructure that imports water from the far-off Sierra Nevada Mountains or the Colorado River. The mission lands that the expedition outlined would become the Mexican land-grant ranchos that have either become massive suburban developments such as Irvine and Rancho Mission Viejo in Orange County, or remain vast private holdings like the Hollister and Cojo-Jalama Ranches, which have preserved the coast but kept the public from accessing it. The gold rush ultimately provided the capital that would push California forward exponentially, but that growth and change was overlaid on a Spanish footprint first left by the "Sacred Expedition."

As far as I knew, no one had ever hiked the Portolá expedition's route before, though it forever changed and shaped this place I and at least 39 million others call home. So I decided to buy a one-way plane ticket to San Diego, for July 14, the day Portolá and Crespí took their first steps toward Monterey. I would walk to San Francisco on their trail, a distance of about 650 miles. My plan was to follow the expedition's path as faithfully as possible, walking at their pace, camping where they had pitched their tents, referencing the journals day by day. We can't always know the precise line the Spaniards walked, but based on their journals, historians have pinned their camps to certain towns, intersections in cities, canyons, or bodies of water where the men and the mules could drink. I would study these descriptions and try to amble the most intuitive route from point to point.

The expedition took three days to walk the stretch beyond Gaviota and make the turn north at Point Conception, but I would cover the territory in one night. Off the point, the currents swirl immoderately. Great white sharks ply the seal waters. Innumerable boats have foundered here. North of Conception, swells race unimpeded across the Pacific driven by prevailing northwest winds, and the fog begins to pile up and consume the hills. There are no Channel Islands to protect the shore or collect castaways. North of Conception, the Chumash didn't set out to sea in their canoes of redwood planks—too rough. In their language, the point was called *Humqaq*, or "the raven comes," that black solitary bird with water in its croaking voice. The Chumash believe that Raven arrives to give the dead their "celestial eyes" in exchange for their earthly ones, which they no longer need. The people near *Humqaq* were said to see these souls drift out over the point's headland. The villagers would cry out and clap their hands, ask their friends and lovers to reconsider, to remain, and those souls might heed their call, circle around, stay a while. Others weren't swayed. They were bound for *Similaqsa*, the afterlife over the ocean. It's said that, as they sped off, these souls shone brightly—like the pulse of today's lighthouse, I imagine—and in the distance there was another clapping, a sound that has been described as that of a gate swinging shut.

Biding my time on the bluffs above Gaviota, I exhaled deeply to calm myself. Gusts swept the water as if someone invisible, with an enormous lung capacity, were blowing again and again into cold broth for no reason. Wavering spots blossomed and died between the kelp slicks. I popped the tab on one of the two Monster energy drinks I had bought at the tiny, expensive beach store below and sipped the fizz as the sky began to fall through its colors. The water settled from deep purple to blue-gray. The taurine began to course through my bloodstream. I looked back at the trestle, the high railroad bridge at the mouth of Gaviota Canyon, knowing that I would have to cross at least two of them in the dark. This one over the beach was dubbed the "Ghost Bridge," and I had been told how some unfortunate souls who had ventured out on it to photograph the sunset had been forced to jump to their deaths as a train came on and trapped them. The night before and all during the day, I had noted the trains as they crossed to see if I could discern any pattern. The Amtrak commuter ran every other hour through the day, but the freights were unpredictable. Now I tried to avoid looking at my watch; the light would tell me when it was time. I would step onto the ties and ballast only when no one could see my edges. I pictured the orange-eyed great horned owl I had watched through my binoculars along these tracks the night before. An owl's feathers are frayed so that it makes no sound in flight.

Alta California

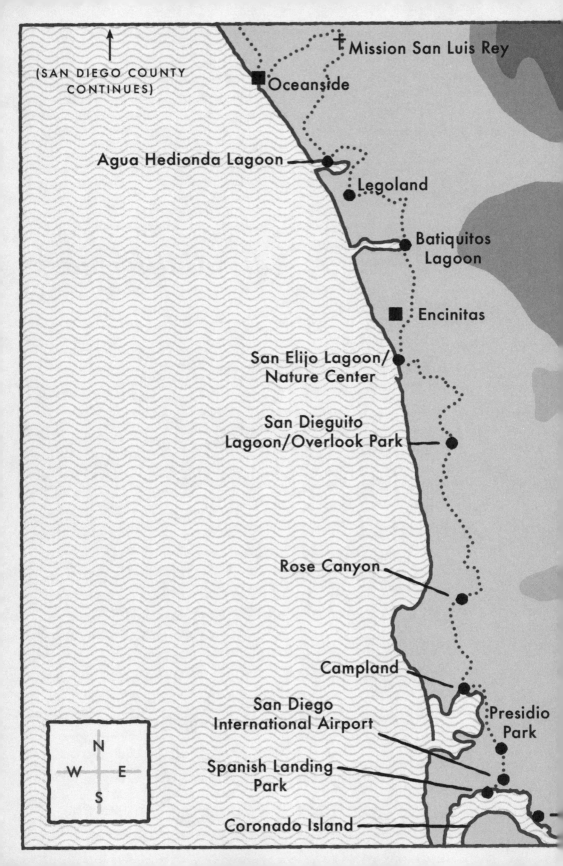

† Mission San Luis Rey

■ Oceanside

(SAN DIEGO COUNTY CONTINUES)

Agua Hedionda Lagoon

Legoland

Batiquitos Lagoon

■ Encinitas

San Elijo Lagoon/ Nature Center

San Dieguito Lagoon/Overlook Park

Rose Canyon

Campland

Presidio Park

San Diego International Airport

Spanish Landing Park

Coronado Island

N
W E
S

San Diego County

✝ Mission San Diego

——— Downtown San Diego

AS MY PLANE BANKED ABOVE the bouldered, cactaceous hills and over untold beige houses and their turquoise pools, each the locus of so many good, anonymous lives, and so many splashing wars, I wondered what I had done. San Diego, from this height, was vast and intimidating, the eighth-largest city in America, and it was only one day's walk of my intended journey. I would be lost among so many streets and people. I had no idea, really, where I was going, and knew next to nothing about Southern California. I'd visited Los Angeles a few times as a kid, and more recently La Jolla near San Diego. That was all. Looking out the oval window on the way south, the state, covered at a mile every seven seconds—not quite the speed of thunder—seemed interminable and awful dry. Then, past downtown's skyscrapers, the ground rose beneath us and shook us like an earthquake of our own making, and with the view gone, everything seemed better, more possible, as the plane rolled up to its wavy distortion in the terminal's tinted plate glass.

I hoisted my pack from the carousel and slipped it over my shoulders, pinning them back. It must have weighed about thirty-five pounds, filled with my belong-ings and supplies for a twelve-week walk. The Portolá expedition left San Diego with three and a half tons of flour, with dried legumes (lentils, beans, chickpeas), two crates of loaf sugar, cheeses, lard, cloves, cinnamon, chili peppers, garlic, a barrel of brandy for the officers and eventually the sick, and a chest of chocolate for a bitter morning drink. Their mules carried all of this. But aside from a leftover burrito from my layover in Salt Lake and a few bags of tea, I hadn't packed any food at all, thinking I could just buy it on my way to save weight. I had my Safeway Club Card in my wallet. I had two T-shirts and one long-sleeve to keep off the sun, a pair of nylon shorts, three pairs of underwear, lightweight camping gear, a recorder, a two-pound laptop, and a host of odds and ends that would quickly feel too heavy: The tail end of a duct tape roll, squished flat. Iodine tablets to purify water. Opera-glass-size binoculars. Several small notebooks. A headlamp. I'd bought a brand-new pair of size thirteen Asics running shoes, which I've always preferred to hike in because they are so light. They'd arrived in Idaho the day before.

Probably I hadn't taken my preparations seriously enough. I'm generally athletic and a former collegiate distance runner, and prior to the trip, my main concern was the minor fracture I'd suffered in my ankle in April when I was struck by a two-pound iron horseshoe. But that seemed to heal up, mostly, and I had heard that you quickly walk yourself into shape on a long trek. I'd ordered an REI army-green backpack, one less conspicuous than my old, heavier scarlet pack, because I wanted to be fairly discreet, if that's possible for someone who is six foot four. For that reason, I had also ordered a lightweight solo tent with a gray rain fly so that I could pose as a rock if I camped on the beach rather than look like an orange buoy washed up. At the last minute I had remembered that my camping stove was defective—the gas leaked and flared around the burner—so I left it at home. I could buy precooked food initially and pick up a stove down the line.

As if to locate the sun, and so myself, outside the terminal I stared up at the rustling palm fronds and the parking garage. Overcast, but balmy. Setting out from a trailhead, there's always a gentle and refreshing surge of adrenaline, and it was no different now. The reverberations of helicopters cruising the shoreline filled the air and my body, and it may be this sound, more than any other, that tells of San Diego, which from the start of colonization was a safe harbor and, soon after, a fort on a hill. The area boasts the largest concentration of defense assets in the world. *Semper Vigilans* is the city's motto. I typed "Spanish Landing Park" into the phone that, rather than armored men on horses, would serve as my scout for twelve weeks. Spinning, spinning, it finally replied, "No known route to this destination." An inauspicious answer. For a moment, I wondered if it was possible that one might not be able to walk out of an airport's concrete curlicues. I should have considered that. But I studied my handheld, backlit map and ventured past the Pet Relief Area and Terminal 2 Parking Lot, with solar panel arrays lofted over and shading the cars (TAKE TICKET WITH YOU FOR EXPRESS EXIT), until I found an access road that turned toward the bay. *Wait, wait, wait,* insisted the traffic sign speaker at North Harbor Drive, in a voice I would come to know well. *Walk, walk, walk.*

SAN DIEGO BAY IS A natural estuary formed by the hilly peninsula of Point Loma to the north and, to the south, a slender, seven-mile-long tombolo—a bar of sand joining an island to a mainland, from the Italian for "sand dune"—known as the Silver Strand, which includes the famous resort of Coronado. These points reach toward each other but, like the fingers of God and Adam on the ceiling of the Sistine Chapel, don't quite touch, allowing passage into the harbor. This is the modest portal that opened to modern California.

In 1542, Spaniard Juan Rodríguez Cabrillo was the first European to enter this harbor in what was probably a two-hundred-ton galleon built on the coast of today's Guatemala. On a voyage to trace the unknown shore and find the Straits of Anian, as the alleged Northwest Passage was known, for six days Cabrillo's ships waited out a rainstorm in a harbor that he named San Miguel. As the oldest history of the voyage asserts, "the port was so good they felt nothing." San Diego received its current name sixty years later, in 1602, when Sebastian Vizcaíno and several other entrepreneur-explorers led the next Spanish reconnaissance up the coast. After more than six months in the prevailing winds and currents, their trio of ships anchored in the same bay. Not realizing that Cabrillo had named it already, they, too, gave it a name in accordance with the Calendar of Saints. It was the feast day of San Didacus of Alcalá, or San Diego, which also happened to be the name of Vizcaíno's flagship. San Diego's major holy work was caring for his fellow Franciscan friars after an epidemic swept Rome during a canonization that attracted thousands of pilgrims, and so disease.

The Portolá expedition was the third to arrive in San Diego, 167 years after Vizcaíno. Portolá had arrived in New Spain in 1764, already thirty years into his military career, and he had been tasked with ousting the Jesuit missionaries from Baja California, thus creating the void that the Franciscans filled before they and Portolá were jointly ordered to probe and expand into Alta California. The expedition's staging grounds were in Velicatá, Baja, just north of the final mission established by Jesuits. From there they departed in two overland groups, consisting of soldiers, muleteers, and Christian natives called *neophytos*, or literally "new plants," the newly converted. After a fifty-two-day trek, the first section, led by Captain Rivera y Moncada, reached the harbor on May 14, 1769. Juan Crespí was among their number. They were greeted by a band of Kumeyaay, soon labeled the Diegueño, of which there might have been six to nine thousand in a region that extended south into Baja and inland to the mountains where they gathered acorns. "Almost all of them of all sexes [are] very much painted in red, white, and black," wrote Crespí, "the men having on large feather headdresses and having their usual good-sized quivers upon their shoulders and bow and arrows in their hands. All of them are very sharp Indians, great bargainers . . . The heathens here would bring mussels but would not part with a single one unless given the item they wished or had taken a liking to."

Crespí and the other men spied, at the bay's north end, two ships that had sailed from La Paz and Cabo San Lucas to meet them, totems of civilization and arrival after so many days of marching through Baja's scrub. "I cannot tell the happiness and joy we all felt upon seeing the hour arrive of our reaching our so long wished-for San Diego Harbor, with His Majesty's two packet boats the *San Carlos* and the *Principe* [the *San Antonio*] lying there." Rivera's men discharged a salvo, white smoke circling upward from their barrels.

They heard a reply at once, but the celebration was short-lived. "Our joy at reaching San Diego was somewhat dashed by finding the entire camp turned into a hospital," Crespí wrote, "with nearly all of the Volunteer soldiers and the sailors . . . perishing from the scurvy, or Luanda disease." Portolá and Serra brought up the rear, following in the footsteps of the first land contingent, and on July 1 finally reached San Diego, where they likewise were confronted with the dismal luck of the ships and their men. Though the *San Carlos* had left more than a month before the *San Antonio*, it had limped into the San Diego Harbor two weeks later than its sister ship after 110 days at sea, having sailed much too far up the coast. Upon arrival, only four of its men had the strength to haul the ropes and manage the ship—the rest lay incapacitated. The Spaniards didn't know the cause of scurvy, or its cure. It's also possible the Spaniards were suffering from having to drink brackish water out of desperation. Ultimately thirty-four sailors would die, some of them after Portolá had continued on toward Monterey. Junípero Serra and another padre would dig "with their own hands" the trenches to receive them.

A stone's throw from the airport, Spanish Landing Park commemorates the reunion, such as it was, of the Portolá expedition's initial overland and oceanic legs. It lies behind Harbor Island, which would have confused Portolá and Crespí because the island didn't exist until 1961, when sand from the bay's floor was dredged and mounded into a hotdog shape for hotels and marinas. *El Desembarcadero*, the old channel of the San Diego River where the Spanish sailors first came ashore, is actually about a mile away, now landlocked and buried under nine feet of rubble and concrete beside an Explorer Elementary School. To the southeast, downtown San Diego rises through the masts of hundreds of white sailboats with dinghies at their margins.

When I arrived at the shore's deckled edge, a girl was endeavoring to push her dog down a plastic slide, but the good-humored dog, with clear blue eyes, resisted with splayed legs. In the shallows, a father cradled his daughter in his muscular arms while his son, wearing floaties, bobbed nearby. Three men shouldered their pontoon fishing floats down the man-made beach, slid on flippers, and kicked away, backward, as they let their translucent lines sail free. "What are you fishing for?" I called out. "For halibut," one shouted. I imagined those bottom-dwellers, with their eyes on the tops of their heads, among the encrusted tires, beer cans, and buried Spanish artifacts. I tried to imagine the 1769 expedition's two ships floating in front of me with their high masts and rolled sails, their mizzens and unicorn jibbooms, the men rowing to shore in their *chalupas* for barrels of fresh water. Their oars dripping, gleaming. Their noisome body odor after months at sea. They would have seemed surreal to the natives, the Kumeyaay, who likely had inherited stories about Cabrillo and Vizcaíno but never laid eyes on a European, not this generation.

Just then a man in a blue tank top sauntered up with a boa constrictor wrapped around his arm like a tuba, and I followed him into the public restroom—cinderblock, but painted an adobe color and with a terra-cotta roof, to befit a Spanish Landing. "That's a big snake you've got," I said, washing my hands. "That's not something you hear too often in a bathroom," he replied. Back outside, I got a better look at them. His name was Jeff. She was a Colombian red tail, sixty-seven pounds, far heavier than my backpack. "She's a tank," said Jeff. "She's my baby." He was burnt strawberry and heavily inked. The snake's diamond pattern blended with his sleeve tattoo, and a topless woman graced his bulging calf. A boy, about ten or twelve, joined us to stare at Medusa. "She'll turn you into stone if you look at her too long," Jeff advised him. "She's got that hypnotism thing." She bobbed her sagittate head, sensing the San Diego heat through her pit nostrils, triangulating the distances, and I wondered if I was now like this snake in some ways, searching with limited powers of vision for some sign or scent of authentic California. Or maybe I was the one who would end up frozen in his tracks on this long journey as the result of too much staring. Dark stripes ran through her pale eyes. "How long does it freeze you for?" asked the kid. "Oh, about a week," said Jeff. "You get to miss school."

SEVERAL MILES INLAND, I WALKED through touristy Old Town, which had replaced a Kumeyaay village called Cosoy, crossing Plaza de Las Armas under its weeping pepper trees. Past a golf course with islands of green in ocher fairways, I found a foot trail that led up Presidio Hill through jumbles of prickly pear and messy eucalyptus. Cottontails skipped across the path. The expedition soon moved camp below this hill to be closer to fresh water, and two days after Crespí and Portolá launched from San Diego toward Monterey, Serra established Mission San Diego de Alcalá, "the Mother of the Missions," on this knoll with a simple Mass given to the seven able-bodied Spanish that remained. The sun was lowering, then blinding, as I climbed the steps of the Junípero Serra Museum, which, with its bell tower and clay tile roof, poses as a mission building and so fools many visitors, ushering us further back in time than 1929 when it was actually built. No visible traces of the fort or mission remain in Presidio Park.

For the first few years, the mission was merely a collection of huts. Inside its brushy chapel, Serra carefully situated devotional objects—the chalice, monstrance, and gold-leaf paintings—that he had gleaned from the Baja missions, hoping they would inspire curiosity and reverence in the Kumeyaay. They did not have that effect. A month after the Portolá expedition departed, twenty or more Kumeyaay waited until several soldiers returned to the ship and then attacked the mission, setting fire to the huts and pulling the bedclothes out from under the scurvy-ridden soldiers, cloth being as novel and valuable as any other treasure. No doubt they decided they had to take a stand against these bearded strangers, who seemed poised to stay, uninvited. Junípero Serra and another padre, Father Vizcaíno (no relation to the explorer), retreated to a hut, and when they raised its curtain to peek outside, Vizcaíno's hand was shot through. Serra's young neophyte servant from Baja tumbled through the curtain with an arrow through his throat, leaving Serra in a muddy "sea of blood," as he later recalled. The four able-bodied soldiers on hand finally rebuffed the attack with their guns, and the Spaniards suffered no losses beyond the boy. The Kumeyaay spared the ill when they could have easily slain them. At least three Kumeyaay were killed and more were wounded. The Spaniards heard the wailing in Cosoy below the hill. Days later, the Kumeyaay asked for peace and a visit from the Spanish surgeon.

The mission, as you might imagine, baptized no one in its first year. Instead, a stockade was built, and tandem brass cannons were installed, though they did little more than boom and blow smoke, impressive enough. Five years later, Serra relocated the mission six miles up the San Diego River for more arable acreage, as well as to gain distance from the ruffian Spanish soldiers, a separation he believed necessary to win over and "yoke" the wary Kumeyaay. Presidio Hill eventually was abandoned to cattle until, in 1907, a businessman bought the scrubland, turned it into a park, and donated it to the city.

Too late to visit the museum, I ambled uphill through pines. A Frisbee floated across a sloped lawn of clover and dandelion. Two men in shorts, their hair so trim they might have been navy, were tangled on a picnic blanket, cocooned in a personal evening. Orange light glanced off their bare legs as the earth spun the sun into the fog that looked like a tidal wave arrested over the ocean beyond Mission Bay. A sharp-shinned hawk called in a pine's armature of shadows. I stopped to gaze at a tall brick cross, slightly menacing, where it's said an original wooden cross had been raised by Serra in 1769. Then, still four or five miles from my destination for the day, I cut downhill toward the whispering highway, past a crowd of homeless or hurting people gathered for a steaming dinner on paper plates, with their bikes and worldly belongings, their milk crates and sun-faded sleeping bags, askew in the grass.

"WE SET OUT AT ABOUT four o'clock in the afternoon from here at San Diego harbor," wrote Crespí on this day, July 14, 248 years ago, "course north-northwestward, over level quite grass-grown land, close by some inlets where there are salines having very good white salt in them, beyond which we started along the shore of the second harbor here in San Diego." He had rested for two months in San Diego, Portolá for only two weeks. The expedition, some sixty-three men, departed with most of the still-healthy soldiers and muleteers in San Diego. Besides Captain Portolá, whom Crespí refers to as "Governor" since he was in charge, three other officers comprised the leadership: Sergeant Ortega, the expedition's chief scout; Lieutenant Fages, who led a band of Catalonian volunteer soldiers; and Captain Rivera y Moncada, second-in-command but the expedition's tactical leader, since he previously had commanded Baja's buffcoat soldiers and had the best knowledge of Las Californias. Other key members of the expedition included a second padre, Francisco Gómez, and the expedition's cosmographer, Miguel Costansó, a twenty-eight-year-old engineer born in Barcelona who kept a shadow journal to Crespí's, briefer but in respects more revealing and emotional.

Already falling behind the expedition, as dusk neared I, too, set out from Presidio Hill and glided over the San Diego River, staring down from an overpass at its thickets of willow, its dead and green escaped palm, its shrubby banks inscribed with human trails. The river was mauve, gunmetal, and as wide as Morena Boulevard, my route north. Once the river had flowed over a braided, woodsy delta with an outlet that, over time, oscillated between the San Diego Harbor and the "second bay" Crespí describes, Mission Bay, but now it is divorced from both and runs straight and narrow to the sea guided by levees. Eyeing the river's remaining bottomland, I wondered how many people would sleep below those tattered palms tonight; and I wondered if I would have been brave enough to pitch my tent there if, considering my late arrival—which didn't leave much time to scout a spot—I hadn't made a reservation at a campground on Mission Bay's north side.

The sky darkened as I walked Morena along I-5. The illuminated signs grew insistent: SANTANA'S MEXICAN FOOD ... ES MUY BUENO; CANINETOFIVE; THE HIGH DIVE ... GRILL BY THE BAY. Passing the Coronado Brewing Co. Tasting Room, I decided to duck inside. My hips and shoulders ached, my skin below my straps was chafing. My trip seemed like potential madness. The warehouse was warm and hoppy, with stainless silos, tanks, and fermenting voices. Dropping my heavy pack against the hardwood bar, I asked for a taster of guava IPA. A Rottweiler named Daisy sidled up with her master, and she slobbered me something fierce when I reached down to unzip my pack. I had to locate a napkin to wipe the foam from my hand. Grossly overweight, she had a mottled tongue that suggested, her owner told me, that she wasn't purebred. "She responds to 'Nazi,'" he said. "No, really—that was her name. She was wandering the streets of Riverside, where all the white supremacists and other trash live. It's even on the chip implanted in her.

The rescue society called her owner and he came down to get her. But when he was asked to pay for her to be spayed, he walked. Left her. She was going to be killed."

Something like melancholy filled me, but wonder is the antidote, and movement is the path to it. As I stepped back into the warm night, a spray of pink and lime-green fireworks erupted over the highway and Mission Bay, which was known earlier as *Puerto Falso*, because when Cabrillo entered the San Diego Harbor in 1542, some of his men went ashore, glimpsed this other large estuary, and panicked, thinking their ships had sailed without them. They were only disoriented, fooled by this "false" bay. I imagined boaters under these showers of sparks. Miles to go still, and I felt, on the one hand, a sense of helplessness and foreboding, as if every day I might struggle to cover the ground I'd planned to walk. Not only because it was far, but because odds were I would be prone to distraction, chasing or waiting for some drifting ember.

But the night was reassuring, too, and soothing: the mind quieter, even if cars seemed louder, the sounds traveling low and crisp through the cooling air. Not less to absorb, only an emphasis on the other senses. On the breeze teasing my arm hair, on Mission Bay's organic musk. Clearing I-5, I came to the bay's light-wriggled margin. Campfires kindled on far beaches, back toward SeaWorld and its illuminated Skytower. Rounding a cove, I slipped between the *tsst tsst tsst* of sprinklers nurturing the park's lawns and more blazing firepits in the sand, where one family had piled wooden pallets to feed the flames. The towhead hair of the children glowed like marshmallows.

Just before ten, I strode up to Campland on the Bay on its promenade of sapphire-lit trees. The gate attendant looked me up and down as he slid back his window. "I have a reservation," I said. "For a primitive site." "Oh," he replied. "I was going to say, 'You have a reservation? Where's your car?'" Probably no one had ever walked into Campland. Here camping mainly meant RVs and their ideal, air-conditioned suspension. Spot number one of the small Primitive Section was next to the skate park, and I slumped at my picnic table, fairly stupefied with weariness and dehydration. "Primitive" was a poor description: any natural campsite would have flowing water. These didn't. But I was just down the way from the fluorescent restrooms, where women were blow-drying their hair. Kids were biking the campground's loops with glow sticks woven through their spokes, while their parents laughed and drank from Solo cups beneath the party-light awnings of their RVs with names like Diplomat, like Cougar and Sundance, like Next Level, Imagine, Seneca, and Weekend Warrior.

For the first of so many times, I pitched my tent in the hard dirt, searching with my headlamp for a rock to drive in its stakes. A few other holdout car campers were set up in this lone row of faucetless sites, but next to their monstrous nylon tents, my slender, two-pound REI solo dome looked lost. I inhaled the second half of my burrito from the Salt Lake airport, shuffled to the bathhouse, and crawled inside my new home to lie on my aching bones and try to fathom tomorrow: I was already running behind Portolá, and I had planned a big second day of about sixteen miles to catch up, one that would take me around La Jolla to the marshes of Del Mar. But for a while I lay listening: to voices down the line, the clink and slosh of dish-washing, zippers galore, trailer latches, snoring. The reality of most campgrounds is that you are far from roughing it and far from alone. Little privacy, and no silence except in the early morning. But there is a sense of community vibrating in the air like one of those RV generators, in part through mutual, mild irritation, as well as a comfort in knowing a space has been reserved in your name, even if it's just a glorified parking space. You belong, temporarily. You have a picnic table.

Before giving up for the night, in my pack I found a hidden baggie of small mashed strawberries from our yard, with a note, stained red, from my wife: "I love you bigger than the state of California. Good luck, Sweets. So proud of you. XOXO, S (+ P)." My cattle dog–collie, Patches. I stared at this slip of wet paper with my headlamp for some time, ate the fruit slurry, and then tucked the note into my pocket guide to the plants of Southern California.

ON THEIR FIRST DAY, THE Portolá expedition filed past Mission Bay and "into a hollow between hills, where there are a good many willows and some sycamores and live oaks." This hollow is hollow no more, for it carries I-5 north: two hundred thousand cars every twenty-four hours. Rose Canyon got its name not because it was a wild rosery, though it was—Crespí fondly called the blooms "Rose of Castile"—but because later a Mr. Rose owned a ranch that included the corridor. There's a Rose Canyon Fault, still active, right under the highway. A Kumeyaay origin story tells of the world's two first men, one blind, who walked out of the sea to create animals and then society. But the blind man was swallowed whole by a crevasse. Now the earth trembles when he stirs, and if he were to roll over in his bed quickly, the ground would ripple and buckle, roads would crack and palms would sway wildly. The Rose Canyon Fault isn't as famous as the San Andreas, but it threatens a six- or seven-point temblor on the Richter scale, enough to seriously unsettle San Diego. It could slip tomorrow or in two hundred years.

At the rear of Rose Canyon Business Park—after wondering if there really was a way forward, as my phone suggested—I found a dirt trail, easier on the feet, behind a spur of chain-link that paralleled the train tracks through the woodland Crespí describes. The canyon's steep, sere hillsides looked gauzy, from a distance, with chaparral. A knot of highway interchange was overhead where San Clemente Canyon joined Rose Canyon, and below was a trickle of algal water, Rose Creek, in a concrete flood channel washed with colorful graffiti: WE COULD BE HEROES, JUST FOR ONE DAY / LUCID / WAKE UP / GET $ / SCUMBAG / SOIL. Crespí, in his journal, fixates on soil from the start, for this was the key to their agricultural vision, to the conversion of this supposedly untouched landscape into a garden, and Rose Canyon had "very good grass upon all sides . . . and very good, even though not very wide, level soil." They followed it as it curved east through an open forest of sycamore, one of California's most graceful trees.

Sycamores, which the Spaniards called *aliso*, have a bark like cracked stucco, a puzzle of buffs, creams, and mints. In the Old World, they're called "plane trees," from the Greek *platos*, "wide," because of their broad palmate leaves, which in Rose Canyon fell casually over the grass like dry, wrinkled hands eager to clasp the ground. They add up to a copious litter, drifts loud to wade through. Birds love their hanging fruits, those hairy pompoms. This whole canyon would have been filled with sycamores, but most were cut for fuel or lumber. Most I would pass in Rose Canyon were secondary growth, maybe forty or fifty years old. Under their canopies the air was cooler, a palpable microclimate, as if the trees were generating their own breeze. A sycamore is a phreatophyte, or "well plant," with deep roots to tap into what little water there is far below.

EASY TO FORGET YOU ARE in a city. Easy to forget that our cities are laced with hidden canyons, those too difficult to build, where you can hike or run awhile out of time among vanished species and people, as well as newcomers, colonists like ice plant, starlings, joggers, and trekkers. After the quiet of Rose Canyon, the cars ascending the mesa seemed like loud animals on migration. Suddenly, I felt the ocean's influence again. I stopped for lunch at Subway and wove through UC San Diego, past dorms and research centers and a hospital, sipping a Jamba Juice. Over these "grass grown tablelands," I walked, where the Spanish had seen numerous hares and pronghorn antelope that could have outrun a Pleistocene cheetah, and then into the Sorrento Valley, which had appeared so lush to Crespí that it "seemed nothing other than a field of corn"—nothing other than the California Dream. They encountered a Kumeyaay village here called Yatsuga and gave its residents a standard offering, or mollifier, of glass beads; some poor mule was carrying a chest of them, along with other "ribbons and trifles."

Traveling I-5 from San Diego to its northernmost suburb, Oceanside, you roar directly over six striking "lagoons," impossible to miss. They're not actually lagoons, but emerald or frittered marsh, some with snaking mud channels, a few with large tidal ponds. In 1769, Portolá's men and their exotic ungulates were forced to trail behind these marshes. The beach would have been a slog and, based on their journals, they took to the sand only a few times. They would have needed a barge to float their stock across the shoreline channels, but the only boats around were the Kumeyaay's slender canoes of bound tule reed. Instead they plodded behind these estuaries, a mile or two from the ocean: a trail that near San Diego is essentially El Camino Real, which ultimately linked California's twenty-one missions. Back of the marshes was the best route for over a century until, in 1881 and 1882, the California Southern Railroad line was constructed between San Diego and Oceanside. Between 1912 and 1915, the Pacific Coast Highway was unrolled, two lanes of miraculous asphalt between the rails and the beach. Finally, in 1965, I-5 was laid down inland of the tracks, another river of commerce right through these marshes. In these lagoons, you can see the history of transportation in California, or in America for that matter, slightly delayed.

As I walked through Los Peñasquitos Lagoon, the southernmost, on a bike path—really an abandoned road, Old El Camino, a glorious retirement—the tule reed shimmied and glinted. The Spaniards had found two clay jugs by a spring in this valley to quench their thirst. Now a marsh wren chattered out of the brake, the coastal sun filtering bronze through its active wings. I imagined its domed nest with one porthole, which they tie to a reed so that, in the inevitability of a severe tide, the woven home slides up the stem, high and fairly dry like a bead on a string. To the west, the silhouette of the seven o'clock Surfliner—Amtrak's commuter train to and from Santa Barbara—cut the view in two. In the distance was Torrey Pines State Natural Reserve, a ridge that holds those endemic salt-pruned trees so iconic of the San Diego coast and its golf.

Running out of sun, I kept on past Peñasquitos like the Spaniards, climbing El Camino to Del Mar Heights. My late-day feet appreciated the wide "grass grown" strip along the sidewalk, though this coarse, spongy Bahia lawn slowed me a step and was certainly a waste of water. There must be an ideal consistency or species of sod for the urban orienteer—not too thatched, not too baked—and already I was becoming a connoisseur. Already I was cutting every corner I could, including through the gas stations I wasn't otherwise using. Down El Camino, another sloughy expanse was revealed, "much better than the last one" wrote Crespí, where the expedition camped beside a pool that might have reflected swooping bats until the mules splashed in. But I felt I had to keep to the ridge. The highlands around the San Dieguito Lagoon were studded with houses, and their residents might see me wade into the marsh. There's safety in heights, in presidios on hills.

At last light, day disintegrating, I veered off El Camino into Overlook Park. Beyond a board fence, lights flicked on inside the houses. To the west, I-5 intensified to a candy-cane stream, and the spotlights from the Del Mar Fairgrounds circled the low marine layer. It was opening day of Race Week at this famous thoroughbred track. But it felt as if those spotlights were also for me. I had completed my first full day, about sixteen miles. Or were those spotlights searching for me as I prepared to bed down illegally? I was nervous about poaching a campsite in suburbia's interstices. Would anyone wander through this park during the night?

Too cautious to even set up my tent, I spread out my ground cloth, pad, and bag under one of the few pines, on needles that crunched and reluctantly settled beneath me. When I began to slide down my inflatable pad, I picked up everything in a bear hug and moved to another nearby tree with level ground, a good lesson. My legs and arms were sticky with sweat and dust. My boxers were faintly damp, but I'd told myself I'd change them only every three days. I lay twitching from fatigue, half under my sleeping bag, which was too warm. The pine branches drooped like the skeleton of a tent and through them a few stars shone. I rationed my remaining water, sipping: so many faucets nearby, carrying water from a municipal spring, but none available to me. El Camino's streetlights were shaped like mission bells, quite intentionally, and their cones of incandescence marched up the incline. All night, cars accelerated out of the lagoon and into my restless eardrums.

PRICKLY PEAR STAINED MY HANDS rosy in the morning. Several ripe tunas presented themselves, purple, not far from my sleeping bag, so I halved one with my Swiss Army knife, which held traces of gritty peanut butter from the last time I'd unfolded it camping, and scooped out the scarlet flesh with a plastic spoon I'd gleaned from the Salt Lake airport. The fruit was as blood-filled as raw tuna from the ocean. The taste is tart and milky, the seeds round and gelatinous as roe. The spines are more like short hairs whorled on tiny jutting chins, and they embedded in my skin and irritated my fingers for hours as I walked.

Around me in Overlook Park was a quintessential stand of chaparral, coastal California's predominant, drought-resistant biome, one that most people walk right past without noticing. The word "chaparral" comes from the Spanish *chapparo*, the name for a dwarf evergreen oak, and more generally a word that means "short in stature"; and indeed, I ran my fingers lightly over a waist-height scrub oak laden with the smallest acorns I'd ever seen, their tips as sharp as fresh pencils. There was manzanita, too, "tiny apple," winding sculpturally with papery, auburn skin and succulent paddle leaves. And there was a gray-barked shrub—its leaves waxy like most chaparral species to slow transpiration in the aggressive sun—that I identified as lemonade bush: conspicuous red berries, pubescent and gooey and shaped like Corn Nuts. They can be cold-steeped for a sour tannic tea, and I thought about dropping a few in a Powerade bottle—I'd adopted these for canteens because they're light, narrow-necked (better for drinking mid-stride), recyclable, and come with a sugary drink, all for a dollar—but I had no water and needed to hurry on.

I followed a trail down an eroded sand- and mudstone gully until I came to a jeep trail through the flatland beside the San Dieguito Lagoon. In the distance, a roadrunner with a hackled crest paused and then skillfully careened into the grass and sagebrush. A roadrunner, or "chaparral bird" as they're also known, is nothing like those loony cartoons. It is a warrior bird that has retained a dinosaur spirit. It will hide among flowers to snatch a hummingbird out of the air. According to the Kumeyaay, the roadrunner was struck on the cheek with a stick by a supernatural being, leaving its gash-red facial stripe. I had not expected to see one so close to the sea.

THE DEL MAR HORSE PARK was overrun with girls in uniform khaki-colored jodhpurs and tall black boots that would have worked in New York City. Saturday, show day, and clubs from all over the county had arrived to compete on the eucalyptus-lined greens. In front of the warm-up arena was a row of "set up" tents with pennant fringes, each with a club's insignia and primly furnished as if via Pottery Barn: drapery, orchids below dressing mirrors, plush wicker furniture, and coffee tables laden with snacks, including a tub of Mrs. Pastures Cookies for Horses. Over the couches hung ribbons for first to seventh place (blue, red, yellow, white, pink, green, and brown). This is what riding had become two and a half centuries after the Portolá party, all men, rode through on the first horses California had seen since the Pleistocene miniatures. Now Mexican stablemen were grooming and saddling, readying the horses for white matrons and their teenage daughters.

A mile down El Camino, in search of water and coffee, I had stumbled on this horse park and its restroom and cafe. After a breakfast burrito, I dropped my pack in the shade, leaned against the railing, and studied the jumping. Occasionally a buzzer and loudspeaker summoned riders to competition. Such a strange world to me, one with its own language. This class of competition was "hunter." "What's 'hunter'?" I asked a group of loitering young equestrians, a few girls and a boy. They must have wondered just who they were dealing with, but patiently explained that it was a vestige of a time when English gentry really did pursue game with their hounds over the brooks and fallen timber of their estates. Now only the form and manner of the horse matters: how fluid its motion, how rhythmic and regular its stride (twelve-foot is ideal). A show hunter should be ridden "deep into the corners" so it doesn't break gait. Vaulting a fence, a mare should arch like a fountain with a perfect roundness or bascule—a French word for "seesaw." In flight, her forearms should rise level and parallel, her fetlocks and hooves should tuck lightly under her chest. Takeoff should be from a distance of six feet. All these rules in pursuit of a theoretical fox.

The horse park was an incongruous sight. Southern California is awash with Spanish/Mexican culture, the idea of it at least, and yet here was this conspicuous eddy of English pageantry amid the Mission-style architecture. What an interesting scene this would have been, I mused, if these gals instead were leaping hedges of scrub oak and rounding patches of prickly pear with lances in their hands and shields tied to their saddles. That would be a good test. Portolá and his soldiers had marched just by or maybe right over this plot beside the dry San Dieguito River. The frontiersmen from Baja were known as *soldados de cuera*, or buffcoats, because they wore long, almost skirted vests of layered hide, deer or cattle, six or seven plies thick. Enough to stop an arrow, but probably not a musket ball. Enough to make one sweat incessantly, and enough to keep those salt stains from bleeding through. Immensely heavy in the rain. Born in New Spain—in Mexico—the buffcoats grew up riding its ranchos and so were skilled horsemen sensitive to the landscape of Las Californias. They would later guard the presidios and missions of Alta California. They carried a shield, or "targe," worn on the left arm, that could deflect a club or projectile, ornately stippled and painted with the red and yellow of royal Spain. From their saddle horns hung aprons of leather that draped around the horses' flanks and the soldiers' legs, protecting both from brush and the blows of an enemy. This garb was the predecessor of chaparajos, those leather, seatless leggings, which owe their name to chaparral. The West's cowboys derived their "chaps," and maybe their swagger, from this word. Portolá himself praised this novel leather getup, lamenting when he first arrived in Baja that "I more than anyone reached here torn and scratched to pieces by the terrible Thorn-trees"—cactus—"along these same trails in this Country . . . a man must have more Cowherder than Soldier in him in order to serve in this land."

THE HEAT DROVE ME TOWARD the ocean, though the Spaniards had stayed inland. This was my expedition as well, I told myself, and I was allowed to make the occasional detour, as the scouts would have done. I studied my own handheld "manzanita," my little Apple, and headed over the Rancho Santa Fe hills on a zigzagging diagonal toward the next lagoon, San Elijo. Crespí actually bestowed this name, *La Cañada de San Alejo*, on the estuary that is one drainage farther north, but as happened throughout California, sometimes a name later drifted a short way, as if slowly carried north or south on the San Andreas Fault. Crespí himself occasionally moved a name when he felt he'd conferred undue prestige on a minor valley by initially titling it after an important saint. The etymology and sedimentology of the coast were both deposited in layers only to be shaken up and scrambled, and these tectonics are still at work.

Inside the spacious concrete hall of the San Elijo Lagoon Nature Center, the County Parks ranger at the front desk, Mark, held a book entitled *Beat Poetry*. With wavy hair and a thick reddish beard, he did look like an Allen Ginsberg acolyte, but he wore the usual game warden uniform: a khaki shirt with a gold name tag and forest-green pants. I asked how his day was. "I've been able to do a little reading, so that's good," he replied. "Kerouac rocks my mind, so I have to take a break now and then to think about it." I told him what I was up to. "I dig your project," he said. "Sounds very noble." A gopher snake was coiled in the terrarium built into the counter; elsewhere fence lizards, a rosy boa, fiddler crabs, California kingsnakes, and an alligator lizard. "Hi, lizard," said a boy touring with his mother. Outside, the marsh channel was silted and windswept. There I also found a table with a 3-D topographic map of the San Elijo Watershed. Like a god, you could pour a jug of water over one end, high up in the Peninsular Ranges near Palomar Mountain, and see it run down Escondido Creek—a thousand-year or truly apocalyptic flood in miniature—to the place where we were standing. I had traversed only the map's tail end, a few inches right by the ocean.

The prospect of a nature center always intrigues me. No matter how hokey it turns out to be, there's dependably one artifact or specimen you could never have imagined. Beside the sluice of the watershed map stood a replica of a Kumeyaay shelter, called an *e'waa*, that had been built "the authentic way." A modest dome, it was about five feet wide, of thatched cattail over a scaffold of bent willow. It seemed to draw inspiration, naturally, from the abode of a marsh wren. It was not so different, I imagined, from the first huts of the San Diego Mission, or any other mission, a reminder that sanctity is the eye of the builder. One portion of the hut was left unfinished to show how it was constructed: still-green cattail draped and folded over the ribs and tied with jute twine (the Kumeyaay would have used cord made of yucca fiber). Now the thatching was tan and brittle. When the lizard kid followed me outside, he beat me to the *e'waa* and exclaimed, "We could have a picnic in here, Mom! We could live in here, and then we could come out and play with the map." "We sure could," she said, but I suspected she preferred her own home.

I crawled inside the *e'waa*'s entrance, which would have had a mule deer hide for a flap, and found a rock circle for an imagined fire. The hut was about the size of a three-person tent, small but a mansion compared to my solo dome. Overhead was a skylight, a blue seventy-two-and-sunny view as they say about San Diego, a smoke hole. Some of the cattail dangled where it had slipped or broken, and the whole structure rustled in the breeze like a low-key aeolian harp. All in all, the *e'waa* had an eerie feel, as if it had been recently abandoned. The cattail was finely corrugated like corn husk and speckled with black rot. There was, in fact, a corncob lying to one side, which made little sense, since the Kumeyaay had no maize, until I realized it had rolled in from the tortoise pen next door. Mojave Desert tortoises aren't found along the coast, but this way schoolkids could meet these gentle, aged burrowers.

Mark popped his head in to check on me. It was the end of the day and he was wiping down the 3-D map and gathering up its jugs, its rainclouds. "This little house could withstand a good deal of weather," he told me. But the previous iteration—which had been built by Kumeyaay tribal members—had been destroyed on the third day of a lashing El Niño storm. It was a typical home for a family of four, said Mark. Took about a week to build. Tightly bunched, the cattail would be waterproof. No mortgage. These were the homes that would have stood in Cosoy below Presidio Hill, before the Spanish drove the villagers away. These were the homes that Portolá and Crespí would have passed by the handful every day. I tried to imagine two adults and their kids living in this dome hardly larger than an office cubicle. It seemed impossible, but I was far taller, probably by about a foot, than the average Kumeyaay would have been. The cramped *e'waa* also suggested a mostly outdoor existence. Southern Californians once spent most of their days on the move or in the shade of tall scrub or sycamore.

I asked Mark how he had come to work at the Nature Center. He told me he had been an assistant to an undertaker. "But once you've seen your hundredth crying couple of the day, you want to move on." He had started at the reserve as a student worker before being hired on full-time. "We close at five," he said, peering in through his sunglasses, "but you can sleep right here, as long as you don't have a car in the lot. No one will notice." I told him that was super kind. "I try to be kind to all walks of life," he replied. He warned me to be careful camping in the open spaces of Orange County, when I got there, because those rangers spend so much time dealing with gang murders in the woods, they don't have time for environmental education.

Maybe I should have stayed in the *e'waa*, but something didn't feel quite right—something about curling up, so soon or so exactly, in the memory or imitation of another culture. Plus I had miles to go before I reached the next lagoon, where the Portolá party had actually camped. I'd turned my day into a long V by detouring toward the ocean. Mark told me that when the Kumeyaay, as hunters and gathers, moved inland seasonally, they carried the willow branches of their *e'waa*s with them to reassemble. More thatching could be found at their destination. But as I left, I noticed this *e'waa*'s willow lattice, sunk deep into the ground, had rooted and sprouted a few determined leaves.

THE HAZARD OF SETTING UP your tent at last light—of "flailing," as I've heard it called—is that in the morning you might crawl outside into a swarm of poppy-seed-size ants, black and frenzied. They crawled through my leg hair, even over my eyebrows, just as the night before I had paced through this burry field near the Batiquitos Lagoon. After a quick dip in the ocean, I headed inland again to my proper place at the rear of the lagoons, and at dusk, down a semi-forested bike path, I had vaulted a low chain-link fence, lingering a moment to make sure the drunkard I'd just passed didn't see me. I paced the tree line, breathing hard until I found a clump of coyote brush. Coyote brush is another staple of chaparral—tall with tiny, sheeny leaves and a long, dogged taproot—and it would become my staple blind, all the way to San Francisco. Coyotes likewise dig it. I could hide my solo tent behind just a bush or two.

On my knees, trying to remain inconspicuous, I fit the poles into the corner brackets of my REI Quarter Dome, snapped the plastic hooks onto the aluminum arches, and slid the gray rain fly over them and tightened it. Gray is the hue of discretion, of sun-worn California meadows. Settling in the grass, I savored the thin-crust pizza slice I had carried from Encinitas and then crawled inside. I was coming to terms with the fact that the down sleeping bag I'd brought was far too warm for summer in Southern California, especially because I seemed to be finishing each day's walk with a relative sprint to reach my intended destination. My metabolism raced on. Through the nylon ceiling, the moon felt almost warm. A crotchety thrum of traffic came through the trees. Too wound up to go to bed, but too wary to use a light or my laptop because my tent would glow like a paper lantern and I didn't want to attract attention, I lay thinking about or rehearsing the day, or neither, just brain-humming, until I fell asleep. This became my pattern.

I wondered what the Spaniards' camp would have looked like. Crespí mentions having his own tent, *una tiendecita*, which he shared with the expedition's other padre, Father Gómez, but most of the others, the non-officers and neophytes, would have slept in the open air. Sixty-three men is no minor campground; they were a traveling, overnight village, as large as many of the Native villages they encountered. The clanging of pots and pans, the crackle and rupture of fire, conversation, and laughter—the Portolá party was the original Campland, minus Solo cups and RVs. Their experience was social, whereas mine, though I was embedded in a population center, a neighborhood unimaginable to them, would be mainly solitary. I would have to keep quiet while camping, and I wouldn't dare kindle a fire because it might be seen or, worse, spread. The Spaniards would have posted lookouts, up all night with the mules and horses grazing nearby, breathing and nickering in the darkness, tethered or in makeshift corrals. There was real danger. Until I slept, I was my own lookout, and I wasn't sure I had less to look out for.

The Luiseño, rivals of the Kumeyaay and whose historic territory I was now entering, had an initiation ceremony for boys: each was asked to lie down, and then the chief poured ants on him from a basket, though these were large, red, and probably furious. The boys had to endure the ants and their bites until, eventually, they were brushed off with stinging nettle: a diffuse pain to soothe a concentrated one. But the ants did not bite me, which seemed a kind of grace. Maybe they were trying but couldn't latch on with their minuscule mandibles. They only crawled over every part of me until I shook and stamped them off. I had camped on their labyrinth, and they had discovered my empty pizza box, with its stains of grease and few strings of mozzarella. Was that a fair trade? Perhaps.

I'D BEEN DEBATING WHETHER TO visit Legoland, and finally decided it was my duty: the Spaniards wouldn't have missed it, and I had already neglected SeaWorld. As with Campland, I may be the only person to have ever walked to Legoland. At 10:11 a.m., cars were streaming up to booths painted like Lego boxes to pay homage and the seventeen-dollar parking fee, but I simply stepped through a gap in the ivied fence, hailed by a symphonic music that suggests, *You Have Arrived*. Strollers were being unfolded from trunks. Young creatures were being strapped into them. An official photographer asked a family if they wanted to jump for posterity and, with their arms overhead, they managed to bounce an ebullient inch or two off the plaza, which of course was tiled with colorful squares. DID YOU PRINT YOUR TICKETS AT HOME? PROCEED DIRECTLY TO A TURN- STILE. I had not, but I talked my way into a twenty-dollar entry fee as "a journal- ist" and was shocked when no one asked to search my giant army-green pack.

Legoland seemed related, by way of Denmark, to California's early adobes, like the kind I had seen briefly in Old Town San Diego and would see all along the coast, including at each mission. It speaks to our impulse to pour into molds, to stack, to fortify. Away with willow and tule! Apart from the rides, Legoland is a 128-acre sculpture garden. More than 62 million Lego bricks are joined by the nubs, including 2 million alone in Bronte, a chubby brontosaurus near the entrance gate. Nearby floated really dirty Lego swans beside warm-blooded mallards dab- bling with their rumps aloft. The smallest Lego creature in the Land is a rabbit, nestled in a tiny magician's hat, made of just four plastic bricks. The place is a zoo of the imagination, an outdoor cathedral to play and to the—now plastic— foundations of civilization, where you encounter simulacra of animals, places, and experiences, and devour thousands of calories. Try the apple fries.

I found myself watching Junior Driving School, ages three to five, not to be confused with Driving School, ages six to thirteen, both rides among the few where kids have any actual agency. When everyone was buckled in, a master button was pushed and the cars sprang to life. Was it some magnetism? You could tell which kindergartners had a lead foot because they lurched forward immediately. "There you go," said a mother, with pride. Then: "Watch where you're going!" The boxy cars, yellow and blue and red, with classic Lego nubs on their hoods, looped around a concrete island/median with a red NO PARKING stripe around its entire length. Already we were instilling the driving culture in the future generation so they could fly down I-5 over the San Diego lagoons. What option did they have? Walking, at least in Southern California, is now for the poor or the eccentric. At the end of the session—the kids had revolved, at most, an eighth of a mile—the boy in front of me burst into tears. "You can go again," said his mother. "You can go again." All things are said twice to a child. He was only half-consoled. As they exited, each student was given an official Legoland driver's license with no expiration date ("Always remember to wear your seat belt," said its reverse).

Afterward I found one of those same licenses drowned in San Francisco Bay, along with oodles of tossed coins. I had not expected to reach my destination so soon, but here it was, in Miniland USA, which was impressively not mini. New York City, New Orleans, and Las Vegas (with aliens crash-landed in the adjacent desert) were also nearby, but my attention remained on California. Emblems of Southern California had been created as if possibly a small preview of my journey—Griffith Observatory, Huntington Pier, and Mission San Luis Rey—but it was the Port of Saint Francis that was most gloriously rendered: the Golden Gate Bridge, with its sweeping tomato cables. Ghirardelli Square. "See, that's Coit Tower," a woman said. "Daddy and I used to live near there." The Transamerica Building, until recently the city's tallest (Salesforce Tower now sails above it). Lombard Street, ever the snake.

Through my binoculars, I began to study the little San Franciscan Lego people, with their blockheads and rectangular limbs, hundreds or possibly thousands of yellow, brown, and white faces, with no eyes, noses, or mouths: even as Lego tried to be progressive, it homogenized. There was a Lego churros stand. There were sea lions made of gray bricks on floating docks, streaked white as if with their guano. A little speaker belted out *Arf, Arf, Arf*—vocalizations recorded at Pier 39. People were fishing nearby. Sharks and Silicon Valley investors, you had to imagine, were circling above the pennies and nickels in the algal moat that pretended to be the bay. "I don't have any change," a passing mother said. "So maybe later." What would she or her child have wished for? Once more I felt like a giant, but as soon as I exited the turnstile and passed the WELCOME sign of a million synthetic bricks, I felt impossibly mini again. It was a long walk to the real San Francisco.

On my way out the drive, I passed a statue of a man with a huge snake, a boa, around his neck: it was Jeff and Medusa from Spanish Landing Park, turned not to stone, but to Lego, life-sized. He had shaved his mustache and removed his tattoos.

FLOATING OVER THE AGUA HEDIONDA LAGOON later that afternoon in a rented plastic kayak—not far from the cacophony of Legoland, as the crow flies, but several hours' walk to my launch around the shoreline, up and over hills—I thought about what it must have been like to drift in almost absolute silence a few centuries ago. Or not silence, but the nasal calls of terns and the distant, ceaseless churn of the beach. Only the voice of your partner, though I had none, or the murmurs of a few others on shore. No highway, which now purrs with more people every ten minutes than lived on this whole San Diego County stretch at the time. Crespí wrote of the San Diego Harbor, "It is very plentiful in very large sardines, rays, and many other fish, and a great many mussels. All the heathens here are great fishermen, having a vast number of tule-rush floats which they use for catching fish in the sea." Tule is a type of tasseled bulrush, by nature a long and skinny pontoon filled with air, and these stalks grow to ten or twelve feet in length, which the Kumeyaay and other coastal California tribes bundled tightly into stable canoes.

But the open water of Agua Hedionda, on which I floated, didn't exist then. The term "lagoon" only came into use in San Diego County in the late nineteenth century. I was suspended over a onetime salt flat—one of those "white glitters" Crespí mentions—that was usually dry or pocked with shallow, hypersaline puddles. *Agua Hedionda* means "stinking water," though the name may actually refer to nearby sulfur springs. Now it is an open bay, the most picturesque of the San Diego lagoons by the usual standards of idyll. We've been taught to admire clear, placid lakes instead of fetid, productive marshes. The estuary was flooded and dredged in 1954 when the Encina Power Station was built; jetties were installed to keep the lagoon's mouth pried wide. The natural gas– and oil-fired plant draws from Agua Hedionda to cool itself and pours the warm discharge into the ocean. Its smokestack looms over the highway.

My paddle flashed in the lowering sun and the wind blew drops of salt water onto my lap. On the lagoon's south shore was a plastic chair, and as I drifted nearer, I saw that above it hung a hat on some scrub, as if the seat were being held for someone. I turned my prow that direction and drove it onto the narrow beach. The chair was set in a windbreak of an old coyote bush cut and splayed wide, maybe by the wind. Inside the woven hat were dried berry stains: someone had used it as a basket. I hung it back on its branch and leaned back in the flimsy chair, in my half-soaked bathing suit, taking in the red-tiled roofs defining the ridge just as they had above the San Dieguito Lagoon. This was someone's yoga or reading spot, or just a place to land. A private *desembarcadero*. In front of the chair was a patch of artificial turf like the kind I had putted on earlier at Legoland, and the kind many San Diego yards employ to save water and lawn mowers. For a table, there was a plywood board on an ammunition box. More seedling ants swarmed over dried fish gunk on its surface. Also a pile of mussel shells in the grass, each smiling with a vacant slit.

On the slender beach, fiddler crabs emerged from their burrows. That faint scurry I had seen as I rode my prow onto the shore had not been a sign of dehydration. The sand was rippled with lacy green algae and perforated with holes, their homes. They stood in congress, each male waving its giant, pearly claw. They were more like maestros than fiddlers, but each species gestures in a different pattern: maybe others more truly play the violin. The sun over the highway poured straight through the exoskeleton of their claws, made them translucent and rosy. Fiddlers wave their arms to ward off other males or attract females, and this crescent of Agua Hedionda was in constant motion, until I came too near. Then they all darted underground.

Around their burrows lay mud balls of various sizes, little BBs and musket balls. The tiniest were "feeding pellets" that the fiddlers regurgitate after sieving the sand for organic matter. The largest, about a half inch wide, were "burrow balls" that they'd excavated and arranged, like boulders in a xeriscaped garden. These actually serve as territorial markers, as monuments to their plot of sand. Monuments the crabs must forever recreate as the tide rises and their handiwork washes away. So they aerate the mud, a boon to marsh plants and the tiniest of animals, known as "meiofauna." When the water arrives, the crabs retreat, slip in sideways, pulling in their massive defense behind them and plugging the exit with a mud ball to prevent inundation. Afterward they dig out their homes all over again.

Since there wasn't a lagoon of this scale at Agua Hedionda when Portolá marched through, the crabs likely wouldn't have existed just here, in this very spot. Fiddlers move as the mudflats do—as we used to, before we built dikes and concrete bridges. Had the Spaniards seen them? Did they see in them a metaphor for their own armor, for the claiming of land, for the rising and falling tides of empire? Did they see a potential meal? Gulls swoop them. Egrets lance them with the thrust of a cricked neck. Gradually the crabs edged out again, as I stood still, and they began to gesture and glow in the light. I walked across the crabs' suburb to my kayak and they disappeared underfoot. All but one. He was dislocated. He sidled toward the lapping water. I prodded him with the broken hinge of a clam shell to gauge his ferocity. He seemed overmatched. He dug himself in. Far across the water, people were paddleboarding as if in a mirage.

INLAND LAY MISSION SAN LUIS REY DE FRANCIA, several hours' walk to the northeast. Striding down Rancho Del Oro Drive, I could see its salt-white facade and robin's-egg-blue dome set in dry fields, with parched hills and one prominent stone outcrop, a small monolith, in the hazy distance. A sign on Mission Boulevard advertised an off-Broadway show, way off, at the parish: LATE NIGHT CATECHISM: COME AND LAUGH YOUR SINS OFF! There was a rippling banner of a convivial Pope Francis on the church's ivory walls, and after hours of walking in the sun I was thankful to step through its ponderous doors into a cool stone interior with slumping votives and celestial ornament. I realized then that, two centuries ago, a mission church in Southern California would have offered physical relief, the first refrigeration.

I paid a small fee, left my pack with the receptionist, and wandered through the mission museum, looking at artifacts and black-and-white photos through time, the mission ruined and restored. Named for King Louis IX of France, a charitable monarch but also a crusader, San Luis Rey was one of the last missions to be established, in 1798, not quite thirty years after Portolá's initial expedition. Eventually it would be known as "the King of the Missions" for its great size. Bridging the gap between Mission San Diego to the south and Mission San Juan Capistrano to the north, San Luis's lands stretched from today's Cardiff to Camp Pendleton across a thousand square miles. "[W]e came in sight of a very large and handsome, all very green valley," wrote Crespí. "This is a grand spot, the best of any we have come across; not even San Diego can compare with it. It has a fine climate; such is its greenness that it appears to be all cultivated: there is a great deal of wild grapevines, looking like planted vineyards, many tall grass clumps, and other unknown plants, so that it is toilsome to pass over its flat." He named the valley after Saint John of Capistrano, but of course Mission San Juan Capistrano was established to the north and thus this place became known as *el viejo valle de San Juan de Capistrano*, until this old name was finally cast off.

Father Domingo Rivas, who ventured from San Diego to witness the founding of Mission San Luis Rey, on June 13, 1798, described its rustic inception. Two basic buildings were erected on day one, a church and a dwelling for the padres. "Neither apartment exceeded ten yards in length and five in width," Rivas wrote, "and their walls were nothing more than poles and branches of trees, so that they are perfectly described by saying that they were *sicut tugurium in cucumerario*, like a lodge in a garden of cucumbers"—a verse from Isaiah. A wild cucumber, known as manroot because its tuber can be the size of a buried child, does thrive in California, but so far I had seen only wild gourd with its golden flowers.

Rivas marveled that the Fathers were founding this settlement "without any other aid than some pickaxes, a dozen plowshares, half a dozen crowbars, some blankets, a quantity of flannel, and two dozen bolts of cloth with which to clothe the Indians." Though they were clothed to begin with, at least the women. Miguel Costansó, the expedition's cosmographer, wrote of the San Luis Rey Valley, "The Indians in this neighborhood, warned of our coming, came out to meet us, so confident, it seemed, and certain of our friendship that they brought all their women." Crespí added: "The women all went very decently covered, with thick bunches of strings in front and the usual animal hide behind. All of these ones here arrived with their bodies covered by a sort of mantlet that they wear from the neck downward, made up of hare and rabbit skins thoroughly twisted together into one." The men wore paint.

Within a month, baptized Luiseño natives had molded six thousand adobes, hauled beams from immense distances, and laid the foundations for five large rooms. These first buildings were completed by the end of the year. Once the adobe was mortared and limed, the walls were more than two feet thick. The roof was a thatch of tule and earth stucco: a hybrid of Spanish and Native methods, part adobe and part *e'waa*. After a year, more than two hundred Luiseño lived in *e'waa*s surrounding these first buildings. This was an immense success, from the padres' perspective, outdoing any mission to date. Father Francisco Palóu, another chronicler and *condiscípulo* of Crespí and Serra, wrote, "Satan must have grown jealous."

Eventually the mission's buildings extended over six acres and typified the layout of the Alta California missions: a grand church was finished in 1815 of quarried stone, 165 feet long with a nave twenty-seven feet wide and ceilings thirty feet tall. The wings and colonnades of the stuccoed quadrangle measured five hundred feet to a side and held rooms for the padres, for storage, and for workshops. Tule roofs were replaced with clay tiles to guard against fire. The San Luis Rey livestock branding iron—a design that looks much like the number 5—was pressed hissing into the hides of more than fifty thousand animals reared from an initial donation of eight hundred cattle and sheep from its sister missions in San Diego and San Juan Capistrano. The Luiseño, or more properly Quechnajuichom, for a kind of stone found nearby, built the mission and tended its lands at the direction of the padres, cultivating fruit, vegetables, and grain, and beef, chicken, and pork. By 1825, the number of Luiseños living at or nearby the mission was 2,869, more than three times the average at other missions. But San Luis Rey's Native population had been more than five thousand before it was devastated by disease. In this way, as well, it was illustrative.

In the courtyard, I listened to the fountains on their domed bases above water lilies. Wisteria grew over the closed side doors to the church (PLEASE ENTER THROUGH FRONT DOORS) and trembled with the breeze. A statue of Saint Francis held up its arms, to the living doves, in a niche in the wall. The bells chimed every fifteen minutes. In the shadow of the corridor were mortars and pestles that evoked the Luiseños who had made their meals here—who had been made to make this place—and were buried in the graveyard next door.

SOME OF THE MOST AUTHENTIC writing about San Luis Rey comes from a young Luiseño named Pablo Tac, born at the mission in 1822, about midway through its tenure prior to the U.S. takeover. Showing unusual aptitude, he paid a high price for his intelligence. He was chosen by Father Antonio Peyri, one of Mission San Luis Rey's founders, to accompany him on his return to Europe along with one other Luiseño boy. Their families would never see them again. Tac left at ten years old, bound for Mexico, then to New York, France, Barcelona, and eventually Italy. In Rome, he was placed at the College of Propaganda, a fitting name. He would continue his religious education for seven years until he succumbed to smallpox at the age of nineteen.

An Italian linguist encouraged Tac to write a Luiseño dictionary, but he got only as far as the Cs, ending with *cupu-*, just twelve hundred words in. It's believed that he wrote his brief treatise, "Conversion of the San Luiseños of Alta California," when he first arrived in Rome at only twelve or thirteen years old, and it is a captivating document, though not entirely trustworthy. Tac is relaying stories handed down to him, and the Catholic propaganda had already done its work. He waxes lyrical about the mission's founding: "This was that happy day in which we saw white people, by us called Sosabitom. O merciful God, why didst Thou leave us for many centuries, years, months and days in utter darkness after Thou camest to the world? Blessed be Thou from this day through future centuries."

Tac describes the mission buildings and, below them, a "sunken garden" and an "ever-flowing fountain" delivered by aqueduct for drinking and washing. Carrying water from the walled garden to San Luis Rey's kitchen, the neophytes had to pass through a wooden turnstile designed to keep thirsty horses and cattle out. Sometimes these swinging beams knocked the clay jug off their shoulders, so that "they return to the house without water or pitcher, dripping with water." Occasionally a bull still found its way into the garden and frightened the women scrubbing at the *lavandería*. In the surrounding orchard, pears, apples, peaches, quinces the color of the sun, pomegranates, and many vegetables grew. The neophytes were not allowed into this Eden without permission, lest they steal these fruits. Pablo Tac relayed that, when caught, a thief would hop the garden walls to escape punishment, "jumping as they know how (like deer in the mountains)." He seems to distance himself from "they," but again, he was only ten years old when he left San Luis Rey. He had been told that his people jumped like bucks—that their ways were more animal than human.

Tac tells a story of a Luiseño who snuck into the garden and up a tree, and there choked on a fig as he stuffed it into his mouth. "He then began to be frightened, until he cried out like a crow and swallowed it," Tac wrote. "The [Native] gardener, hearing the voice of the crow, with his Indian eyes then found the crow that from fear was not eating any more. He said to him, 'I see you, a crow without wings. Now I will wound you with my arrows.' Then the neophyte with all haste fled from the garden." The threat of punishment pervaded the missions, even in its gardens. I peered through the locked iron gate of the garden's remaining entrance arch and down its cascade of brick steps, both of which Pablo Tac describes, to the excavated foundation of the waterworks, and I tried to imagine all that bounty within. Beyond the ruins, over Mission Boulevard, was a strip mall. The mission had planted prickly pear along the garden's edge to keep you out and off the fragile, melting adobe walls—a common strategy in Southern California, I began to notice. PRIVATE PROPERTY, read a sign, PLEASE DO NOT PICK THE CACTUS. It seemed Mission San Luis Rey wanted it both ways. I didn't steal any tunas, which here were mostly green, but through a gap in the wall I did slip into the garden for a minute to the side of the unearthed troughs where water had once flowed and men and women had washed.

EVENING APPROACHED AS I STROLLED west, back toward the ocean, past San Luis Rey's trailer parks and down the river levee's bike path, vaguely looking for a place to camp or simply reassurance that there would be a place to camp if I walked a few more miles. The river channel was a bottomland of scrub, deadwood, and patches of sand, with larger cottonwoods shivering, a revelation of groundwater. Hard to imagine a flood in this dry land that would warrant a levee of this size, but history must justify it. Several figures in a culvert raised my guard as I first approached the levee, but it was only three kids with their pit bull, sharing a joint.

In the distance, parachutists were swinging in descent. Camp Pendleton marines, I thought at first, but the base was north of the river, beyond a ridge. These were just civilians falling toward the Oceanside Municipal Airport for a thrill and the evening view. On Benet Road I crossed the river, seeing on my phone's screen another dotted line, a trail, one that might be less traveled. Maybe I could camp there. Past the driveway to Prince of Peace Abbey, past a scrapyard with battered cars piled up, I came to a sign where the road dead-ended: NO TRESPASSING — AREA PATROLLED. A man was changing the oil of his old vehicle just there. When I asked if anybody went down that way, his mumbles were unintelligible, but my impression was, No, it was a bad idea. A semitruck idled nearby with its driver hidden behind tinted glass. Feeling a little desperate, I turned around.

Back near Benet, I scrambled down an embankment, away from the river, into a weedy triangle of meadow at the mouth of a minor canyon, and I waded toward an unruly stand of what looked like bamboo, hugely tall, segmented, dusty to the touch. Inside this thicket were low caves you could walk through hunched, a warren of cane tunnels. I thought about pitching my tent inside one of these caverns, but they were dim, and claustrophobia set in. Unsettled, nearby I found a patch of ground between some bamboo and giant fennel, stalks my height with yellow umbels. Again too nervous to set up my tent, at last light I laid out my pad and bag and put my lime-green earplugs in, rolling them delicately between my fingers. The world dampened. Very quickly I had learned that earplugs were essential urban camping gear, suppressing the restless engines and guttural compression brakes, the choruses of dogs and the distant trains. At the same time, they made me feel more vulnerable.

Sometime after dark I heard a man's voice and pulled the foam from my ears, kneeling in my sleep bag. Was he wandering toward me? Car doors opening and closing. Muffled voices. After about five minutes, I relaxed. Through the wind, I heard a man say, "Obama's not such a bad president, if you really think about it." Which put me at some ease. Then later, "Oh yeah, this is mountain lion country. . . .

They're the apex predator." Pablo Tac told of a cougar in Mission San Luis Rey's horse pasture: "Here too the workmen found a California lion . . . and because they were many, the lion was afraid of them and the cries which they let out following it. It ran leaping here and there around the pasture. The Indians hidden behind the trees threw stones at it until one struck the middle of the forehead and it soon weakened, falling. He then died." But I was less scared of a mountain lion than of a couple of humans stumbling upon me.

The voices didn't come closer. They only faded in and out with the breeze and my own pulse. In the darkness, an impressive drill within Camp Pendleton then came to my ears: the *whomp whomp* of choppers, the boom of shells or noisemakers. It was like hearing a war over the ridge, though I have no way of really knowing what war sounds like beyond movies and news clips. Lying on my pad, I imagined young marines on belay or running through the sage with night-vision goggles. They were negotiating their nerves, like me. Did this happen every night? Were they about to charge over the ridge? Yet the noises closest at hand were equally startling. Several times I awoke when rodents rustled in the dry cane. A rabbit, I believe, flashed once in the moonlight that silhouetted the stalks above me like inside-out, shredded umbrellas.

In the morning, bushtits, my friends, filtered through the fennel and cane over my sleeping bag as I opened my eyes—a rambling flock of about a hundred, though it is always impossible to count these rapid gray Lilliputians. I watched as they bathed in the dew beaded on the bamboo leaves, then shimmied and puffed their downy undercoats in the sunlight. I studied their eyes: the males have golden irises, the females all dark. Also saw or heard yellow chat, house finches, goldfinches, warbling vireo, California towhees, and a fox sparrow. Nearby, a dozen beehives to capitalize on the fennel. When I walked out of the weeds, a jeep and a sedan were double-parked in a pullout along the meadow, their doors cracked for air. Inside was a tangle of blankets, heads, and shoulders. Other people camping here for lack of a better option. Those voices.

FIVE MILES DOWN THE San Luis Rey River bike path, on Oceanside Beach, I saw a bird perched on a post, but when I raised my binoculars, it was a lost flip-flop. An aircraft carrier floated on the horizon, probably nuclear powered and with over five thousand personnel. An Osprey—a hybrid helicopter-plane—was flying loose circles around it. Camp Pendleton was hosting a monthlong international war game, I learned, the biennial Rim of the Pacific Exercise, which explained the barrage of noise overnight. Units from Canada, Mexico, and Chile were on hand to train, strengthening cooperation between allies. I could see smoke rising from the guns of the carrier below its control tower: phantom enemies, out there somewhere.

Brown pelicans soared low, classic, in formation until each peeled off from their V, one by one. Parents were doing their honest best to defend their kids' skin with mists of spray-on sunscreen. Through it all, you could hear the Osprey reverberating, and I began to wonder if rotors and warships meant something quite different to those who live on the San Diego Coast, something more like beach volleyball. On Oceanside Pier, which stretches nearly two thousand feet into the Pacific, a fisher in a hoodie sat on a pail eating a dripping mango as he waited for sand shark. He'd caught one recently with store-bought shrimp. South of the pier, grandstands and tents had been erected for one of the world's largest women's surf contests, the Paul Mitchell Supergirl Pro. I had missed it by one day, but some of the women had arrived to practice. They stretched on the beach before throwing themselves into the waves. I leaned on the pier's fish-gut railing to watch as they studied the waves' particularities, found their timing before tomorrow's heats, with sun-fried hair that might have caused Paul Mitchell to turn a one-eighty in his grave. They gouged the ocean, gliding to a feathering crest before snapping their hips to cut the other direction, "rail to rail," from one edge of their boards to the other. They were writing on the fleeting page of the ocean, staying ahead of collapse.

I HAD JUST STEPPED OFF the beach, readying to head north before I ran out of daylight, when I heard a commotion across the reedy mouth of the San Luis Rey River impounded behind sand. A dozen or so young men were jogging slowly, exclaiming and chanting with feathered staffs lifted in the breeze. They were headed for the breaker, and I turned back, wondering what this gathering could be about. Clearly it was tribal. They beat me to the shore, where they left their sneakers and socks and waded into the shallows up to their shins. Surfers bobbed beyond them. Over the onrush and sibilance of the froth, they said "Ho!" as they turned to face each direction with their scepters: skyward to honor the heavens, then down at the shallows to honor the water, and finally toward the beach to honor the earth.

A woman named Kimmy, in oval shades and with swaying brown hair, explained this to me as we watched. She was Apache, but many tribes, she said, were represented, including Luiseño. I had encountered the Peace and Dignity Run. These guys were running as a group—relay-style, a mile or two per leg—from Alaska to Panama, where they would meet other Indigenous runners who had begun in Tierra del Fuego. "This fulfills the eagle and the condor prophecy," one runner told me. "When they meet in the land of the quetzal, there will be peace on earth." It is a prophecy forever waiting to be fulfilled, since the relay has occurred every four years, on an Olympic schedule, since 1992.

Several of these men were so dedicated as to go the whole way. They had started in May. Others had joined for only a few days or just an afternoon. They were sleeping in community centers and on hardwood gym floors. They had spent the night at Mission San Luis Rey. I asked Kimmy where she had started. "I started just over there, in the parking lot!" she said with a laugh. "I have my kids, and I have a lot of health issues. But I told my daughter, in four years I'm going to do it with them."

When the runners left the waves, a circle formed on the sand and, to my surprise, I was invited to join. I was reluctant, but they insisted. My intuition was to observe rather than participate, but how could I say no? Taking part, when invited, is better for the soul. Mel Vernon, captain of the San Luis Rey Band of Luiseño Indians, lit a sage bundle with his orange lighter, and a young woman smudged us in turn, clockwise around the circle. She drew circles around my face and down each of my freckled limbs, as if conjuring an invisible figure before me. The smoke unwound on the breeze, pungent and brief. She turned me around and smudged my back, tapping me on the shoulder when she had finished. It would take her the whole ceremony to smudge everyone in the circle.

Mel greeted us briefly. He was not a chief, but a volunteer. "If it were paid," he later told me, "people would have beat me out for the position long ago." He had kicked off his sandals and his gray ponytail spilled from a red ball cap. "Thank you all for being here," he said. "Whoever put the ocean here had a good idea. The Creator! Back when he was doing things the right way. When water was pure, and fish were safe. This was the highway for our people, the river"—Kimmy had mentioned that, once, canoes could travel inland to the mission—"and it's just an honor to be a part of what you're doing with the Peace and Dignity walk, and what that represents. This is a wonderful thing for our tribe, and an acknowledgment of our culture."

Many others stepped forward:

"My name is Emerson. I'm Diné, Navajo. This run had a little bit more meaning for me, because Camp Pendleton was my home for eight years. This was a very powerful run for me. I felt like I had warriors around me, running with me."

"My name is Randall. I don't think any of us could have imagined a more perfect place to end our day than in the water, where we could reach down and touch the second of the four sacred elements. And just the hospitality that we've been shown. Some of us started in Alaska. We are almost three months into a seven-and-a-half-month run. The only thing that surpassed the beauty of nature that we ran through was the generosity of the communities that we went through."

"My name is Willy. I wanted to say that I had a vision once in which Jesus Christ, our Lord, came to me, and he said, 'It's good that you believe in me, but don't discredit your ancestors, because they gave their life just like I gave my life for my people.'"

Finally the visitor was asked to introduce himself. I took a deep breath, because I was afraid or even a little ashamed to say that I was following in the footsteps of the Spanish, though my project was wholly different from theirs. I couldn't bring myself to do it in the moment. I hedged in front of the group:

"My name is Nick. I just started walking from San Diego to San Francisco, so I guess I'm going the wrong direction. It's great to run into some fellow walkers, runners . . . whatever mode of transportation you take. Thank you for inviting me into the circle. I'm glad to have been on this beach. And yesterday I had the opportunity to visit the mission. It was a humbling experience to learn of the hardships there, and also of the triumphs."

"Fresh legs!" yelled Emerson.

"Not that fresh!" I replied.

The runners rolled out four blankets of various sizes in the middle of the circle and, below them, a little altar was fashioned: a conch shell, a rattle, a dish of cut glass filled with ocean, and a spotted gourd. After everyone had spoken, the men began to retire their staffs. Each was laid on a blanket, and some of the carriers turned a circle before doing so. There are circles within circles within circles. "We're all one," another runner told me, to explain why he participated. "We bleed the same." Decorated with ribbons and beads, each staff had been gifted to the runners by a different tribal nation during the journey. The most captivating was a length of skeletal cholla cactus wound with a desiccated gopher snake, a version of the Rod of Asclepius, that emblem of healing and medicine. The blankets were bundled and tied. They would be unrolled tomorrow morning, for the next leg, but I would be miles north by then if I could pass through Camp Pendleton.

THE PORTOLÁ PARTY HAD TO veer around seaside mountains, and I would have to veer around military bases. I knew from the start that Camp Pendleton would be an early roadblock, so I had called ahead to see about receiving permission to pass through. For three days, the expedition had traveled from the San Luis Rey Valley through the heart of what's now the Camp over rolling sagebrush hills and through canyons that impressed Crespí. He named them Santa Margarita and Santa Praxedes; he was mainly in the business of naming valleys, not mountains, which were of little use. "Of all the places we have been coming across, not one is bad," he wrote. "I have greatly enjoyed viewing the beauty."

I reached the camp historian finally, and she kindly helped arrange a tour. Walking through the base was another matter. I had half imagined being escorted along the roadside by a disbelieving marine, but no tax dollars were devoted to this. You can apply to bicycle through Camp Pendleton's southwestern, coastal portion, but Portolá's route was inland, and I didn't have a bike, and I wasn't sure I could ride with a heavy backpack on. That could end badly in a ditch or on the grill of a Humvee. Highway 101 dashes through the Camp, but California Highway Patrol would pick me up if I tried to stroll those eight miles. Nor can you travel the beach; you would have to sneak through something called Assault Craft Unit 5. Maybe there is some way to walk this stretch, but I took the expedient, less honorable route. I walked to the I-5 on-ramp near the Camp's south gate and, with a few swipes of a finger, hailed a car. Portolá did not have that luxury. But he did have a horse. My incredulous driver ferried me eight miles to the next exit at Las Pulgas Canyon and left me under an overpass.

It was another ten miles or so to San Onofre Bluffs Campground on the old coast highway, also technically through the base, though outside its main gates. Frankly, I wasn't sure I was allowed to walk this stretch either, but several cyclists reassured me, and soon I relaxed and stopped glancing over my shoulder for a detail of black cars. Off to my right, a two-thousand-acre brush fire had erupted over the brown hills in the Camp, no doubt ignited by one of those military exercises, which often include live fire of blank ordinances, and I thought about how the Luiseños, before they were Luiseños, would have seared this ground regularly. "Over most of this march we found it burnt off by the heathens," Crespí wrote, a refrain in his journals.

Tribes throughout California tended the landscape by setting yearly fires. Along the coast, lightning strikes and ignitions are rare compared with other parts of the West, so normally coastal sage scrub and chaparral torch only once every few decades. This relative stability allows the shrubs to reestablish dense, climatic stands that, from a foraging perspective, are less fruitful than grassland. They're also thorny. Coastal natives came to depend on the seeds, foliage, fruits, and bulbs of the herbaceous annuals, which, after a fire, quadruple in diversity to capitalize on the newly cleared space and rich ash. In particular chia seeds, *Salvia columbariae*, were prized, and, pound for pound, this grain delivers five times more fat than other grasses and three times more than acorns, which are also less reliable. All along their journey, Portolá and his company were presented with baskets of gruel or porridge made from chia or other minute kernels that existed in bulk only because California's natives set blazes, creating a mosaic of grassland and shrub. This tending-by-fire was so rewarding, so nutritious, that it may be why agriculture didn't develop in California. History shows that typically it would have among such a sizable population, but there was no need.

Now flame was racing in the nowhere of Camp Pendleton. Behind the foothills, which had generous firebreaks plowed on their shoulders like long epaulets, the dull-orange and jaundiced smoke mushroomed and roiled into the troposphere with an intensity and alacrity that, from this distance, looked soft and leisurely. I spooked once when a muscular helicopter whomped down the coast and hovered nearly overhead to land on a bluff-top pad, for training I guess. A peloton in its Technicolor jerseys whirred through a tunnel under I-5 that framed a metallic blue, a raw oval of ocean, and I followed it. Soon this old highway emptied out at the San Onofre Bluffs Campground, where I descended one of its famous paths, Trail 6, and walked the kelp-laced cobble, the shore's original road, until, cold and worn as a beach stone, I climbed again at dusk with heavy thighs and found the campsite number I'd reserved. It was across from a Highway Patrol checkpoint, its floodlights blazing all night. De facto, Camp Pendleton's two hundred square miles are one last defense against smuggling and undocumented immigration, though it's far from the Mexican border. At least by foot. Maybe that's why it's impossible to walk this lovely coast from Oceanside.

A CALIFORNIA THRASHER THE SHADE of the bluffs drank through its decurved bill from a morning puddle, maybe my own, below the outdoor shower, its gullet pulsing. When a train passed along the highway, the bird danced a nervous circle, head tall, but returned to crouch and sip until my neighbor's pit bull puppy, Juno, flushed it into the chaparral. *Juno, get back here! Juno!* At nine, Richard, my guide, picked me up at Trails, as San Onofre Bluffs is better known, in his Jeep Grand Cherokee. It was surprisingly satisfying, cathartic, to again throw my pack into a back seat. An easy talker, Richard had a chalk-white beard and mustache around full lips, a black felt cowboy hat, and a white vest over a blue checkered shirt. His teak bolo tie was inlaid with turquoise. He was a former marine, but had never been based at Camp Pendleton, though he had been discharged there in 1967 after three years of service: "I said, 'I'll see you guys later.'" As we drove, he rattled off the famous breaks nearby that fell under the umbrella name of Trestles—Lowers, Middles, Uppers, Cottons, Church. Surfers had to park a fair hike from the beach and carry their boards underarm, a second pair of arms swaying at their waists like neoprene shadows. "I mean, this is world-class stuff," said Richard. He'd become a Camp Pendleton docent five years ago and almost never gave solo tours. "I was real skeptical, too. I said, 'I'm not going to give a tour to one guy.' Then I said, 'Well, who is this guy?' And I looked you up. Ah, you're serious. You're rocking and rolling." I told him I wasn't so sure. "No, you are. So I said to my wife, 'I've got to show this guy around.'"

"Do you have an ID, just in case?" Richard asked as we drifted up to Camp Pendleton's north gate and stopped in front of a marine with a camouflage cap riding high on his shaved head. I reached for my wallet.

"Good morning, Corporal, how you doing?" said Richard, flashing his credential.

"I'm living the dream."

We laughed. "That's good, buddy," Richard said. "Have a great day. These guys . . . living the dream . . ."

He turned up some classical music as we turned left, up Cristianitos Canyon. It was on this day, July 22, that Crespí and the expedition's second padre, Father Gómez, performed the first baptism in Alta California here in this canyon. A white wooden cross ten feet in height marked the pullout, and I assumed that was the entire commemoration. But Richard began to crunch down a gravel path lined with white painted stones. "Where are we headed?" I asked. "We're headed down to the actual site," Richard replied. The path took us past glossy manzanita and down concrete steps to the base of the river terrace, where there was of course a dry gravel wash. As the steps ended, we entered a glen of sycamore and willow. "There's the well they had, supposedly," said Richard, pointing. It looked like a campfire ring of river stones, only filled with the wrong element. The baptismal font sat on bare dirt beneath a wooden roof that the marines had built on two posts to keep off the rain, leaves, and sun.

The Portolá party had camped lower in the canyon at "a middling-sized pool of very good fresh water at a dry creek," which Crespí dubbed the stream of San Apolinario. "On our reaching this spot," he continues in his journal, "the scouting soldiers told us that they had seen yesterday a girl infant in arms who was dying. We requested the Governor for two or three soldiers to go with us, and then we two Fathers went to the village to try to see this infant in arms and baptize her if she was in danger." The padres would have walked up the valley Richard and I had just driven, the hem of their robes fragrant with the sage and swishing through long grass. "We did find her in her mother's arms, scarcely able to nurse, but the mother would not in any wise let us see her. We gave her to understand, as well as we could, that we did not wish to harm the child, only to wash its head with water, so that if it died it would go to Heaven. As well as he could with her clutched to her mother's breast, Father Fray Francisco Gómez baptized her; she was named Maria Magdalena, and I have no doubt that she will die and that in passing by we have won this soul's passage to Heaven." It was the feast day of Mary Magdalene, the apostle of apostles who stood by the Crucifixion and witnessed the Resurrection.

Imagine the terror of this Juaneño woman: her daughter, barely hers, is on the cusp of death, and she is being asked to hand the child over to utter strangers, their pale skin an anomaly or possibly a disease. They gesture that they want to trickle water over her. That this will send her to the sky. In this both tender and invasive moment, California begins to tip. The land itself goes through a small rite that honors one culture at the expense of another.

"Whoa," I said to Richard, "that's some undrinkable water." The contents of the font were as pink and viscous as strawberry yogurt, thick with cyanobacteria or some maroon algae. The former, I'd guess. It was a red tide welling up. You could not look into it without thinking of the blood of California's natives, soaked in the alluvia of this creek, and of the blood of Christ, which swept through this region to bury them. The dappled ovals of light that poured around the sycamore leaves played across the well's glossy surface. My own shadow moved at its edge when I leaned over to look in. Three gray, half-polished river stones rested at its bottom, fallen or pushed in from the well's gap-toothed rim. On the bank above us, about fifteen feet away, grew a single ornamental rose as if it had drawn this red water directly into its petals.

Who had built this rustic stoup? Richard didn't know, but we imagined it might have been stacked and mortared before the ranch became Camp Pendleton in 1942. Old concrete steps and chunks of wall were half-buried under leaf litter and sycamore root. "The water is still here," said Richard, "there's still water underneath." All this green testified to that; it was a refreshing bower, a place where several *e'waa*s might have stood to avoid the summer light, and maybe a seep had been dug then. "God, what great trees, aren't they?" said Richard in a high-pitched hush, looking upward past the felt of his brim. "Oh man, wow. Gosh." He was reveling in the breeze, the simmer of leaves on petiole. We were both imagining what it would have been like to be here, in a village, in 1769, under these sycamores. "Ah man, God," said Richard, "that baby is huge." He whistled quietly, *shwoo*. We estimated that one tree was a hundred feet tall, circled in places with sapsucker holes, where the woodpeckers would harvest insects drawn to the sweet stickiness of the wells they had made. We could hear, but hardly see, lesser goldfinches in the canopy's motions.

Through the willows of the gravel wash, out in the mown field of the valley that no doubt was once cultivated with lima beans, you could see the plain beige boxes of mock dwellings—"combat placements," Richard explained, with dark empty doorways and windows. The marines use them for training. They would storm these huts imagining themselves in Desert Storm, leaning against the jamb with their rifles tucked upright to their pounding chests before swinging into the open-ing, barrel first, clearing one structure after another. Scattered in clusters throughout Camp Pendleton, they can't help but evoke the *e'waa*s that once were here. Yet they stand in contrast: sharp lines and edges, all drywall, more Lego than woven dome. Crespí and Gómez stood on this ground. Their uniform was of the cloth, not of the military, whose camouflage now steals its design, it seems to me, from the bark of a sycamore. But the distinction is tenuous. When the padres visited this Juaneño village with a guard of soldiers, they were also going door to door, searching and converting. They were the first. Portolá's soldiers gave this place the alternate name of *la Cañada del Bautismo*.

Before we left, I wondered aloud about the font's depth. "Let's see if I can get a stick," said Richard, but I found a suitable one first, a sycamore poker. Bubbles rose as I prodded the mud below this anoxic soup, only a few inches deep—an act that, I realize now, might have been a touch sacrilegious. "Oh, it's stinky," I said.

"Ohh," said Richard. "I bet it is. Oh man."

"You wouldn't want to be baptized in that now," I said.

Richard guffawed. We imagined this pink slime running down our foreheads. "No way, man, no way," said Richard.

WE DROVE SOUTH ON SAN MATEO and Basilone Roads, two days back in time by the measure of Portolá's progress. Past 62 Area, with its barracks of beige cinder block and brick-red sheet metal that reminded me of college dorms. Several dozen recruits, "new boots," stood in rows. Retired tanks were on display like boulders washed out of the mountains. Roadside obstacle courses, ropes to ascend and logs to hurdle. We passed a lap pool with a high dive that, in this heat, almost looked inviting. "They do a lot of training there," said Richard. "It's not fun. You got a whole pack and gear, and you got your rifle, and they shove you off that high deal. You land like a rock, man, and you gotta try and survive. Oh, it's a bitch! God, I remember it really well."

We sailed by an elaborate training complex that posed as several blocks of a Middle Eastern city, dropped out of the blue. Richard told me it was wired with cameras so a session could be replayed, the way a football team studies postgame footage. "It's so they can critique a guy and say, 'Hey man, you just killed thirteen people in that hut. You killed them all, and they were civilians.' It's that kind of training that saves lives." Sometimes actors are even hired so that soldiers have to negotiate a busy town or chaotic market street. Women sidle up to distract the marines in a foreign tongue; other performers carry baskets and plastic water jugs. There are food carts with fake kebabs on the grill. There are sheep mannequins for good measure. After mock bombs go off, and insurgent gunfire rings out, casualties are staged and these actors become an angry crowd that must be pacified and controlled. The dream is peacekeeping, but from another angle, it is pretend invasion and colonialism.

We rolled over these parched hills, "out upon tablelands very clad in dry grass, save a few wild prickly pears and sagebrush," as Crespí wrote. Past bulldozed firebreaks a hundred feet wide that ran up ridges with pockets of oak in their folds, and past blackened tracts where only cactus had survived a burn. Tough, scorching land for vaqueros or marines. "This is nothing compared to Afghanistan," said Richard. "It's got humidity, a hundred twenty-five degrees. It's insane. It is really insane." After about fifteen miles, almost back to Oceanside, we reached the base's southern end, where the Portolá expedition had camped on July 20, the night after their stay in the San Luis Rey Valley. Crespí had called this valley *Santa Margarita Virgen y Martir*, and the Santa Margarita River still occasionally floods the base's airfield, which was once the site of the area's largest Native village and, afterward, the mission's vineyard. I thought to photograph the tarmac, until Richard gently stopped me. "They *really* don't want you doing that," he said.

At the intersection with Vandegrift Boulevard, we arrived many years into the future, from Portolá's day, when we pulled up a slight rise to the manicured oval driveway of the Santa Margarita Ranch House, the base's historical gem. Low-slung and red-tiled, surrounded by palms, this house tells of the evolution of Camp Pendleton and of California, which is a history of marches and confiscations, of a transition from one kind of rangeland to another. This land had belonged to the sixty Luiseño "souls" that visited Portolá's camp and seasonally ranged from shore to summit. It had become an outpost of Mission San Luis Rey as described by Father Antonio Peyri, where those same natives were made to work: "To the north, at a distance of one league and a half"—the Spaniards' standard league was about 2.6 miles—"the Mission has a place with a house and garden, and near the beginnings of the sierra a vineyard. This site, lying in a cañada, is called Santa Margarita. The land is cultivated and wheat, corn, beans, and barley are raised. The fields are irrigated by means of the water from the sierra, which, though not plentiful, assures good crops." After Mexican independence and secularization, it had belonged to the last governor of Mexican

California, Pío Pico, who had built the hacienda's first two rooms before he deeded the rancho to his brother-in-law, John Forster—also known as Don Juan—in exchange for his help settling an astonishing gambling debt. In 1882, the 181,000-acre ranch was then bought by James Flood—one of the "Bonanza Kings" who invested in Nevada's Comstock Lode, the richest silver strike in history. His family owned it until the marines, in the War Powers Act of 1942, "borrowed" some 125,000 acres and afterward paid $4.2 million for it, when they decided not to give it back. The Ninth Regiment and the First Battalion of the Twelfth—three and a half thousand marines, some of whom would fight at Iwo Jima—marched for four days from San Diego in Portolá's footsteps, putting in longer days than I had with heavier packs. There were no suburbs around the lagoons then, just sage and farms.

A marine in camo trousers and an olive tee was waiting to let us in, and he followed us from room to room for lack of other assignment, or maybe because we might swipe an antique. When the marines arrived, the hacienda became, of course, an officers' club, and the butcher room, still with iron hooks on its walls to cure the beef, had been converted into a handsome bar. This was as the war escalated. "You can only figure some of the conversations that took place here from 1942 to 1945," said Richard. On the wall was a black-and-white photo of vaqueros, the ranch's cowboys, wrangling a herd of white-faced cattle with conical hills in the distance: one cowboy mounted, his lasso tight to a calf, while two others in their hats, frozen in time, moved to tie it, castrate it, brand it. The ranch's TO branding iron—"Texas Oklahoma," the origin of Santa Margarita's cattle, another long march—also hung on the wall and looked strikingly like the marines' own symbol: a spread eagle perched on the globe (with an anchor through Earth's molten core). In the sunlit courtyard was a hulking bougainvillea, more tree than vine, that Richard claimed was the oldest in the state at more than 170 years in age. It was as gnarled and swollen as the elephantine face of Pío Pico, who probably suffered from acromegaly, an excess of growth hormone. I imagined generals sitting in its magenta shade.

We wandered the wings. The room that had been the chapel of Pío's sister, Ysidora Pico, with her rosary beads and kneeler still in one corner (*Holy Mary, Mother of God, pray for us sinners, now and at the hour of our death*), is now known as the Presidential Room after Franklin Delano Roosevelt asked if he could spend a night there in 1942. There was the room, too, where in 1944 Roosevelt had asked if he could use the phone, and of course, Mr. President, go right ahead, and so he called

Senator Truman and asked if Truman would join his ticket as vice president. And in the oldest room, one of Pico's originals with hand-hewn beams from sixty miles away, Richard showed me the hatch to the attic where the ranch's maidens, mainly Native servants, were cloistered each night under the watchful eye of Ysidora, who kept the key. "Up the wooden hill they would go," said Richard. Later, during Prohibition, the attic hid a cache of gin, other spirits. There were iron bars across the windows of this particular room to keep the vaqueros out.

ON THE WAY BACK TO San Onofre, Richard and I made one last stop, at the Las Flores Ranch in Las Pulgas Canyon, where my ride from Oceanside had left me only the day before, though it now seemed like ages ago. I had turned a huge circle, even more in time than space, over the last twenty-four hours. "Now the name, Las Flores, came from the Portolá expedition," Richard explained as we drove. "When the troops were here, they camped there. And one of the senior officers said—and I can't repeat the name—we're going to going to call this place 'Las Flores of the *dablalagahadahaga*.'" Richard couldn't remember that name either. "And then somebody else said later on, 'Let's just call it Las Flores.' Because flowers were everywhere. Flowers and fleas. That's where 'Las Pulgas' comes from. The fleas were unbelievable." At this canyon's watering hole, Crespí and Father Gómez marveled at a "good-sized garden" of wild roses and grapes: "It had been burnt off by the heathens not long since, but the roses were springing up again with very handsome shoots, and we were still able to find a very fragrant rose blossom that I plucked, and could see a great many withered rose buds amongst the burnt matter." He called it *Los rosales de la cañada de Santa Praxedis*. But a subsequent group had been bitten alive. I wondered aloud what the fleas subsisted on, before Spaniards: Maybe small mammals? Richard had no answer.

Quickly it became clear that Richard's mind was on one thing, and it wasn't roses: "We have one of the original grapevines from the ranch at Las Flores here. Last year, we must have had a hundred bags of grapes off that vine, and these grapes are like no grape, I would say, that you've ever tasted. But they're not ready yet."

He was so wrong. At this Monterey-style adobe—U-shaped and plastered white, with two stories on the oldest wing that once enjoyed an epic ocean vista, before the ranch's trees grew up—someone had hung bunches of grapes, a wine varietal the color of honey, on the wire fence. "What the heck?" said Richard, in surprise. "Bob must have cut some and put them out here, and they're ripening." We were both smacking our lips, teasing the granule seeds between our teeth, savoring the sun-warmed pulp, *mm mm*. "This thing is going nuts," Richard gushed. "Somebody is giving it plenty of water." He tiptoed through the wavy sprawling vine to see the extent of the spoils. "If only we could get a stick, so we could raise it up and take'm," he said. A stick is the world's most useful tool.

The Las Flores adobe was built in 1868 for the son of John Forster after he acquired the ranch from Pío Pico. After years of neglect and fighter jets rattling its mud walls, now it was being painstakingly restored and retrofitted to withstand earthquakes. But Las Flores's history was older: it was first the site of an *asistencia*—a way station—between Mission San Luis Rey and Mission San Juan Capistrano, built in 1823. Passersby could rest for the night and feed themselves and their mounts. This place of assistance and its large white cross were so prominent on the brown seaside tablelands that ships mistook them for Mission San Juan Capistrano. Richard led me to the ruins, but first he pointed to the grapes and said, "Grab a stack and take them with you." We walked toward the ocean over land once sown, in all directions, with lima beans and now with ground squirrels and the coyotes that pounce on them in an elegant, mangy arch.

A dirt road materialized with a seepage across it at willowy swale that we skirted, pushing back some branches. "Honest to God, this is the El Camino," said Richard. "There were monks and priests, Indians, walking on this trail." El Camino was less a single road than a braiding of paths that meandered like a stream. Unlike today's straightened highways, the original El Camino bends and turns organically around phantom shelters and stands of brush. Here it was dust and vanished footprints, the ruts of trucks. "That one section back there," said Richard, "I remember walking on it and getting a feeling like, 'Whoa.'" He shivered. "I had, like, a moment." Spirits also have been reported in the Las Flores adobe: a brown-robed priest like Crespí at the foot of a bed and, more recently, a skinny vaquero. A conservationist working on-site confessed to Richard and me, "He does not like you peeing on his cactus, from what I've experienced."

We moseyed up to the ruined *asistencia*, a melted hump that belied its onetime size and looked more like a termite mound than a human creation. Even from a distance, you could see white specks in its molten shape and, at my feet, in the local mud, were hundreds of tiny white snail shells and other calcareous artifacts of a former ocean that had been dug and poured into molds—uplifted first by tectonics and then by shovels and hands. The *asistencia*'s remains were fenced in by chain-link, a large perimeter indicative of its real footprint. What was left, marooned at center, had been covered by a sun roof to keep it from eroding further. I was probably standing on liquidated adobe.

We listened to the swaying-grass *woosh* of the highway and thought about travel in former times: three miles an hour if, like me, you're walking. "Just think about this property with no sounds," said Richard. "Birds, ocean crashing sometimes . . . Boy, what a piece of property. You know, if the Marine Corps didn't own it, can you imagine what it would look like? Oh, yeah—the Mission Viejo Company would have developed it." It's estimated that Camp Pendleton's land—twenty miles of shoreline with inland ocean views and one of the most desirable climates in the United States—would command at least $5 billion from developers.

Brea Canyon

Santa Ana
River Crossing

Grijalva Park/
Santiago Creek

Orange

Portola Springs
(Tomato Springs)

Irvine

Trabuco Canyon

Mission Viejo

Esencia

Mission San Juan
Capistrano

San Clemente

N
W · E
S

Las Flores Adobe

Orange County

SANTA ANA
MOUNTAINS

Cristianitos Canyon/
Baptismal Well

■ Camp Pendleton
(SAN DIEGO COUNTY CONTINUED)

PORTOLÁ'S ROUTE

● Rancho Santa Margarita

WHEN I ARRIVED AT THE San Mateo Campground at the foot of Cristianitos Canyon, I stood in a shower stall and drained my fifty cents' worth: four minutes of blessed hot water. Showered again in the morning, because why not, and took my time breaking camp. It was too damn hot to hike through the whole middle of the day. At a shady picnic table, I jotted a few notes while I borrowed a charge for my camera and phone, a constant concern, from an RV hookup. By mid-afternoon, RVs were lined up and idling at the campground entrance, the weekend crush. I crossed the road and waded through tall, burry grass in my sneakers toward a jeep trail that led up the northern, buffy ridge of Cristianitos, thinking about Richard's admonition: "I'd definitely have boots on if I were to walk through here." Rattle-snake country. This was Camp Pendleton land also, and again I wasn't sure I wasn't trespassing.

I was headed inland, into Orange County, almost due east toward the Ortega Highway—Ortega was the Portolá expedition's lead scout. In the chaparral, more ghostly combat placements stood with their vacant windows, like cardboard boxes tumbled into the scrub, and I imagined the marines orienteering between them, humping a pack like me. From above, I could see and hear a few of them acceler-ating on Cristianitos Road back to 62 Area on motorcycles like Tom Cruise in *Top*

Gun, though that elite navy flight school long ago moved from Miramar to Fallon, Nevada. Under humming, stick-figure electrical towers, the road climbed the ridge. The Portolá expedition must have remained low in the canyon, but I couldn't walk there. Soon I was trudging up and down a massive firebreak of soft, tilled soil, the width of three lanes, an invisible fence dividing Camp Pendleton from San Clemente suburbia. Mountain lion prints in the dust, I was pretty sure, wider and more oval than a dog, clawless. The hills the color of a cougar. How can I describe the shades of brown that are Southern California and its straw-filled terrain? Dirty blonde and rosy brown, invasive khaki, coffee with milk, the rusty umber of California buckwheat, potato skin to the horizon. But studded with green. With oak, manzanita, and toyon, wherever there is leakage or a little luck, a dearth of fire.

Looking into the valley, I tracked the bone-white roadside cross that marked the Cristianitos historical site as it passed behind me, and out here in the empty scrubland I could imagine myself a traveler in former times. "The ranchos," Richard had told me, "they all had these crosses as a sign to travelers to say, 'You're welcome here. You can come here and get a meal, your horses will be fed. Spend a night, spend a week—no bill.'" There had been one above the Santa Margarita hacienda and one beside the Las Flores *asistencia*. Of course, this cross in off-limits Camp Pendleton meant no such thing.

The soil passing beneath me was flecked with mica, a rifle shell crushed and bent, a scattering of scrub-jay feathers from some minor unnoticed catastrophe— the end of a particular blue. Coyote and bobcat tracks, too, and the unbroken snake-bellies of bikes. Quail whirring, clucking, into a thicket that had snagged a Mylar balloon. Even looking through binoculars around here seemed a risk, like I might get in trouble for spying. And I was spying on everything.

For the first time, I had decided to wear my long-sleeve shirt, and already I knew it would save my skin on this journey, though already it was soaked through. I salvaged an empty water bottle from the trail, just in case I found a spigot: in the sun, you start to second-guess your preparation. The long hillside was a crisscross of sidewinding roads, firebreaks, and single track; then all of a sudden an office park appeared, which looked surprisingly like a bloated combat placement, as well as the utter oasis of a golf course, Bella Collina, a counter-vision to the sage and chaparral. A golf course in Southern California can use as much water each day as a family of four does in five years. It was a glimpse of a different, artificial season, and it made me wonder if this landscape might have been lusher when the Portolá party walked through. This green was so obviously false, titillating, pornographic, but the interface of pastoral and scrubland was somehow irresistible to the eye: a work of art. Someone was sweeping up balls on the unirrigated driving range—yet another rangeland—in a cart with Plexiglass sides, a plume of dust rising in his wake. From the clubhouse, a wedding rang out—pop music, the cheers after the couple was announced, "We invite you over here for a cocktail hour, while the family is taking pictures"—and it made me feel alone. But around the bend, above Avenida Pico, I found rubescent house finches feeding on thistle heads big and spiny as artichokes—*bracteate*, armored as if by "plates of metal"—and watched them tease the seed free and sever the kernel from the cottony pappi, which floated into the air, all of it lit like a torch in the sunlight. I thought of my wife. She would love to paint these thistles.

AVENIDA PICO DEAD-ENDED IN A cul-de-sac where some teenagers had parked their Audis and Mustangs in a fan and were milling about, taking pictures by these sleek hoods, as if they'd only just gotten their licenses, which was more or less true. "Let's go meet the BMWs," said one of them, in all seriousness, before they sped off. The cul-de-sac and Cristianitos Road, which I'd planned to take north to the Ortega Highway, were blocked by a tall fence and gate, and the finer print of the NO TRESPASSING sign read RANCHO MISSION VIEJO. Reluctantly I started down a walking path that traversed the hillside in my general direction. But when I saw the fence had fallen away, I took a deep breath and dropped down the dry-grass slope onto Cristianitos Road. The day was escaping me, and this was the direct and historic route, *más viejo* than Mission Viejo.

Richard's words about Camp Pendleton echoed in my mind: "The Mission Viejo Company would have developed it." I was at the southern end of Rancho Mission Viejo, the remainder of John Forster's and, later, James Flood's enormous ranch, one that combined the Santa Margarita y Las Flores, Mission Viejo, and Trabuco land grants: 230,000 acres in total, or 359 square miles. Obviously, you could walk a straight line in such an acreage for days without coming to its end. When the marines co-opted Rancho Santa Margarita y Las Flores, they took the entirety of the rancho's coastline. A "mere" fifty-two thousand inland acres remained, the Trabuco and Mission Viejo tracts, and it belonged to the O'Neill family.

How the O'Neills came into the picture is an unlikely story that speaks to James Flood's enormous wealth: he didn't much care whether he gave away an enormous ranch. Richard O'Neill was a butcher and then a meat wholesaler in San Francisco's market district, and he supplied Flood's saloon, the Auction Lunch, with fresh cuts each morning. They became friends. Then Flood became one of the wealthiest men in the world when he finagled a controlling interest in the Consolidated Virginia Mine, one of the Comstock's largest. It produced about $136 million, and ever after Flood invested in all directions. His Bank of Nevada seized the struggling Chowchilla Ranch near Merced in the Central Valley, and Flood asked his friend and meat-seller O'Neill if he would manage the ranch. O'Neill knew his beef and made it profitable.

Looking for a ranch of his own, Richard O'Neill eventually inspected Rancho Santa Margarita y Las Flores when it came up for sale after Forster's death. He approached Flood, and in 1882 they made a handshake agreement: Flood would pay the $450,000 price, and O'Neill would manage it, with his portion of the earnings going toward a half share. The deal was never in writing, but amazingly Flood's son made good on the promise in 1907. When the Santa Margarita Company dissolved in 1939, Richard O'Neill Jr. took hold of the inland Mission Viejo and Trabuco Ranches while Flood's sister and descendants kept the coastal Santa Margarita y Las Flores. Three years later, the marines came calling and suddenly only Richard O'Neill Jr. was left with land. In this way, the O'Neills were again lucky.

My first coyote of the trip appeared in a field beside the road, but by the time I wrestled my binoculars out of my back pocket it had slipped into the tree line. From then on out, I kept my binoculars in my more capacious front pocket for quick access. The road crossed a dry creek and came to an intersection with another gate, waist height with another Mission Viejo NO TRESPASSING sign. It would be hard to argue I hadn't seen this sign, but I'd come this far; I hopped it and accelerated, feeling like those San Clemente teenagers in their convertibles. "Just think about this property with no sounds," Richard had said, and now I experienced it. There was nothing mechanical, not even planes, only the notes and scratchings of birds and an anemic breeze. I could hear myself think. Then a barn owl flushed from an oak window, startling me, pale and golden with rounded wings and a heart-shaped face. Like so many large, empty land holdings, these Mission Viejo miles were in many ways an effective preserve.

I knew this road through Mission Viejo was Portolá's route because, even from the heights of Camp Pendleton, I'd seen the formations that Crespí wrote about: "At some knolls upon a tableland ... we went through the midst of two mines situated at ground level with very good red-earths and ochre, which had been dug out a bit by the heathens in order to get the paints which are their party, and Sunday, clothing." Even from afar, these banded slopes reminded me of the famous Painted Hills of Oregon, where the clayey strata of white and red are so steep and alkaline that nothing grows. Finally I neared them. The white layers were likely a soft mudstone of ash, while the reds were a sign of a warmer time that had leached the stone and left iron oxides. The natives wore these colors for ceremony and sunscreen. I wanted to gather some of this pigment for myself, but this "mine" was behind yet another gate, down a short road. I thought about what I would do and say if a ranch hand or patrolman came upon me: I'd gotten lost; I was trying to find my way out. Maybe I could dive off the road into some brush. But it was lined with barbwire, woven through with cactus and poison oak.

Suddenly two cars were up ahead, and I stopped in my tracks, stutter-stepped, and then just kept walking. A young man in an SUV with a "Real Estate at Rancho Mission Viejo" decal on its door looked at me with something like amazement as I raised my hand in mock naivete. Behind him was a sedan full of old ladies with glasses. I wondered where they were going. I wondered if they would make a call about me. I picked up the pace.

Then up ahead I saw something else moving, crawling, across the pavement: a tarantula, the size of my palm, and hairy. Its bristles were tinged with red, especially on its bulbous abdomen, which looked almost like a filbert paintbrush. I hovered over it, and when I reached down with my camera, it slowed on its eight legs and circumspectly raised its rump in warning: their abdomens can release a cloud of urticating (stinging) hairs with barbs that irritate the eyes and nose, or fingers. It walked with a metronomic hitch, each hoary foot meeting the pad of another as it stepped. It slowed whenever it sensed my hand or foot, and once two fang-like spinnerets emerged from its abdomen, an intimidating bluff.

This, I've learned, could have only been a lone, mature male—females almost never leave their burrows during the day. I saw several others crossing the road. We were wandering Mission Viejo all together in the warm evening. Normally they hunt insects, and even lizards and frogs, by night, injecting their venom into the animal to predigest it, but these tarantulas were on a different mission: each in search of a female in her burrow lined with silk to keep the walls from caving in. He might travel as much as three or four miles each night until he found her. He would follow her scent to the den's opening and rub the strands of its silk funnel and, if she was receptive, she would emerge. Afterward she might eat him.

NEARING THE HIGHWAY, I HOPPED another gate. Just as I was about to breathe easy, three more cars came down the road from a sandpit facility. I wondered if they'd gotten word from that earlier caravan and were out to intercept me. But they drove past me and stopped at a second gate at the highway, and several of the men left their cars, but only to open and shut the gate. I walked west on the shoulder of narrow Ortega Highway until, at last light, I dove back onto Mission Viejo land through a gap in the barbwire where the fence tapered to a massive concrete culvert. I thought about sleeping in the culvert itself, but went up the hillside. Too nervous or tired to set up a tent, I kept imagining that someone might spot me from the ridge above. But in a ranch of this size it was unlikely. The night was warm and I unzipped my bag, turning it into a blanket, and I lay underneath it. A few stray ants found their way in. Big ones. I tried to ignore them, even after one bit me between my toes. Bright moon, unsteady dreams.

Sometime later I shot upright when an animal called loudly twenty feet from me. It sounded like "Whoa," or "Nooo," or "Zoe"—a gruff exhalation, almost human. It was like no deer snort I'd ever heard. I fumbled for my headlamp and swung the light. Only bare earth and grass. I didn't think it was a wild boar. I wondered if it was a mountain lion. My heart was racing, and for a few minutes I sat upright in the moonlight. I told myself that, whatever it was, it was gone.

Later I confirmed it, after listening to recordings of vocalizations. It was a mountain lion: an animal that can leap eighteen feet into the air, and up to forty feet across the ground. That can easily weigh 150 pounds and will take down larger prey by leaping onto its back and severing its spinal cord at the neck, biting its jugular, or clamping its windpipe shut until it asphyxiates. I wonder if this ghost cat kept walking, unsure and ultimately afraid of what I was. They walk six or so miles each night on a much larger territorial circuit—almost the distance I was averaging each day. They need roughly one deer a week to survive. Or did the cat sit nearby and watch me settle back into sleep, its muscular tail flicking silently in the lunar glow?

IN THE MORNING, I WALKED a few minutes to the mouth of Cañada Gobernadora, where the expedition camped before it went north up the canyon. But I had decided to stay on the Ortega Highway and detour a few miles west to absorb Mission San Juan Capistrano. The Portolá party hadn't walked through the valley where Capistrano is sited, though the scouts may have ventured that way. But the mission was an important bridge between Mission San Diego and Mission San Gabriel in Los Angeles. After secularization, Don Juan Forster then bought its ruins for $710 from his brother-in-law, Governor Pío Pico, and lived there for twenty years before Abraham Lincoln returned the missions to the Catholic Church and Forster moved south to Rancho Santa Margarita. Now Mission San Juan Capistrano is billed as "the Jewel of the Missions." So I wanted to see it, at the expense of my legs.

Mission San Juan Capistrano is a startling contrast to Mission San Luis Rey. Immaculately restored, with extensive gardens, it has a booming street-front, picture-window gift shop, part of a recent renovation that cost well over $3 million. The third most-visited attraction in Orange County behind Disneyland and Knott's Berry Farm (not a berry farm anymore, but another amusement park), San Juan Capistrano drives home the commercialization and fetishization of California's missions, trafficking in mystique and fantasy. More than half a million people a year visit the roofless Great Stone Church, ruined by an earthquake in 1812 just six years after it was completed, including gaggles of schoolkids and not a few brides and quinceañeras. When I visited, newlyweds were holding each other in the shade of the east transept's walls, her long veil lifted in the breeze, "Until death do us part" surely echoing in their endorphin-flooded minds as it was in mine. Two photographers and a videographer cooed positional suggestions. On a nearby wall, I found a fossilized scallop in the mortar, an inclusion laid by neophyte hands and now dark, smooth, from the oils of centuries of passing fingers. The Great Stone Church has been preserved and retrofitted with steel rods so that it is earthquake safe, but it hasn't been rebuilt, offering a romance of collapse and decline. Yet there are no weeds. Time here is imagined to have stopped.

The mission is the town's centerpiece, and as it grew increasingly famous, its neighborhood has become increasingly bourgeois, with fancy restaurants (good house-made veggie burgers) and a Starbucks immediately across the street, and fancy houses on the surrounding hills. In the courtyard, Crespí's wild Roses of Castile have been tamed and pruned in a broken circle around a fountain of lily pads with koi schooling through their drifting roots. People lounge on the lawns under strawberry trees, a close, imported cousin of the madrone that is now common in California on streets and in gardens. The courtyard would have been simply functional in the mission's working days, with Acjachemen women combing and spinning wool and, rarely, something like a rodeo in its dusty enclosure with spectators on its dull-orange pantile roof. The courtyard gardens of the missions are a modern invention, part and parcel of the importation of water into Southern California. They attract birds. As I sat under a tree, a mockingbird rose from a cross on the rooftop, again and again, belting a convincing imitation of a kestrel's *kee kee kee*. Mockingbirds can learn up to two hundred sounds. This one did not stoop so low as to include a car alarm in its repertoire. Again and again, it lifted, with flashing white-and-gray wings and a liquid voice. The Kumeyaay of San Diego believe that mockingbirds are the souls of the dead reincarnate, that they know all languages, and that they can speak to their owners, even in dreams. Kept in an arrowweed cage lined with rabbit fur for warmth, the bird was always released after its owner's death, as if to sing his praises or rendezvous with him elsewhere. Perhaps the Acjachemen held similar beliefs.

At a table under an umbrella was an adobe-making station. Normally this activity is reserved for kids, but the attendant, Josh, let me have at it. Blue buckets held semi-wet mud, clumping, the texture of cauliflower. I squeezed a handful of this dark earth into a square wooden mold that looked like a window frame for an elf, pressed the wet adobe flush against the table with my palm, and then pushed the brick out carefully. Ta-da. "You just need to put it in the sun, now," said Josh. This brick would fit on a sill and dry in a day or two. The mission's bricks, however, were poured into ladder molds set on the ground; they weighed sixty pounds each and took a month to dry. It's clay that holds adobe together. Sometimes straw or other organics, like dung, are added to help bond the adobe, but if your dirt is right, apparently it's not necessary: straw and grass fiber provide tensile strength, while adobe is all about compression. "What is Adobe?" asked a faded laminate sheet on the table, with all these materials depicted. The gratuitous close-up of a wet, swirled cow patty was a turnoff, but I imagined it played well with kids. Poop in the walls! I took my bricklet to go, in a handy, slick cardboard box the mission provided. It fit perfectly. "People are going to think I'm carrying gourmet chocolates," I said to Josh, though I wasn't exactly sure who was going to be looking into my backpack. "Yeah, just let them try it," he replied. Sometimes the kids do try to eat the adobe, he said, which looks not unlike brownie mix. Those who don't scrutinize the laminate.

WHAT MADE SAN JUAN CAPISTRANO famous, what put this cow town on the map, isn't the mission per se, but the story of the swallows. Maybe you've heard about the swallows of San Juan Capistrano, how they miraculously return each year to build their mud nests under the eaves of the Great Stone Church and the older Serra Chapel on the Feast Day of Saint Joseph (though some "scouts" arrive early, and some "laggards" trail behind). How they return to Jerusalem in the fall, carrying a twig in their beak to use as a raft as they cross the oceans. These are cliff swallows, and in fact they migrate to and from South America. They have dark blue blacks, rusty throats, square tails, and a white "headlight" on their foreheads. And they are doubly a quintessential mission bird because they likewise build adobes; they descend to puddles and collect mouthfuls of mud, or "pellets," which they then spit up to create a hanging nest under a ledge or, in modern times, an eave. Each mouthful adds another brick to the foundation or curving walls. These "adherent cups" eventually grow into a gourd shape: a globular nesting chamber with a tubular entrance that makes it more difficult for predators to enter. A cliff swallow nest is an accretion of over a thousand mouthfuls. They patch up their nests, reuse them from year to year. A century ago, in the ruins of this and maybe other missions, the birds may well have scooped up genuine melted adobe and so recycled the mission's bricks to their former heights.

There are reports of swallow colonies at Mission San Juan Capistrano from the nineteenth century, when the Great Stone Church's ruins would have been a passable cliff rising lonely in the pastureland. But it was Father O'Sullivan, the man who resurrected Mission San Juan Capistrano after the turn of the century, who spun their myth and importance in his 1930 book, *Capistrano Nights*. While strolling in the town one day, he apparently happened on someone knocking nests from the tall eaves of a new hotel. The swallows were frenzied. "The poor birds were in a terrible panic, darting hither and thither, flying and screaming about their demolished homes," wrote O'Sullivan. As he recalls in his memoir, he confronted the hotelier, resulting in this exchange:

"'What in the world are you doing?' I asked.

"'Why,' said he, 'these dirty birds are a nuisance and I am getting rid of them!'

" 'But where can they go?' I continued.

" 'I don't know and I don't care,' he replied, slashing away with his pole, 'but they've no business here, destroying my property.'

" 'Then come on, swallows,' I cried. 'I'll give you shelter. Come to the Mission. There's room enough there for all.' "

As the story goes, the very next day O'Sullivan discovered these swallows rebuilding under the eaves of the Serra Chapel and the Great Stone Church. It's a Franciscan parable if there ever was one, another recycling: give shelter and succor to the animals. O'Sullivan's book caught the attention and imagination of other writers, and in 1936, an international radio broadcaster told the world that "the skies were blackened with swallows" on Saint Joseph's Day in San Juan Capistrano. A few years later, Leon René wrote the song, "When the Swallows Come Back to Capistrano," which made the mission truly famous. The song became a hit on records by several bands that, together, have sold more than 3 million copies.

On the mission's south wing, at the crux of the cracked stucco wall and the eave's black beams, were several swallow nests that I and several other visitors tried to wrap our minds around. No ticking, squeaky calls emanated from their interiors. Because they were made of plastic. These fake nests seemed like a crass deception, but they were designed by ornithologists to help lure swallows back to Mission San Juan Capistrano, the equivalent of a duck decoy. The swallows have disappeared. It's thought that the restoration of and scaffolding around the Great Stone Church, that disturbance, might have caused the birds to turn elsewhere. The mission has also tried playing their calls from an iPod in the greenery behind a statute of Junípero Serra and a neophyte boy. But cliff swallows now have innumerable nesting options, like highway overpasses, with fewer gawkers and more bugs in the air.

"Come to the Mission," O'Sullivan wrote. "There's room enough there for all." The swallows have become a symbol of inclusion and loyalty. But they are heroes in a narrative which, in truth, has no relation to or bearing on the mission's real history. As Jacque Nuñez, an Acjachemen woman, once said at the start of the town's spring festival, La Fiesta de las Golondrinas, "Before there were suburbs and towns here, before the ranchers, before the settlers, before the missionaries, before the Spaniards and Mexicans, there were swallows that flew here, coming from faraway Goya [Argentina]. And those swallows that flew over this land long ago also flew over a people, my people, the Acjachemen. Those were the first people that lived here. And those were the people who built the mission when the missionaries came. It is their craftsmanship and handiwork that we admire today when we see the mission. They—we—are *still* here."

I CAMPED IN DRY SAN JUAN CREEK, laced with sandy horse trails and their crumbling road apples, and then hiked back up the Ortega Highway to Cañada Gobernadora, which the Portolá expedition followed north. The distant hills were washed out, a few serrations of the coastal Santa Ana Mountains barely visible. Antonio Parkway carried me across the creek's wash to Cow Camp Road—Rancho Mission Viejo had once gathered its vaqueros here for its yearly branding—which led me to a development called Esencia, a place still very much coming into being. The steep road cuts were newly mulched and planted with ornamentals. I passed the loneliest sapling in a sidewalk so new you could smell the cement; it looked like they'd forgotten to pave a square and instead decided to plant a tree. Trucks hauling something, trucks hauling nothing, and trucks hauling a Caterpillar or tractor to haul or shove something else. All of them big. Trucks with their final axle flipped onto their own trailer bed, like you might see on the logging arteries of the Northwest. Perhaps that was the source of all this lumber. Cow Camp ended abruptly in an unfinished, barricaded dirt lane, and I turned uphill toward the coffee shop I'd spied on my phone. I hoped to camp out for a while like a cow in the shade. I also desperately needed coffee.

The planned community of Rancho Mission Viejo ultimately will have eight "villages" and fourteen thousand homes. On my walk from San Juan Capistrano, I had passed the first village, Sendero, "the path," and watched retirees play paddle tennis. Sendero had been named America's "Master-planned Community of the Year" by the National Association of Home Builders. Now Esencia, "essence" or "indispensible," was underway: twenty-seven hundred homes, plus apartments, on 890 hilltop acres, the highest geography of Rancho Mission Viejo. If you paid a little extra, from your window, on a clear day, you might be able to see a touch of ocean near Dana Point. A K–8 school was planned. A high school would follow as those kids grew. Whole blocks were being assembled. The hammers were like a chorus of harsh frogs during a spring mating. All of Orange County had been built this way, one development at a time.

The outdoor patio beside the coffee shop at Esencia's Canyon House community center overlooked an oak canyon, and a small public "farm" stood next to it, really just a garden of raised beds. In the afternoon I hoisted my pack again and, on my way out, ran into two older women who asked me where I was going. "Into the wilderness," I said, though technically I was only going to walk past it.

"You are? Do you have enough water and everything?" replied one.

"By yourself?" said the other. "Don't go by yourself. You're going to make us worried. We're worriers."

Short of the wilderness, down the block were the Aurora townhomes. I left my backpack on a bench around the corner for credibility and then, for lack of a clear entrance, hopped a rail toward a door that read, MODEL 4. "Hello," I said in the foyer, hearing voices. It was the TV, some Disney movie: a prince was taking a princess's CGI face into his hands for a drawn-out kiss. "Hello," I called again. No one was home.

But around the corner was the sales office for Aurora at Esencia in a first-floor space that would become a two-car garage once even the models were sold. Debbie, with sandy hair, a floral blouse, a sporty voice, welcomed me in. I told her I was passing through, that my wife and I were thinking about moving from San Francisco. It just seemed too far-fetched to say I lived in Idaho. That definitely would give me away. People from Orange County were moving to Idaho, not the other way around. And fortunately, I had just visited a laundromat in San Juan Capistrano, where I'd stripped down to my bathing suit and washed everything. "It's a special place," Debbie told me. "Plus the open space is awesome. Tons of hiking trails, and even docent-led walks. We'll be here through March–April next year. We have everything released now except our last phases." She handed me a colorful site map with about a hundred townhouses in horseshoe configurations, each townhouse size a different pastel. She began circling possibilities, scribbling prices: 637K, 613K, 611K, 516K...

"Do you have a price point that you're trying to stay in?" she asked.

"Um, I mean, this is all doable," I said. "It just depends on so many things."

"So is it a job move?"

"Well, potentially, yeah."

I was terrible at this. She homed in on the two-bedroom units, perfect for a young couple or someone way out of their league. Someone wearing dusty sneakers and burr-filled socks who was clearly dehydrated. "This one at five-sixteen, this one at five-oh-four ... both of these are going to be ready in September and they come with a ten-thousand-dollar incentive." She trotted me outside, back into the heat, and down the flower-lined railing toward the corner model, Unit 1, the cheapest in Esencia, the essence of "starter." "This is a driveway, by the way, normally. Everything has two-car garages with direct access. You have elevated living, with the master bedroom on the third floor. Sometimes it will have a deck off the master, sometimes it will not." She left me at the door to explore on my own.

I was grateful for the air-conditioning and to have escaped Debbie's questions. She was likely onto me. The lights were on. New-carpet smell, new-everything smell. Newness, it seemed, was the essence of happiness. Music piping discreetly, on both floors, in sync. The shadows of a glossy tree cast by a tall floor lamp onto the ceiling were perfect. "Happiness is a journey, not a destination," argued a pillow on the master bedspread, just behind an alabaster breakfast tray with two mugs and a matte-finish jet-black bowl. An odd maxim considering they were selling a destination. The time on the stove, 1:00, was perfect, though it was actually 3:50 and I had better move along. The refrigerator was empty and thirty-four degrees, but you wouldn't starve because two canisters of handmade pasta sat on the counter. The mention of a cobweb would have been profane. Hell, I could probably enjoy living here, I thought to myself. Then I opened the sliding glass door to the balcony, which looked out on almost identical condos—"sometimes it will have a deck off the master," Debbie had said, "sometimes it will not"—and heard nothing but jackhammer.

"Thanks again, Debbie," I said, popping my head back in. "I enjoyed it." She sprang up from her rolling chair, introduced her colleague Lauren.

"It has a more rural feel than San Francisco," Lauren said.

Debbie nodded, and added, "It's the wave of how they're building things . . . more farm-to-table and environmentally conscious, and it's kind of like . . . more trails, more dedicated open space."

"It's the way of the future," said Lauren, nodding.

"And of the past," I said.

"Well, it always comes around," said Debbie.

JUST AFTER FIVE O'CLOCK, ABOUT three miles north, I strode into an empty, 5-million-gallon water tank, brick red, that was still under construction. There were two of them, in fact, to supply water to Esencia's more than twenty-seven hundred projected homes. I had followed a freshly cut dirt road up to the area's highest knoll and suddenly the tanks were revealed, one far from finished, with a roof of steel rafters that radiated across the sky like the veins of a Mexican fan palm. The other was almost buttoned up. Only a doorway remaining—a doorway large enough to drive a semitruck through—and a few open portals for eventual pipes that cast ellipses of sun across its metal bottom. The tank seemed as large as an aircraft hangar, and it boomed with each step. Dusty tire tracks from the lifts wove across the floor like snakes. I wondered if birds, maybe swallows, might roost or nest inside it only to be trapped and inundated as the water level squeezed them against the ceiling. "Echo," I said aloud. "Echo," the tank replied a hundred times at once. It felt like an inchoate cathedral to which all of Southern California might come to worship before it was sealed off.

And where would this water come from? In theory, it would have come from the 750-acre Irvine Lake, a reservoir that sits in Santiago Canyon but, because of the extended drought, was only at 13 percent of capacity. But until the reservoir rose again, the water that would fill these tanks would drain from the Sierra Nevada Mountains to the Sacramento-San Joaquin Delta—once a marshy confluence in the Central Valley the size of Rhode Island and not far from my ultimate destination, the San Francisco Bay. Either that, or this water would come originally from the Colorado River. It was going to be bought from the Metropolitan Water District of Southern California, which imports from all over, in particular from Northern California. The State Water Project is the longest and most complex conveyance system in the world—about 700 miles of aqueduct, tunnel, and pipe—with three dozen reservoirs and more than twenty pump stations. Two-thirds of California's population relies on this network. Here was a new terminus. It rang like a bell as I clapped my hands.

I sat in the shade against one of the tanks and drank from one of my Powerade bottles, which I'd refilled in the Canyon House community center bathroom. This water was also from somewhere distant, and it would drain shortly through me into the grass. Santiago Peak, 5,689 feet above sea level, dominated the horizon. It was the right shoulder of the Saddleback formation that defines the eastern skyline of Orange County, the highest peaks in the Santa Ana Mountains and the oldest rock in Orange County. As I thought about it, that "saddle" was like a constant reminder of the Portolá expedition and the vaquero days that would follow. Below those peaks, in the foreground, were the terra-cotta-soldier houses of the exclusive community of Coto de Caza ("the hunting preserve"), built in 1968. There was no snow on the Santa Ana, nothing to feed this civilization but Northern California, and all along the way much of that water would evaporate into the sky, and the fish of the Sacramento-San Joaquin Delta would continue to struggle for lack of it. And here I was leaning up against and drinking from this reality, complicit and grateful. I was so thirsty.

Two ravens sat on the dusty lip of the new road as I left, their scaled charcoal feathers ruffling in the wind, their bills agape as if they were also thirsty. Down the ridge, another new road ran back toward Esencia. The water pipe must be right underneath it. The distant knoll it arrived to was graded, covered with bedrock. Yellow machines—dozers, shovels, rollers, water trucks—were lined up for the night like cars in an airport lot. As I walked, the ravens dropped off, falling out of view and then rising up in swirling play. Their tails balanced the air, their heads rotated. They had no idea where they were going, but happiness was the journey.

THROUGH THE THOMAS F. RILEY WILDERNESS PARK, all grassy knolls and oak. As soon as I stepped around Mission Viejo's last gate, I felt freer, rid of the anxiety that comes with trespassing. PLEASE SHOVEL MANURE FROM PARKING AREA, read a sign, the sweetness of alfalfa lingering. There was also a posting that warned of mountain lions, but I didn't need a reminder. Acorn woodpeckers laughed in the live oak. My trail dead-ended at Kingfisher Court, where three boys were playing stickball in their driveway, hurling a tennis ball against their folding garage door and swinging at the rebound (and missing), pitcher and batter standing almost side by side—a recipe for a broken arm. I was half-staring at my phone. "Pokémon Go?" asked one of the kids. "No," I said, "I'm just trying to figure out where I'm going."

Soon I was going up Oso Parkway, my pockets full of equipment—recorder, camera, binoculars, notebook—bulging and swinging around my thighs. I flushed a bevy of bushtits that scattered like loose change through the chaparral along the sidewalk, *peep, peep, peep.* I found a pen that said, I SAVE WATER—DO YOU?, made of 76 percent pre-consumer recycled plastic. Eventually I followed a street called Meandering Trail into the community of Las Flores—another thousand-acre Mission Viejo Company development. Since the real Las Flores had been lost to the marines, they stole its name and built another one, just down the way from their version of Rancho Santa Margarita, which has the longest name of any California city. Near dusk, I found a trail into Trabuco Canyon, a deep, wild, welcome gash in Orange County's plain of planned community. The sky was the most sultry orange imaginable. My feet were barking. The dogs that belonged to the distance were barking.

Down canyon, I pitched my tent in the noisy leaf litter under a sycamore with a huge ball of parasitic mistletoe hanging from it like a chandelier. And in the twilight, I scrambled up the precarious slope below an overpass to reach the warm interior of a Taco Bell, where I bought a root beer and danced a little to Top 40, to the amusement of the women with their hair tucked under their caps, as I waited for my cinnamon twists so that I could crunch them loudly and surf the internet mindlessly, and lick the sugar off my just-washed fingers, and feel like a normal person before I plunged back into the abyss of midnight deer, whose steps in the dry grass always made me hold my breath.

TRABUCO CANYON IS SO NAMED because when the Portolá expedition camped here, one of the soldiers lost a variety of gun called a trabuco. It was stolen by a Juaneño, or at least that's who they and history blamed. I had seen a trabuco, in English known as a blunderbuss, in a vitrine at Mission San Juan Capistrano. It had the look of an ornate sawed-off shotgun, all polished wood except for its flared iron muzzle, trigger, and flintlock. Its cocked hammer was wrought like a whale or sea monster, as if on an illuminated map. Flint is harder than iron, so when the hammer falls and it strikes the frizzen, microscopic bits of iron are shaved off and they combust due to the friction. These sparks fall into the gun's pan, which ignites a dab of powder, which through a pinhole ignites the rest of the powder inside the barrel. *Boom!* Blunderbuss is a corruption of the Dutch *donderbus*, meaning "thunder pipe." It's good for relatively short ranges. The soldiers would have carried theirs in leather holsters at their sides.

A stone-and-concrete historical marker sat neglected on an open, grassy bench above the creek: SAN FRANCISCO SOLANO, NAMED BY THE PORTOLÁ EXPEDITION THAT CAMPED HERE ON JULY 24TH AND 25TH 1769, WHILE OPENING THE FIRST OVERLAND TRAIL THROUGH CALIFORNIA. Crespí had officially named it this, but his name had ultimately lost out to the soldiers' nickname. I sat in the shade against a plywood shack that housed the remains of the Trabuco Adobe, swigged my bottle, and surveyed the historical marker, which was grown over with dust-covered mint behind an iron fence—very cemetery. The adobe was built around 1810 as a two-room outpost of Mission San Juan Capistrano. It was where the mission's horses were reared and broken. When the French privateer Hippolyte de Bouchard anchored off Dana Point in 1818, the mission's gold chalices and crucifixes were carried to this adobe before the mission was raided; later Pío Pico hid here in 1845 while evading American troops on his way to Mexico. Eventually it fell to shepherds, and now, far past the point of conservation, it is boarded up.

I had been hearing the sound of a machine, and suddenly a tractor emerged from the arroyo's trees, as if this canyon, too, were being developed. But the tractor was only dragging a huge bundle of bamboo like a long peacock tail. Maybe it wasn't bamboo, but it was the kind of reed I had slept beside in the San Luis Rey Valley when I'd heard the Camp Pendleton midnight exercises. In this canyon, half-dead thickets of the stuff bowed under its own weight, creating, in places, a tunnel over the trail. Some restoration must be underway. The tractor dropped its load next to a white dumpster, and when I followed it back down the road into the creek, I found eight or ten men sitting along the Stream of Francisco Solano, which was running cold and clear with a surprising amount of water. They were on break, eating out of Tupperware beside a few camp stoves for tea or coffee. Several men were playing cards on the cobble in camp chairs. Music trickled from a portable radio. It was a vision of the Spaniards resting 250 years ago, only in jeans.

Then they went back to work, walking upstream a short distance. The ponytailed restoration foreman, Rob, was busy building a child's rock dam in the creek so he could rig a pump and tamp down on the dust in the tractor's wake. He told me this bamboo look-alike was an escaped cultivar known as arundo: *Arundo donax*, also called giant reed. It grows to thirty feet tall, in clumps, and spreads rhizomatically. In North America, said Rob, arundo usually doesn't produce viable seed, it just creeps laterally or grows from root fragments washed downstream. "It's hard to kill, it's very hard to kill," Rob said. "It is definitely tough stuff, it doesn't give up. They say one acre of the rhizome, of the roots, will propagate ten acres. And they can set them, those roots, on the shelf in the sun for twenty years, and it will still rehydrate and grow." In places like Tijuana, he told me, arundo is so aggressive that it can clog a river like a dam. The water, when there is some, has to flow over the banks to get around it. And though arundo looks like bamboo, it's useless, he said. You can't eat it, you can't use it for building because it dries brittle. Well, you can make ethanol out of it. It is the ultimate invader. It was dense in the Los Angeles River before Alta California was even given to Mexico. It was thought to have come from the Mediterranean, since the padres introduced it—*Carrizo de Castilla*, Grass of Castile—but turns out it only invaded there too, in antiquity, from the Indian subcontinent, which is perhaps why I picture elephants and rhinos in this towering cane. Here there was only a tractor. "The last contract," said Rob, "we had guys dragging it out. It was tough, my guys were ready to hang me."

This restoration was, indeed, like a minor military operation. It was not dissimilar from the way the Portolá expedition would have broken trail, with machetes, through dense canyons and passes. These men were using loppers to cut the hollow canes, one by one—chainsaws were too dangerous, in such close quarters—and then stacking and tying them for the tractor. Others raked away debris so the stumps could be sprayed with herbicide. "It's like a brick wall," said a man named Jeff, who was stacking. "And after we cut the reed, the root-bound underneath is very much alive." They would have to dig it out. After the removal, sycamore would be planted—one of the tractor operators told me Trabuco Canyon had one of the oldest sycamore stands around—and even poison oak, which wildlife loves.

Leaving this plain of San Francisco Solano, I noticed a sign with red lettering in the grass along the trail: WARNING!! POSSIBLE UNEXPLODED ORDINANCE (UXO) OR PRACTICE BOMBS MAY BE PRESENT IN THIS AREA. DO NOT TOUCH!!! REMAIN ALERT TO POTENTIAL DANGERS. EXERCISE CAUTION IN YOUR ACTIONS—STAY ON PARK TRAIL. This canyon, I learned, had been within the Trabuco Bombing Range, used through the Korean War. Mostly "practice" bombs were dropped, explosives that only produce a cloud of smoke but are dangerous nonetheless. When Rancho Santa Margarita was developed, seventy tons of unexploded bombs were carted off. But the undeveloped canyons like Trabuco weren't cleared, not comprehensively. I thought of the men cutting the arundo jungle along the creek; I thought about how I had tramped through the grass off-trail in the dark the night before.

THAT AFTERNOON, MILES TO THE west, I walked Irvine Boulevard with an oily grapefruit in my pocket, one I had picked from an overhanging limb in a Lake Forest neighborhood. The road ran through leafy commercial parks, and then, as if emerging from a tunnel of civilization, was suddenly entirely exposed and unfinished on a bare plain that swept south toward the San Joaquin Hills on the coast near Laguna. A white feather lay on a bedrock shoulder, where a sidewalk would exist soon, and I imagined it would become a fossil, the wet slurry entombing its vanes and barbs for others to find in thousands of years, though in truth the concrete would last only a short while.

Beyond a fence was a vast dirt field, once chaparral, and then ranchland, and then Marine Corps Air Station El Toro. Decommissioned in 1999, it was now awaiting houses on its northern fringe, though enormous hangars still loomed. Probably you could see this empty lot and its dust from space. The eight- and ten-thousand-foot tarmacs would look like an enormous cross laid on the land. In the distance, in front of the seaside hills, was a cluster of high-rises—the Irvine Spectrum—and an enormous orange globe. Turns out this is a balloon in Great Park, a developing recreational park of over six hundred acres on the old El Toro land. Thirty passengers at a time can ride the balloon four hundred feet into the air for a forty-mile view on a clear day. Walking along the chain-link between me and those raw miles, I began to imagine all this hard- and soft-scaping as nothing but coastal scrub and chaparral, nothing but coyote brush with white-crowned sparrows and towhees erupting from sprays of pungent green; all twists of manzanita with Anna's hummingbirds zipping through to draw from bell-shaped flowers.

The land that is Irvine was consolidated by brothers Benjamin and Thomas Flint, their cousin Llewllyn Bixby, and another partner, James Irvine, a San Francisco merchant. Together they bought Rancho San Joaquin, Rancho Lomas de Santiago, and some of Rancho Santiago de Santa Ana, in total eight miles of ocean-front and 110,000 acres. Like many others, including James Flood, they bought when the 1860s drought wreaked havoc on Mexican American rancheros. It was a period when there was a major turnover in ownership. At the same time the Civil War generated a demand for wool, so the Flints and Bixby wanted to expand their sheep business, centered around Monterey, to Southern California. Irvine bought out the others in 1876, and the Irvine Company was formed by his son in 1894, not long after Orange County was established. So began the transition from grazing to growing. Beans, barley, and corn; then celery, cabbage, peas, and lettuce. Finally citrus groves went in. All of it created a demand for water that led to the building of reservoirs that now feed homes.

When Los Angeles suburbs bumped up against the ranch, the Irvine Company began to focus on development, at first mainly around Newport Bay. The completion of Disneyland in 1955 and the Santa Ana Freeway further shifted attention from Los Angeles and decentralized the region to the company's advantage. From 1950 to 1960, Orange County's population more than tripled to 704,000 people. At that moment, the University of California also decided to build a new campus, and the company smartly donated a thousand acres for UC Irvine, around which they developed a comprehensive master plan for "a garden city": a self-sufficient community of interspersed housing, business districts, and open space. The architect, William Pereira, claimed to want to avoid vast parking lots and instead "restore the land to the pedestrian" by lacing it with neighborhood and regional parks. The Irvine Company and others like the Mission Viejo Company imagined they were pushing back on mass-produced, amenity-poor suburbs. Of course there was nothing but money in it, too. The houses were twice as expensive as others in the county and tailored toward white, upper-middle-class families. Ultimately, for all its gardens, you could argue that at heart Irvine is inefficient suburban sprawl. But people moved in and led rich lives. The Irvine Company is still developing and the population of Orange County is 3.2 million.

Not far from where the expedition had camped, a Portola Court was springing up between Still Night Street and Irvine Boulevard. Only the corner condos were finished, the rest still in plywood, as if the colony was spreading from an artesian well. Crimson bottlebrush grew on the newly mulched embankment. An advertising banner hung on the noise-canceling wall of textured cinder block and plate glass offered an enormous bird-of-paradise flower. Here was paradise. You could look in, see your future residence. From within, you could look over Irvine Boulevard toward the blinding orange over the ocean. Stacks of tile on the roofs. A construction worker had spray-painted a figure on one plywood wall: two nippled boobs, an hourglass waist, a smiley face. The future owners would never know of this hieroglyph. Across Still Night, behind a row of pines, was a genuine orange grove, one of the last.

As I walked up Still Night, two coyotes began to howl and cackle as the orange in the sky turned a certain ripe intensity and began to rot into the horizon. *Eeh, eh, eeeh, eh*, one called very close by. Something so hyena in the tenor of the trickster. I crossed the street to try to find them and from the sidewalk looked down at a vacant corner lot, a depression below the road overgrown with brush and grass. At least for this day, they had denned here. *Eeh, eh, eeeh, eh.* The dogs erupted in reply. A glass door slid open beyond a wall, a man said to his dog: "Get inside—be quiet!" I would have been barking too. One coyote moved into view, then another. They looked directly toward the lava sun as it disappeared. This was their hour; they could gauge the time precisely. Their noses worked the breeze. Cottontails scattered as I moved a few steps closer, and the coyotes heard me, it seems, because they quieted. They looked right at or past me, standing as only a dog can, so still and so comfortably, listening, and then trotted into the grass for a veil. They lay down. One was skinny and mangy, and through my binoculars, I saw it begin to gnaw on its irritated skin as if it wanted its own marrow. It snapped after a fly, twice. I thought of my own dog, Patches. She does that. In my mind, I heard the clack of the jaw. Between the coyote's ear tips and its nose, you could draw a perfect triangle. Young sycamores were trained to stakes at the lot's edges, and just fifteen feet from the road, the coyotes sat under them waiting for the cottontails or the night, whichever came first.

AT DUSK I REACHED TOMATO SPRINGS, also known as Portola Springs, also once called the Springs of San Pantaleon by Crespí. The martyrologies tell that, in the fourth century, Pantaleon was a physician to the Roman emperor before he was convinced that Christ was the one true physician. "What use are all thy acquirements in this art, since thou art ignorant of the science of Salvation?" he was asked by a priest. He healed several on faith alone and was ordered to die for this magic. He was burned, scalded with molten lead, drowned in the ocean, given over to beasts, stretched on a wheel—in each case, Christ intervened. When the executioner's sword bent on his neck, the headsman was converted instantly. It was only when Pantaleon welcomed the sword that his head fell and milk flowed instead of blood.

These milk and honey springs, Tomato Springs, were hidden in a cleft below a hillock at the very edge of Irvine's development, which I suppose is civilization as we imagine it. A little oasis of green announced the water. Beyond was the Foothill Toll Road and, above that, a wilderness or former rangeland depending on your perspective, the Limestone Canyon Nature Preserve, which the Irvine Company opens to the public only for docent-led tours. Beside the spring was a cul-de-sac of freestanding condos three deep. A small rush-grown creek was channeled between levees behind these homes, and a rusted pedestrian bridge crossed over Portola Parkway for speed-walkers and mothers with their strollers.

I had thought to camp farther from the road and the springs, but was deterred by a taut barbwire fence and another PRIVATE PROPERTY sign. So from the walking path, I went up the short knoll above the springs, where I found something: a Portolá historical marker. Many of them are unmapped and unmentioned, and it felt good to have found this one by intuition. There was just enough room to put down a pad at the top. I slung down my pack immediately so that it would seem as if I had just come to this minor prominence for the view. No tent tonight; it would be too conspicuous. It was the kind of spot that teenagers might seek out to drink beer or make love on an old quilt: an endless view of Orange County with the ambient light of the city sifting down.

Across patches of darkness that in a year or two might be lit and filled with homes, the horizon twinkled. To the southwest was the Ferris wheel at the Irvine Spectrum, lit alternately purple and blue and red as it revolved through my binoculars, as well as two neon buildings like something out of Las Vegas. The great balloon of Great Park glowed just as the sun had as it descended into the unseen ocean moments ago. Darkness fell and Portola Parkway below me became an alley of incandescent globes only rarely guiding a car, each with a different shush.

Then in the great distance, far to the north, fireworks erupted: Disneyland. It must have been. Dandelion clocks lifted on the horizon and broke apart; heart-shaped pink arrays, sideways stars, and missile streaks. This was where I would go tomorrow, so far away that the fireworks looked minuscule and I could blot them with a finger. Still, they were uplifting. The show was long, fuzzy in my binoculars. The thud of the explosions was soft, friendlier than the practice mortars of Camp Pendleton. Eventually a fountain of light, the finale, a bouquet that illuminated its own smoke cloud, which must have covered the city for miles. Nothing more to see. I began to rub the dirt from between my toes, but the booming continued in the darkness. Continued for longer than I could believe before it rose to a crescendo and finally died. If thunder travels a mile every five seconds, then I was looking fifteen or twenty miles into my future.

COYOTES IN THE NIGHT. I had heard them cackling faintly, and now I pulled out my earplugs and transferred my batteries from my recorder to my flashlight in case the pack preferred this hill and I would need to ward them off. Kneeling in my sleeping bag, I saw their shapes, their motions . . . vague in the city glow. There must have been three or four within a hundred feet, and they were calling tremulously to the ones I had seen earlier a half mile off. But they silenced, and I put my earplugs back in, and my body filled with warmth. They broke into an uproar one more time, but I didn't budge, just opened and closed my eyes.

Beeping woke me in the morning, two-toned: *Uh-uh, Uh-uh.* Beeping and the ratchet of tractor plates. The yips of coyotes and cries of machinery bookend suburbia. I opened my eyes and the world was sideways: a long post of green and brown against a thick wall of ashen blue. Earthmovers were working in each direction, grading and clearing. The tanker trucks were suppressing the dust with fans of water behind them. When I opened my pack, ants were again crawling over everything; they encircled the grapefruit like miners on an oily planet, searching for a seam.

The Irvine horizon brightened to a dirty lilac. I sat on the low sandstone outcrop that had thrown an extra half hour of shade on my sleeping bag and spread Jif on a raisin bagel with the handle of a broken plastic knife. Each house below had a black panel on its roof, a thermal water heater, I thought, to bolster their showers. Trash day: green and blue bins curbside. More joggers on Portola Parkway. A California gnatcatcher, a bird threatened by these suburbs, popped to the crown of a sagebrush and flicked its long tail with a wheeze as it darted after gnats, aphids, other sage insects. Gnatcatchers twitch between islands of brush, sometimes ascending through the weave to look out from a sprig. Blue-gray with a dark forehead. As I began the day's walk, I kicked open a dried coyote scat and big seeds rattled across the concrete path. I wondered if last night's pack was bedded down now in these Tomato Springs.

"Happy summer," I said to a boy on his silver Razor scooter.

"Thanks," he said.

"How you doing?" I asked an older Indian gentleman strolling under a red "Monaco" ball cap with his hands behind his back.

"Very good morn," he replied without a smile.

A FOR SALE sign in front of a Portola Springs home had the last word: I'M GORGEOUS INSIDE.

AFTER A RESPITE AT THE oasis that is Starbucks, I walked down City Stroll alongside Mission Bell and hung a left on Iceberg Rose—which wins some kind of award, as street names go—to Nature. Nature Street looked quite similar to City

Stroll. Soon I was on Arboretum, which was mainly planted with eucalyptus. A girl pedaled by, said, "Hold on tight, here we go," to the stuffed animal belted to her handlebars. On a ball field, under some outfield trees, a counselor was feeding Wiffle Balls underhand, from about eight feet, to boys hunched over a rubber plate. Finally, his bucket emptied. "You can pick'm up, and water break," he said. "Water break, Team Awesome. Water break." The kids scrambled. The counselor stooped to snatch a sycamore fruit, a hairy pompom, out of the grass, and he hit it with his fungo bat, *ping*, harder than any of his protégés had swung. We watched it sail, the original Wiffle Ball.

A real tomato spring is at the corner of Bryan Avenue and Jeffrey Road, a fruit stand lined with sunflowers on a seven-acre urban farm. That is more or less all that remains of agriculture in Irvine. In the nineteenth century, James Irvine gradually converted his grazing land to crops, starting with thirty-one thousand acres of barley. Lima beans also thrived and, in 1911, he boasted that he had "the largest bean field, under one management, in the world." He laid thirty miles of concrete pipe to raise rhubarb, artichokes, celery, potatoes, and corn; to grow walnut, olive, and citrus groves. Thirty-eight hundred acres of Valencia orange were ripening on the ranch by 1938. But by the forties, agriculture began to give way to development. Come World War II, some of Irvine's best bean fields became El Toro Marine Corps Air Station. About 257,000 acres were farmed in Orange County in 1946. Now only 7,000 remain.

Long tables held pints of varicolored tomatoes. I asked after the sweetest cherries. "Either of these," said Juan, "try them." "Mmm," I said. "They're both good." For over twenty years, the owner of this farm had been growing organic vegetables on this plot leased from the Church of Latter-day Saints next door. But organic farming in Irvine is a battle. Last fall, a coyote took a single bite out of twenty to thirty watermelons each night. A single bite. The farmers propped a mannequin in a truck, they set up spotlights, they ordered wolf urine off the internet and sprinkled it around. Nothing worked. They also released sixty thousand predatory mites to combat the vegetarian mites that are bloodthirsty for strawberries. There is constant weeding. But the threat of development is the largest anxiety. Land is so valuable in Irvine that a farm can't expect to lease or last forever.

Juan had a thin mustache like dark peach fuzz under an Under Armour ball cap. Most of his week was spent at farmers' markets in Manhattan Beach, Redondo Beach, as far as Escondido near San Diego. "Do you live in Irvine?" I asked.

"No, it's too expensive. I live in Anaheim."

I asked about the Disneyland fireworks.

"Oh yeah, it starts around eight or nine. Every night. I used to live, like, right next to Disney. I couldn't go to sleep, I used to hate it. It was really loud. Right next to Disneyland, but now I live a little bit farther."

He asked me if I was going to go, and I replied, "Nah, I've already been to Legoland." When I told him I was walking to San Francisco, he raised his eyebrows and let me have a basket of tomatoes, a purple plum, a cucumber, and a squash for three dollars. It was highway robbery. I asked him if he knew of Santiago Creek, where the Portolá expedition had camped next. He didn't know it. Heading up the long sidewalk, I passed the farm's rows of tomatoes with many fallen or tossed to the ground, melting wrinkled into the eager soil, doomed because of some blemish. But more hung on the vines: creamy green as they begin, then every slant of yellow, and finally scarlet. I toyed the skin of my sweet cherries between my teeth for miles.

FOR SEVERAL DAYS NOW, I'D hiked roughly parallel to Santiago Creek, though it could not be seen because it was behind the buffy foothills. The creek begins near Santiago and Modjeska Peaks, the Saddleback formation that I had seen from Mission Viejo, and flows west to Orange. I met it near dusk at Grijalva Park, where men and boys were playing basketball and others were jogging a crushed-earth path on the perimeter. Santiago was an empty wash of willow. Miguel Costansó wrote of the stream, "One could see . . . that it was diminishing each day on account of the dry season, the water gradually sinking into the sand," but it "appeared to have a considerable flow in the rainy season." Just downstream of Grijalva Park, its bed has become a parking lot, one you wouldn't want to rely on during a flash flood out of the Santa Ana Mountains.

A shirtless man with a bedroll dawdled erratically along the riprap boulders, and I decided, after five nights of camping, that it would be okay, it would be fine, to spend a night in a motel. I would walk several miles in the dark to it, stopping once to sit on a wicker lounge chair by the outdoor gas pit at a Dunkin' Donuts. I did have a donut. But for a long while I sat on a park bench as the same people passed me on the cinder track, round and round: a mother and daughter speed-walking in tights, a boy on a time-trial run in basketball shorts as silver and flowing as the steelhead that once swam up Santiago Creek. The park lights brightened as the frayed horsetail clouds held the last orange of Orange County in the bruised sky. A few higher contrails like fading lead ropes. A man held up his phone to it and turned a full, slow circle, saying to a friend on video, "Can you see it? Can you see it?"

I spent two nights in the City of Orange nursing my sore legs. The expedition periodically took days off, so I would lose no time. In the afternoon of my rest day, I rallied and left Motel 6 for the Bowers Museum in Santa Ana, where I saw a carriage that had belonged to Pío Pico, all black with just two wheels, each as tall as the carriage itself. It had been donated by the granddaughter of Don Juan Forster and Pío's sister, Doña Ysidora, and there also, hanging, was Don Juan's leather vest, which I imagined he wore at the Santa Margarita hacienda. There were paintings of oranges in their crepe papers, and local packing labels, for example: OLD MISSION BRAND, VALENCIAS, GROWN & SHIPPED BY PLACENTIA ORCHARD COMPANY. The label showed three friars in their brown habits (tufts of white hair jutting from their caps) around a table under a mission colonnade, remarking, it seems, on the unrivaled roundness, color, and aroma of the Valencias that must have reminded them of their home country, Spain, a place they would never see again.

From the museum, I caught a bus to Anaheim and bided my time in a brewery before buying a nosebleed ticket to the Angels' game against the Red Sox. In Boston, in 1769—the year of the Portolá expedition—the cobbled streets were rumbling with carriages and discontent. Merchants were becoming increasingly annoyed by British tariffs. The Boston Massacre would unfold the following year. I poached a seat in a lower section, one better than I'd paid for, but after a while ambled to the stadium's other side and sat as high as I could, where no foul ball could possibly reach me. From there I could see through the lights to the Puente Hills, where I was headed. It was the last series that lumbering David Ortiz would play in Anaheim—he was on a glory tour—and the Angels' players lined up for the anthem wearing rainbow-tinted wraparound sunglasses and gold chains, patented Big Papi. The hitters were feckless or the pitchers were sharp; it was impossible to tell from my height. Bottom of the ninth, Red Sox up 1–0. The Angels load the bases and, fielding a grounder, the Sox's third baseman throws home. The ball sails wide of the catcher. Two runners score—the game is over. It was Girl Scout Cookie night, and, already full of peanut butter Do-si-dos, after the upper decks had cleared I walked the stands scavenging unopened boxes of Thin Mints, caramel Samoas, and short-bread Trefoils. Who would leave these? I carried out a dozen boxes, gave one to my driver as he left me back at my motel. In the morning, I would give the rest away, already half-melted, to men washing cars in the unrelenting sun.

ON THE MORNING OF JULY 28, the Portolá expedition came across "a good-sized river going through the midst of the plain," shallow and sandy. "Its bed must hold at least ten yards' worth of running water, with a depth of a half a yard," Crespí wrote. "By what we have noticed from the sand along its banks, this river must plainly carry very large floods, and we had some trouble fording it even now, in the depth of the dry season and the dog days." Camping by the river, they felt three earthquakes in the span of an hour. "The first and most violent must have lasted the length of a Creed, the other two less than a Hail Mary; a great shaking of the ground, however, was felt during all three." Miguel Costansó observed, "One of the natives who, no doubt, held the office of priest among them, was at that time in the camp. Bewildered, no less than we, by the event, he began, with horrible cries and great manifestations of terror, to entreat the heavens, turning in all directions, and acting as though he would exorcise the elements." They named the spot *El Dulcissimo Nombre de Jesús, del río de los Temblores*, but the river became the Santa Ana. Eighty years later, early German immigrants would call this place Ana*heim*, or "home by the Ana."

The Santa Ana River is the longest coastal river in Southern California, running ninety-six miles from the San Bernardino Mountains to the Pacific south of Huntington Beach. Crespí describes catfish, and once the river held thirty-inch steelhead trout at the southern end of their range. Over time the Santa Ana has been tamed. The fish have disappeared. East of Orange, the earth-fill Prado Dam was built for flood control in 1941 following a huge flood in 1938 that spread a silver sheet of water through the banks' orange groves. Once there was nothing but orchard on either side of the river. Now there is nothing but housing and warehouses, which have made the land more valuable but the flooding potential worse. After another flood in 1969—on the two-hundredth anniversary of the Portolá expedition—the Army Corps deemed the Santa Ana the greatest flood threat west of the Mississippi and, in 1987, the 3-billion-dollar Mainstem Project began. The Orange County portion of the river was straightened and channelized and a second dam, Seven Oaks, was built far upstream. In the City of Santa Ana, the channel is entirely paved, but over 80 percent of the river at large still has a natural bottom.

Glassell Street took me over the Santa Ana, but not before I explored underneath. The bridge had debris fins extending from its piers to deflect a flood's logs and boulders. But here the river was a wide, sandy, flat-bottomed trough. Grass in some places and only bare, cracked soil in others. I sat in the shade of the overpass, feeling and listening to the concrete tremble from the weight of trucks, *los temblores de automóvil.* Pigeon guano ran down the piers like showers of sparks. I thought there was no water in the river at all until I climbed the levee across this first channel and discovered a second, parallel channel on the other side, this one ponded and reedy. T- and L-shaped levees had been built across it to slow and spread the flow, encouraging more recharge and creating habitat: Black-necked stilts wading up to their chests. Mallards. A glossy ibis probing its own reflection. Snowy and great egrets on the fringes. The Orange County Water District heavily manages the river and, via ponds like these, more than triples the recharge of Orange County's aquifers. Earlier in the century, these underground reservoirs were seriously overdrawn. Rubber dams divert storm water into percolation ponds on its sideline, like a bumper on a bowling lane. Water from treatment plants far downriver is pumped inland back to "spreading basins" in Orange, some of which absorb ten acre-feet a day. Two and a half million people in Orange County sleep on a sandy, flowing water bed hundreds of meters deep, and these subterranean reservoirs are their lifeblood. Just twelve inches of rain falls on average each year.

The fractures in the dried river mud were six inches deep. A baseball was locked in that mud, and I thought I saw a snake, but it was a leather belt. Crespí reported that the Santa Ana was rich with cottonwood, sycamore, and willow, but the only trees now were behind a bike path and probably planted. Signs beside the path read, CAUTION BIKE WAY SUBJECT TO FLOODING/DEBRIS AND MAY BECOME IMPASSABLE and NO CAMPING, NO STORING OF PERSONAL PROPERTY. There was a faded flier, some personal debris that would loosen and fly off with the dry Santa Ana wind: REWARD FOR LOST DOG. YORKSHIRE TERRIER. PLEASE CALL ME IF YOU FIND HIM. I wanted to call the number given and tell her that everything would be all right. But I couldn't.

Walking north through Placentia, I passed one of those recharge ponds. Bluebird or swallow nest boxes were tied to their chain-link fences, but some of their entrances were plugged with large corks, I presume to keep the starlings from colonizing them. From across the street, the horns of mariachi came to my ear, and down an alley behind a warehouse was a party under a white tent. They saw me listening and waved me over, offering me rice, beans, tortillas, and cabbage salad from aluminum chafing dishes, and a Corona to keep me light of step. It was the anniversary of a small electronics business and the ninetieth birthday of the owner's father. The old man sang karaoke tenderly.

I SPENT THE NIGHT AT the damp edge of a creek off Brea Boulevard as it begins to climb the Puente Hills several hours to the north. Best I could do at last light. Lower in the canyon I'd found homeless encampments, towels and sheets strung up like laundry through the runty trees, so I kept on up the road, farther than the homeless would want to be from convenience, until finally I had to just crash down a grassy slope and make do. Late into the night, cars roared not fifty feet above me, their headlights flickering through the renegade palms surrounding my *tiendecita*. I couldn't help but imagine a car plunging off and down into the creek, some drunk or distracted driver. I put in my earplugs and tried not to think about it. In the dewy morning there were orange koi finning, as if escaped from the fountain at San Juan Capistrano. An oleander grew beside the stream, as it does on the medians of California's highways, and it had dropped pink, five-petaled flowers into the water, which had a dusky or smoky tint. I wondered if that greenish hue was from a natural or unnatural oil seep.

This was in the Brea-Olinda Oil Field, the divide between Orange and Los Angeles Counties. The Puente Hills, which rise a thousand feet off the valley floor, run from the southeast to the northwest and divide Brea and La Habra from City of Industry and West Covina. The Portolá expedition crossed these black-gold heights, not knowing oil was underneath. An obelisk marker commemorating the Portolá expedition is found a short distance up Brea Boulevard, a marker that's been repainted many times since it was put into the ground in 1932. But the date it lists is two days off: the Portolá party camped here or near here on July 29, not the thirty-first. And studying the description in Crespí's journal, it seems likely the expedition actually camped at the base of the more modest Coyote Hills just to the south, in today's Fullerton, before continuing across a plain to the Puente Hills in Brea. It's a reminder that our historical markers, and our histories, are provisional, impermanent, best guesses, calculated arguments, biased, fallible.

Behind the marker, in a chain-link enclosure, was some sort of minor oil collection facility in a concrete well, pipelines running in and out of a humming tank. NO SMOKING BEYOND THIS POINT, a rusted sign advised. Plastic Chardonnay bottles, Woodbridge by Robert Mondavi, lay in the gravel. Across the road was a fenced-off lot with sheds, larger tanks, and other buildings for petroleum collection. There was also a great beige pile of fronds below shaggy palms, and two orange trees, their golden spheres hanging in their round canopies, behind a long, unhitched tanker trailer. On the horizon all around were oil derrick towers, each a memorial to extraction and abandonment and fast cars everywhere.

The Spaniards made no mention of *brea*, Spanish for "pitch," in the Puente Hills, but they would come across it before long elsewhere in the Los Angeles Basin. Petroleum rises here, however, in the Whittier Fault Zone. In the opposite fashion of the aquifer recharge ponds, tar seeps up through porous material or along faults until it hits solid stone, an incidental cap. The first well in the Puente Hills was drilled in 1880, and this little range became the first oil field in the Los Angeles Basin. By the 1920s, Los Angeles would become the state's largest oil field, at the time responsible for one-fifth of the world's oil. Over 400 million barrels have been extracted, and 19 million barrels are thought to remain accessible in the Puente Hills. We think of Los Angeles as the city of highways, as the angel of the car industry, but from this light it has been a center of fuel culture for far longer. More than four hundred wells are still active in the Brea-Olinda Field, which is laced with a maze of dirt access roads blocked by gates. I had thought about hopping one of those gates to find a place to camp, but thought better of it.

As I strode back down Brea Boulevard, I watched scrub jays glide overhead. Nodding pump jacks squeaked and complained just off the road like industrial birds pecking the ground for seed with rusted bills. I stopped again at the Portolá marker, hoping to feel something of their presence. Had they really camped here? The oil collection well behind the marker hummed and let out a slight hiss. Ground squirrels had dug a warren between the road and creek, and I thought about how we had also riddled these hills, burrowing thousands of feet.

A native California walnut tree grew along the creek, and I dropped my pack to take it in and maybe collect a few nuts. It was a chaos of multiple trunks and shaggy branches bowed to the ground, a green fountain, somehow more shrub than tree. Its leaves are made up of more than a dozen leaflets that run opposite each other down long stems. The fruits have the color and stippling of a green Anjou pear, but these mostly were shriveled and cracked. I could see or poke a finger into the interior fibers, black with rot as if charred by a fire. Inside is the hidden shell. Native Californians gathered and ate walnuts, and they made dice of the split shells, too, filling their interiors with asphaltum—a particularly sticky tar that often rolls up on the beach from oceanic seeps—and inlaying shards of abalone for pips. These dice were thrown into shallow baskets, landing either up or down. High throw wins. Over time, the pale ridges of the walnut shells were worn smooth and dark from use. Natives employed tar in numerous other resourceful ways. They plugged the breathing pores of abalone to turn them into bowls, helped affix obsidian blades to wooden shafts, mended fractured mortars, and much more.

A man and a woman came down a trail along the creek, pushing bikes. They had spent the night in one of those camps I had glimpsed. This was their home. He had gray hair and a mustache. She had dyed brown hair and a pink-and-white shirt. He gave me a nod, seeing that I was studying the messy tree. "Macadamia nut," he said.

"I think they're walnut," I said.

"No, macadamia."

"I really think they're walnut."

"Nope, macadamia."

I collected about twenty walnuts, breaking off and crumbling the dried fruit and skins between my thumb and fingers before I slid the wrinkled nuts into a plastic bag for later.

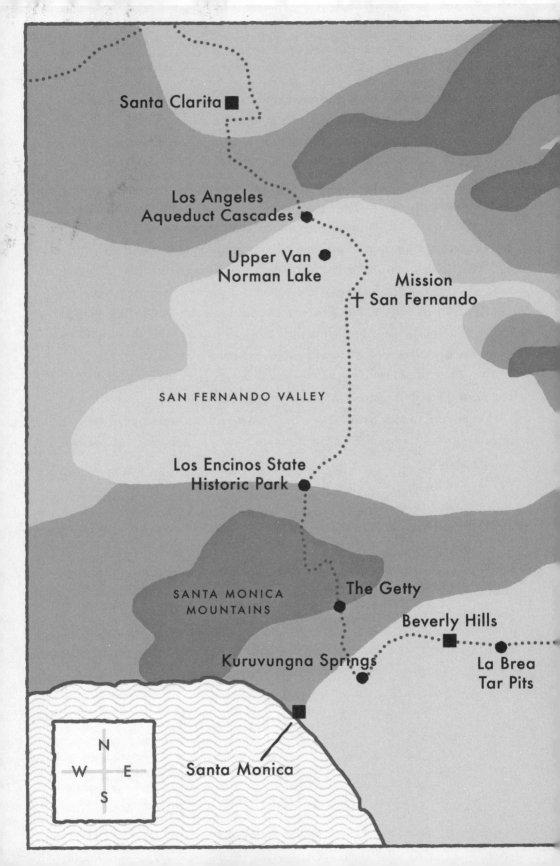

IN NEIGHBORING LA HABRA, WHICH means "the pass," honoring the Portolá expedition's climb over the Puente Hills, I began up steep Citrus Street. Crespí ultimately called the Puente Hills "a middling high range," though it took them three hours to follow its canyons up and down through oak and sycamore. I thought it was steep enough. The higher you climb, the tonier the houses, with the occasional oil derrick. For a breather, I picked up a dimpled lemon from below its tree on a lawn; like a fragrant coal, it radiated warmth after a morning of sun. North Citrus met Avocado Crest Road, which met Hacienda Road, and I detoured down it a mile to see the house where the first Hass avocado tree grew. The original tree is gone, but another one cast shade in front of the garage: How could it not be its progeny? Seemed like no one was home, so I hopped the low gate and scavenged an *aguacate* off the driveway. At a nursery up the road, the owner told me avocados were his best sellers. He had Hass, Fuerte, Pinkerton, Stewart, Holiday Dwarf, and Reed. "What's the best time to plant?" I asked. "This is California," he replied. "Any time is good."

By the time I had reached the other side of the hills, Sarah had arrived. She had flown from Idaho to join me for two days, and took a car from LAX and met me around noon below the Hsi Lai Temple. Promptly I suggested she use the back of the temple's entrance wall for a pee blind. Welcome to the urban hiking life, dear. But even this suggestion made me consider, again, how much more difficult and intimidating this journey would be for a woman, for all sorts of reasons. Especially solo. I could just press up against a hedge and let the river run through it.

We bantered like sweethearts for a few miles, and I was self-conscious about speaking into my recorder in front of her, but that was exciting, too, because now someone was actually listening, maybe. We walked past Manzanita Park, where there was no manzanita, and down Turnbull Canyon Road past tanks and buildings with a chemical or refinery aspect. "I don't think we took the most scenic route," I offered. "But this is the City of Industry." We were nearing the City of La Puente, also the name of the area's rancho. The Puente Hills, the City of La Puente, the Puente Junction, all of them were named because Portolá had to get his mules across this marsh. The expedition camped on the banks of a stream here on July 30, and the next day the soldiers constructed a bridge, *un puente*, to cross it. Crespí named it *La puente del arroyo del Valle de San Miguel.* "This seems to be a large swamp," he wrote, "with level black soil that cannot be bettered . . . a great many very lush grapevines looking as though someone planted them here; countless rose of Castile bushes; so much of what we thought to be cumin that double-hundredweights' worth could have been gathered." Like so many other marshes, which are forever villainized as worthless and empty though they are one of the most biologically productive habitats to be found, and beautiful as even Crespí saw, this one had been filled and paved over with industries.

We stood on a bridge above San Jose Creek, a tributary of the San Gabriel and likely the stream by which the Spaniards camped. It was a concrete trough with vertical walls, warehouses, and more tanks on either side, and a bike path on its south "bank." The waterway was straitjacketed, a shadow of itself, but still kicking: water about a half inch deep flowed toward the Pacific. It was flood control at its best and worst.

"That's so sad," said Sarah, seeing it.

"This is more water than I've seen almost anywhere," I said.

Sarah leaned against the bridge's railing with her hands on her knees.

"You okay, dear?"

"Yeah," she said. "Sarah's not sure how you're doing this," she said, as if it were me speaking into my recorder. The heat was tremendous and added weight to the walk, as it had done ever since I had left the coast at Cristianitos Canyon and Camp Pendleton.

"You adjust," I said, smiling.

We tried to imagine the Spaniards' *puente*. Was it a bundle of branches or something more official? The journals offer no clues, but it must have been sturdy enough for the mules. Below our feet was a bridge of steel and concrete, all function, the width of the creek itself. The span bounced perceptibly as a truck crossed. It was built of the kind of materials produced in the warehouses along this creek. We relied on it and them. Incredible that we could stand here, on this minor engineering marvel, and not think twice about it. From under us a pigeon flushed and clapped upstream, the bird's reflection and its shadow racing side by side across the gloss. The water was spread so thin that as much must have been evaporating as flowing forward. Miniature islands of sand were in the flow, and tufts of grass had rooted on their edges, growing fast and doing their best to hold on and make things softer and more permanent.

WE STARTED DOWN THE BIKE path into the lowering sun, and for the hours we strolled, we saw no cyclists. Puente Creek soon joined the San Jose, another concrete channel. A killdeer skittered below the runny cascade of an outfall. Two black-necked stilts yipped nasally, and the echoes of their cries in this concrete canyon turned them into a great flock. Were they trying to distract us from a nest, or from a precocious chick camouflaged on one of those islets of sand? We spotted none, but we did see tire treads: someone had driven down this creek. It was as much a road as a stream. Lonely rocks seemed tossed onto the concrete, but they were harbingers of high water, much higher. A yellow ruler painted on the wall measured sixteen feet, suggesting the possibilities. The sheet of water gathered on just one side of the channel, and then inexplicably streamed to the other side like runoff from a hose. The creek was hugging an imperceptible curve, Sarah pointed out. I wished I always had a partner on this journey to learn and steal from. What else had I missed these past weeks? So much, and especially her.

We spotted a man and his son riding a palomino tandem on a dirt path on the opposite bank. Stepping just faster than us, the horse's stifles quivering powerfully, black tail swishing. Stables were carved into the terrace above the river and the path, and stairs led down from houses past oleander to them. Clearly it was a long tradition to ride this creek, the San Jose. Another rider approached from the west, and soon the horsemen passed each other with nods and mutual dust. It seemed a vision of another Los Angeles, of rancho days, but it was now. This was a random vein east of Los Angeles. These men walked their horses here every evening, and that was life.

WE SPENT THE NIGHT IN a Motel 6 in El Monte, only the very best. I wasn't about to make Sarah camp in urban Los Angeles, nor was I particularly keen on the idea for myself, though it would have been easy to poach ground by the San Gabriel River. In the morning, we shook out our sore legs and started toward the Whittier Narrows Natural Area, a four-hundred-acre preserve along the San Gabriel River. "Due in this same southerly direction, the range has a gap," wrote Crespí, "through which this valley connects with the long spacious plain which we left behind on the 29th when we set out from the Earthquake River of the Most Sweet Name of Jesus." We, too, were headed toward the water gap between the Puente Hills, now mainly behind us, and the El Monte Hills up ahead. Really they are the same "middling" range, with a passage—a narrows—cut through at the confluence of the San Gabriel and Rio Hondo Rivers about fifteen miles from the ocean. A more famous water gap is the Delaware Water Gap, where the Delaware River slides dramatically through the ancient Appalachians.

These hills rose on the same faults that allow oil to the surface; and the impasse of bedrock under this range also forces water out of the aquifers on its northern side, thus the Whittier Narrows Area is famously marshy—or was. "We . . . were struck with wonder," wrote Crespí. "We came upon such a vast number of extremely lush rose bushes . . . From horseback, I myself plucked more than four dozen of them that came into my hand, very pink and sweet smelling . . ." The City of Industry was a wet field of roses miles long. He wrote of antelopes across this plain, "traveling in large bands just as though they were goats," and after making camp, the soldiers rode out to hunt them. There were numerous hares and the droppings of elk "like those of cattle," and tales from the Tongva they encountered of grizzlies in the San Gabriel Mountains, which, Crespí mentions, "become very snow-covered in season, the snow lasting upon them for a long time, indeed months." Such a snowpack above Los Angeles sounds impossible, but the Portolá expedition journeyed during what's now called the "Little Ice Age," which lasted from about 1300 to 1850. At its peak around 1700, temperatures in the northern hemisphere were on average about 3.5 degrees Fahrenheit colder than today.

There was more water then, more wildlife. More black-necked stilts and kill-deer and phoebes. "Unexpectedly this afternoon, there came a large meine [troop] of birds that intruded in among our messes, but since all of us were caught unpre-pared we were able to catch only a single one that came right into our hands; they were thrushes, a bit smaller than the Spanish ones, having a bit of red on their wings; and we noted that they were being pursued by a bird of prey . . ." There were red-winged blackbirds in their clouds of thousands, and more falcons—peregrine, prairie, merlin—hunting them.

DURFEE AVENUE TOOK US PAST the Whittier Narrows Nature Center, where we met a raccoon named Mr. Magoo pacing restlessly in his cage. Back and forth, back and forth. He had been blinded by pepper spray or weed killer. "They were going to put him down," Grace, a volunteer in a Hawaiian shirt, told us, "but we said, 'Well, we'll take him.' Yeah, you're a silly boy. Yeah, come on. Yeah, you know we're here, don'tchya." Through the preserve, pulses of heat brushed our cheeks and ruffled the golden currant. We passed Bell's vireo enclosures, built to help protect these endan-gered birds, but saw no vireos. We had to find a hole in the fence to find our way out of the preserve. A fire had ripped through some of the narrows to Durfee Avenue, charring trees and bubbling and curling a bike-path sign. At the intersection with Rosemead Boulevard: LONG BEACH, 20, ⇐, PASADENA, 13, ⇑.

We swung left toward the narrows, walking the incline of the horseshoe dam as it carried the road. Little red ant craters along the sidewalk were miniatures of this giant earthwork. Toward Whittier, the land of Nixon, and toward Montebello and Pico Rivera. Pío Pico had owned the narrows until 1892 and, along the *rivera*, built a hacienda that was ultimately stolen when he signed away the deed thinking it was merely a loan, because he didn't read English. Walnut and citrus farms and houses had sprung up around the narrows, but flooding in 1938 compelled the dam. Con-struction finally began in 1950, displacing more than five hundred homes. Now the dam protects half a million people from flood.

The empty San Gabriel passed under us into the vast "recharge basin" behind the dam, but in 1769 Miguel Costansó noted "a river of fine water—from sixteen to seventeen yards wide—that rises near the gap," the Whittier Narrows. This place was a *discharge* basin then, with an artesian river emerging to light. Under a rainbow umbrella, we bought a cup of tejuíno from a street vendor with a Red Sox cap and a wooden cross pendant slung down his white T-shirt: TEJUÍNO ESTILO JALISCO, FRUTA, FRESCAS, Y COCOS, hand-painted on a board with battered corners because it had blown over innumerable times. Of ancient Mesoamerican origin, tejuíno is a mildly fermented slurry of corn dough and unrefined cane sugar. He poured in baking soda to give it fizz and planted a pink straw in the shaved ice. "Drink of the gods," some call it. Sarah couldn't stomach it. I barely could. It has a bright lime start, but the soda aftertaste is sticky and strong. It was cold, though.

We stepped over the yellow bar gate and out onto the dam that held back these dry rivers, the San Gabriel and the Rio Hondo. The recharge basin was all grass, willow, scrub, and impenetrable brakes of arundo with cottonwood, eucalyptus, tree of heaven, and maybe sycamore rising in its interior along a swallowed channel. It was threaded with horse or dirt bike trails, and I wasn't sure I'd want to venture into this enormous bowl of trembling and choked scrub alone. Give me a woods or slim river buffer, which is somehow more comforting, airier. Easier to see through and escape from.

Our path was blocked above the floodgates for security reasons. Downstream, the exit flume and channel slid into the suburbs of Pico Rivera, the homes' baked tiled roofs well below the levee. Dogs who would never meet were woofing and yapping on either side. We stepped down the dam's upstream incline of poured concrete, along a chain-link fence topped with coiled razor wire. The dam was at least fifty feet tall. Its gates were convex by design, but it was as if an immense flood had bent them toward the ocean. They opened like eyelids. Some of the gates were raised just a crack, others entirely. Concrete fins between them stretched upstream to deflect the cars and cottonwood trunks that might travel with an exceptional flood. There were a few sun-gold road apples at the start of this concrete channel, and some cobbles the size of grapefruits reminded of the rivers' potential to convey those mountains we could see to the sea. Atop the San Gabriel peaks stood radio antennae and a few white observatories like remembrances of the snow Crespí saw, the snow that would melt and tear away at the range and occasionally transform the narrows into a broad and wet bronco. Recently the Army Corps determined the Whittier Narrows Dam is structurally unsound: like the Oroville

Dam in Northern California, it could fail if seepage erodes the sand beneath it. Even if it doesn't rend asunder, these gates might fail and release twenty times more water than the channel can carry, devastating neighborhoods from Pico Rivera to Long Beach.

IN A NICHE IN THE wall of the Mission San Gabriel Church is an old tiling with this greeting: "Visitors! The spirit of 1771 welcomes you – Behind this arch, the beginning of California & modern civilization is written in massive walls and rudimentary though genial factories. Inside you will breathe an atmosphere of many years. Every inspiring psalmody of the church, fragrant and comforting with virtues and heroism of the Friars and Missionaries who brought the blessing of Christianity to pagan Indians and to us."

It was on September 8, two years after Portolá and Crespí walked through, that Padres Pedro Cambon and Angel Somera held Mass in a glen near the narrows, beside an impressive river, on the feast day of Archangel Gabriel. A memorial to this *Misión Vieja* stands near the narrows at Lincoln Avenue and San Gabriel Boulevard near The Shops at Montebello. Under an olive tree is a bell that swivels without a clapper, marking the original El Camino. In its early days, the mission by the Rio Hondo consisted of a square, timber barricade with a chapel at center; several larger buildings, perhaps workshops, those "factories"; and about a dozen huts of thatched roof for the neophytes or soldiers. All of the earliest versions of the missions appeared more or less this way. They were quickly built frontier settlements in open space. They looked less like the California missions of today than the French trading posts of the far north more familiar in American history.

"In every way a very grand, excellent spot for a very large plenteous mission," Crespí wrote of this valley, which he named San Miguel at the Puente marshes. But he didn't imagine the flooding. When the Rio Hondo spilled its banks in 1775 and ruined the year's crops, the missionaries sent the neophytes to gather acorns and other wild staples from the mountains, tacitly conceding that a foraging lifestyle was better suited to this landscape of change. That wouldn't do. The year after, the mission was moved about five miles to the north, in the middle of what, in its honor, became the San Gabriel Valley.

The Spanish were determined to grow their wheat and corn, so they sent neophytes to the San Gabriel foothills where a necklace of springs, an "artesian belt," existed at the canyon mouths. About three miles northeast of the mission, near today's Huntington Library in Pasadena, was a seeping oasis of tule and trees known to the Tongva as *Acurag-na*, or "Woodville." It was the place where firewood could be had. There and elsewhere the San Gabriel neophytes were made to build rustic dams of brush and earth to divert water, creating Los Angeles's first reservoirs on their sacred grounds. Not to stem a flood, but to redirect it to the mission and its fields through ditches, zanjas, that the neophytes dug and later lined with stone and tile. A dam built in 1821 called La Presa, or quite literally "the dam," still stands. Ten or twelve feet high, a fifth of the height of the Whittier Narrows Dam, it is now the headquarters of the Sunny Slope Water Company, one of the region's oldest. The handprints of the Tongva, who became known as the Gabrieleños, are visible on its smoothed lime.

SARAH AND I WALKED NORTH to Alhambra and, the next day, visited the relocated Mission San Gabriel. The clerestory windows cast a pallid green on the church's interior, as if the pews were underwater. The church initially had a stone arch roof, but it was replaced with a flat timbered roof after damage from earthquakes. Seven Franciscan padres are buried under its floor, the first in 1803, the last in 1850. Near the center of the building is an annex baptistery that we ducked into. It has a hammered copper font. In a niche is a mural of Christ, shin deep in water with his hands clasped in prayer as he is baptized by the figure of God, who pours water over his dark locks from an abalone shell, a distinctly Californian, opalescent touch.

The museum was overfull and dusty, a warren of smudged vitrines. The interpretive placards were written in a wobbly, looping cursive that seemed straight from the hand of a fourth grader. In a case of old books (NO FLASH PHOTOS OF BOOKS) we saw a length of wood polished from use: "Arm from chair of the Franciscans. Was it used by Fr Serra?" Nearby was a baptism register penned by Serra in 1778, his recognizable signature ending with an elaborate flourish like a tendril on a vine—something old signatures included to prevent forgery. Numbers running down the left margin read, 433, 434, 435, 436, 437. Under them, *adulta* and *juyuvit*. It was an accounting of souls. Seven years after the mission's founding, San Gabriel Arcángel was climbing toward five hundred converts.

A Seth Thomas clock on the wall, at the mission since 1880 and once used to begin services and time the Angelus bells, had been frozen since 7:42 on the morning of October 1, 1987, when an earthquake shook it to the floor. Outside, in the courtyard, was a sundial, forever ticking silently, with an inscription in Latin: EVERY HOUR WOUNDS, THE LAST ONE KILLS. Most of the garden had been redone with native plants to recognize the Gabrieleño-Tongva people, who had relied on cactus and sage, and more, before they were forced to tend to the mission's cultivars, to stomp wine they weren't allowed to drink. The planters were lined with red volcanic rock and pieces of polished black granite headstone: just the dates of someone's life lifting from the soil. A cross at the garden's middle recognizes the six thousand Tongva buried at San Gabriel, many of whom died of cholera and smallpox.

OUTSIDE THE DAYS INN IN Alhambra, Sarah got into a car to the airport, and I walked west past car dealerships and big-box stores. Past bungalows that looked mostly similar, except that iron bars crept over windows and lawns dried up as the neighborhoods, the zip codes, seemed to shift. Banana trees along stucco walls. Hammocks of spiderweb catching purple jacaranda blossoms in hedges. HAPPY BIRTHDAY was strung up in front of a red house, plastic leis draped over its picket fence. "All the way home, all the way home!" yelled a boy with a bat beside an overturned shopping cart, like those I'd seen in dry riverbeds, as his kid brother one-hopped a tennis ball toward this backstop and imagined plate.

Hills up ahead: Omaha Heights, Monterey Hills, Montecito Heights. I followed Huntington Drive toward the city. An ice-cream cart sounded like a white-breasted nuthatch. I passed a Portola Avenue, a Portola Pharmacy. Outside a variety store stood a folding table with an array of loose, used Lego figures: LEGOS $1. Another sign: POKÉMON, CATCH 'EM ALL—UNLIMITED DATA PLAN. As I neared downtown, the sidewalk petered out. L.A. should be a walking city, with its fine weather, but it has a long way to go. Fingers of bougainvillea reached out from the noise reduction walls and pushed me onto the road; an orange local bus whirred by with a startling push of air. Houses and apartments climbed the hills as Huntington wended through a canyon toward downtown—was it the same "hollow" the expedition took? The streetlights each had a solar panel, just high enough to avoid vandalism. Black-eyed Susan growing through chain-link, a few stalks bent so that their petals swept the pavement. I heard goldfinches among them. IN A WRECK, NEED A CHECK? 323-REAR END. At a light, the bumper sticker on a pickup with

a jumble of purple and pink girls' bikes in its bed offered: DIOS ES MI REY, GUA-
TEMALA MI PAÍS. A white pickup: JESUS WAS A JEWISH LIBERAL.

I swung a right and climbed Lincoln Heights on North Broadway, at one time
the Historic Route 66. Portolá probably wouldn't have climbed any hills here, but
I was eager. The skyscrapers were like stair steps to the southwest: hardly any definition on these enormous buildings, their edges lost to haze and sidelight. Straight
down Broadway was Elysian Park and the peekaboo lights of Dodger Stadium. The
feathered shadow of a tree of heaven was a moving fossil, like imprints in shale.
I stopped to watch tasseled lanterns swaying scarlet over the Vietnam-Chinese
Friendship Association parking lot; BREEZY, said graffiti on the sidewalk right in
front of them. Mexican *panaderías* advertised that they accepted food stamps. In a
pet shop, I homed in on a cage of five lovebirds, native to the plains of the Serengeti:
one was a bright custard lemon, but with a naked pink head from disease or too
much stress in a crowded space.

PORTOLÁ TOOK HIS MEN DUE west from the narrows. They marched for about
three leagues until, through these gentle hills, they came to "another good-sized,
full-flowing river with very good water, pure and fresh, flowing through another
very pleasant green valley." Crespí had trouble describing and differentiating these
flourishing places, of setting them apart in writing one after the next, something I
completely understand, though these rivers and valleys are now more varied than
ever. But he knew a promising location when he saw one. "Good and better than
good though the places behind us have been," he wrote, "to my mind this spot can
be given the preference in everything, in soil, water, and trees . . . A grand spot to
become in time a good-sized mission of *Nuestra Señora de los Ángeles de la Porciúncula*." It was the feast day ("Indulgence," he writes, an established day of repentance)
at the founding chapel of the Franciscan order, the Portiuncula, which means "a
small portion" in Italian. The chapel is so named because the Benedictines gave to
Saint Francis that small portion of land belonging to the ruined Chapel Saint Mary
of the Angels near Assisi. A place of international pilgrimage, the Portiuncula now
stands *inside* the cathedral built around it.

In one of the dusty rooms of Mission San Gabriel, beside a small pipe organ, I
saw the processional crucifix, with the Savior hung from it, that is said to have led
the way twelve years later when the pueblo of Los Angeles was founded by forty-

four *pobladores*, or townspeople, recruited from Mexico's Sonoran Desert. They walked Huntington Drive, as I did, some seventy years before Huntington, the railroad magnate and Los Angeles booster (and book collector), was born. In fact there was no such grand procession and, in 1781, these first hardy Mexican-Spanish-Californians arrived in Los Angeles in waves: four families were sent west in June from the mission, the rest in September. They built a pueblo on a bench above the river, beside some defensible hills now called Elysian. They were a diverse lot: eight of the adults were Indigenous, ten of African ancestry. The pueblo was arranged in a traditional style around a central plaza, not too close to the river, with fields on the floodplain's lower terraces. A zanja would carry river water past the town and along the agricultural plots. But as usual the flood potential was underestimated, and the pueblo itself was moved several times.

I paused on the historic Buena Vista Street Viaduct and looked into the Los Angeles River, not far downstream from its confluence with Arroyo Seco, which Crespí describes as having an even wider gravel bed and "many dead trees that must have come down from the mountains" in a torrent. "On either side of the river there are very large, very green bottomlands, seeming from afar to be cornfields because of their greenness," he wrote. Now there was concrete. Running straight as an arrow north to south, the flood control channel was like a six-lane highway, its slanted banks painted with white squares, graffiti ghosts: What messages lost? Down the middle was a ragged lane of water, green with algae. That drove it home for me: a river is the flow itself, not its bed. It is the ceaseless or intermittent water that doesn't care what surface it's given, though the whole ecosystem suffers if only concrete is provided.

The L.A. River fell forward in idyllic ripples, and if you were to concentrate on just one spot of moving water and gaze awhile, you wouldn't know this river wasn't "wild." But upstream a light-rail train, the public metro, clattered over an overpass, with a healthcare ad on its side: MIRACLES ARE CLOSER THAN YOU THINK. Two concrete pads below me—all that remained of an old bridge?—posed as squat boulders, and a raft of mallards bobbed the wavelet train to their eddies, where one by one they scooted out to preen and sun, and tuck their heads under their shoulders, stub tails waggling. Downstream, booms shifted the river as if from one set of railroad tracks to another around the pillars of another viaduct under construction.

The Tongva greeted the Portolá expedition with "bowstrings removed" among other gracious gestures: they threw three handfuls of beads to each of the men, and blew three puffs of smoke on each from their clay pipes, and brought two or three baskets of "very delicious" sage that Portolá apportioned. Their village of several hundred, one of the largest in the Los Angeles Basin, was called *Yang-na*, which the Spanish settlers dubbed *El Aliso* because it was near an enormous and sacred sycamore. The region's Tongva held meetings under this tree, "the council tree," whose canopy is said to have measured two hundred feet across. When it died in 1892, four hundred years were counted in its rings. The site of *Yang-na*, found after having been lost for 150 years, is under the Hollywood Freeway, a stretch of 101 near Union Station. The settlers whittled at the village, taking the Tongva's small portion for themselves, until in 1846 the remaining villagers were relocated to the river's east side. Two years later Los Angeles forced them to disperse, too, handing them twenty-four dollars, total, in compensation.

ACROSS THE RIVER, EVERY SURFACE of the Elysian Park was gently or violently graffitied: signs, dumpsters, electrical boxes, eucalyptus trees (the cursive of the red lettering blended surprisingly well with its twisting, shedding bark). The historical landmark sign pointing vaguely in the direction of a "Portolá Trail" was no exception. It seems a common misconception that the expedition camped directly under these hills; in fact they tented on the river's east side and crossed the next morning. Searching for the historic marker, I wandered down a dirt trail overlooking the river from the sheer bluffs it had shaped. Lots of baby wipes, napkins, toilet paper, and condoms (purple, wrinkled): all the signs of late-night rendezvous, of a cruising area, of a desire path in the original sense. Worn bamboo mats were nestled in spaces carved out, as if by the wind, in the manzanita. I sat on a sandstone bench (this graffitied, too) and watched an Anna's hummingbird hover in the golden light near a toyon. Moving a few inches at time, point to point, side to side; dipping and rising with invisible manipulations of wing and tail. It looked addled or absent-minded, but it was harvesting barely visible gnats: "no-see-ums" that I could, in fact, see through my binoculars—the kind of bug that, when you walk into a cloud of them, you hold your breath. As if with chopsticks, the hummer was snatching flies. Then he would rest on the power lines slung across the Lincoln Hills and the San Gabriels. Hunched, singing, he was a gray dot you wouldn't know from an electrical line fixture unless your ears were savvy to his treble warble. A second hummingbird danced not far off. These were the little green angels of the city.

Elysian Park, once known as the Rock Quarry Hills, is the second-largest park in L.A. at six hundred acres. As with Presidio Hill in San Diego, urban heights that today would be coveted real estate were once thought to be marginal, if not wastelands, saving them from development. Up Buena Vista Hill, I indeed found good views into Dodger Stadium and its sea of blue seats, skyscrapers beyond them and "cotton candy skies," as announcer Vin Scully would have put it. The Mercedes logo atop the scoreboard's L and A seemed to speak volumes about its fandom. In a eucalyptus forest, on the crumbling pavement of a fire road, there was an eighteen-hole disc golf course, the sound of the discs rattling the chains soft and musical. A foursome of young men told me they played this course almost every day. They had satchels of fifteen or twenty discs, drivers and putters for every distance and bend. I tried to imagine what it must be like to be up here during a ball game: the hum and roar after a base hit or home run. Instead, in a moment of relative silence between gusts of eucalyptus, I heard feral parrots.

Farther up the hill, people were lingering at a pullout with a big view directly above I-5: teenage boys with their car doors wide and bumping; a family taking snapshots before the San Gabes, those successive folds and pleats and wrinkles, with patches of white strata like erased graffiti. These mountains look like many of the semi-arid ranges I've seen isolated in Nevada or Utah, so it was incongruous to see so much civilization before them. The bare ridgetops were dotted with multi-tiered houses and the oases of trees planted around them. Directly below, the westbound I-5 was ponderous. A Ralphs grocery truck inched by with enormous strawberries printed on it. I left Angels Point Road and climbed a short, zigzag trail with some bushtits, where I found a lone tree and swing that carried its swinger right out over the highway and into the view, or seemed to, the mist or smog beginning to purple the mountains. The swing had a Little Tikes rubber seat scribbled all over with Sharpie. It was held up by a chain on one side and nylon construction rope, orange and black, on the other. I didn't have the guts to swing on it.

A helicopter was circling low, repeatedly, and now, focusing on it, I realized it was landing on a nearby knoll. A fire helicopter, I saw, as it banked and caught the last of the day. So I went toward it like a moth. An engine was parked in an empty lot and when the helicopter touched down, two firefighters in their helmets moved forward carefully, hunched below the rotors, to refill its tank. They detached the hose, and the chopper went back up with a whirl of dust and a spray of water that just missed the men. *Fire Attack*, said its white belly. I asked a fireman what was up: there was a brushfire off a highway somewhere out there, eight or ten miles away. Again and again, the chopper dwindled and disappeared to the southwest, and again and again it returned with its blunt, aggressive nose, circling and whomping low. It seemed a mighty puny machine to keep the world from burning. Nearby an Anna's hummingbird rose and hovered and landed again in a toyon, the bush with red berries for which Hollywood is named, and though I couldn't see it, I knew the bird's throat was aglow.

"YOU'RE LOOKING AT ONE OF the largest ground sloths we've found here, Harlan's ground sloth," said a docent named Connor in the La Brea Tar Pits Museum. He was a retired mathematics professor who had come back to an early passion: His first painting, he told me, when he was in third grade, was of a saber-tooth tiger. On the table before him was a replica of a sloth's claw, but behind him a genuine tar-black skeleton reared up on stocky hind legs in what looked like an unfriendly posture: teeth, claws, and bones bared. But the pose may just as well have been the sloth reaching into a tree for leaves. This sloth, Connor said, would have weighed over a ton. It was a grazer, a browser, a mixed feeder. It had giant claws for digging and defense, and embedded in its skin were dermal ossicles (the diminutive of "bone" in Latin), a natural chain mail. This sloth had stepped into a tar pit and become stuck and flustered, until it tipped onto its flank and became devastatingly mired. Tough to think of the particular anguish that each of these animals experienced as they became engulfed. In the museum, an interactive display invited you to "Discover what it's like to be trapped in tar": I pulled up on a cylindrical piston embedded, below Plexiglass, in a vat of tar, and it was enormously taxing. It was a strange workout device that the gyms in Los Angeles should embrace and patent. "That is disgusting," said one woman, as the tar sucked and slurped.

A mired animal or carcass attracted predators such as dire wolves and saber-tooths, and often they might come away with a leg or two: most of the skeletons found in the pits are partial. But this scavenging also resulted in a fatal chain reaction. Nine predators are found at La Brea for every one herbivore, suggesting that, one after the next, wolves and cats waded into a baited trap. In the museum, a whole wall of dire wolf skulls is backlit with orange like the glow of the fire of aeons. It looks like a paleontological wallpaper, a grim and grinning reminder of time and the relative uniformity of individuals. Coyotes made it out of the Ice Age, but dire wolves are gone. Slightly shorter than our gray wolves, they may have been too specialized to survive. Another docent explained it this way to a child: "If you only eat Taco Bell, and then all the Taco Bells closed down, you'd be out of luck. But if you ate, like, Taco Bell, McDonald's, KFC—hopefully something healthier, too, to balance it out—you'd be better. You'd be good to go."

The La Brea fossils are ten to fifty thousand years old, the tail end of the last ice age. Two thousand saber-tooths have been found, six hundred species of animals, 5.5 million individual fossils and more being processed every day. In the museum there is a Columbian mammoth skeleton and the tusks of Zed, another Columbian, who was found when the art museum next door dug a parking garage. There are prehistoric bison skeletons, with their fin-like, elongated hump vertebrae—animals that some people believe helped drive all these other creatures extinct when their great herds roamed across the frozen Bering Strait and proliferated, an invasive species before species were invasive. Later people walked over those same ice fields or paddled the shoreline—most likely waves of people over time—to become the first Californians.

"Our Captain and scouts reported that about half a league or more from this spot where we made camp"—from the newly named *La Porciúncula* and its river—"to the west, they came upon volcanoes of pitch coming out of the ground like springs of water. It boils up molten (and that there must have been about forty of these springs, and perhaps many more, they said) and the water runs off one way and the pitch another." Crespí gave them the name *los volcanes de brea de La Porciúncula*, and he expresses considerable frustration, for him, about being unable himself to visit these gassy vents of tar, "large swamplands of it, enough they said to have caulked many ships with." They had felt four earthquakes at dawn along the Los Angeles River, and since reaching the Santa Ana River, Crespí writes of "hearing" fourteen earthquakes in total (showing the limits of his education, he was probably confusing the Castilian and Catalan-Balearic terms for "feel" and "hear"). Now he attributes those earthquakes to the La Brea volcanoes. "Although we wished to, we did not ourselves have the luck to see these pitch volcanoes; instead, as it was some distance out of the way we were to take, our Governor refused to have us to go by them."

I did not refuse to let myself go, and I tried to imagine the Spaniards' amazement, to imagine the scouts riding by these molten ponds and over bones they couldn't have imagined, with their own sabers on their hips. If the wind is right, you can smell the pits before you reach them. As you walk through the park's east gates, Lake Pit, the largest, is immediately on the left. Actually it's an excavation from an asphalt mine that helped seal Los Angeles's roads and roofs. Wilshire Boulevard was paved over mammoths with the very substance that dragged them to their sticky graves. Eventually this pit-mine filled with water, becoming a brown lake of dull rainbow swirls with tule and cattail at its fringe. Methane bubbles rise like jellyfish from the oil field below and burp. A trio of mammoth sculptures forms an agonizing tableau at one end: a mother mammoth is trapped in the tar, sinking to her haunches (actually floating and tethered to shore, so she can rise and fall with the lake). Her tusks are raised to the L.A. sky as she bellows and trumpets (the remains of a bird nest in her mouth look like grass she was eating). From the bank, her calf reaches toward her in vain as another adult, presumably her mate, stands helpless. The science since 1968 suggests that this artistic interpretation is a little off: males probably kept to themselves, and so they were more often trapped by La Brea. No companion was nearby to pull them out.

Beyond its fence, another pit, much smaller, was covered with sycamore leaves and pine needles, showing how detritus could hide the pits' surfaces. Or the pits might have been covered with shallow water, making them look like inviting watering holes. BEING STUCK IN THE LA BREA TAR PITS WAS A TERRIBLE WAY TO DIE—BUT A GREAT WAY TO PRESERVE FOSSILS! cheered another sign. I wrapped my fingers around the fence of Pit 9 and peered in: tarred pinecones, a plastic sandwich bag, chips bags, the serrated jaws of a palm frond. A plastic bottle blown or tossed in would become a fossil. A soccer ball tarred and leafed had been fished out by an employee but left on the railing's far side. Indeed, a few young men were playing pickup on the lawn, and they'd set up small cones to mark their goals. Their *futból* pitch was about fifty feet long. But other stray green traffic cones said STICKY or GOOEY in official stenciled lettering, and picking one up, underneath I discovered a little tar seep, a nascent pit that might grow and grow, I imagined, until it became a lake. The cones looked like skinny volcanoes.

I watched a perfect, auburn, glassy bubble form in an itty-bitty pit in which two green acorns were lodged, just the seeds of the mammoths they might have become. Fossilized plants from the pits show that the Los Angeles of ten to fifty thousand years ago looked much as it would have today if not for humans and their sprawl: plains of grass with valley oak; sycamores and arroyo willow along the creeks; chaparral on the hills and mountains; and in some of those canyons, redwoods, California bay, and dogwood—those last three now found only farther north. In the museum, in one display case, is a tar-coated Monterey cypress cone and a walnut, just like the walnuts I was still carrying in my pack from the other Brea behind me, where pump jacks were exploiting the seeps. A lime wedge trapped nearby, a wine cork. Through the park, the bubbles rose viscous and unhurried, each becoming a complete sphere, almost, before it popped so gently that it was less a "pop" than a gentle or reluctant withdrawal, a slow collapse.

But what was strangest about the La Brea Tar Pits, when I visited, was that everyone was looking at their phones. Absolutely everyone. They traveled across the grounds staring at their screens like zombies on a Hollywood set, which is a cliché, but a precise description. If the pits hadn't been fenced off, they might have fallen in. This was amid the Pokémon Go craze, the app that recast the 1990s computer game. Already, almost no one remembers this momentary worldwide trend, but it was real. It was a surreality—a virtual reality, if you employed your phone's camera, though it drained the battery. Through the tar pits people ambled searching for mythical digital creatures—Pokémon is short for "pocket monsters"—while monstrous statues of creatures lost to time stood around them. They trod over the real, prehistoric bones that rested in "jumbles" far below their feet, in as yet unexcavated pits.

I caught up with two young fellows and asked them about the game.

"There's this Pokémon that everyone's looking for here," said Berland, "Charizard. They're trying to get that one."

"Charzar?" I said.

"Yeah, Charizard, a dragon guy."

"Have you caught him?"

"Well, I don't have him completely. He evolves. There's like a baby one, Charmeleon." He had that one and showed me on his screen. It was much like a stegosaurus, only with a tail of fire. The game was tied to key search words on Google,

Berland explained, so that Charizard was found here, where something like dino-
saurs, at least in our imagination, once roamed Wilshire.

THE PORTOLÁ EXPEDITION CAMPED AT a sycamore springs near South Long-
wood Avenue and Saint Elmo Drive—*El ojo de agua de los alisos de San Estevan*,
Crespí called it, an "eye of water," their usual term for a spring-fed pool. For lack
of a better idea, I camped in a hostel on North Fairfax, using my old student ID
for admission. A bunk in Los Angeles costs more than a motel room in most towns
across America, and I had to use my earplugs here, too, among ten other shifting,
snoring young men. In the morning I set out west through Melrose Place and
its boutiques, into Beverly Hills and its boutiques. Up and down Rodeo Drive I
walked, past those flagship boutiques, while luxury, sport, and muscle cars cruised
by. I wended through Westwood past high-rise apartments until I crossed the 405
and, near the Santa Monica border, arrived at University High School. The football team was practicing on the field, cheerleaders were practicing to egg them on.
Whistles and rah-rahs filled the warm air. I was looking for a spring, and soon I
found the fenced property of two and a half acres, another small portion, that the
Gabrielino/Tongva Springs Foundation leases from the school district, though of
course it should rightfully belong to them.

   The Kuruvungna Springs are open to the public just once a month, and not
knowing exactly my plans or when I'd arrive, I hadn't called ahead. The gates were
locked but through their wire diamonds, in a small frittered field, stood several *kicha*s,
dome shelters much like the *e'waa*s of the San Diego tribes, only with dried grass for
a roof rather than tule, as Crespí noted, and here armatures of beige plastic pipe. The
property had a central building, the size of a mobile unit. It was a onetime horticulture
classroom that had been abandoned and invaded in the eighties by heroin addicts
before it and the park were reclaimed as the Kuruvungna Springs Cultural Center and
Museum. But I couldn't see any water. Was it gone? Where was it hidden?

   I snooped up the block and a little rise to the high school's back entrance,
where I stashed my pack behind a bush so that a parent, driving out, wouldn't call
the cops on a sweaty backpacker with a burgeoning neckbeard. Then I spied the
dumpsters: REPUBLIC SERVICES, they said. One was blue for recycling. They were
along the fence. The ethics of jumping into a sacred space seemed dubious, but I had
come this far. I would be otherwise respectful. So I climbed onto the dumpster's

floppy black corrugated lid, stepped on the fence's top, and hurdled over, feeling the impact in my day-worn knees.

Behind the cultural center, out of view of the street, was a tender and secret garden. The spring itself was a well lined with slate paver stones. Braided clumps of algae floated on its surface, and through the well's sandy bottom—a soft, organic sand that looked like curdled milk—rose a cold and constant boiling, water under pressure releasing from gravels deep below. The stream it created flowed into an unseen outlet and under a stone pathway to a pond with a grand, 150-year-old Mexican cypress rooted at its edge and an island of bowed ferns and grasses. Two white domestic ducks came waddling up a crushed-gravel path like guardians, but they were only expectant. An empty chicken-feed dispenser sat nearby.

The Portolá party camped here on August 4: "On going two hours, all over level soil, [we] came to the watering place: two springs rising at the foot of a high tableland, their origin being higher up than the large plain here. A small channel of water rises from each of the springs, each one having its separate course . . . [The] little tableland is one single patch of roses, while the two little channels are filled with very tender cresses." Kuruvungna means "a place where we are in the sun," and though this place was shady and surrounded by buildings now, from this tableland Crespí saw the San Estevan Spring campsite they had left that morning, and he could see the ocean and the Santa Monica Mountains.

"I called it *The two springs of the plain of San Rogério*," wrote Crespí. A half dozen "very friendly, compliant, tractable heathens" visited them from the village by these cold geysers, some of the men painted, each offering a bowl "of the unusual seeds"—chia—"and good sage." They presented a necklace of white and red shell to Crespí, who wondered if the red was coral. The soldiers caught an antelope that apparently had been shot and maimed the day before—a wonder that they were able to track it down. "Very good meat," Crespí remarked. The soldiers named the two springs *El Berrendo*, the antelope. Legend has it that this pair of springs gave the area its name: they looked like the weeping eyes of Santa Monica. Legend also has it that Junípero Serra said Mass here.

Until recently, the second spring that Crespí wrote of was a small waterfall above the high school's upper field. But the cascade has been piped into a drain, at least temporarily, by the school district because high levels of tetrachloroethylene, a solvent and likely carcinogen used in dry cleaning, were detected, as well as chloroform. What was once so life-giving has become a liability. NOTICE: NON-POTABLE WATER, read a sign next to the spring as I sat by it. Now its pool runs into a storm drain. It has been confined, shaped, and manicured. But twenty-five years ago the Gabrielino/Tongva Springs Foundation defeated a proposal for a parking garage nearby that likely would have cut off the source of this spring. It still flows with about twenty thousand gallons a day and remains a refuge in this tremendous city.

During construction at the school in 1925, the year after it opened, artifacts and even a burial from the Tongva village were found. These students are studying on top of Native bones. We are all standing on them. But if anything had to usurp and colonize this particular village site, a high school seems one of the best possibilities—a place of learning with a diverse student body ready to embrace this complex history. Times have changed: University High School was the home of the Warriors, but activists brought attention to the racism inherent in such a mascot in the seventies; twenty years later, in 1997, the school district finally eliminated all Indian mascots. University High School is now the home of the Wildcats.

I sat cross-legged by the pool for a long while, listening to the football players' jumping jacks. A spring is a portal to a subterranean world. It's the entrance to a path that doesn't end at mountaintops, but leaps into the sky, continuing up the curve of the water cycle. In many cases, a spring is also a wavering window into the human life that once drank from it and grew up around it. The ranunculi on its doorstep, the buttercup or monkey flower, are like flags. Innumerable springs have been capped and lost in Los Angeles, but this one has persisted, a reminder of the wetlands the basin hosted amid the fluctuating rivers. Rancho las Ciénegas, which once occupied most of the core of Los Angeles, means "of the swamps." Watts and Compton were marsh; Inglewood a floral grassland. I sat with the ducks as even the dusk evaporated and the fluorescent lights of the shoebox museum began to reflect on the water. I could have stayed the night on my ground cloth beside this sacred spring without attracting attention, but I had intruded enough already, and so climbed the fence again and rode the bus up Santa Monica Boulevard to a bunk at the same hostel. I would bus back in the morning.

"*BIENVENIDO A GETTY*," THE TRAM's speaker advised as we glided uphill through oaks, with the 405 below and the Los Angeles Basin expanding before our eyes. "When you arrive, explore our five gallery pavilions, presenting nearly twenty-five hundred years of European Art. Stroll the garden, discover modern outdoor sculptures located throughout the grounds, and hunt for fossils in travertine stones." The main atrium, and all of the museum, whispered with rubber heels and the ocean breeze that had bypassed the city below. The stone was full of pores and swirls, of divots and grooves and crystals. I stopped to orient myself at a metal model of the museum and its grounds, which reminded me of one of the mission models that every California fourth grader makes, only extremely fancy and on a travertine table. The whole place had a sepulchral feel, as if Getty's bones were hidden behind some unidentified stone block, with his wife slid into a vault beside him. A plaque near the entrance said as much: THIS MUSEUM IS A MEMORIAL TO J. PAUL GETTY (1892–1976).

Jean Paul Getty's career began in Oklahoma, where he joined his father's oil company at the age of twenty-one. By twenty-three, he had made an independent fortune through his own oil speculations and shortly moved to Los Angeles. He continued to amass companies and new reserves through the Great Depression and after. In 1949, he paid $9.5 million to King Saud for sixty-year rights to an unproven field between Saudi Arabia and Kuwait. When this gamble began to yield more than 16 million barrels a day, Getty became the world's richest person. "The meek shall inherit the earth," he famously said, "but not its mineral rights." Most of his estate was left to the museum, where his personal art collection is showcased. The museum holds the bones of a certain slice of Western culture, the things we wish to revere or are told to.

In the South Pavilion, I visited a special exhibition, *Unruly Nature*, devoted to Théodore Rousseau, who explored the boundaries of light, season, and time of day as he elevated the once-"lowly" genre of the landscape. His intimate, dense, primeval Forest of Fontainebleau looked quite unlike what I had seen so far in Southern California, though some of his heathscapes reminded me of coastal scrub or chaparral. I found Van Gogh's liquid *Irises*, and nearby, Degas's *Milliners*, and around the corner, some of Monet's snowy wheat stacks. They looked like frosted muffins, or perhaps I was just famished. And around another corner was *Bullfight, Suerte de Varas* by Francisco José de Goya, painted in 1824, just four years before his death, a fact that seems reflected in the subject: A bull stands proud with a pink gash on its neck. The picador is beleaguered, exhausted, nearly slumped on his mount with his lance under his armpit. His horse is done for, its intestines unraveling on the arena's dirt. Clearly Goya's sympathies are with the bull, which, as the Getty's curators argue, is "noble in its staunch resistance." The spectacle of the bullfight, it seemed to me, would stand well for an allegory of Portolá, his soldiers, and Spain's project in California. They carried lances up the coast to tame this wild place for all the world to see. Goya, I realized as I stood there, was alive and working in Spain while Portolá was marching toward Monterey.

On the patios overlooking the Los Angeles Basin, museumgoers pointed out the neighborhoods to each other. I had left my binoculars inside my pack, which I had to check, and without them I couldn't quite locate University High School and Kuruvungna just below. The beaches of Santa Monica were clear. In the other direction, UCLA's khaki buildings and a high-rise cluster known as Century City stood out. Much farther east, downtown L.A. was faintly visible if you knew where to look. An interpretive panorama on the railing showed us where Santa Catalina Island should have been. We couldn't see it on this day for the smog, but maybe Portolá had.

I watched a bougainvillea sepal turn circles in a travertine corner with several mint wrappers and half a straw wrapper. All in a lonely dervish. On account of the drought, the Getty had turned off its water "features," and people circled and studied them even more reverentially as a result. The orange water stains on the fountains' stones, normally submerged, looked like honey light on distant islands. Here, in miniature, in my imagination, was Santa Catalina, and a preview of the Santa Barbara Channel. If drought ever ends in California, the Getty should leave one of these features dry and let us remember how it was. A memorial.

But the museum couldn't bear to turn off its main fountain below in the garden. Down a long, zigzagged path was a large pool with an island maze of concentric hedges, interlocking rings of green. A waterfall poured into it. Errant pennies and dimes glinted on the pool's bank. This was the spring that Getty and his despoiling industry had built. The water was piped uphill, I imagined, to create this modern English garden. I walked the maze beside the fountain as I left—at the museum, you have to move the Getty's way, up ramps, down ramps, through mazes—and I paused near a boy and his mom as they surveyed the pool. "If you look at it from here, it's almost like Mickey Mouse," he said. He was right. They hadn't thought of that.

"THE SCOUTS WENT OUT TO look for a watering place, and they say there is no way along the shore past the ranges falling steep to the sea," wrote Crespí at Kuruvungna, his springs of San Rogério. "They say many high rough mountain ranges run along to northwestward and northward, but in one of those directions we shall have to go, in whatever way God shall assist us in doing." They chose northward, since the Santa Monica Mountains at Pacific Palisades and Malibu were, for many years into the future, impassable, too sheer. Instead they climbed up the future Sepulveda Pass past the future Getty on the future 405. "The mountains through which we were passing are quite high and rather steep; however, very grass grown on all sides with large sycamores, large live oaks, and white oaks and also with a great many small walnut trees laden with quantities of small round nuts with very good meat, only their shells are quite thick and hard to crack." They crossed the future Mulholland Drive at the crest, descending to Encino in the San Fernando Valley, where they found two villages near a large spring pool: "a large one, with turtles in it, and a great deal of tule-rush patches and swamps surround it; it is of hot water, very good and pure, however, once it is cooled." They set up camp nearby in the shelter of an enormous white oak, *un encino blanco.*

This pool is now an oval duck pond with a granite lip at the Los Encinos State Historic Park, and I put a quarter into the duck-food dispenser and watched my cupped hand fill with pellet, seed, and corn, which I parceled over the railing to see the frenzy. The spring was part of Mission San Fernando's holdings, and then it belonged to the 4,460-acre Rancho El Encino, a modest acreage because it was originally granted in 1845 by Pío Pico to natives. Not many natives were so lucky. Their petition: "We, Tibercio, Roman, and Francisco, Indians of the Mission of San Fernando, before Your Excellency, appear and say: that after having spent the greater portion of our lives in the service of said Mission, that was given us a reward for the service a tract of land in the Encino, and on this land, we have made a vineyard: having forty horses and some cattle, and for this reason consider ourselves owners of this land, but as the simple concession is not sufficient, we pray Your Excellency to be pleased to order a title to be issued to us, including our square league."

Just beside the spring stands the De La Osa Adobe, built by the next owners in 1849. The ceiling was hidden behind swooping cloth, as it would have been a century and a half ago to catch the earth and dust as it fell from the rafters. When the 1994 Northridge earthquake occurred, a wall collapsed and had to be rebuilt, and it was discovered that one room's walls, under several more recent layers of paint, once had been hand-painted to look like veined marble—to give this salon something of the Old World grandiosity that the Getty also aspires to. The French Garnier family had lived at Rancho El Encino from 1869 to 1878, introducing sheep to the landscape as others did when demand was high during the Civil War. But when this bubble burst, Garnier went bankrupt and had to sell. Soon these lands grew barley that the new trains carried all the way to Chicago. In this manner, the ownership of Encino and its uses continued to shift, but the springs continued to run and be admired. In the 1870s, one man wrote, "Horse and cattle will come for miles to drink from this spring, which, compared to other water, to the quadruped, is like champagne to cider." Now Valley people come to eat and imbibe at the Lakeside Restaurant & Lounge under oaks strung with party lights.

ALL DAY I WALKED NORTH through the Valley, which Portolá's soldiers called *el valle de los Encinos*. Through the Sepulveda Recreation Area, past the Encino Municipal Golf Course, and over the Los Angeles River, which here was full of water. Past the Woodley Park Cricket Field, where I dropped my pack and watched Indian and Pakistani men in their whites bowl and bat on the circular fields. Then back onto six-lane Sepulveda Boulevard, the longest street in the county. Here it was mainly a strip mall. Seven-day Tires, Diego's Mufflers and Auto Repair, Gharibian Auto Repair, Four-wheel Parts, Vicar's Father Gentlemen's Club (TOTALLY NUDE), Valley Animal Hospital, Lorenzo's Alignment, Sepulveda Tires, MobilityWorks of Van Nuys, Precision Smog Check & Repair, Western Bagel, Luna's Radiators-Mufflers, Extra Space Storage, Chio's Peruvian Grill—all of these within a few blocks, while I thought to record it.

The San Fernando Valley is a 260-square-mile basin with an eastern outlet, another narrows, from which the Los Angeles River flowed into the great city and coastal plain before a dam was put in. The valley is contained by the Santa Monica Mountains on its south side, the Verdugo Hills to the east, the San Gabriel Mountains on its northeast, the Santa Susana Mountains to the north, and the Simi Hills to the west, all of these mountains draining water to the aquifer beneath that is tipped toward L.A. Once the valley was a grassland that hid grizzly bears and was prone to dust and sandstorms, especially after agricultural engineering changed the drainage patterns. Now how much pavement had been put down in this valley? I hadn't thought to ask that question in L.A., maybe because that answer would have been even more unfathomable. About 1.86 million people live in the San Fernando

Valley today, making it larger than every city in the United States except New York, Chicago, Houston, and the valley's conjoined twin, Los Angeles. A third of the valley's residents were born outside the United States, suggesting just how quickly it has filled and with what diversity.

The sun was intense, and it reflected off the concrete, so I kept to Sepulveda's west sidewalk for the afternoon shade thrown by two-story apartments. As a mother and her baby in a stroller passed me, I imagined the milk in his bottle curdling or becoming butter. I studied a cell phone tower that pretended to be a palm tree: the tallest palm you've ever seen, with fruits of wires and tubular boxes, yet somehow more convincing or less glaring than coniferous cell towers. Real palm fronds rested on the sidewalk like the ribs of a large animal, and starlings, long ago arrived from Europe, rained down the trees' seeds, the new acorn, having eaten the fruit around them. Green crosses dotted the landscape, some of them illuminated, for medical marijuana. Many places in California, in America, you have to pick either suburbs or strip malls to walk through for miles, and both are fascinating or boring depending on your mood.

In late afternoon, almost all the way across now, I stopped at Del Taco, where I bought a Dr Pepper for its delightful fizz and the right to use the restroom. A buzz-cut white guy in his twenties wearing a black hoodie walked in with a Del Taco cup, and he headed for the soda fountain, too.

"Are you going to pay for that?" said the cashier. From a switch below his counter, he turned the machine off, mid-pour, when the man didn't answer.

"I'm just getting a refill," the customer said.

"No, you left long ago," said the cashier. It seemed like the man had tried this trick before.

"I'm dehydrated," he said. "Turn it back on—I'm fucking dehydrated."

"Sorry, you have to pay for it."

"Turn it on or I'll fuck shit up in here. I'll cut you—I've got a knife."

He walked up to this young Hispanic manager and tried to goad him into coming out from behind the counter. Then the man stormed out, slamming the door. A second later he was back to retrieve the lit candle he'd set down on a table when he came in. I hadn't seen that detail. "You gave my candle bad energy," he said. "You're a disgrace to your people, you nigger."

"Shut your mouth!" the manager shouted, as the man left. He slapped the counter. His fury built. "Let me go out there," he said, pacing behind the cash register. "I'm going to go out there."

His coworkers talked him down, and he apologized to everyone in the restaurant, though no apology was necessary. There weren't many of us, but we were gripping our tables.

BLUE TRASH CANS ON THE curb. "If tears could build a stairway, and memory's a lane, I'd walk right up to heaven and bring you home again," hung on a front door. There was only one row of houses between Woodley Avenue and the Department of Water and Power's Van Norman Lake Complex, which started at the ridgetop above them. People had built stairs in their backyards up to that high fence. A few had even built decks for the view, which was what I was searching for. At last I found an empty lot, one just too steep and narrow to build on, and scrambled up to the fence, conscious of the barking dogs in the adjacent yard.

Upper Van Norman Lake lay before me, the terminus of the Los Angeles Aqueduct from which water is distributed to the city: a broad concrete bowl of 175 acres, rimmed with levees. It can hold 3.3 billion gallons, or about three weeks of water for Angelenos. Yet the reservoir seemed mostly empty, as if it were just a black expanse of caked mud. At its southern end, up against the slanted dam, was a sliver of water with a loose raft of white gulls. That was all the water? It couldn't be. Through my binoculars, at the lake's other end I spotted the inlet gushing into the reservoir, but the water seemed to vanish. I couldn't understand why it looked like tar paper. Then I realized something must be floating over the surface.

Turns out that 96 million black plastic "shade balls" have been poured into Van Norman. Which makes the reservoir the world's biggest and most depressive McDonald's ball pit. The cost was $34 million. The idea was that the balls would tamp down on surface wind evaporation, but it was quickly pointed out that black absorbs heat and might accelerate thermal evaporation while fostering bacteria. It's speculated that the ulterior motive behind these shade balls is to provide "a covering" that brings the reservoir into compliance with a new Environmental Protection Agency rule for reservoirs of treated water.

After crossing the San Fernando Valley, the Portolá expedition camped in the vicinity of Upper Van Norman Lake, in "a hollow upon the north of this level, with a vast amount of swampland and a great amount of lush greenery." But nothing grows in today's Van Norman Lake, which is precisely the point; where once there was a wetland, now there is a sterile reservoir to feed hundreds of thousands of dispersed taps and yards. Crespí mentions an intermittent stream of broken pools, a water source he was pleased with. "And so let this watering place be kept in mind for a more thorough survey of the location, showing whereabout is best suited for a town, whether at the pool"—the springs at Encino—"or here, whenever comes time for laying out a town." Little did Crespí know that the town would come to fill the entire valley that he had walked across that afternoon for three hours. It would swallow both locations.

To the northeast was Newhall Pass, which divides (or bridges) the San Gabriel and the Santa Susana Mountains. It would be my way out of the San Fernando Valley tomorrow. Where the canyon began to narrow toward the pass, I spotted a zig of pipe running out of the mountains: the last descent of the famous Los Angeles Aqueduct, which carries water to the reservoir from more than two hundred miles away in the Eastern Sierra. Straight across Van Norman, meanwhile, was the low finish of the San Gabriels, smudge-orange at its humped crest as if the grassy peaks were smoldering in the dusk.

I'd left my pack below as I scouted this view of Van Norman, but I retrieved it now, setting the dogs off again, and climbed up once more, hunched. Along the fence I crept to a narrow strip between DWP's land and the backyard next to this empty lot. There was just enough flat earth on the ridge for a pad, not a tent. A hummingbird flew in to the yellow tube flowers on the house's yard fence high above its roofline, one last sip, as I cleared several thorny sprigs and laid down my ground cloth. On one side of my sleeping bag was a vista of the wide-open landscape of the reservoir; the other direction was an undulation of houses and trees. A slit moon appeared. Great horned owls called a soft fore, *fore-fore*, over the golf course beyond Woodley Ave, while a white truck drove slowly with its headlights along Van Norman's cracked-and-sealed levee. Was it a patrol? I-5 became an aqueduct of light. The lake drained away to darkness, filling all the while with long-traveled Sierra meltwater.

An hour into my rest, the homeowner below slid open his door to smoke a cigarette—I could see its one orange eye dilate as he inhaled. He hushed his dog as it growled, smelling me. Dogs are rarely wrong. The door slurped shut. When the trash truck and a pack of coyotes woke me in the morning, the view over the reservoir was bright with mist.

VEILED TODAY. THE MOUNTAINS AS if behind a screen. As I trudged up San Fernando Road along the commuter rail and then I-5, I stopped to stare across the highway at the pipeline I'd seen the night before, from afar, on the western-most shoulder of the San Gabriel Mountains. Looking like a segmented earthworm coming over the hill, it was what filled Van Norman Lake. Beside it descended an open channel of rushing water. Lower on the hillside, another channel of exposed tumbling white, this one discreet by comparison, emerged from a tunnel: "the Cascades."

It was on November 5, 1913, that the Cascades were dedicated here below what was then the San Fernando Pass. William Mulholland, the great water architect of Los Angeles, was of course on hand for the ceremony. In their suits, caps, and fine dresses, people had made the trip from Los Angeles to see this deus ex machina Mulholland had engineered as chief of the Bureau of Water Works and Supply. He had begun his career as a simple ditch digger, *un zanjero*, and this was some ditch. It would deliver an inland mountain river to the semi-arid coast more than two hundred miles away. Round-trip tickets on the train from downtown L.A. were a dollar. Thirty thousand people are said to have attended. The *Los Angeles Times* reported, "As all roads led to Rome, so all roads led yesterday to San Fernando."

They lined both sides of the channel and climbed the cliffy rocks above the tunnel, and stood in the fields. After a number of speeches and musical performances, Mulholland spoke. "No one knows better than I how much we needed the water," he said. "We have the fertile lands and the climate. Only water was needed to make of this region a tremendously rich and productive empire, and now we have it." He words rang out with an almost Catholic fervor. "This rude platform is an altar," Mulholland said, "and on it we are here consecrating this water supply and dedicating this aqueduct to you and your children and your children's children— for all time."

At 1:10 in the afternoon, Mulholland unfurled an American flag, the signal. The silver wheels were turned to open the gates and, after what must have been several breathless, humming minutes, the Cascades rushed to life. Water poured forth and began to race at eighteen miles per hour down this last stretch of aqueduct.

Stairs had been built to slow and splash the water, creating a spectacle, and these stairs were embedded with blocks to further froth and slow the water. The mass of people lining the base of the Cascades must have braced themselves as the tongue of water, dirty at its tip, came straight toward them, but it slammed into a dogleg with a spray and raced and frothed and licked on toward Los Angeles. Smoke from the ceremonial cannons hung over the whole affair. Famously, Mulholland then turned to the mayor of Los Angeles and, beneath his walrus mustache, said, "There it is. Take it." The people rushed to the water with their tin cups to taste it, and children and adults alike waded into this captured river.

The water came from a diversion on the Owens River 233 miles away, between the Sierra Nevada and the White and Inyo Mountains. Without inflow, the shallow Owens Lake, the river's terminus—a lake twelve miles long and rich with life, especially migrating birds—began to evaporate. The people in Owens Valley had been led to believe that the aqueduct would carry off only unused water, but Los Angeles took it all, everything they had a right to, and then they started pumping the groundwater. The aqueduct was sabotaged with dynamite more than a dozen times in the twenties in an effort to save the lake and the Owens Valley economy. In 1924, its intake near Lone Pine, the Alabama Gates, was occupied by farmers and other citizens. But their cause was lost. Owens Lake dried up in 1926 and began to swirl with toxic dust storms. The aqueduct was soon extended farther north to the tributaries of Mono Lake, which began to dry up, too, before it was saved by the resourceful Mono Lake Committee.

As I stared at the mesmerizing descent of water, I-5 grunted with the compressor brakes descending Newhall Pass. There is no fanfare here anymore, and perhaps there shouldn't be since this water grab is now sometimes referred to as Los Angeles's "original sin"—though the original sin was surely against the Tongva, and later the city's own marshes and waterways. But the agony and accomplishment of the aqueduct remains extraordinary. At the time, it was the most ambitious water project in the world and also the most expensive at $23 million. One hundred forty-two tunnels were dug—fifty-two miles of tunnel in all. From the Cascades, the water flowed into the older San Fernando Reservoirs before, in 1921, the water was redirected into the Van Norman Reservoir above which I had slept. By then, Los Angeles had more than tripled in size to over three hundred square miles, which included the annexation of the San Fernando Valley. The city's population had almost doubled to half a million people. Today the city of Los Angeles is 465 square miles and has a population of 4 million.

As I continued up the road past the Cascades, I crossed a manhole in which I heard a wooshing. Only a minute later did I realize I had stepped over the Owens River.

THE PORTOLÁ EXPEDITION WAS GUIDED over today's Newhall Pass by two natives: one from the village from which they came, another from the village toward which they were headed. "It was necessary, once having climbed this high pass, to get down a long descent, which we had to do on foot, it being so steep," Crespí wrote. Upon their arrival, villagers were waiting to receive them and offer baskets of gruel and "tiny little raisins": elderberry, I imagine, berries even smaller than peas. I had seen them shriveled along the road on my own descent from the pass, had eaten them by the bunch since San Diego and let them color my fingers purple. These people were the Tataviam, who later were pulled into Mission San Fernando's orbit and labeled the Fernandeño. Crespí admired their generosity and their craftsmanship: "There were two old women who were making two very large rushwork-wickerweave baskets like large hampers, very finely done, made of some large grasses . . . so close-woven that they fill them with water and not a drop escapes." A crucial invention in this dry land.

After a night in Santa Clarita—Crespí named this long valley *la Cañada de Santa Clara*, and it stuck—I walked down Railroad Avenue and veered into Newhall Creek. Who can stand to stay on a sidewalk when there's a waiting riverbed just parallel? A western kingbird bounced on a stalk of yucca, the bird ashen, windswept, its chest a warm butter. Through the sagebrush and rabbitbrush I wound, and, in a grove of cottonwood and willow, came across a knee-height memorial cross, IN LOVING MEMORY OF TRAVIS NEWMAN, 9-21-87 TO 10-6-13. Not three years dead. Born less than three years after me. Faded nylon flowers were placed at the cross's foot, as well as an American stick flag and two ball caps: one embroidered with "LA," the other with "Love." I wondered if his ashes were scattered here or only other bones washed out of the hills. I wondered if he had taken his life in this dry, rustling grove. Someone besides me had visited. There was a Dr Pepper bottle, half-full, condensate beaded on its interior, and a dirty, sun-bleached sleeping bag: the bed of the bereft. All around were heart-shaped, serrated cottonwood leaves in windrows, some brittle from last year, some a soft bright yellow.

Whine of insect in the building heat. Humps of sand where once bushes had grown. I was glad to be in the riverbed, but I sank with every step: nothing rushing about this channel. I hurdled several low concrete dams that seemed designed to slow a flood, but now were fairly useless because the drop behind them had filled. I imagined a muddy torrent pouring over them and overwhelming the memorial for Travis, carrying his plastic flowers toward the Santa Clara River, toward the sea. That was my route. A wood-rat nest leaned against a cottonwood like a pile of sticks lodged by a flood. Why do cottonwood leaves and all those of the aspen-poplar family tremble and quake? I didn't know, but I know now that it may be to avoid overheating in too much sunlight. It may be to keep a fresh supply of CO_2 circulating or to throw insects off balance.

"We feared that the more we penetrated into the country the greater the difficulties might be, and that we might be led very far from the coast," Costansó wrote. "It was decided, therefore, to follow the canyon in which we had camped, and the course of the stream, if possible, as far as the sea." I followed it west, too, traversing the thirsty Santa Clara River on a bike path that crossed Lost Boys Bridge, as it's locally known for starring in an eighties vampire movie: undead teenagers hang from the trestle as a train blasts over, testing their stamina. Vaux's swifts were cruising the bottomlands, ascending higher and then diving into the wash. The cottonwoods were suffering. Many dead, just snags and snarls, and no doubt the swifts nested in them, one pair to a hollow. Through my binoculars, I saw one of them, an untethered anchor, cut across the observation tower at the center of Santa Clarita's Six Flags Magic Mountain amusement park, far in the background. The people on the roller coaster were feeling the forces that these swifts feel with every turn. I imagined I could hear them screaming. The swifts seemed to gather in a loose coil as though preparing to migrate south. But it was too soon, wasn't it? Maybe they were just corralling some swarm. Nearby, the expedition had found another village with "no other protection than a light shelter of branches in the form of an enclosure," as Costansó put it: *La Ranchería del Corral.*

IN 1971, A BLIND THRUST fault slipped and the 6.5 magnitude San Fernando Earthquake occurred, its epicenter in the San Gabriel Mountains about nine miles north of San Fernando. Instantly those mountains rose seven feet. The earth buckled and broke on a ten-mile line that made evident a previously unknown fault.

Lower Van Norman Dam partially crumbled and liquefied, and was a hair's breadth or another aftershock from breaching. It held back 3.6 billion gallons of water. Had it broken, the unleashed tidal wave possibly would have killed between 70,000 and 120,000 people in the San Fernando Valley. As it was, 80,000 people were evacuated for three days while the reservoir was drained and shored up. If the quake had occurred when Van Norman was filled with 6.5 billion gallons, as it had been one year earlier, the dam would have failed, no question, and it would have been the largest disaster in American history.

Such a disaster also would have been an eerie, much more devastating, repeat of the Saint Francis Dam failure in 1928, though no earthquake was involved then. Built under the direction of William Mulholland in the San Francisquito Canyon above Castaic Junction, near Santa Clarita, the thirteen-hundred-foot-long concrete dam provided a backup source for Los Angeles. Three minutes before midnight on March 12, the dam failed catastrophically, unleashing twelve billion gallons. It would have supplied Los Angeles for two years, at the time. Instead the lake surged down the canyon into the Santa Clara River Valley and turned for the Pacific. It took five and a half hours for the wave to travel what the natives told Crespí it would take four days to walk, about fifty-five miles. "See you later, if the dam don't break," valley residents had quipped to each other after it was built. Survivors said they thought it was an earthquake at first. No warning was given to the towns downstream until an hour after the rupture.

Pieces of concrete two stories high were washed a half mile down valley. When daylight broke, at least two hundred people had perished in the deluge. The toll rose to four hundred. Now the figure is thought to be at least six hundred, because of the number of undocumented workers in the area. Bodies were found as far south as the Mexican border, washed out to sea at Ventura. In the Santa Clara River Valley, they were still being discovered decades later. Just the center of the two-hundred-foot-tall dam was left upright—"the Tombstone"—until the Bureau blasted it. The dam, it was concluded in the aftermath, had been built against shoddy rock, and water had wormed its way through under pressure. Mulholland accepted blame for the disaster, which was generally seen as the result of unchecked ambition and hubris in the face of nature. Before long he stepped down as the Bureau's chief engineer and general manager. But it's now thought that the eastern side of the dam was built on an ancient landslide, something geologists at the time couldn't have identified. This old landslide likely shifted under the weight of the dam and its water. The dam exploded all at once.

All along the expedition's route, California's natives had heard from their neighbors, as in a prolonged game of telephone, that Portolá and his peculiar retinue were coming. Often villages lined up waiting for the Spaniards' arrival, sometimes in their finery, the way the citizens of Los Angeles later awaited the water of the Cascades on that morning in 1913. Crespí wrote of the Tataviam in the upper Santa Clara River Valley: "Upon their head the village chiefs bear a certain kind of a stick, so well carven, polished, and smooth, with such different-colored shell inlays intermingled with each other, that they make a great effect to see." He marveled at how they could inlay so finely with just bone and flint. What the natives didn't realize was that the Spaniards were more like the first tremors of a flood from a broken dam, a flood that would reshape and rename everything.

NEAR CASTAIC JUNCTION, I PASSED a historical marker along a farm field: AP-PROXIMATELY ONE MILE SOUTH OF THIS POINT WAS THE ADOBE HEAD-QUARTERS OF RANCHO SAN FRANCISCO, ORIGINALLY BUILT ABOUT 1804 AS A GRANARY OF MISSION SAN FERNANDO. THE RANCHO WAS GRANTED TO ANTONIO DE VALLE IN 1839. Henry Mayo Newhall then bought the upper valley in 1870, and his heirs still own most of it. He had come to California for the gold rush, but made his money from a San Francisco auction house and built a railroad down the San Francisco Peninsula. When Southern Pacific purchased it, Newhall had a fortune that he would parlay into land all across the Golden State, including the Rancho San Francisco, which he bought for two dollars an acre. It bridged Ventura and Los Angeles counties.

Newhall used his influence to make sure that the railroad connecting Northern and Southern California ran through his ranch and up and over the pass that now bears his name. Over the course of a year, Chinese laborers dug a 6,966-feet-long tunnel through the joinery of the Santa Susana and San Gabriel Mountains. The first train emerged on the south side, in the San Fernando Valley, on August 12, 1876, a foreshadowing of the aqueduct. The Newhall Land and Farming Company still exists because of the foresight of Henry's sons, who decided to stop selling land only to divide the earnings and, instead, began to reinvest it in the company. With the help of the aqueduct, they eventually grew rich, though they almost lost everything in the Saint Francis Dam Disaster. Reparations were later paid by the city of Los Angeles. Eventually, as in Orange County, grandiose developments cropped up, the first of them Valencia, across the river from Santa Clarita. The development continues: in 2017, a deal was reached with environmental groups to let a $13-billion, 21,000-home suburb called Newhall Ranch go forward on the hillsides just downriver of Six Flags.

As I headed down the valley, one of Newhall's fields was stippled with bright red chili peppers, tens of thousands, millions of burning seeds that set my throat aflame just looking. The buildings across the road fell away and suddenly I was on a sidewalk along nothing, to nowhere, brand new but already overgrown with a prickly weed that cast a black lace shadow. There were no sidewalks in portions of L.A., but there was one here. Someday, a commercial strip would line it, but for now it was an art installation. To my chagrin, the road turned to a highway, State Route 126. I would have to walk it a long while. The deep green agricultural fields ran to a cottonwood tree line and cliffs half in shadow, to chaparral slopes, to brown tablelands, to rolling foothills, and finally to the soft, uneven knife of the Santa Susanas in the sky's grip.

Soon it was five o'clock. Soon it was six. Thanks to a final stoplight, miles back, there were moments of peace. Then the cars and trucks blew past in a roaring necklace. The valley was narrow, a half mile wide. A double-decker trailer passed by hauling new cars to dealerships in Santa Clarita, so that those cars, once sold, could gun it back to the cool coast. The holy red palms of an In-N-Out cup. A water bottle of sunflower seed husks, like a ravaged bird feeder from someone's lips. The air—it was filled with the sweet, soapy aroma of peppers. How can I ever make a list that resembles anything close to the real experience? The roadside was crowded with holes and held the most lizards I'd seen all trip. There were plenty of ants for them to eat.

I found a barn owl in the gutter. Just its bone shards catching the up-valley light, its striped feathers trembling in the push of passing semis. It was an accidental dam for roadside debris: sand, slips of straw, wood fragments, a few bits of plastic. Just down the road at a turnoff was a sign. Why do signs always seem to convey so much more than they mean? WARNING: ABANDONING ANY ANIMAL IS PUNISHABLE BY FINE AND IMPRISONMENT.

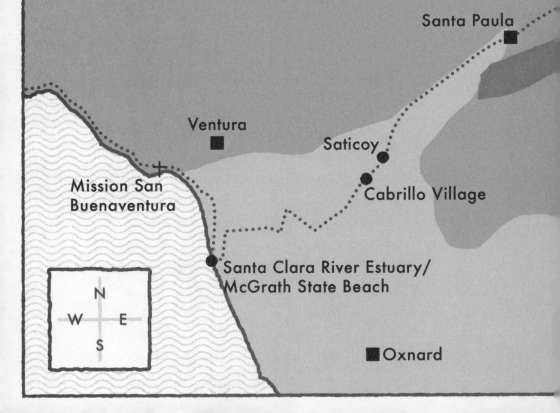

TOPATOPA MOUNTAINS/
SESPE WILDERNESS

Santa Paula

Ventura

Saticoy

Mission San
Buenaventura

Cabrillo Village

Santa Clara River Estuary/
McGrath State Beach

N
W   E
S

Oxnard

"STEPPING OUT OF THE TENT around midnight to see the stars for the first time in a while. In part because of where I've camped, motels . . . also just being in cities. But here in the middle of this ranch land, in this dry river channel, suddenly they're revealed. Bright lights to the east toward Santa Clarita, over the hills. Light of the road, lighting up the bluff, to the east.

"Right when I pissed . . . it was on sand, but the sand was so hard, I felt it spatter back on my legs, on my sandaled feet. Then glancing up at the sky I saw an amazing shooting star that left a kind of halation, at least on my retina. It was heading west, like me. I saw a couple other little minor ones as I stared up, but nothing major.

"The spears of the arundo, breaking into the sky. Their dark silhouettes. They're quite beautiful. I try to identify constellations. Thought I might be able to see the Little Dipper. But doesn't it pour into the big one? And I couldn't find that. Felt like I was seeing Jupiter straight up. But I don't associate planets with straight up. Maybe that was the North Star. Thought about how often my dad had pointed out constellations to me, to us, growing up, especially in the hot tub on summer nights, or winter. And still, I can't . . . I can't identify much. I thought I might have identified the Southern Cross, but I need to . . . I need to look at a star map.

"I was thinking earlier about . . . since I'm having trouble sleeping with the highway . . . about how contaminated valleys that have highways are, sonically. You can't . . . you can't camp in this valley, really, and expect to be able to sleep, even in the distance, without earplugs, and earplugs don't do the trick here. I'm not far enough. I'm only a couple hundred meters, through, you know, brush that doesn't block the sound. You need noise-canceling headphones like babies wear at sporting events.

"The little loud putters of the semis, like they're traveling over the margin where there might be those cuts in the pavement that make that whirring sound on your tires. Strange brake noises and accelerations, and cars that are designed to make noise . . . it's just ludicrous. And I have to put earplugs in so that I don't get to hear the little insect hum and chiming cricket, which are so minor and so much more preferable. A moving sedan isn't so bad. It's the bigger ones.

"When I get out of my tent I'm wobbling, my legs are tired. I have trouble getting my balance. Dizzy going from this little tiny dome to the big dome of the sky. Really light out, though no moon. So I guess that's starlight. I wonder if you'll be able to . . . there you go. . . that's the sound of a truck crossing over the divider. I wonder how much of that ambient noise this recorder is picking up.

"I'm staring up at the sky in my boxers, with my fleece cap on, and my little down jacket on. Thin, fairly thin. I'm wearing it to bed because it's cold. Dizzying to look up at the sky for too long, though. Combination of my tiredness [yawn] . . . I'm tired . . . and dehydration.

"That's all for tonight.

"I forgot to say how distinct the Milky Way was. I can see the . . . I can see the sweep, the wash of cloudiness, that is the Milky Way. And I had been thinking earlier how certain trucks literally send a vibration through the air that I feel not as a sound but as a little quake. And just thinking about all the little birds in the arundo, or wherever they're roosting, or the coyotes, their skulls filling with that vibration all the time, and all of us are feeling those vibrations."

BIRD-CONTROL CANNONS SCREAMING IN THE morning—whistling pops that brought me back to Camp Pendleton. And eerie white ghosts, scarecrows, hanging from the barbwire along the tableland citrus. Less than a mile down the road, I came to Rancho Camulos, which the son of Antonio de Valle, Ygnacio, had inherited and safeguarded after his father's death. A Tataviam village here was called

Kamulus, or "juniper"; there must be some in these foothills. The 1860s drought caused Ygnacio to sell off most of his rancho, but he saved the core of Camulos. The place became famous as the alleged inspiration for Helen Hunt Jackson's wildly popular novel *Ramona*, since she visited shortly before the book was published in 1884 and many of the details match up, including a rip in the altar cloth. Camulos was overwhelmed by visitors as a result—the Southern Pacific Railroad promoted a whistle-stop at the ranch on its spur from Saugus to Ventura—while it also capitalized on the attention, establishing itself as "The Home of the Ramona Brand."

The museum was closed when I arrived, but I wandered in the open gate. The ranch's fruit stand was shuttered, too, but advertised that the ranch was a Sunkist grower. An old picking trailer with a rickety elevated platform stood in the drive. The hacienda was behind a fence, but I admired its gardens and the granary that the ever-laughing acorn woodpeckers had punched into a legacy oak. This must have been such a peaceful spot before the railroad. Still was. Shriveled balloons lay on the ground from a wedding. I gleaned three oranges and three grapefruits from below their trees and savored one of each as I walked, flicking the juice from my fingers and rinsing them with a trickle from one of my bottles. Would have taken more if I didn't have to carry it. A grapefruit's bitterness lingers wonderfully.

NOT LONG AFTER, BELL PEPPERS were being harvested, the sweet cousin of the chili peppers I'd seen yesterday—the lone *Capsicum* that has lost its heat, due to a recessive gene. The pickers were squatting and hurrying to white totes at the row ends, their cars in a gleaming line far across the field. I wandered off the highway and met Susana, supervising in a long-sleeve navy blue shirt and a lifeguard-style woven hat. She wore white latex gloves as she inspected what the pickers poured into a tote, one five-gallon black bucket after the next. Actually these buckets were retired nursery pots that once might have held a tree. The workers would lay the peppers gently into the new crate, dipping their buckets low so the peppers hardly fell. The peppers squeaked as they tumbled against each other and nestled into their cranial folds. Some ruby red, others a gradated swirl of green and yellow-orange that would ripen on the way to Safeway, all of them spotted with dust and shine. A bell pepper is indeed an ephemeral, sealed bell with hundreds of silent clappers— the seeds around its core. "Smells so good," I said to her. "Smells great." Soapy and sweet. But her tepid assent and expression suggested that the scent's charm had mostly worn off.

Susana was a tax accountant, as well, and her role as foreman likewise involved accounting. She would run her hand through the new peppers, assessing them, and then punch a hole in the yellow card each picker kept in a back pocket, or tied to their person some other way. The rate was a dollar and five cents per bucket, so they literally jogged up and down the rows with their buckets over their shoulders, catching their breath only as they picked, as they twisted and broke stems. Most picked a hundred-plus buckets a day. One man recently had managed 305 buckets.

"Yeah, he's amazing," Susana said in a deep voice. "Nobody else can do that. Running *all* day long."

I replied, "They probably put in more miles than I do on my walk."

Each time, the pickers had to go farther and farther out the row, so the returns gradually diminished. There were about twenty or twenty-five peppers per bucket, about sixteen buckets per tote. I tried to do the math in my head. I tried again. That was upward of three hundred peppers a tote, I guessed, maybe close to four hundred. But it looked like more. In California, an acre of bell pepper might yield fifteen to twenty tons of fruit, with a gross value of about ten or eleven thousand dollars. This is what the bells of the El Camino Real had sought to produce.

As you'd expect, the rows had black tarp at their margins to suppress the weeds. Wooden stakes guided white cord to help the plants stand tall and clear of the furrowed aisle. Discarded peppers lay crushed and dried in those well-worn trails, and Susana was on the lookout for imperfections. A single blemish, any thumbprint of rot, was enough—meant curtains—and Susana tossed it into the slight ditch between blocks where the forklift ran over it (*beep beep beep beep*), mushing these succulent treats back into that from which they came. Which means the sky: over 90 percent of a bell pepper is water. Of twenty tons of peppers, nineteen is groundwater. Some of them looked as if a magnifying glass had been held to them, burning a little black hole in this carnal flesh. Susana let me take one of these throwaway peppers—it was ideal, huge, a specimen except for its broken tip. I would snack on it later.

They picked Monday through Saturday, would go until September. "We have a lot of ranches," Susana said, "all over the place." She and most of the pickers lived in Oxnard, where I was headed—on the coast, at the mouth of this dry river—and some would pick strawberries come winter. I thought I could see coastal moisture hanging in the air down valley. Maybe that was just hoping. Between the pepper blocks, a pickup was hitched to a trailer that held a pair of Porta-Potties and a picnic table, for breaks, with a pop-up awning. I could hardly believe how many of the farmworkers wore sweatshirts, but the sun; but the dust and the white antifungal residue that was sprayed onto the peppers, only at night, as a liquid; but the pepper plants' own exfoliation. You wouldn't last more than a day doing this work in anything less than a long-sleeve. They wore bandannas in every style: around their mouths, around their ball caps, around their necks. The man who said, "What's up, friend?" as I left wore a cap with the California flag embroidered on it. "How you doing?" I said, acknowledging his pride.

THE TOWN OF PIRU (*Pie-roo*), at its turnoff on State Route 126, is marked by an Arco station with an am/pm. The place was founded by an evangelist who bought land from Ygnacio de Valle to create a Garden of Eden in the Santa Clara River Valley, and so he planted all the fruits of the Bible: dates, grapes, figs, olives, pomegranate, and apricot. Now the gas was $2.39 a gallon, the lowest I'd seen in California. I recharged there in various ways, sitting in the eave of Arco's shade with a hot coffee and my legs crossed. People arrived and departed with a beer in a bag or some other cheap delectable. Noontime; I was always getting my coffee too late. A blue-lined handicapped space in front of me. Across the route was a nursery with boxed palms that waved without resistance. The mountains rose up over them, all brown, as if the wind was whittling away at those hills to create this haze, and beyond those Santa Susana Mountains was the San Fernando Valley and the nearly 2 million people I'd left behind two days before.

You have to ask for a token to use the restroom in Piru, and the manager slides one across the counter at you. When I bought my thawed burrito and coffee, he said, "What about the Powerade?" I thought he had said, "What about the power?" since I'd asked if I could charge my phone in the store, and he had replied, "If you can find a way to do it, do it."

"I'll plug in a minute," I said. I had scouted the outlets.

"No, what about the Powerade."

"Oh, I'll buy those later," I replied. I had pulled out two of them from the refrigerators: two for $1.89. White cherry and classic lemon lime. But I wanted them cold after my coffee.

"Where did they go?" he asked.

"I put them back," I said. He looked over that way as if those particular bottles would stand out to him in their neon rows.

"You put them back," he said. "Okay."

"I promise you," I said.

Outside, a man in a blue shirt moved from trash can to trash can with a black five-gallon nursery pot that looked exactly like the one the pepper pickers were using. He was scavenging recyclables. When he turned, he was startled to see me at his feet on the gum-pocked and spill-stained concrete. At the next trash can, he extracted a Gatorade bottle. I was going to buy two new Powerade bottles, I realized. I pulled out an old, empty bottle that I had carried for perhaps a hundred miles, and then I tried to chug the water in another, but I had to pour out the remainder on the curb to give it to him. A waste. There's not enough water in this land.

"Thank you, my friend," he said. "Money for gas."

ALL DAY I ATE ORANGES. Oranges without compunction. There must have been twenty to fifty under every tree in these orchards. Windfall, it's called. The waste was unfathomable, but a boon to the fruit that remains, which ripens all the sweeter for it, I imagine. I would swerve a little and gather an intact, good one from the rotting many: black and scaly, ringed with mold (pale white on the outer ring, like alkali at the edge of a desert lake; then sage green; and finally, at the fungal epicenter, a powdery blue). Many were cracked so that they seemed to smile. I stepped on one long-dark and it compressed and rebounded like a sponge. I stepped on another, still with some color, and it spurted hot pulp and a hundred or so lethargic bugs, something between a fly and a beetle. They began to scatter through the sand. Something more skittering than maggots. In places the oranges were piled into the water ditches that gave them life, lodged in fresh silt as new grass waved around them. In the Santa Clara River Valley, you can buy a twenty-five-pound box of oranges or grapefruit for three dollars. So I didn't feel abashed about gleaning them from the ground until my stomach hurt. I dug my thumb under the thin skin of a Valencia and, after it was done, shook the juice from my fingertips. Sticky hands soon collect dirt (the downside of Powerade is you can't wash with it). A warm orange on a hot day every few miles.

COMING INTO FILLMORE, I VEERED off Highway 126 in favor of a stretch of railroad, the first time I'd done that. These were the same tracks that created this town when they were strung through in 1887. J. A. Fillmore, it turns out, was a Southern Pacific superintendent. Leaving the shoulder was, is, a relief I didn't know I needed. A highway a hundred yards away, when it isn't the only path, is a much better friend to a walker. A jeep trail followed these rails into town, and I saw a white egret in a pool of water in a fallow field, a spill of irrigation. There were ridges in the pool where tractor wheels earlier had made ruts while turning, and in places the slick was dense with algae: scum, even from a distance.

The egret lifted as I neared, but in that same instance a green heron, our smallest common heron, landed with a raised crest, the only green about this bird. Their throats are auburn with a white gullet, their bodies slate blue. It sat perched on one of those ridges of mud amid the pool. Those ridges, with algae on their sides, looked in miniature quite like the Santa Susana Mountains and their sides of oak which hold this valley. The bird morphed into an almond shape, with a recoiled neck. Then it stretched out horizontal, readying to strike: less a dart than a pluck. A tadpole? There were killdeer around the pool, also. Horned larks arrived, and two mourning doves came to its edge. Mourning, mourning. I went to its side to look in: the algae snapped and popped like Rice Krispies. A few flies walked the soup, but above all it was covered with tiny snails, little black spirals—field periwinkles. A pool of accidental water in a farm field can be an oasis.

WALKING TOWARD THE BIKE PATH at dusk, I met a kid on a low-ride bike. "Where you walking to?" he said.

"The bike path," I said.

He circled around and pedaled lazily beside me. I was carrying a Subway sandwich and a Modelo in my pack and, in my hand, I had a grande drip from Starbucks that would be an ice coffee by morning. It stained the creases of my palm as it sloshed hot through its lid.

"Where did you come from?"

"From . . . from . . ." I honestly couldn't remember the name of Piru though I'd been there just hours before. "From up the valley."

"Where are you going?" he said.

"To San Francisco."

"No way," he said. "Did you hear about the guy who is walking the whole border of America? My dad is following him online. His knees are swollen *this big* from his pack. I thought about biking from the Ventura Pier to the Statue of Liberty. I've got nothing but time."

"You'll want a better bike," I said, "one you can extend your legs on."

"That's what my dad said. Why?"

"Better for your knees and you get more power. What you're riding is for style, a town cruiser."

"I got it out of the trash," he said. "Rebuilt it."

Finally, I asked him, "What about Sespe Creek, is it safe? Are there homeless people down there?" I wanted to believe I was in no danger camping in the dry creek beds of suburban and rural California, but it was hard to the shake the feeling of risk, so I tried to be cautious and make sure that no one saw me when I slipped into the willows for the night.

"Oh nah," he said. "You'll find nothing. You won't have to worry about homeless people until you get to Ventura."

Moonlight has the same quality as my laptop on its dimmest setting. I drafted this recollection in a grove of dead mustard and arundo, just above dry Sespe Creek, named after a nearby Chumash village and also where Portolá camped on August 11. As I moved down the Santa Clara River, the moon moved forward an hour each night and grew toward full, and it was just about half when I reached Fillmore. When I stared into my screen, writing at night, I lost the world; I suppose that also happens during the day. But at night, you realize this especially when you look up again and you are enveloped in black, vulnerable. Animals stir everywhere. Crickets rule. Something was chewing vigorously in the stand of arundo about twenty feet from me. Wood rat, I hoped. The birds were vocal at dusk, but afterward they became a rare flap of wings, a ruffle in search of comfort. Two sounds from the crickets: a constant whir, a trifold chirp.

SUN UP. OUTSIDE MY SOLO dome, I let my salty shirt dry before setting off, hanging it on a rack of withered mustard. Agave and prickly pear nearby. A translucent spider had woven a delicate web, already flecked with dust, across the cave-opening of my sneaker. It hung there above the blue sole. Luckily I noticed it. I wondered: Just how bad did my shoe smell if this spider thought it was a standout location to catch flies? Smelled fine, actually. With a sweep of my finger, I cleared the web and shook out the filamentous creature. Nearby there were red ants: they always quicken in their concave cities when I step toward them, as if feeling tremors and preparing for a flood. A hooded oriole, yellow-orange with a black throat and mask, from a willow. A Gatorade bottle, no label, stream-worn, in Sespe Creek wash, which was filled with reddish sands and silt. Apparently there are rosy sandstone boulders in the mountains from which the Sespe runs, first west to east through the high wilderness and then south through Fillmore. Plastic, I've noticed, scuffs rather than polishing like stone. It seems I had begun to stop differentiating between animal, plant, and trash. They're all worth cataloging. They all travel the same waterways. Wading through the brush, across Sespe Creek and to the highway through a gravel yard, my pockets soon filled with frangible plant debris, and I had to keep blowing out the lenses of my small capless binoculars.

IN THE SANTA CLARA RIVER VALLEY, orchards run up the coffee-colored hillsides, reminding me of the fincas in Central America which go up the rain-forest volcanos. Except here I was in a land of drought. You could see the pale green of the lemons and mandarins, the larger, darker greens of avocado or orange, and the newly planted orchards that were an audacious stippling on a parched, rolling canvas. One orchard I passed had grown prickly pear along the fence to deter people like me, loose cannons and scavengers; I caught sight of an orange impaled on two spines, where it would desiccate on a slow-motion rotisserie, the sun for a fire.

On the road into Santa Paula, I lost myself in a pomegranate. It had been broken into by a bird, so I had no qualms about picking it from the sidewalk tree. The cavity the avian had made was like the work of a small blast of dynamite and there, inside, you could see the ruby fruit kernels. They might have been a day or two less than ripe, but they were more than worth eating. Again and again, my hands were sticky. Eating a pomegranate in the hand is like eating a strange corn on the cob, ingrown and filled with blood. All these niches, these crevices, to explore with my dirty fingernails. Dirty because of days of fruit.

THE CREEK BESIDE WHICH THE Portolá expedition camped in Santa Paula is starkly channelized, confined by twenty-five-feet-high concrete walls. The stream is perhaps a hundred feet across with a line of willow flowing down one side like a verdant approximation of a flood. They have experienced big, stony floods in Santa Paula and are not messing around anymore. But the water here is fleeting. In this valley, Costansó wrote, "We halted on the bank of the stream which, at the time of our arrival, flowed with considerable volume, but, shortly after, dried up with the heat of the sun—just as the scouts told us they had noticed on the previous day. This peculiarity we afterwards observed in other streams; they flowed by night and became dry by day."

I was loitering on Telegraph Road where it crosses Santa Paula Creek, staring blankly downstream, when I began to hear it. The bridge began to sing: a low, building whistle. It was the sound of water lifting into the sky. It was the west wind through the slats of the metal rail. Only a few seconds, ethereal. Then another fluting note. When the wind was at just the right angle, this pleading sound rose up again. It was stronger on the southern rail, and it was irregular, scattered, notes sometimes few and far between. A woman with a stroller passed by as the bridge began to sing, and we looked at each other as if to make sure we were not alone.

I stood there for fifteen minutes. Suddenly I began to hear everything else: the clinking crash of recycling as it was tumbled into a dumpster; the trucks on the highway, which had none of the bridge's haunting melody; the staccato beep of a truck announcing its reversal; a loyal dog barking protectively. The willows in the channel swayed in circles, enmeshed in each other, waiting for nighttime's respiration. The channel led south under the highway to the Santa Clara River and pointed straight up the mountains to the SP for Santa Paula, built of painted rock, and higher still to a few radio towers, blinking, at least in my imagination, in my memory.

The Boys and Girls Club was a few minutes' walk farther, down Harvard Boulevard, from the singing bridge of Santa Paula. Beside it, in Harding Park, I found a marker that didn't mention Portolá, but did mention that the place was "named the Holy Martyrs, Ipolito and Casiano," on August 13, 1769. Odd, the date was one day off: Portolá and Crespí actually camped here on August 12. Did it matter? Was the date important? When you're walking a long distance, time becomes more malleable, less certain. You feel mainly the sunsets and the seasons.

I put my pack down against a picnic table as a table saw whined somewhere across the street. I thought to put my recyclables from last night into the blue can below a rustling live oak. But it was so filled with trash, none of it recyclable, that I knew nothing would be sorted, the whole lot would be tossed. So like a madman I saved my Modelo can and Starbucks lid for a better depository. There was a circle of sand in the lawn where you could play a volleyball game. If you brought your own net. A white dove winged across, maybe a racing pigeon. Particles began to obscure the northern mountains, dust or smog. The oaks in this park were elegantly limbed and cast cauliflowers of shade. A man rested his bike on the lawn and lay down with his head against its tire for a pillow.

IN THE CALIFORNIA OIL MUSEUM, in downtown Santa Paula, there is a life-size model of a cable-tool drilling rig, the machine by which the black gold of California was extracted more than a century ago. It is housed in its own building, with tall glass windows that allow bright light on the hand-hewn beams of this hulking contraption. It is massive, but there is nothing too complicated about its design. Simply put, a steam engine powers a wheel that rocks a beam that lifts a rope with a heavy drill bit tied to its end. Up and down, up and down, up and down, goes the drill, pulverizing the rock below. Drilling lower and lower. A graduated series of pipes, called casings, would be slid into the well to prevent its walls from caving in, and another wheel, the sand wheel, would haul up the minced rock periodically, the "cuttings." Cable-tool rigs have also been dubbed "pounders," "percussions," "spudders," or "walking beam rigs." I got stuck on that last name, "the walking beam." That beam was the main seesaw lever that lifted the rope over and over again. Its work was methodical, marching—"walking beam" was a perfect and poetic name, only rivaled by what it sat atop, the Samson beam. At full speed, the walking beam in this model would rise and fall every two seconds, thirty times a minute, but it was walking slower here. I understood: the museum was trying to spare these old parts.

The first gusher in California was discovered just west of Santa Clarita in Pico Canyon, in 1876—Pico Canyon No. 4, it's called. Alex Mentry had drilled three other wells before he tapped into it, what's now considered the grandfather of the state's oil wells. From a depth of 376 feet, the well produced twenty-five barrels a day—a modest gusher, by modern standards. When the well was extended several hundred more feet in its second year, the crude was said to jet to the top of the derrick as in the legends and movies. Pico Canyon No. 4 produced more or less continuously until 1990, when it was finally capped, long after it had become one of Los Angeles County's first two National Historic Landmarks. There had been an earlier, short-lived oil boom—a boomlet—in the 1860s, but it was Pico Canyon No. 4 that inspired an acceleration of oil exploration. The number of barrels produced in California leapt from five hundred thousand in 1879 to more than 4 million in 1881. Small oil companies eventually consolidated into larger ones. The California Oil Museum itself is housed in the original offices of the Sespe Oil Company (whose field is in the hills north of Fillmore, above Sespe Creek where I camped), the Hardison and Stewart Oil Company, and the Mission Transfer Company. Farther down the Santa Clara River Valley, the Ventura Oil Fields, the tenth most productive in California history, are found in the hills between Ventura and Ojai.

An interpretive sign stapled to the model rig in the museum says this machine would have cost $3,400 in 1889, quite the sum, and a half dozen men would have needed several weeks to build it. If oil were discovered, the rig would remain on the well and be converted into a pump. The pump jacks I had seen in Los Angeles County and in a few places coming down the Santa Clara River Valley are the direct descendants of this cable-tool rig. Their horse heads nod thanks to the energy of an electric motor rather than a steam engine, but the mechanics, and certainly the outcome, are the same. Pound, pound, pound until you find oil. Then plunge, plunge, plunge to create a vacuum to pull it up. Send it to a refinery. Put it in your car. Turn it into plastic bags that will blow and tumble and snag along the roadside.

FOLLOWING THE RAILROAD TRACKS TOWARD the Santa Clara River, where I planned to camp for the third night in a row—the channel widening, but no water still, just sand and gravel, willow and arundo—I came upon the Sunkist Saticoy Lemon Association Plant 3. Beyond chain-link, four big semis were idling, lights on, ready for a nighttime haul. The loading dock held shrink-wrapped pallets of white boxes with blue-and-gold sides, the colors of California. TRUCK DRIVERS, said a large sign on the wall, PLEASE COUNT YOUR LOAD AFTER BEING LOADED. SIGNATURE ON BILLS MAKES YOU FULLY RESPONSIBLE WHEN YOU LEAVE. The air, it smelled so sweetly of lemon, as if the whole neighborhood were a tall draught of garnished ice water on a summer patio table. Especially when a hint of Pacific breeze came up the valley. If you're going to live next to a factory, I thought, better to live next to a lemon plant than a meat-packing facility or a pulp mill.

I was just standing and gazing and sniffing, when a man approached wearing a black ball cap. "How's it going?" he asked. No doubt I appeared lost or intoxicated by lemon fumes. "Great," I said. "I was just passing by, and stopped to take in the plant." I was sure he had come to chase me off, but he invited me in with a casual wave. "Want to take a look?" he said. He was Mario, who grew up in Santa Paula but now lived in Oxnard. He was security, but the kind of security I admire, more ambassador than hard-ass. He had nothing to prove and plenty of time. "Oh shit," he said, when I told him I was plodding toward San Francisco. I asked if he knew where these trucks were headed, and he said not precisely, but as far as New York or Florida. "They don't grow their own lemons in Florida?" I said. "No," Mario said. "And Florida sends their oranges here." Such is modern commerce. I had just walked orange groves for days and gleaned many from the rotting masses. In the Santa Clara River Valley, a frugivore could survive on windfall year-round.

"Want a bag of lemons?" Mario said, as we walked toward the loading dock.

"Ah . . . no," I replied, with a laugh. "I mean, if they were oranges I would take them, but lemons I can't eat on the go so much, too hard. Too hard to make lemonade."

They had them to spare. That day, and every day, the plant shipped out fifteen hundred boxes, fifty-four boxes per pallet. They would go to Safeway, they would go to Walmart. They were going to China, Japan, and Korea, as the characters on the cartons showed. The edges of the loading dock, the edges of stairs, the poles and chains, the hard hats the men were wearing—all of it was lemon yellow. It conveyed both caution and regality. Stand-on-top forklifts hovered in and out of the plant quietly, and one of the drivers pulled up short to say hello. "Is it hard to drive that forklift all day?" I asked. What a dumb question. "It gets tiring, yeah," he replied. "Thirteen hours a day. I didn't want to go school, man—biggest mistake ever. Yeah, I never went to school, you know. But it's like riding a skateboard, you know."

Inside the plant, women wearing hairnets were cleaning the fruit. "As far as pictures," said Mario, "you might want to wait until the ladies leave because they might get a little offended." Stacked pallets were being shrink-wrapped on a glorious lazy Susan, light gleaming off the thin film. One hundred fifty people work in the plant, typically until nine o'clock, but the plant was closing early today. Depended on orders.

Mario took me in another bay to the refrigerated main-level warehouse. I'd never been in a cooler this grand. The floor was painted with yellow lines, like parking stalls, on which individual orders had been arranged for shipping, an airport garage with a heavenly scent. The stalls were labeled A-15, B-12, and so forth. And how many lemons were in each box? "It all depends on the size," said Mario. In the field, the pickers filled up bags, one after the next, and filled their own totes— forty-five dollars a tote. "They bring them in and they get washed, and then they get sized, and then shade and color. Like see these, right here, they are a little green. So they're probably going to sit here two or three days." Some varieties like Saticoy, "our top fruit" as Mario put it, were huge: the platonic ideal of a lemon, 115 per box. On the other end of the spectrum was Brimfull, the size of a lime, 235 per carton. "See how ugly they are?" Mario said. I tried to defend those Brimfull; they were elegantly pimpled, more expressive. But they would become cocktail wedges or lemonade. The plant didn't bother to wax them—that gloss was reserved for Saticoy.

Looking at one pallet's label, I saw the invoice was for $6,400. That was nothing, Mario said. Lemons going to Asia commanded higher prices. He had worked at a plant that sent eighty pallets of avocado to Japan daily for ten grand each, shipping not included. "And that was just that one brand," said Mario. "We still had local, we still had what we were shipping across the States."

He took me downstairs to a sprawling basement cold room, a catacomb of fluorescent lights and crates. The old concrete walls were chipped and pocked— they looked like they'd been through a few earthquakes—and the floor glistened and was sticky with decades of natural oil. The aroma was surreal. "My god," I exclaimed, "I wish I could bottle this smell and take it with me."

"When the season's really good, everything here is full," Mario said.

Hundreds of thousands of lemons, stacked to the ceiling. And around the building's side was a lemon silo, of sorts, under which a semi could pull up and fill its trailers with blemished fruit for lemonade and concentrate. The Santa Paula plant was 190,000 square feet—and it was the smallest of the Saticoy Lemon Association's three plants, the others in Oxnard and Ventura, all three of which have operated for over eighty years.

Citrus in California is a more than 3-billion-dollar business, of which lemons are a modest part, though Ventura County's lemon groves cover almost 17,000 acres and provide about 70 percent of the country's lemons. The Saticoy Lemon Association, established in 1933, pays for the privilege of calling its fruit Sunkist, giving up a percentage of all sales. As I stared at the word, I began to fixate on "kist." Kist, kist, kist. Give me a kist. It was a brilliant and awful reduction, a bid for copyright and recognition. It worked. Originally called the California Fruit Growers Exchange, Sunkist has wormed its way into the minds of most Americans as the premier citrus brand. It is headquartered up the valley in Santa Clarita.

When we circled back to the loading dock, the hills were turning amber. Beyond wind-rippled palms, limestone bands stood out on the Santa Susanas, and a fog bank was floating up valley. The coast was near. I thanked Mario and hurried on in search of a patch of ground. "It'll be cold camping in the creek," said Mario.

"Not as cold as it is in those fridges," I said.

WHITE DOVES RACING CIRCLES OVER an orchard house on Telegraph Road, on my way toward the Pacific. There was a coop in the rear, and the birds were out for exercise. Roundabout they dashed, in silence, in shimmer, through an alley of pine and palms. They thought of settling on the roof, and a few did, but most accelerated, revolved again. Flock mentality. Through my binoculars, I saw that each had a blue band on one of its pinkish legs, identifying them as belonging to this yard. Two dozen young avocados in black plastic pots. Two turquoise dumpsters. A silver Toyota pickup with the lids of its toolbox open. An antique wooden chair in the dirt, beside it, in need of mending. The motion of the pigeons was unadulterated, an expression of the need to burn energy. Of the color ivory. Of one family or person's care for these creatures.

I veered off Telegraph onto Pistachio, encouraged by its name, and wound my way toward Saticoy, a neighborhood technically in Ventura. Ate three large sweet figs on the corner of Pistachio and Casa, and then, having whetted my appetite, succumbed to a Jack in the Box Garlic Fries advertisement: enormous flecks of parsley, the suggestion of oil. I ate those as I crossed the freeway overpass into Saticoy. The median's pinkish oleander swayed with the ocean breeze and rush of cars. These people would reach Santa Clarita in forty minutes. It had taken me three days to walk that distance. I sopped up the garlic oil and ketchup in the carton with my last fries and licked my fingers, gingerly transferring the carton between my hands so I could take a snapshot of the vibrant mustard field beside the highway. I was seeing lemon everywhere. By legend the missionaries threw mustard seed along El Camino to color the way, to turn it and eventually the state golden, and there's a modest truth to this: we know that black mustard, one of California's first invasive plants, did in fact arrive in the late 1700s, since its seeds and pollen have been found entombed in the adobe of the later missions.

On a Friday, the street sweeper in Saticoy seemed to be chasing me as I wandered, raising as much dust as it collected. Saticoy gets its name from the Chumash village here along the river that, Crespí wrote, "brought out two barbecued heads of mescal plants for us"—century plants, probably, a giant agave. On the stuccoed wall of the 3 Amigos Market was an "Old Town Saticoy" mural depicting its past and present: a Chumash woman wove a basket, a man flaked a stone for an arrowhead. On the modern half of the mural, a woman pushed a stroller and a painted car hood read, UNIDOS! honoring the auto body work that now goes on in Saticoy. Portolá was nowhere to be found.

The historic train station, originally built by Southern Pacific in 1887, was boarded up with plywood whose knots in the grain looked like so many eyes, staring out, and along the rusted tracks its pale walls were painted gray to head height. Already new graffiti, gang tags real or pretend, had been layered on: OLD TOWN SATICOY LOCOS 13, ESSATICOY, FUCK THE REST ESS13. In town, new squares of concrete around a telephone pole had been etched with sticks or fingers before they dried: OUR GOAL IN LIFE SHOULD BE TO LEAVE THIS PLANET BETTER THAN HOW WE RECEIVED IT. / DON'T FORGET ... BE AWESOME! / REVOLUTION HAS NEVER BEEN A SPECTATOR SPORT. / TODO PARA TODOS. Elsewhere the sidewalk was imprinted as if with branding irons, a nod to the ranchos. As I stood looking at Saticoy Auto Body & Truck where a vintage car was getting a fresh coat or some other detailing, the owner of the shop paced out onto the street and said, "I don't want you snooping around here." I'm sure he had his reasons.

I HAD READ ABOUT THE Cabrillo Village in Saticoy, which has a famous history as former Saticoy Lemon Growers Association housing. So I went. The village had its start in 1936 when the Growers Association constructed its first housing for Mexican workers. But Cabrillo Village was cheaply made and so neglected by the growers that in 1975 the Association offered its tenants five hundred dollars each to leave the village so that it could be razed. The workers didn't want to abandon their homes, of course, and they enlisted Cesar Chavez to help them try to remain. Ultimately they stood together with elbows linked, a human chain, as the bulldozers approached and then backed down. The people of Cabrillo Village were able to collectively buy their homes and the land itself for eighty thousand dollars. It was the first time that Mexican American farmworkers were able to purchase their homes from growers. Only in this light did the village's name, Cabrillo, after this coast's pioneering European explorer, truly resonate.

Cabrillo Village's avenues were 16 de Septiembre, Si Se Puede, and Cinco de Mayo; its cross streets were the back of the alphabet, Q, R, S, T, U, V, through which girls on bikes were riding circles. The homes were a tan stucco with small yards surrounded by low cinder-block walls, each painted pastel and topped with cast-iron fencing; some of the yards were overflowing with semitropical plants, with fan palms, lemon, orange, and grapefruit. There was a small office at the village entrance and a resource center dedicated to Saul Martinez, a California Highway Patrolman who had grown up in Cabrillo Village, worked for United Farm Workers alongside Chavez, and been killed on a dark desert highway by a speeding car as he pushed a fellow officer out of harm's way. Several thousand people came to his funeral. The center's paint was peeling now, but Saul's brothers and sisters had worked for a week to freshly paint it before the dedication and, the night before, others slept inside it to make sure it wasn't vandalized by rival gang members. Now it houses the Catholic Charities Food Pantry.

For generations, the people who lived in Cabrillo Village had picked the fragrant lemons I'd seen the last few days. These were their kids and grandkids, and great-grandkids. I went left on V Street and found a dry ball field worn to dirt in patches, such as in front of the *fútbol* goals whose unraveled nets looked like spiderwebs. You could see the faint chalk or spray paint of the penalty area. Beyond the far goal, two stairways led, it seemed, to the horizon, which was hazy with mountains and a denim blue: the levee. Cabrillo Village is hemmed in by the Santa Clara River and new suburbia.

A few men were loitering under eucalyptus along the field's perimeter, some of them on benches. A tennis ball was overthrown and bounced my direction, and one of the men walk-jogged to retrieve it. I lifted my hand and pointed at the ball, gesturing that I'd help him out and lob it back to him. When I did, he came right up anyway. "Ulysses," he said, holding out his hand. His cheeks were angular and led to a black goatee. He wore a skater hat. "How you doing?" he said. "What are you up to?"

I told him that I was interested in the history, that I was just walking through Cabrillo Village to see what it was like, that I was retracing the route of the first Spaniards. "This exploring about the history, like, what's it for?" he asked. It was a good question.

"I'm a writer," I explained, "so I'm going to try to write a book. This is an adventure, but it's my work too. It's fun, interesting. You see something new every day. . . . Do you live right here?"

"Yeah, I live in the area." I could tell he was hedging. Ulysses was uncertain about me. He had a slight build, but he was confident, though he struggled at times to get out the right words, stuttering a little. At least in English.

I tried again to explain myself: "I just read . . . It was on Wikipedia, actually . . . that the Camarillo Village . . ."

"Cabrillo Village," he corrected me.

"Cabrillo, sorry, Cabrillo . . . um . . ." There was a quaver in my voice, because it was true: I knew nothing of this place, and I felt his suspicion, which bordered on aggression.

"You're not a cop or anything like that, are you?

"No," I said. "If I were a cop, would I look like this?" I wore a blue plaid long-sleeved shirt, tall socks stretched up my calves, and a broad-brimmed straw gambler hat I'd picked up at the hardware store in Santa Paula.

"Or, you're not associated with any of that?"

"No, no, I promise you. . . . If I were a cop, I probably wouldn't be carrying a giant backpack."

"They come in many disguises . . . You're not associated with any organizations or anything like that?"

"No. No, I know why you would say that, but . . ."

"You're just a traveler?"

"I'm seriously just a traveler. . . . Yeah, I'm carrying, like, all these oranges from up the valley." I was looking for a way to validate myself.

"That's good. Can I have one?" He was calling my bluff, though it wasn't one, and I began to rifle through my pack for a Valencia. Just then Ulysses began to feel ungracious. He was taking fruit from a stranger, a vagrant. Though I certainly didn't mind giving him an orange.

"I'll trade you for one," Ulysses said. "Do you like Arizona drinks? I've got some food right here, for your travels." He motioned toward the house behind him.

I tried to politely decline and change the subject. "Do you know anything about this neighborhood and its history?" I asked.

"I really don't know much," he replied. "Other than they marched . . . they fought for their rights, you know what I mean, during that time. If you want to know about this area, you got to know more about that time. This is one of the beginnings of that . . . Let me give you some food for your travels. Thanks for your blessings. I'd like to bless you, too. Just wait here."

"Okay," I said finally, giving up my protest. "I'm going to look around."

"Careful, don't look around too much, because they don't . . ."

"I don't want to alarm anyone," I reassured him.

I listened to the jingle of an ice-cream truck as I waited. Two Eurasian collared doves mewing, fluttering. The girls passed by on their bikes again. Ulysses reappeared.

"You don't want to be staring," he said, with a brief laugh.

"What," I said, with a half laugh of my own. I was just standing there, looking around like a normal person, gazing over the ball field. But I wasn't a normal person because I was wearing an enormous backpack and looked as if I had just stumbled out of the bushes, which was true. And to him I must have looked something like the boa I had seen in Jeff's tattooed arms on the first day of my walk, at Spanish Landing Park: a potential predator, observing.

"You don't want to be staring . . ."

"Milk?" I said when he handed me a plastic bag with two small, foil-capped drinks and a nectarine. I was eager to just move on, to change the subject, to leave Cabrillo Village.

"You're not allergic to anything, are you? You want to poke two holes . . ."

"Thank you," I said. "You know, this is too much . . . I'll just take one."

"They're really good, you're going to want another one," he said. "They're good for your health."

"Made from lactic acid bacteria," I said, reading the label. "Like a yogurt."

Ulysses paused and said, "If you walk over this levee, there's a path that takes you to Oxnard."

"All right, sure. You mean, you feel like I'm not safe here?"

"Let me . . . 'Cause it's a small neighborhood, it's a neighborhood actually, you know what I mean? If you want to take a view of it, you can walk the perimeter of it. You're kind of like . . . you're like an outsider. There's been, like, rival gang shootings here."

"Really?" I replied. I tried to make it sound like I hadn't read about that. Then for some reason I told him about the graffiti I'd seen on the boarded-up train depot in Saticoy.

"I don't know . . . I don't know about that," Ulysses said, reflexively. It was a stupid thing to mention, because I was fueling his suspicions.

"All right, yeah. No, I was just curious. . . . You poke two holes in this, huh?"

"It's like a coconut."

"Cool, thank you. Can I give you a lemon? Yeah, let me give you a lemon. I was going to make some lemonade . . ." I had gathered several after all.

"You can have that for yourself . . ."

"Here, no, it's only fair," I said. "Well, it's not fair—I think I got the better end of the deal."

I handed him a Santa Paula lemon, still warm from sitting at the top of my pack, and then Ulysses more or less escorted me across the dry ball field, past the soccer goals with their frayed nets. As we strolled he told me that in years past the field was more of a gathering ground, a place where his grandfather and others played music and celebrated.

"So you grew up right here?" I asked.

"No, but I got family."

"What do you do?" I asked.

"What I do . . . I just am."

"Well, me too, right now."

"I hope you're successful in obtaining all that you want to know, and success . . . successful on your book."

"Thanks, I appreciate your well wishes. Do you consider yourself, like, a guardian of this place?"

"No, I just am. This is one of my last paradises."

Having climbed the stairs from the ball field, we stood atop the levee and surveyed the broad wash of the Santa Clara River with its swirls of sand and shrub. The roofs of houses peeked above the far levee on the opposite side, a quarter mile away. It was an expansive view, and suddenly we both breathed a little easier.

"I'm going to a mall called River Park, or something . . . you know of it?" It was the biggest mall in the area. I was seeking out an REI, to finally buy a stove.

"No," he said. "Down that tree path, you hit Camarillo. Down that levee over there, you hit Oxnard."

"That's where I'm going, through the arundo. Any water ever flow through here?"

"It's been a while. But at the entrance of the river, at the beach, they kind of like seal it, and there's some there. . . . Oh, you've got binoculars. Can you see across? How strong are they?"

"They're ten by twenty-five. They're really cheap. But waterproof. You want to look?"

"How cheap are these?"

"They were seventy bucks . . . Cheap for binoculars."

"Where at?"

"I got them online."

"These are fucking . . . I mean, excuse me . . . these are awesome."

"Yeah, they're good, and they . . . I like to watch birds and animals, and mountains . . ."

"Interesting . . ."

"To each their own," I said. "Ulysses, have you ever read *Ulysses*?"

"I tried to."

"I've only read the first part of it," I said. I had savored the episode on the Sandymount Strand but gotten bogged down not long after the entrance of Leopold Bloom.

"Yeah, I've read a lot, but I can't read the whole literature . . . the whole book. To read like the ones at universities, no, I can't. One other question I got: Are you Libra?"

"I always forget," I said. "I was born December twentieth. Does that make me Sagittarius?"

"Capricorn. . . . If you want, you can walk along the levee and look into the village."

"No, that's all right," I said. "I got a sense for the place. I don't want to bother anyone, seriously. I got a quick feel. The streets named by letter. Seems like the old part is in the center there, and these apartments are newly built. Seems like a good neighborhood. . . . All right, dude, later on. Thank you. Be safe."

"You as well," he said.

I paused in the river bottom, unsure for a moment of which direction to go now that the view was lost to arundo and willow taller than me.

"Hey, Ulysses, this way?

"Yeah, just follow the path."

AS I WAS WALKING THE far levee toward Oxnard, a dirt biker scared the bejesus out of me. Somehow I didn't hear him coming until he passed like a fighter jet over my shoulder wearing a helmet and a backpack. A motorcycle down a barren riverbed is one of the swiftest ways to travel in California, and here the sand was tracked and rutted. Old sagebrush, coyote brush, and fennel grew to my height. I was half-sure I glimpsed another roadrunner from afar—probably hunting lizards or cottontail in the riprap. Their movement tricks the mind, makes you wonder if you imagined the motion. YOUNG METRO. DON'T TRUST'M. SHOOT YA, read graffiti on an outfall clogged with tumbleweed. "Best served chilled," read Ulysses's drink. It was still cold and tasted like watery strawberry yogurt. I was grateful for it. California towhees on brown branches. Periodic cottonwood. Sprinklers arching across a field beside a new development with men still hammering the roofs even at 6:30 on a Friday. This unfinished neighborhood had fenced me out already, but Cabrillo Village had no fence along the river, just the levee.

After a visit to The Collection mall in Oxnard, where I finally picked up a new camping stove and dashed into Whole Foods for a sandwich and beer, I returned to the Santa Clara River through an office park lot that had a gap in the fence. A great horned owl sat on bent scrub on the levee's slope, bobbing in the breeze, its pale feet visible in the dusk. Mid-river, I pitched my tent on a flat sandy spot surrounded by arundo. I'd gotten into the habit of hiding my valuables in the interior of a nearby bush, just in case. In the middle of the night, I awoke to hard, fast footsteps not far from my tent and sat upright in my sleeping bag liner, heart racing. The steps retreated—whoever it was had just walked past quickly. Only the sounds of birds and Highway 101. The wind had died, so the traffic was louder. I tried adjusting my earplugs.

Bleary-eyed, I wove downriver in the morning through willow and sage. The dry riverbed was flowing with Anna's hummingbirds. I heard them in each ear, from different directions, sometimes three or more at once, and I watched a young male as he sang from several low islands of brush. A first-year bird: the iridescent red on his chin small and asymmetrical, no crown yet, like a young man with a bad beard. He was defending no flowers so far as I could tell, but this was his territory. Vociferously, he flew from perch to perch, as if testing them. When he landed, his wings remained a blur for a moment, as if he were trying to find his balance. Once he wiped his bill, both sides, on the stem he clasped. Anna's don't migrate. I wondered if a hummingbird born in this wash might never leave.

Nearing the highway, several times I hit a dead end of arundo or willow and had to backtrack because it was too choked to punch through, and I recalled Rob, the restoration foreman in Trabuco Canyon, telling me that it grew so thick it sometimes dammed rivers. Sweeping spiderwebs from my face, I slunk through a corridor of green that finally opened up, all at once, to the concrete pillars holding up roaring 101. Underneath was a vast clear expanse like an unused parking garage. Two blue shopping carts were tipped over in the sand. A few minutes later I found myself in a Carl's Jr. for coffee. I had a stove, but no grounds. Red globe fixtures and soft rock from the ceilings. TELL US IF YOUR VISIT WAS A 5 STAR EXPERIENCE, said a sign on the table. It was, Carl, thank you.

As I left, I made lemonade outside on the narrow table of a bike rack. It would have been a bad idea to open my Swiss Army knife inside. The lemons were from under a tree in Santa Paula. I'd gathered five, given one to Ulysses, and carried the others twelve or so miles. I cut two, squeezed them into my lone Nalgene. The seeds emerged, plopped, and sank. The wrung-out lemon halves and their fringes of pulp looked like ragged sunflowers. I tore through those smiling Carl's Jr. stars on the sugar packets and endeavored to shake out every grain. Eight packets. The lemonade was good and my hands smelled fragrant and were cleansed.

STRAWBERRY FIELDS STRETCHED OUT AS I neared the ocean. From afar, they looked like salt flats, pure white, each row covered tightly with plastic from which the plants burgeon through slits, their flowers also white. Only green berries, in this field. I loitered at a fruit stand where a luxury tour bus had let off Chinese passengers to shop. It was a bonanza, a strawberry frenzy, the cash register ringing merrily. I asked where in China they were from, and a lady told me, "Los Angeles." I was chastened. This was just a weekend trip, a getaway to Santa Barbara. They bought flats of the massive scarlet berries for the drive and took photos of each other with iPads. One boy washed two strawberries in the parking lot, dousing them carefully with his water bottle before easing them into his mouth.

I took half of my black bean burger and fries to go from Brophy Bros at the Ventura Village Harbor and walked south on the beach about a mile in search of the McGrath State Park Campground. It was the first time, I realized, that I'd walked south on my trip, and bizarre to have the afternoon sun on my right side. The Portolá party hadn't veered this way, but I thought McGrath was my best bet for an official campsite on a Saturday. I also wanted to see the mouth of the Santa Clara River, see its estuary, a fitting culmination after four days of walking down-valley.

There was no mouth, only a berm of sand that blocked the water from reaching the sea, just as Ulysses had said, only it was a natural feature. Some years the ocean or the river breaks through. Most of this water was from the discharge of the Ventura water reclamation plant. Brown pelicans floated in the pond; willets, sandpipers, and a curlew nestled in the sand. But the main attraction was a large colony of California least terns, a federally endangered bird. All of them faced the sea with their bellies on the toasty beach, black-capped, stripes through their eyes, a forehead white as glare. Lemon dagger bills. When I put my takeout down to wrestle my binoculars from my grimy shorts, they didn't like the look of it and lifted all at once in a jangling formation that quickly dissolved like salt thrown over my shoulder.

MCGRATH STATE PARK WAS A ghost town. There were only a few RVs and tents, a dozen families or so, and I couldn't understand why. I wandered toward Harbor Boulevard looking for the park's front entrance, for a sign with instructions and a deposit box beside it, but then gave up and called out, "Hello?" in front of the host trailer. DEBBIE AND RALPH, said the sign.

"How'd you get in?" said Debbie, as she stepped out of their RV, with orangish hair.

"I walked down the beach," I said. "I came from Ventura Village Harbor."

Debbie explained that the park had been closed for two and a half years due to frequent flooding, which was hard to fathom. I'd seen no water in the river for four days, and a few miles inland it was hot as the dickens. Counterintuitively, the drought was to blame. The drought and us. For years, the river hadn't mustered enough force to cut through the berm at the river's mouth, and as a result the water treatment plant's quiet discharge just spreads sideways. The water—our reclaimed toilet flushes and showers—swallowed the picnic tables, the firepits, the roads. It killed most of the trees. Debbie and Ralph, who wintered in Arizona and, for tax reasons, were residents of North Dakota via a mail service, were posted here to keep out the homeless.

But occasionally people were allowed to stay at McGrath if it was dry enough, overflow of another sort. This weekend a church group with a bungled reservation at another campground had been redirected here. They also didn't turn away "hike-bikers" like me, though a cyclist would have to lift his bike over a locked gate to inquire. Debbie told me to have a look around, to choose whatever site I wished, and I chose the spot next to them in the pocket-lee of a purple-flowering bush. The bushtits swarmed it in a rush of gray like a spray of sand. The shower was free—not the norm for a State Park. So was the campsite for that matter. Good omens. It felt wonderful to be back on the coast and settled earlier in the day than normal, in a sanctioned spot. Why always scramble for a campsite at the last minute? I had been doing far too much of that.

I roamed the listless grounds and sat to write on a picnic table floating amid pickleweed and other frittered grasses and forbs. The floods had brought this wash of weeds, but neglect and maybe a drought of coffers had let it stay: a park can be closed without being abandoned. On the whole the campground had a post-apocalyptic feel; it was a California far into the future, once the water had finally run out. Then tents and RVs, running on who knows what, might truly be a way of life. The tenantless concrete loops were shaped like gears, the orderly pullouts the teeth around each wheel. Grass had taken to the cracks like sparks up a copper fuse. The cottontails were wary, as if they rarely saw a person or even each other. But there was the scent of s'mores on the sea breeze. The church group was huddled around those rusted-out firepits, which now looked particularly fitting. And the sun—the sun was a burning marshmallow.

CRESPÍ AND PORTOLÁ LEFT THE vicinity of Saticoy on August 14 and "saw the sea far off, where there is a sort of a very large embayment in the land, closed off, in the direction toward where we were keeping on, by a sort of half moon, or C." This must describe today's Pierpont Bay in front of the pleasantly grungy and countercultural City of Ventura. The expedition was advised by Saticoy's natives to travel the dry creek bed. It was their highway to the sea. They found a large village of at least four hundred Chumash near the shore. Crespí counted "thirty well-built, large round grass-roofed houses," "round like half oranges," each of which by their estimate could house sixty people. Inside they found women processing seeds and weaving baskets "of rushes, with such patterns and pictures, as to strike one with wonder," and Costansó tells that they bartered for some of these, as well as for wooden bowls made so well, without iron or steel, that "not even those turned out in a lathe could be more successful." Likely these bowls were made of sycamore burls, carved while still green, finished with red ocher and squirrel fat; the Ventureño Chumash word for sycamore, *qsho'*, was also the word for "bowl." On the roofs of the houses were smoked fish curing in the sun. The chief was out fishing in one of three *tomols* in the bay, so instead they were welcomed by his wife. When the chief landed, he visited the Spaniards' camp beside the Ventura River to offer them not only "gruel," but also "bonitos"—a type of tuna—"and very large needlefish, all just freshly caught." Crespí estimated the bounty would feed the expedition for three meals and ultimately declared, "They are very good folk." All along this coast, the Chumash provided the expedition with ample fresh fish, and Costansó would later bemoan that they had no salt to cure it and carry it with them.

Thirteen years later, Mission San Buenaventura was established here, named for Saint Bonaventure, not just a theologian but a true philosopher, one of the "Doctors of the Church," the Seraphic, who lived in the thirteenth century (the City of Ventura has lost its *Buena* for the sake of convenience). Among his many arguments, he believed that all the world's creatures were footprints of God, shadows and vestiges created in an originary moment. San Buenaventura was the ninth mission founded, the last during Serra's tenure, the final of six he personally dedicated. Its cross was raised on Easter morning, 1782, at *la playa de la canal de Santa Barbara*, not far from the estuary of the Ventura River, which is much smaller than the Santa Clara River, flowing only sixteen miles from its headwaters. The mission harnessed this water, building a seven-mile aqueduct that drew directly from several tributaries in the mountains. A settling tank of bricks still stands behind the church, and traces of the aqueduct, which was still in use until the 1860s, are found behind homes off Ventura Avenue. It made the mission bloom. Just a year after it was founded, the British Captain George Vancouver described San Buenaventura as amazingly fecund. Even bananas were grown, a delicacy that was trade bait for mariners.

At Mission San Buenaventura, the wind chimes in the courtyard's pine mixed with the rumblings of motorcycles cruising Main Street, which is lined with bric-a-brac and thrift shops. The upper classrooms of the Holy Cross School, built on a mission cemetery and so on the bones of the Ventureño, overlooked the courtyard, and beyond those high windows, eucalyptus crowned the hill. At the courtyard's center, a fountain fell on floral tiles, blue, white, and gold. The Virgin statue spread her arms to store-bought flowers, red lilies, white roses. People had rubbed smooth the toes and sandal straps on Junípero Serra, bringing out a reddish patina, and I thought of my own broken-in feet. Could I have managed this walk wearing sandals? Though the padres usually rode. And the California indigenes wore even slighter sandals or went barefoot. What you're used to is what is comfortable. At the courtyard's edge was a wooden olive press, a wheel rimmed with a metal band that turned to crush the oval fruit. OLIVE PRESS, said the sign. ONLY ONE LIFE TWILL SOON BE PAST. ONLY WHAT'S DONE FOR CHRIST WILL LAST. I will admit, the wheel's heft was more pronounced next to such language.

The church is the only part of the original mission that remains. More or less original. The first church was destroyed by a fire in 1793. This one was finished in 1809, and reconstructed with buttresses in 1816 after an earthquake. Now the whole north wall seems to be leaning ever so slightly toward San Francisco. The hand-hewn ceiling beams were dragged to the mission by oxen from the San Cayetano Mountain area. On the walls, as usual, are the Stations of the Cross, as well as a portrait of pursed-lip Junípero Serra. A Sacred Heart burns on the wall like these hillsides once did and will soon again. During my visit, Gregorian chant played softly. I sat on the first pew awhile, taking in the altar and the array of votives below a bleeding Christ. I used my binoculars to study the gold tabernacle. A small sheep was painted on it.

On the jamb of the side door was a holy water font, a clear Pyrex bowl, just like the kind you'd use for mixing dough at home. Held by a bronze mount, it cradled a film of water, hardly visible. A mother and her two children stepped into the church. Her son asked, "What is that for?" She said nothing, just dipped her finger and touched his smooth forehead and each side of his chest. He wore a Dodgers cap and a gaming T-shirt that read, I LOST MY HOMEWORK IN A CAVE SOME-WHERE, above a pixelated man wielding a pickax. She did the same for her younger daughter, who had a pink-and-white ribbon in her hair and a T-shirt that proposed, TIRED OF BEING A PRINCESS? LET'S BE UNICORNS.

BEFORE I LEFT MISSION SAN BUENAVENTURA, I stopped to study two large bells in one of the museum's display cases. They were made of wood—some of the only full-size wooden bells in the world. Riddled with insect holes, cracked from top to bottom, they were cinched tight with leather or rawhide that ran between carved grooves. One of these old straps had unraveled as if to let the cup breathe. These bells never had clappers. Instead they had two opposite metal plates on their inner walls. Someone would climb the belfry and rattle a stick or club between the plates to make the bells "ring." Quieter than cast-iron bells, they may have been fashioned of wood to avoid attracting pirates in the Santa Barbara Channel.

Bells are a complicated mission icon. They are celebrated as a sign of divinity and of the celestial—the music that calls to worship each morning, or every Sunday. But they also were rung to remind the neophytes of their obligations. They were the sound that woke them, told them when to arrive at the church, told them when to go to the fields, told them when they could come home, told them when curfew had begun and they had to remain in dormitories, huts, or houses. They were the sound of conscription and, in fact, of slavery. These mission bells, beautiful as they were, seemed strangled in their sinuous bands, complicatedly bound.

IN THE EVENING, I FOUND myself at the Ventura County Fair, "A Country Fair with Ocean Air," having caught the scent in town. I had heard the fireworks from my campsite in the Santa Clara River, near Oxnard, and now here I was. It was the last day of twelve. People were walking that direction, and I followed them from my motel and bought an "Admit One" red carnival ticket. Inside there was roasted sweet corn with butter, cheese, and paprika, and deep-fried watermelon. Belgian waffles on a stick and funnel cake with powdered sugar, a weakness of mine. "Do you take Visa cards?" asked a twelve-year-old boy at a game booth. "No, we only take tickets," replied the carny, incredulous because all of the games only took tickets. Was this his first rodeo? I also overheard a man say, "What the fuck's a fern?" walking past some potted greenery. His girlfriend replied, "It's a little tree."

PLEASE NOTE: GRANDSTAND SEATING IS FIRST COME, FIRST SERVED, SO I made my way past the rides and food booths toward the eruptions of cheers. The aluminum bleachers already were full, but after a few minutes I was allowed in. I tried to sit high up on an aisle stairway, but was shooed off by security. Sweetly a woman had her family scoot over on their bench to make room for me. Families, most of them Hispanic, filled the stands, wearing skate shorts and zoris or their western finery: jeans and silk shirts, silver buckles and Stetsons with upcurled brims of suede or tight-knit straw, stiff as the day they were conceived. People had come from the interior to see the rodeo with their sweethearts and their six-year-olds. There were corrals of strollers at the base of the grandstand. I counted at least thirty. "A calf got fecal on my calf," quipped the rodeo clown. "Does anyone have a baby wipe?"

Men say, but moreover do, such stupid things. They wrestle steers and tackle calves, and they try and usually fail to ride broncos and bulls bareback. When they get up out of the dirt, best case they walk away with a serious hitch in their already bowlegged step. One bull got a horn on the leather-vest back of a rider, and he left grabbing his vertebrae. Another cowboy held his wrist as if it were broken. *"¡Un aplauso!"* urged the Spanish announcer. "Pay the man!" implored the other MC. "Don't let him walk away with nothing." Many people just stomped their heels on the bleachers. The arena rumbled and rang. "The more noise you make, the bigger that loop gets!" said the announcer, as a vaquero wheeled his lariat around his horse. Here were modern-day cowhands, on tour and in the stands, in their finest, in chaparajos and *chalecos de cuero.*

The moon had risen above the grandstand's lone skybox, dust on the horizon as if from under the hooves of this arena. The hills beyond Ventura tapered lumpish to the south, above a row of white trailers and pickups. A crane cut into the paling blue with an American flag at its tip, and as the light faded, the crane itself and all the other rides began to blink and glow neon. Thin marine clouds floated across Ventura, and to the north, fog gathered, a premonition of the cold Crespí would complain of in Northern California. The cowboys started breaking down the gates and rails of the arena the moment the show was over. The bleating calves were loaded into a big trailer. The collective scream from rides like Kamikaze and Super Spectacular Evolution came in waves. A train whistle. Later in the night, as the crowd thinned, teenagers gathered in circles on the napkin-strewn grounds, leaning on each other and flirting, their faces and hair flashing dimly with the whirling bulbs, most of them looking like they'd sprung from the loins of surfers.

And before then, but after the rodeo had finished, motorcyclists gunned their dirt bikes off a ramp and did flips in the air, throwing their legs off to one side and even letting go of the handlebars entirely—floating with the bike, like an insane pair of satellites—before grabbing hold again. Was this the end result of Portolá's ride through this brush-filled land?

THE ORTEGA CHILE COMPANY WAS started on the road out of Ventura. The next day I stopped to see the original adobe. An El Camino Real bell stood out front, guiding me north. José Francisco Ortega was not only the chief scout for Portolá, but afterward the first commandant at the Santa Barbara Presidio. Ortega accompanied Junípero Serra on the trip to found Mission San Buenaventura, and later he earned a rancho, *Nuestra Señora del Refugio*, to the west at Gaviota, where I was headed. His grandson built this unassuming adobe in Ventura, and it was his great-grandson, Emilio Carlos Ortega, born in 1857, who ushered the cultivation of gentle Anaheim peppers from New Mexico to California, where he perfected their roasting and canning in his mother's *cocina*, the kitchen of this little adobe. His Pioneer Green Chili Packing Company became the state's first commercial food enterprise and it moved from a wooden packing shed here, where a dozen employees produced about a thousand cans each day, to Los Angeles in 1900.

The adobe's foundation is Ventura River cobble, and its roof is held up by salvaged redwood beams from another adobe on Rancho Sespe. *Arundo donax*, my loyal accompaniment, was laid across these beams in a mat, bound with rawhide, covered with grass, and slathered with local tar. So arundo did have its uses after all, even in 1859. Later, clay tiles for the roof were acquired from the mission after it was damaged by a quake. The lot itself was former mission property, of course, which Ventureño Chumash had been granted after secularization and then sold to Ortega. Holes in the thick and cracked plaster had been left un-patched to show the honey-combed beams and adobe brick with grass or hay poking from it. Since the adobe's grounds were a public parklet open dawn until dusk, the structure's doorways were crossed with bars, which made you feel as if you were looking into a jail cell rather than a home. Initials carved into some of the bricks had been worn to faint traces. Aroma of urine on the back walls. The dried ribcage of a Cornish hen, ants streaming from it. A bloodied maxi pad in a niche in the adobe like a holy relic. Before I left, the *cocina* door slammed shut in the breeze, startling me. I propped it open.

CRESPÍ NOTED THE VENTURA RIVER was full of bramble and rose bush, and at high tide, became a large inlet. Crossing on an overpass, above its dry wash and the footpaths of the homeless, I was too far inland to see it run into the sea. Their crossing was difficult. "The water came up over my stirrups and I got my feet wet," wrote Crespí. I strolled under Highway 101 just before Emma Wood State Beach and emerged on the north side of Surfers Point. Far to the south was a power plant near McGrath State Park, my ghost camp of several days ago. Windsurfers in the foreground were in imitation of the pelicans that hung in the air for a split second to line things up and decide if they should go through with it, before plunging like heavy spears.

State Beach Access Road was lined with RVs, all daytime recreationists. They leveled their rigs, pulled out their awnings, unfolded semicircles of chairs. One man, Ken, peered from his doorway with bad teeth, a white shock, and a faded fleece vest with Olympic rings on the breast. He asked if I wanted a snack, some cashews, but I politely declined. The inside of his motor home looked a bit like a hoarder's nest. Three pictures of Jesus were taped above his kitchenette. He lived in his RV, parking it at night in Ventura's industrial section, and spent his days at different beaches. I asked if he was going to go swimming. "I'm eighty-one," he said, "I don't need to go swimming. But I surfed this whole coast in the fifties."

A Channel Island, just the peak, was visible—the first I'd noticed. So were periodic call boxes and their west-facing solar panels, and the Mission Trail bells below the zipper of the guardrail, its traveling car roofs. The Santa Barbara coastline trends east-west, as Crespí observed, and I headed toward the lowering sun to reach Pitas Point, where the expedition had camped. Crespí wrote of a "coast as calm and clear as though it were a pool of oil or a lake," but it was windier for me. When I reached the point, Faria Beach Park was full up, but I asked around sheepishly and found a young woman willing to let me pitch my tent behind her Mercedes. She was a Chinese student studying at the Rhode Island School of Design, and she had borrowed a friend's car while visiting Los Angeles to steal away for a night. She'd bought a cheap tent, pad, and sleeping bag at Walmart. Mainly she sat in the driver's seat, out of the elements, and stared west into the oncoming churn and fog with her earbuds in. Nowhere much to go, especially because everyone had already walked the beach most of the day. The stairway down the riprap was blocked by the dusk tide, the waves climbing the stairs in white leaps.

Crespí and company had been warned there was no water here for their horses and mules, but they carried enough for themselves. A small village welcomed them and, into the night, from a distance, the Spaniards heard wooden flutes, which Crespí noted these Chumash carried around their necks. Played with the first two fingers of each hand, they were made from pithless elderberry until the missionaries introduced arundo—yet another use for the giant cane. The music kept the expedition up and worried Captain Rivera, Crespí reports. He doesn't add why, but Rivera, as the former captain of the presidio in Baja, was savvy in ways that none of the other Spaniards were. Having heard stories of Native attacks from the southwest earlier in the century, he clearly thought the fluting might signal ominous preparation. "Plainly it was all done in order to entertain us," Crespí concludes. Costansó found it "very disagreeable." The point was given the name of *los pitos* or "the whistles." The name slipped sideways to *pitas*, Spanish for agave, which is likely also found on the patchwork chaparral hillsides here, its spines whistling with the wind, faintly.

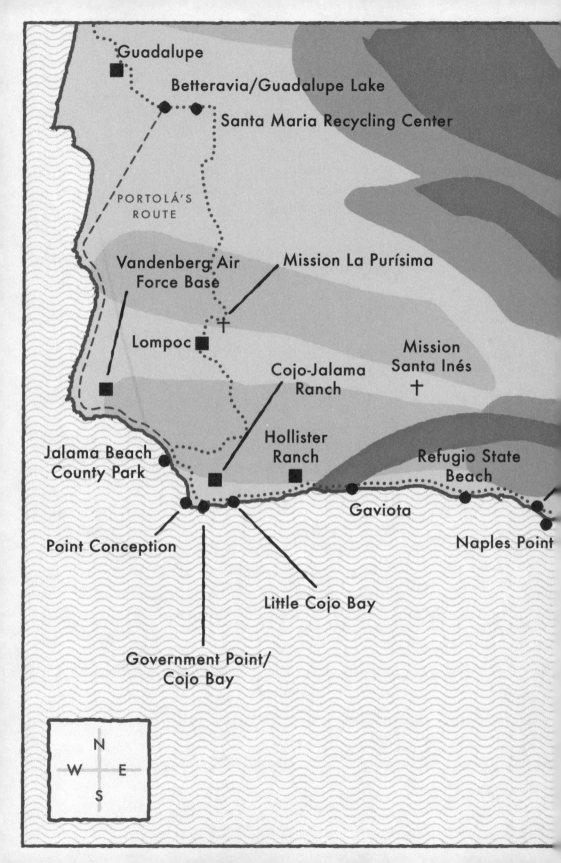

Guadalupe

Betteravia/Guadalupe Lake

Santa Maria Recycling Center

PORTOLÁ'S
ROUTE

Vandenberg Air
Force Base

Mission La Purísima

Lompoc

Mission
Santa Inés

Cojo-Jalama
Ranch

Hollister
Ranch

Jalama Beach
County Park

Refugio State
Beach

Gaviota

Point Conception

Naples Point

Little Cojo Bay

Government Point/
Cojo Bay

N
W   E
S

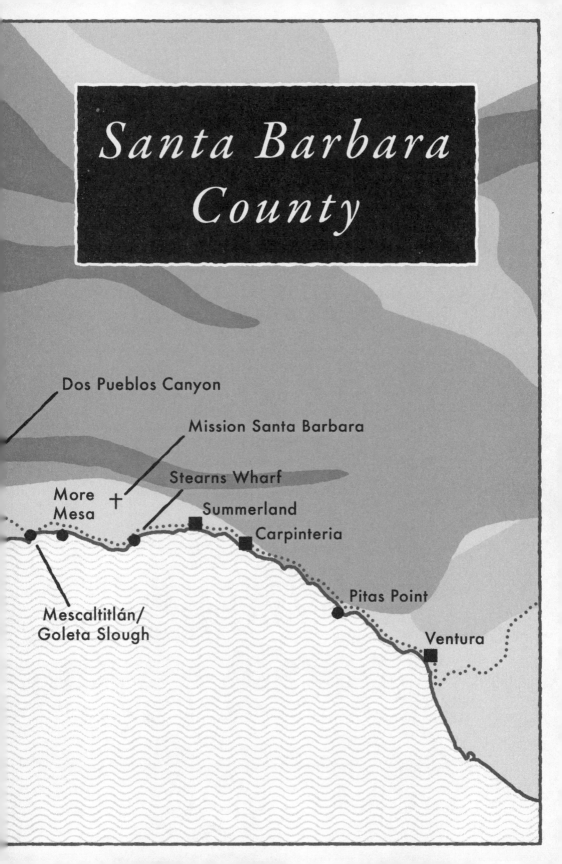

Santa Barbara County

Dos Pueblos Canyon

Mission Santa Barbara

Stearns Wharf

More
Mesa

Summerland

Carpinteria

Mescaltitlán/
Goleta Slough

Pitas Point

Ventura

NEARING MUSSEL SHOALS AND RINCON ISLAND—an artificial island built just a half mile offshore in 1958 for an oil platform—I came across self-proclaimed "Crazy Mike" above the wrack line. Lean and muscular, he had a narrow, handsome face and silvering hair that feathered back from a part, and he was shirtless, his collarbone prominent. A ring tattoo looked like a tourniquet around his bicep, a captain's band. For weeks, he had been building a miniature railroad of dried arundo scavenged from a weathered play shelter just down the beach, someone else's creation. Mike called the cane "bamboo," but it was arundo, all right, I knew it by heart now. It grew green in a stand along the riprap—hardy enough to weather the occasional flood of salt water. He scored the cane with pliers and it snapped cleanly. His creation made a figure eight in the sand, an infinity sign. The track was about twenty feet long by a foot wide. "I come out here every once in a while," said Mike in something like a drawl, "so I figured I'd make a little beach art. Come here with my girlfriend, with other friends, and we put the E-Z up over it."

He was alone today, no shade tent, but there was an orange bottle of 35 SPF sunscreen upright in the sand. Seven or eight days, he'd been working on this rail. Soon he would finish the figure eight by completing the bridge over the lower rail. Then he would put crosspieces down the whole thing, approximating a roadbed.

Mike had worked in the railroad for his career, as had his father, for Union Pacific. Building bridges all over, fastening. "Tehachapi, Minnesota ... you name it." He'd also run trains, mostly freight. "I've worked hard all my life," he said, and his outsized hands, his nails that looked like they'd been flattened like pennies on a rail, proved it. Blacksmith forearms. Now he was taking some time to play. But his play, like the figure eight he'd inscribed in the sand, was railroads. Clearly he loved locomotives with his whole life force. He told me that, in the loft of his house, he had a model train set; he stained the strip wood, laid the tiny ties, affixed it all with daubs of glue. Thousands of pieces. A loft was less dusty than a garage. That was key. "That's the most important thing," he said. "Clean wheels, and clean track."

The modern history of California is of course closely tied to the advance of its railroads, which began when four Sacramento merchants—Charles Crocker, Mark Hopkins, Collis Huntington, and Leland Stanford, some of the biggest names in California even today—bought into the dream of a transcontinental line and formed the Central Pacific Railroad. It took more than six years for them to meet the Union Pacific's line in Promontory, Utah, where the Golden Spike was driven in 1869, just a century after the Portolá expedition. Eventually the company merged with and became the Southern Pacific, which built or secured all of the forty-seven hundred miles of standard gauge in California and thus held the state in a vise. Governor Leland Stanford helped secure federal land grants so extensive that they amounted to more than 11 percent of the state, as well as federal bonds to the tune of $59 million, which they only paid back forty years later. They poured this money into their own construction companies to do the grading and riveting, and then they sold land along the lines to foster business. They acquired subsidiary transportations like ferries and steamboats, cutting everyone else out, and were notorious for raising and lowering freight costs capriciously. As the lemon industry took off, for example, Central Pacific suddenly charged more to carry the fruit; when growers felt this squeeze and began to plant other trees, the railroad dialed back; and when a tariff on foreign lemons was then imposed, they raised the rate all over again, in each case charging as much as they could get away with. Yet for all its avariciousness, the railroad created a sustained agricultural and development boom in California. Wherever the line went, so did money and population and workers like Mike.

Bridge-building and railroad work in general have changed, Mike told me on the beach. "They're all more concrete and steel now, viaducts," said Mike. "Now it's all automated. A machine comes along and shakes the track, and then puts it down again. It's all done by computer now, everything." This sand track was quite the opposite. The arundo pieces were set by hand, all of it perfectly balanced. Only a few joints had been tied with strips of bark or grass, though he was thinking of bringing some wire so that it would last, barring teenagers, until winter. We were above the high-tide line, but storms would surge to the rocks. His circuit was like a sand painting, in this way—the hand of the ocean and the breath of the wind would sweep it off. But the arundo was pretty strong; it had been used in the roofs of early adobes, after all. Mike had built his track with the same Xs and triangle shapes he'd created in real life with the help of cranes and pile drivers. He demonstrated the railroad's worth by gripping two crosspieces and doing a push-up without a quiver. "I was wanting to make something that was strong enough to stand on, but I don't think it's going to happen," he said. "I'm sure I could, though . . ." When I walked up the beach to leave, he walked with me to harvest more arundo from the sagging tepee-like shelter, carrying four or five good poles back with him. How one thing becomes another.

BELOW RINCON PARK, A WOMAN, Norma, walking with her friend on the beach, said I couldn't make it along the bluffs just then during high tide. So I turned about and walked with them for a moment, scaling the bluff path again. Norma told me she'd recently walked from the Mission San Buenaventura to Mission Santa Barbara, the current leg of my pilgrimage—I was impressed and glad. I could take the "old tracks" to Santa Barbara, she said, if I wanted. Some of the spikes had popped up from the rails like budding mushrooms: we needed Mike to pound those back in. The rails were well-rusted, but silver and slick down their middle—these tracks may have been old, but they were still in service. Nineteen sixty-six was stamped on them, fifty years ago. One-fifth of the way to Portolá. He and Crespí would have killed for a path as straight and level as this, I thought. It was peaceful. No people, no trucks, no surf. Or would the horses and mules have hated the ballast, the loose rock under the ties? It's true, I walked alongside the railbed in the dirt for better footing.

Seven oil platforms on the horizon—at least seven—perfectly spaced. Two trawlers, the *Matthew* and the *Frances B*, anchored near in. Pelicans soared at eye level, at least two hundred feet off the beach, above waxy manzanita and coyote brush. Towhees chipping. A whistle sounded behind me, and I looked behind to a notch in the hills where the highway was visible, its streaming cars, and farther back to Rincon Island and its causeway. Nothing, so I kept walking. A few minutes later, the scintillating sound of the tracks—that electric popping—as the northbound commuter train rushed by with its dull nose barreling into the sun. SURFLINER, SURFLINER, SURFLINER, SURFLINER, it said as it passed, and I heard it whistling again into Carpinteria, ahead of me. I'd spend the night there beside the dunes at a campsite I'd reserved, too tired and late to much enjoy it.

As the train and I approached town, a row of eucalyptus rose along a fence and scattered its buttons, each acorn etched with a tiny cross. In Carpinteria you can cross the tracks to tar-blobbed beaches, portions of which are closed as harbor seal sanctuaries. Women jog the bluff trails past snags that seem to mimic a running motion. A dog bag dispenser is dedicated to J.P., a lab: HE LOVED THE BLUFFS, JULY 14, 1992–MARCH 17, 2007. Fourteen years, a good run. I watched a red-hulled boat that serviced the oil rigs as it churned in reverse to stay backed against its dock, below a crane flying an American flag. Then it throttled forward and charged out for the rigs with a billowing wake. The moon was almost full as it sifted in and out of southern clouds. The oil platforms' first lights came on: three amber, three fluorescent green, as if port and starboard on a boat without a hull traveling with the tectonic plates. Men live on these platforms. They float above a seeping hole in the ocean floor.

"Further along after the tar pit sign, I stop to watch the train"—the southbound Surfliner, this time—"as it rounds the bend. Glows . . . glows gold with the light that's coming due east, I guess. I thought I had been walking north, almost, just by instinct. As it curves around the bend, it catches the light. There's a man standing with his arm around his wife, an older man. And there's a young woman wrapped in a towel, her hair wet, her bikini-bottom slightly clenched from the cold, shivering, goosebumps. We all watch the train as it goes by."

"WE SAW AT THE VERY edge of the sea a large village or very regular town here at this point, appearing from a distance as though it were a shipyard, because at the moment they were building a canoe that still had its last topmost plank lacking from it (and this spot was dubbed by the soldiers *La Carpinteria*)." So California's seaside carpenter's shop came to be. Crespí had already noted numerous *canoas* as they passed other villages along the Santa Barbara Channel. "The biggest canoes they have are about some seven or eight yards long," he wrote on August 14. "Two or three heathens get into them with their nets and very large fish traps made of rushes . . . and whenever they wish they can go a great way with a single stroke. . . . So light are these canoes that two men can put them into the water and out of it." Called a *tomol* by the Chumash, these canoes were used for journeys miles across the ocean to the Channel Islands. The Portolá party discerned that a number of these canoes had been sent to the islands "so that the people from there could come to see us." The Spaniards were a sight to behold, a spectacle worth traveling for. *Tomols* were equally used just offshore for fishing. Crespí wrote, "The entire village came over with a great many bowls of gruel, and brought us an amount of fish vastly greater than any of the preceding ones [villages], of both fresh and barbecued bonito, so that no one cared for fish anymore and it got thrown away." Consensus was that Carpinteria, which Crespí labeled *San Roque*, would be wonderful grounds for a mission, for cultivation. "We may say the same in a mystical sense," Costansó added, "as the gentleness of this people gave us great hopes that the word of God will fructify equally in their hearts."

In Carpinteria, a fiberglass *tomol* can be found at a park near the end of Linden Avenue. When I arrived, a kingbird was making its rattling call from a sapling sycamore and a man was sitting on one of the canoe's three benches while his daughter tested the slide. It was a halting descent. "That's not a very comfortable slide, huh?" he said. The *tomol* was embedded in a blue rubberized playground surface much like an all-weather track. It put a bounce in my step as I walked across it, this fake water. Two fiberglass dolphins were breaching from the rubber, reminding me of those I'd seen barreling in the surf at Faria Beach Park. There were fiberglass seals, too, hauled out on a "rock," and their big tar-black eyes were baking, scorching, when I touched them. The park had fiberglass grass shelters, one of them half-finished. There were real cattails planted along the edge, as if this inlet bordered the Carpinteria wetlands I'd later walk, the marsh wrens a-chitter in the mud channels. Here was the last Chumash village in Carpinteria, a reminder of *Mishopshno*, the village the Spaniards had encountered.

When the father disembarked, I took my turn in the *tomol* and sat awhile on this shore's edge, just where its bouncy surface waved from blue to blue-green, to blue-green sprinkled with beige, to beige sprinkled with blue—all bits of recycled sneaker or tire or plastic bottle. Hard to say if the water was coming forward or receding, or if the *tomol* was being launched or landed. That was left to imagination. Actual *tomols* didn't have built-in seats, but I appreciated this one, hot as it was. Fake stitches joined the fake planks. Really, milkweed or some other fiber would have been used to lash hand-hewn planks of driftwood cedar or pine about an inch in thickness, joined in an imbricated pattern to form the hull. The Chumash also used redwood washed down from Northern California. Apparently it could take as long as six months to finish a single *tomol*. They were ultimately painted, often with red ocher.

Perhaps the most authentic *tomol* model, built by a native for the Panama-California Exposition in San Diego in 1915, measured twenty-three feet long and weighed 325 pounds, its prow and stern upturned like wings. It had protruding strakes—like the slightest of ventral fins—at center on both sides, likely just for handholds. It was sanded with sharkskin. The seams of *tomols* were caulked with tar and the entire craft was sealed with pine pitch. Asphaltum is available right on the shore in Carpinteria. The tar pits are second in significance only to La Brea, and near my campsite, below a cinder-block lifeguard tower on the beach, I'd found a mass of hardened tar that looked like lava, like Hawaiian pahoehoe. There were fresh glistening seeps, Pollockian spatters. Sandstone boulders were written in dripping black with the words and names of lovers. The tar had preserved the sandstone underneath, thus creating a relief as the stone wore away: BJ. KDG. CASH. SALT. Crespí noted the tar seeps, writing, "We saw, before reaching here, at a small ravine about a dozen paces from the sea, springs of pitch that had become solidified, half smoking."

I had thought I might find kids at play here in the park: they would be brandishing invisible double-sided paddles, calling each other "chief," saying "Land Ho!" quoting *Island of the Blue Dolphins*. Instead it was quiet. Only the kingbird, laughing acorn woodpeckers in the distance, and the whir of the cooling fan of the Island Brewery across the tracks. Sunflower seeds flecked the blue rubber where some dad had spat them as he watched his kid paddle the air. Finally, two boys arrived. "There's nobody here," one said to another. "Except for that guy."

I WALKED THE CARPINTERIA MARSHES and then Padaro Beach, with the sun pouring hot through the glass of the tony beach houses. The ocean left bubbles on the sand like you might blow in your chocolate milk. They jiggle-wavered in the breeze before bursting and leaving a ring of spittle. *Poof.* A one-legged man crutched past me in the opposite direction, in a steady rhythm, wearing camo shorts and a golfer's hat. A veteran, I thought. For a while I tracked his postholes in the sand: six feet between his swings. The print of his five-toed shoe. I noticed the little Vs where the water had retreated and scoured the sand around a pebble, so that each pebble looked like a grounded comet. The Santa Ynez Mountains and their high boulder fields were on my right, the Carpinteria oil platforms far out to sea on my left. When the beach dead-ended at a point, I asked a woman with a child if there was any chance she'd let me cut through her yard to the road. "I'd rather not," she said, "I'm sorry." I understood; I didn't even stew about it.

I backtracked a half mile and tiptoed along the cemented riprap of Arroyo Paredon Creek where it meets the ocean, and went out a home's garden gate rather than contorting myself around the overhanging barbwire along the creek that was meant to deter people precisely like me. The Spaniards on this stretch beyond Carpinteria encountered several villages burned to the ground, made "ruins and ashes" perhaps several months before. The Chumash guiding them explained that people from the interior, "mountain heathens" Crespí called them, had raided and destroyed these shoreline villages and killed most of their people. Ever observant or opportunistic, Crespí noted that both ruins were beside good running water, and I wondered if Arroyo Paredon Creek, which I had used to escape the beach, might be one of those sources.

At the lot for Loon Point Beach, there was a sign: HORSES PROHIBITED ON BEACH 10 AM TO 5 PM, MAY 1 TO NOVEMBER 1. But at 6:53 p.m., a group of horses ventured down in front of me. They raised the dust, the U shapes of their shoes pocking the path and the wet sand, where they were erased by incoming waves. Their tails swishing circles, the same hue as the shining kelp. Their oval rumps jostling. Trailing them, I imagined that I was trailing the Spaniards. This would have been the vantage point of the soldiers and others who walked behind the clergy and the officers, and the vantage point of the muleteers. Nine riders. Their English-style helmets gleamed as they plodded due west. Sun down each hair of those manes. Through the slosh of easy waves the horsemen walked, just where a protrusion of rock half blocked the beach, but they had to pull the reins about, gently, only a little farther at a bluff. "Was it higher than you expected?" I asked as they passed, swishing and huffing. "Yeah, little bit," said one man. I used my phone to check the tide for the first time on my trip: high tide at 7:43.

When I reached the bluff's base, I scrambled up on a tumble of sandstone boulder and concrete debris. There was rusted corrugated sheet metal, cables, and chunks of brick and mortar, too—relics of the derricks that once peppered this curve of the coast. I had reached Summerland, in this never-ending summer land. Here, in 1896, the first offshore oil production began on the West Coast. By 1899, piers laced this stretch and were dotted with twenty-two oil derricks, with more soon to come. Now that infrastructure and its implements had been thrown up on the shore, the wreckage of industry, and oil production had been pushed far offshore. Looking back south from the train track heights, I saw that the riders had paused in front of the lone eucalyptus before they would turn uphill again. I admired a black-and-white Appaloosa through my binoculars, then I began the long hump to Santa Barbara, which I would reach after hiking through the remaining evening and into the dark, pausing briefly in Montecito; and on a road shoulder where I laid an injured swallow under a tree out of the headlights, its wings still flapping and its heart pumping pumping pumping; and beforehand, at the Summerland Post Office where ice plant was draped down chipped murals that showed the vanished derricks pulling up that black blood from their piers.

DAY OFF. I POURED COMPLIMENTARY batter into the iron on the back deck of my hostel and enjoyed a waffle with artificial syrup in the partial sun. My legs were shot from the long walk the night before, my arches flattened and sore. Late morning, I hailed a ride to Mission Santa Barbara, which rests up the valley about two and a half miles from the ocean—a good distance from which to spy pirates. The "Queen of the Missions," Santa Barbara was founded in 1782 by Junípero Serra, but the governor of Las Californias at the time wouldn't actually give permission for its construction, only for the presidio that's now been excavated and reconstructed downtown, where a papier-mâché horse stands on a bed of straw in one room, a de facto stable.

So Mission Santa Barbara wasn't built until four years later, after Serra's death. It was the first mission overseen by Serra's successor, Father Fermín Francisco de Lasuén. Mission Santa Barbara evolved in stages into an iconic sandstone church, which was finished in 1820 in a Greco-Roman style inspired by the writings of Roman author and architect Vitruvius. It has an ocular window over the entrance and red Ionic columns whose volutes recall curling waves. A second bell tower was added in the 1830s so that the facade would be symmetrical with two red domes.

The mission slowly collected about a third of the Chumash who survived in the Santa Barbara area. At its height in 1803, about 1,800 natives lived in an adjacent pueblo of about 250 homes—one of California's first planned housing developments, you could say, though modest by the current standards of the Mission Viejo, Irvine, and Newhall companies. The neophytes' homes adjoined each other like condos. A drawing of a Chumash house in the mission museum shows a ladder leading to a loft, dried meats and vibrant vegetables hanging in wreaths from the wall, and an outdoor kitchen with a plastered *horno* or domed oven. Indoor kitchens were a recipe for disaster. The pueblo rendering looks like a Mexican village, and that's exactly what it would officially become.

In 1824, Santa Barbara took part in the largest Native revolt that occurred during California's mission days. The Chumash had been reduced to two or three thousand from what might have been twenty thousand before contact. There was, of course, ample distrust between the natives and the Spaniards, especially the soldiers. At this juncture, unrest was fostered in particular by the declining economic conditions of the missions after New Spain became Mexico and secularization occurred. The Franciscans also had less control over the soldiers then, since they were often paid late.

Santa Barbara was one of three Central Coast missions involved in the revolt. It began at Mission Santa Inés, inland of Santa Barbara, when a visiting Chumash man from Mission La Purísima asked a Mexican soldier if he could see his imprisoned relative. The soldier refused, and apparently the native responded, "Is it perhaps that the king deprives relatives from speaking with a prisoner?" It hardly seems an insolent question, but any question at all was. The soldier allegedly responded, "There is no longer any king but the captain," and he had the man flogged. It ignited the revolt, one that, it seems, had already been planned for the very next day. It was an incidental spark just as the fuse was going to be lit anyway. The neophytes burned most of the mission complex at Santa Inés, but were forced to retreat west to Mission La Purísima, where they took control and sent the soldiers and priests packing in the other direction. In Santa Barbara, when the Chumash heard that the element of surprise had been blown and the revolt was on, they raided the arms cache and seized their mission, too. The soldiers from the presidio besieged Mission Santa Barbara, trying to win it back, but were unsuccessful. The Chumash then retreated into the hills and finally into the lower San Joaquin Valley, "tule country," once covered with marsh.

Father Lasuén and Santa Barbara's padre, Father Ripoll, journeyed the sixty miles to the inland Chumash camp and after three days persuaded them to return with the promise of amnesty. Or perhaps the Chumash were convinced by the lieutenant of infantry who supposedly said, "For almost three days I have been exposed to the weather night and day. If they do not decide to surrender before tomorrow at dawn, I am going to lead the charge." All in all, about twenty Chumash died during the rebellion. Seven were executed afterward. One Spanish soldier was killed.

In the mission museum are several rusted and pocked cannonballs that the presidio's forces fired at the mission during the revolt. They were extracted from the facade during a renovation in the 1950s. There is the weathered statue of Saint Barbara—missing her arms and buffed of most detail by the elements—which fell fifty or so feet during a 1925 earthquake and is now pieced together and resting on her side, in a corner. There is a *ladrillo*, or tile, on which an anonymous Chumash soul stippled a hieroglyph: a figure with arms of three fingers and legs of four toes, lizard-like, on the otherwise smooth brush marks of the clay. There are the whale-bone markers that the Chumash often used as headstones, and a whale vertebra stool that is centuries old. There are donut stones, which look exactly as they sound and were used to add weight to digging sticks or fishing nets. And there is a copy of Scott O'Dell's Newbery Medal–winning young adult book, *Island of the Blue Dolphins*.

IN THE WALLED CEMETERY OF the mission, on the stone of the left bell tower, at about chest height, is a plaque that reads JUANA MARIA, INDIAN WOMAN ABAN-DONED ON SAN NICOLAS ISLAND EIGHTEEN YEARS, FOUND AND BROUGHT TO SANTA BARBARA BY CAPT. GEORGE NIDEVER IN 1853. It was her life that was the basis for O'Dell's book, which all California kids read and romanticize, and which sticks with me still.

As the story goes, in 1835, when the people of San Nicolas were being forcibly removed by the Mexican government to the mainland—to the port of San

Pedro, near today's Long Beach—a young woman leapt from the ship and swam back to the island in search of her child, who had escaped or been overlooked in the roundup. She then lost her child to the island's wild dogs. But this dramatic story was first told in the 1880s. More likely the woman who became known as Juana Maria was accidentally left behind and the ship simply did not turn back amid the difficult surf.

San Nicolas is the remotest of the Channel Islands, sixty-one miles from the continent. It's far south of the four islands visible from Santa Barbara, and to the west of Catalina Island. George Nidever was a fur trapper, explorer, mountain man, sailor, gold miner, rancher, and otter hunter. He and his men had been camped on San Nicolas six weeks, hunting sea mammals, when on their last night they discovered footprints on the far part of the island, where they had never been before. They spent an extra day searching for this lone drifter. "Charley and I struck up toward the head of the island," Nidever recalled. "Reaching the place where he had seen the footprints the day before, he followed up the ridge. Near its top he found several huts made of whale's ribs and covered with brush. . . . Looking about in all directions from this point, he discovered at a distance, along the ridge, a small black object about the size of a crow which appeared to be in motion. Advancing cautiously toward it he soon discovered it to be the Indian woman, her head and shoulders, only, visible above one of the small enclosures resembling those we had before discovered. He approached as near as he dared and then, raising his hat on his ramrod, signalled [*sic*] to the men who were then recrossing the low, sandy stretch, and were plainly visible from this point." They came up the ridge from the other side and surrounded her, and she made to escape, but then gave up and offered them some wild onion she had been preparing.

Nidever described her as "medium height, but rather thick. . . . She must have been about 50 years old, but she was still strong and active. Her face was pleasing as she was continually smiling. Her teeth were entire but worn to the gums." She might have been continuously smiling because she was overwhelmed with nervousness. She wore a dress adorned with cormorant feathers that nearly reached her knees, a cape of gull skins, a necklace of keyhole limpets threaded with sinew, and sandals. She hid her dried abalone and fish—and perhaps sea lion, too, from a rookery that, from her hut, she would have heard through the night—in fissures in a nearby outcropping so the wild dogs could not reach it. In wintertime, she is thought to have spent time in a cave, one that has since filled with sand and hasn't been fully excavated.

The woman was taken to live with Nidever's parents in Santa Barbara, where it's reported she would lean on the railing of the porch, extend her arms to the Pacific, and speak in a language no one quite knew. She was given the name Juana Maria. Only four of her words were recorded. It's believed that the Nicoleño spoke a Shoshonean language like the Gabrieleño or Fernandeño and were more closely related to them than to the Chumash. Seven weeks after leaving the island, she died, and in that moment she was baptized. She was buried somewhere in the mission cemetery. Some of her belongings were sent as a curiosity to the Vatican, where they were lost if they didn't disappear, one way or another, in the crossing. A few of her things were also sent to the California Academy of Sciences in San Francisco, where they were destroyed by the flames of the 1906 earthquake.

In 1939, a historical sleuth named Art Woodward journeyed to San Nicolas in search of Juana Maria's hut location and Juan Cabrillo's grave, which is believed to be on one of the Channel Islands. With *The Life and Adventures of George Nidever* in his knapsack, Woodward rode to the west end of San Nicolas with the island's caretaker, where he describes shell middens that extended up the sandy ridges. "Abalone by the thousand cluster on the rocky reefs along this section of shoreline," he wrote. "The sand dunes covered with middens are acres in extent. No wonder this well-watered island was a favorite haunt in spite of the drawback of fog and wind."

Based on Nidever's description, they located the remains of the whalebone hut on the ridge's prominence, where there were nineteen large ribs and fan-shaped scapulae lying in a loose circle, along with flat rocks. A year later, Woodward and others returned, made a sketch of the bones as they lay, and then endeavored to reconstruct the hut. The rib bones propped up the wide scapulae, so that there were windows to the ocean under the shoulders of these lost giants. This skeleton would have been covered with brush to better block the wind. Woodward's assistant, an archaeologist named Marion Hollenbach, squatted amid the circle of bones, with just her black hair visible over the top, to reenact the discovery of the woman who, at death, was christened Juana Maria.

The island now belongs to the navy and is used for training and weapons testing. In fact, San Nicolas was closely considered for the first atom bomb test before White Sands ultimately was selected and became the Trinity Site. I wonder if those whale bones are still there, or if they have been pulverized by bombs, or if they were stolen as relics. What it must have been like to live in a shelter of whale bones, bones born of krill and fortified by the depths. It seems unlikely that the Nicoleño could have hunted whales, but they would have been expert at scavenging the strandings that occurred, dead or alive, ultimately dragging the bleached bones upslope for their walls and rafters.

WALKING THROUGH DOWNTOWN SANTA BARBARA is like walking through a hall of vaguely historical mirrors, many of the buildings imitative, Mission style, some built to appear like three-sided rancho haciendas. Nothing but red tile roofs in Santa Barbara. I entered the tsunami hazard zone, and finally made it to the famous Stearns Wharf, which streamed with people. There was a sign for NO BARE FEET. A sign for NO GOLF CARTS, NO HIGH HEELS, NO DIVING, NO SKATE BOARDING—all the fun things are a bad idea on splintery wood. Over the rail, on the sand below the wharf, were sheets with penny-tossing games, an ingenious scheme that was as satisfying and probably as lucrative as any game at the Ventura County Fair.

Tan bodies on towels. Terns over the water. A cross-country team, in the shortest shorts—already loped by. In the sand, a boy was building a presidio. "Are you building a fort?" I asked. "I don't know," he said. He was. There was a moat. The tide would surge. In the surf, a pit bull huffed water from its shaking jowls. Farther out, people were paddleboarding, a slow instrument whose value the Chumash might not have fully understood. "You don't want to have a hard grip, you want to have a soft grip," said a shirtless man teaching his friend to spiral a pigskin. His words felt true about my passage through these landscapes, about life in general.

In Santa Barbara, Crespí wrote, "the roofs were invisible because of all the fish laid out on them." They were tiled with sardine and bonito, such was the bounty of the coast via *tomols*. He estimated a village of seven hundred "souls," all of them lined up weaponless as the expedition passed. When the Spaniards greeted them, the Chumash "answered us with great noise and laughter." Imagine these sixty-three men parading past these seven hundred: the vulnerability, the spectacle, the bravado, the beginning of the end. These Chumash gave fresh-caught barbecued fish to the Portolá party, who made camp by a lake bordered with tule, and in exchange the natives were given beads and ribbons. Chumash had journeyed from the islands to see them, Crespí wrote, and the chiefs were identifiable because they held long flint knives on staffs. The dancers were painted and wearing feathered headdresses. Crespí named the place *La Laguna de San Joaquin*.

"We broke camp rather to get away from the annoyance of the natives than to make a day's march," Costansó admits. Near the vicinity of Santa Barbara's harbor, the expedition left the shore and swerved inland, heading northwest along the mesa that lies west of downtown. Losing track of the journals, however, I instead skirted the boats and their symphony of clanging masts and climbed to the high bluffs on Shoreline Drive, watching the kiteboarders and, far out, one lone kayaker, his blades glinting as if he had just crossed the distance from the islands that seemed illusionary, just mounds of ocean moisture. One two, one two—a brisk pace, as if he was nervous. The trees of Shoreline Park were salt pruned, zagged like bolts of lightning. A fire was suddenly burning beyond the hills northwest of the city, over millions of red tiles: white smoke, then beige or brown higher up, and finally, where the particulate thinned, gray at its petal edges.

After several miles, I descended to Arroyo Burro, which is probably the "deep dry creek" that Crespí describes crossing only a half league from their next camp. Manzanita, coffeeberry, coyote brush, and cattail. A hang glider floated over the cliff of swirling sandstone below which the creek jogged to sea. Two beach balls had blown back into the narrow estuary, and I thought I saw a third, but it was a motorcycle helmet with a clear visor. The suggestion of catastrophe. I also mistook a black-crowned night heron for a trash bag, until, from a slit, it opened its crimson eye.

What I remember most of Arroyo Burro, though, is that as I stood on the sand and took in Santa Cruz Island, lord of the horizon, a young blind man in a ball cap and turquoise shirt walked the beach with a woman. Not sure she was his mother. His cane, with its red tip, was collapsed like a tent pole and bundled in his hand. He walked easily. The sight astonished me, and I closed my eyes. What must it be like to approach the beach and not see? It must be one of the most rewarding sensory encounters all the same: the breeze on your ocular orbits, the audio of waves, of children and birds. You would never know of the hang glider, or the island across the waves. Or perhaps you would somehow sense them, imagine them. There is always an island in the back of the mind, a California. And through your shoes you would feel the sand, feel the depressions other feet had made. The two of them turned toward the parking lot and finally she grabbed his upper forearm to lend support. His pole snapped together as they approached the concrete steps. He found the rail and tapped out each. He wore sunglasses, as we all did, in the wind and vanishing glare.

I SPENT THE NIGHT IN the scruff of More Mesa, a coastal bluff and open space preserve of about three hundred acres, having walked through the mega-rich neighborhoods of Cliff and Marina Drives, where signs remind you that the roads are private and that public passage is revocable at any time. The mesa has been threatened with development many times, and recently was sold to a Saudi developer, raising speculation about its fate. For now it remains a sanctuary for raptors and strollers. The mesa's chaparral was hardly taller than my waist, so I put together my tent from my knees, last light as usual. UC Santa Barbara students were walking the trails, and I felt vulnerable. Even more than a month into my trek I was still paranoid about being discovered and rousted from my camp, though my worry was likely needless.

Afterward I sat on the bluffs and watched the calming surf. The fire burning in the Los Padres National Forest behind me colored the sunset a navel orange. Crespí had said that the grass on this stretch had been burnt by the Chumash in many places but not in others: "the unburnt were so tall that they topped us on horseback by about a yard." Damn, that's tall. He also wrote, "On the plains here are so many rose bushes that in some spots nothing was to be seen but grass and roses." It was difficult to imagine such glorious herbage. It was, most likely, the direct result of frequent burning, of boom and ash, and unadulterated blossom.

Planes descended over the mesa to the Santa Barbara Airport, but the night was lightly trafficked. I awoke only once when a great horned owl screeched from an adjacent bush. Around six fifteen, when I climbed from my tent, the ocean was gray, calm. Low tide. A raft of five rhinoceros auklets, a long-billed curlew. I was so tired I thought I could sink back into the gray for a few hours. But I did so for only a few minutes, sliding down onto my ground tarp and pulling my hat brim low. When I opened my eyes, a common yellowthroat was between my knees twelve feet away, probing a coyote bush. Other yellowthroats were calling. I think of them as marsh birds, reedy warblers, but here they were. *Bandidos* like me, skulking with black masks. The fog still hung overhead. It was as if the world had rolled over and pulled a coarse, warm blanket over its shoulder. I leaned on my pack as my tent fly dried and wrote some of this.

Slightly anise scent of coyote brush. The lulling beyond the bluffs, ocean. Apart from all the people on the trails, this would be the perfect site to camp a few days. Before I left, I scraped sand filled with cottontail pellets over my own feces in the shallow pit I had dug with a coyote brush spade. Anna's in my ear. Anna's always.

IT WAS A RELATIVELY SHORT distance over the mesa, and down a road, and along a bike path, to the Goleta Slough, above which sits UC Santa Barbara, in the city of Goleta. In Portolá's day, the slough was a vast lagoon and a significant Chumash harbor. "We came to a watering place, a populous town where there is a large inlet that, viewed from afar, seems a lake, and has good fresh water," wrote Crespí. "Here we made camp, and it was a two leagues' march." In the middle of the lagoon was an impressive village, *Helo'*, on a tree-filled island that, Crespí adds parenthetically, the expedition's soldiers nicknamed Islado Pueblo or Mescaltitlán, "there being, so they say, at Tepic a town that is similar to this one." Tepic is the capital of the Mexican state of Nayarit. Legend has it that the Aztec civilization began on an island there in the Mescaltitlán Lagoon before, in today's Mexico City, they founded their great city of Tenochtitlán, also on an island. When Hernán Cortés arrived in 1519, Tenochtitlán may have had a population of over two hundred thousand people, larger than all but perhaps a handful of European cities.

The scouts reported seven additional villages around the lagoon, and Crespí observed three of them: more than two thousand people in all, it's estimated. The lagoon was called *sitiptip*, or the place of salt, named for its white crystal flats where snowy plovers must have nested in numbers. It was a Chumash metropolis of a gentle and sustainable size, the most natives Crespí had seen along the Santa Barbara Channel. So many, in fact, that later, when deciding where to site a presidio, the Spanish thought better of choosing Goleta. "The village lying thus islanded is an extremely big one in its heathen population: so far as we could tell from the distance at which we were viewing it, there must be over a hundred very large round, very well roofed houses, and we guess that there cannot be less than eight hundred souls in this village alone." Villagers visited the Spanish and brought "such quantities of these kinds of fish"—bonitos, needlefish, sardines—"that it was needful to tell them not to bring more, as heaps of fish were lying cast away upon the ground."

This place is unrecognizable by any of these descriptions now. The Chumash are long displaced from its edges. Its edges are gone. No salt glitter. Few fish. During the floods of 1861 and 1862, runoff from the overgrazed ranchos—soil stolen from the dead roots of torn-out grasses—filled the lagoon with silt, transforming it to marsh. Then, in 1928, the area's first landing strip was leveled on the slough's north end. The marines took over during World War II and solidified most of the marsh's remainder, bulldozing much of Mescaltitlán as fill and confining its creeks with dikes. When Mescaltitlán was being razed, a burial was uncovered, an important woman perhaps. She was face down in a flexed position on the scapula of a whale, which had been inlaid with abalone and with beads, hundreds of them glinting in a grout of asphaltum. Who knows how many other artifacts were scattered throughout the slough and now lie under tarmac. The highway and a portion of the university were also built over the onetime lagoon.

I pondered this long chain of events while sitting in a viewing area at the end of the Santa Barbara Municipal Airport, SBA, the descendant of the air base, whose terminal is Mission style with a faux bell tower. This ground was the bulldozed remains of Mescaltitlán, I was sure, mashed and pushed into pickleweed. Small prop planes lifted from the tarmac, tilted back and forth as they gained speed toward the Pacific. The "overlook" was surrounded on three sides by chain-link with a barbwire overhang. It also served as a cell-phone waiting lot, as if one was necessary at this Podunk airfield. ATTENTION! DO NOT FEED THE BIRDS AS THEY POSE A SEVERE HAZARD TO AIRCRAFT. PLEASE COMPLY SO WE CAN KEEP THIS AREA OPEN FOR YOUR ENJOYMENT. Beyond Tecolotito Creek, on the far side of the airport, was a row of UC Santa Barbara buildings including an impressive parking garage. Three vultures kettled over the revolving orange radar dish. What it must have been to see the *tomols* coming and going in this estuary, like the planes now come and go, only more of them.

Goleta means "schooner," and this place is so named either because schooners once took refuge in the lagoon, or because the first American ship built in California was built here in 1829, or because quite a number of ships wrecked on the sandbars that guarded the baylet. All are true. In the Santa Barbara Presidio, I had seen two Spanish cannons that fittingly had been discovered on the Goleta Beach after a great storm. Imagine coming across those iron heads lifting from the sand, the same kind that fired at the mission during the Chumash revolt. But a *goleta* will never anchor inside those sandbars again. Or could one un-fill a thousand acres, if there were money and energy to do it?

Just one sliver of Mescaltitlán island remains across the road, a minor hill that seems as if it has been contoured on all sides, probably true. It has the look of a memorial mound to the heyday of a culture. To be frank, it looked like a grass-and-coyote-brush-decorated Twinkie. Once apparently it held groves of oaks, an island "whose verdure and trees gave great pleasure to the eyes," wrote Costansó. Now it is also behind chain-link. A gas company owns it. There is a sewage treatment plant beside it. That's all that's left of this once-prized and -hallowed ground, the center of the world for a subset of Chumash, some of whom had danced all afternoon to entertain and honor the Portolá expedition (and, in fact, had to be sternly disinvited when they returned that night, so the soldiers could sleep). I had tried to find a way through the fence, but in the end, couldn't quite understand what would be gained by climbing to the top of this diminished feature. So I just clung to the chain-link and looked through.

BEYOND GOLETA, THE SOUTHERN CALIFORNIA coast becomes lonelier, suddenly longs to be Northern. I managed to leave my camera charger in the UCSB Library, where I had taken shelter during the heat of the day. Turning back added a couple of miles, but I needed that charger—I stashed my pack in a bush—and three times I went past the same kids at their soccer camp on artificial turf. At Tecolote Canyon, just before the Ritz-Carlton, I ventured down to Haskell's Beach, but was told by a pair of men that it would be folly to try to round Naples Point. Actually, what they said was, "Nope. No fucking way. You'll be swimming." They advised I take the railroad. "Oh wait, where you from?" said one. "Idaho," I said. "Oh yeah, take the tracks. If you were from L.A., I would have said, 'Yeah, keep going, minus tide, all clear.'"

I scaled the grade through the sickles of a pungent eucalyptus corridor that ran for days, intermittently, along the tracks, and I didn't look back except to see the sheer and calving coastline or step off the grade when a train, phantom or real, appeared. On the rails, immediately I felt more relaxed. So many decisions had been taken out of my hands, and I wasn't trespassing on anyone's land but Union Pacific's. All I had to do was go forward and not get run over, and the odds of succeeding in that were far greater than along any road. Walking the tracks was far saner than plodding Highway 101, which on this stretch was the only alternative. Sometimes, across the fields, like running animals, I would see the backs of cars and semis. Always I could hear them.

For days, I also listened to one eucalyptus creaking against another, to their rustling. Their acorns collected at culverts to the sea. Was this what the Australian Outback was like? Eucalyptus seeds were bought to California during the gold rush, and the state immediately found an appetite for these robust, fast-growing trees to populate its sparsely forested coastal hillsides and central valleys. The railroads hadn't yet materialized to create easy access to the great timber reserves of the Sierra and northernmost California. Firewood was often scarce and expensive—even the Portolá expedition sometimes had to carry it with them—and no fossil fuels were handy until oil was found in Southern California in the 1890s. The economic and environmental conditions were perfect for eucalypts to take hold and become an iconic, shaggy figure of the Golden State. They flourish in soils that stunt other trees, and they withstand droughts by storing water in special roots, "lignotubers." In particular, Tasmanian blue gum was cultivated widely, *Eucalyptus globus*, and it spread like the wildfire to which it's adapted. Its hard fruits do look like globes, like jingle bells or buttons X'd with thread. Now you can drive whole days on California's highways without losing sight of eucalyptus. You can walk for a week on the railroad along the Santa Barbara Channel with this lovely invasive, which now seems as natural as the natives, to keep you company. California, railroad, eucalyptus—it's all of a piece. But not quite. In Carlsbad, near San Diego, I had visited a fifty-three-acre grove planted by a man who had thought to sell the wood for railroad ties until he discovered eucalyptus was too twisted and split-prone.

One of the earliest blue gum devotees and promoters lived right outside Goleta, just where I hopped onto the tracks. Ellwood Cooper was a Quaker who moved from Pennsylvania and embraced the coast wholeheartedly. "This is the Italy of America," he wrote to his friends back home, "the paradise of the western world, the climatic perfection of this globe!" Yet he clearly missed Pennsylvania's forests, because he did nothing but plant trees, it seems, across the two thousand acres he dubbed Rancho Ellwood. His orchards and gardens became a tourist attraction, producing olive oil, persimmons, almonds, and many other fruits. He also planted eucalyptus: 150,000 of them across a hundred acres.

Cooper's eucalypt enthusiasm was such that he published the state's first treatise on the genus, *Forest Culture and Eucalyptus Trees*, which offered a grand plan to preserve and generate arboreal California. The only impediment was a dearth of rain and a surfeit of wind, he argued, but something could be done about that: "Moderate the winds, increase the rain, and we have perfection." He proposed planting a continuous band of eucalyptus all the way up the state, one hundred feet wide. This minty and miasma-reducing "shelterbelt" would slow the wind and even compel rain, he explained. He also wanted to line all highways and roads with blue gums as reinforcement. Any farmer who joined the cause and seeded eucalyptus, preached Cooper, "increases the certainty of his crops, decreases one fourth his labor, beautifies his home, improves the climate, doubles the value of his land, receives inspiration from this work of his own hands" and so on forever.

Though Cooper sounds like a crackpot, for almost two decades he was president of the State Board of Horticulture and, in fact, he was a staunch supporter of "diversified planting." Rather than the monoculture of the enormous wheat fields that had spread across the former ranchos, he imagined a plentitude of small-scale, tree-heavy sustainable farms. But his eucalypti may have gotten away from him a little. I wondered if all the trees I saw west of Goleta's last neighborhood, Ellwood, were escapees down the tracks.

THE BANKS ABOVE THE RAILS rose and fell and let through troughs of ocean, crescent windows. I brushed my hands through umbels of fennel with their yellow and their societies of bees. I studied the swirls of upthrust sandstone and touched the cobble deposited at the mouth of some river ages ago, tumbled along the beach, locked in place and lifted. If the coast landscape itself were exposed strata, its basic layers would be ocean, the crashing surf, the beach, the bluffs, my railroad, the highway, and finally the Santa Ynez Mountains with their hanging gardens of boulder. Beyond all these, smoke trailed my direction, west, from the Rey Fire in the Los Padres National Forest. I had looked up the conflagration's name. Far in a southern direction were the peaks of moisture-shrouded islands and one white oil platform with its antennal derrick.

Naples Point was named by an Italophile, John Williams, who decided he would build a resort and development, Naples-by-the-Sea, beside Dos Pueblos Canyon in 1887. His co-investors were Southern Pacific executives, but as it turns out that was no assurance. The railroad reached as far west as Goleta, then stalled for over a decade. Williams grew so desperate he erected enormous white letters on the bluff, N A P L E S, to entice passing boaters, but the E and the P, the L, N, and S, blew down in the channel winds. He went bankrupt and died before the railroad moved forward. His wife, who built a chapel in his honor and buried him in its vault, then had him exhumed so that his casket could ride into Santa Barbara on the first train south, and then back to Naples, in 1901.

Thus, most or all of Naples Point is still private ranch—cows staring through eucalyptus fence lines. On a short trestle—short, but it made me nervous nonetheless—I crossed over Dos Pueblos Canyon from which I saw, down below, a parking lot and a manicured lawn above a private beach. White folding chairs and white umbrellas were set out for a wedding. Portolá and Crespí had camped on the tableland south of this arroyo, where six or seven hundred "souls" were reported at two villages, *dos pueblos*, "at the very edge of the sea." The original Naples. Crespí named it San Luis Obispo, a name that would migrate a week's walk up the coast. Now only the lucky few live here and rent their land for parties.

The stress of camping illegally wears one out, and to avoid it, on occasion I'd just as soon modify my own expedition slightly so long as I was seeing the places Portolá and Crespí had seen. So I kept on, thinking I could reach El Capitán State Park and its campground before nightfall. About five minutes later, I passed a wedding dress rehearsal on a bluff just above the tracks, Dos Pueblos Orchid Farm. I stood and watched from afar. They had arrived on a black school bus that read #HOLYMENDOMONY in large white print. The groom was a ginger, his hair afire in the cross-ocean light. There were nine bridesmaids.

At the head of the Santa Clara River Valley, Crespí mentioned "what we gathered to be a bride" at the Tataviam village below Newhall Pass. "She was wearing a great deal of paint and very much decked out in their fashion with all different sorts of their usual shell beads." Though of course distinct from the Tataviam, in the Los Angeles Basin a Tongva bride was dressed in beads, paint, feathers, and skins, and then escorted to the groom's village accompanied by family and friends, who threw food and seeds at her feet as she went. Later, when she sat with her groom, seeds were poured over the couple—a blessing and a sign of plenty, a show of wealth.

This contemporary couple went through the motions as I watched from the tracks, and then he fake kissed her and grabbed her and arched her over like a sailor just back from war. Their laughter cut through the shush of the surf and breeze, and I could see the coordinator telling them to go, touching their arms in turn. The groomsmen took the arms of the bridesmaids to process up the aisle. I also could have sworn I saw Ozzy and Sharon Osbourne sitting in the front row, but it must have been this exclusive locale getting the best of me.

FROM EL CAPITÁN STATE BEACH, where I found water, I ignored the signs and slipped through a fence to a bike path about to collapse into the ocean, which I walked a mile or so to Refugio State Beach. At last I had come into "hike-n-bike" territory, where for five or ten dollars, a non-motorized traveler can pitch a tent on a communal lawn or patch of dirt. Touring bikers with their saddlebags are common on the California coast, and in summer you reliably find four or five of them spending the night at a State Park. There aren't any hikers; my whole trip I never saw or heard of one. The coast, like our cities and suburbs, isn't walker friendly. You have to trespass or stride along the highways or walk the rails, all different kinds of picturesque illegality. Or you have to time the tides just right, and even then, there are impassable points.

From Dos Pueblos Canyon, the scouts took the beach to the Refugio, but on the way back were forced inland by a high tide, where it was slow going through deep gullies. So the expedition rested a day to time the tides and utilize the beach in the early morning, one of the few instances they marched on the sand. They cut inland over El Capitán Point. No one called them trespassers, though they were. Crespí was particularly unsettled by transvestites they encountered near Refugio: "We have been disturbed to note that in these most recent villages there are some men who wear the good-sized deerskin skirts worn by all the women here on the Channel, and go about more bedecked and bedizened with beads and shells than the women themselves; these men so dressed go around with the women, doing the same tasks, or so we have understood ... Who is wise enough to tell what mischief this might be?"

Refugio was a gently curving white sand beach lined with palm trees and a loose grid of RVs. Once this half-pint bay held a Chumash village, *Qasil*, though it was abandoned when Portolá passed through. The expedition camped one drainage farther west, but Crespí had preferred Refugio and named it *San Guido*. Apparently *Qasil* was reoccupied by 1776, because when Juan Bautista de Anza rode through with settlers destined for San Francisco, he noted the village in his journal. It was a trade node with a trail through the mountains to the Santa Ynez Valley. People from the islands visited to exchange goods such as steatite, also known as soapstone, for acorns, and I find it stirring to think of those *tomols* laden with shelled acorns pushing back through the waves. Oaks do exist on the large islands, but only a modest amount. The acorn trade was robust among the inland, coastal, and off-shore Chumash, and it's possible that the high genetic diversity of oaks in the region is a result of this flow of seeds.

In 1786, the coast from this bay to Point Conception, where I was headed, was lent for grazing to the Portolá expedition's head scout, José Francisco Ortega, who named it *Rancho Nuestra Señora del Refugio*. He was the original Ortega, the great-grandfather of the founder of the chile empire in Ventura. It was the only Spanish concession in today's Santa Barbara County; they offered the land to him in part because he owed a sizable debt to the army and could pay it off by raising cattle. Ortega built a home on the rancho in 1794 and died four years later when he fell off a horse above this beach. But his sons would secure a proper Mexican land grant and come to run over a thousand head of cattle. They also ran a notorious smuggling business in the cove with American ships, one that even the Franciscan padres conspired to help toward the end of Spain's hold on Alta California, when they were starved for resources. In all, the dispensation was more than twenty-six thousand acres, and the Ortegas successfully filed a claim for it after cession to the United Sates.

Mainly I rested my legs at Refugio State Beach, but I also began to worry. From the start, I had known that I would encounter another serious roadblock in the form of the famous Hollister Ranch, now an exclusive housing association, a property that began one day's walk past Refugio at Gaviota. Beyond Hollister was the even more remote Cojo-Jalama Ranch, also private. I had been in touch with both of them to try to obtain permission to cross through. Both had turned me away. That sealed my determination to trespass, in some ways. But I had come to the conclusion that walking through in the light of day would be too risky. They both had patrols. If they found me, likely they would just dump me back at the gate and I'd lose time. Potentially they could prosecute me, especially if I tried to pass through a second time. Yet circumambulating those ranches on Highways 101 and 1 would be longer and more dangerous, and I'd miss a pivotal leg of the expedition.

I FOUND A SOUNDING BOARD for my predicament inside the Refugio Beach Store, 8 AM – 7 PM, CAMP SUPPLIES, SOUVENIRS, ICE, BEVERAGES, GROCER-

IES, FISHING BAIT AND TACKLE. The place was little more than a mobile unit with a deck, a trailer bent on gouging your wallet. I had gone to order a vegetarian sub and ask if I could charge my phone and laptop. Paul was manning the cash register, and he obliged me, and we started talking as I hung around for my batteries. He wore a black ball cap, a six-inch white beard that forked subtly like a snake's tongue, and a tattoo sleeve. Each day he rode his Harley to Refugio to make the campers slightly uncomfortable as they bought their Dippin' Dots, the store's best seller. But you could tell he was a sweetheart under that veneer. He made a point of welcoming everyone as they walked in, to help them get past his biker appearance. It was Paul's birthday that day, and I asked if he had plans to celebrate.

"Yeah," Paul said, "you know, when I woke up this morning and took my first breath, I was happy. Then my wife smiles and goes, 'Happy Birthday.' That's good. I've had four heart operations, and her health isn't too great. So when we wake up, we're happy."

I was amazed to learn that he had grown up on the Cojo Ranch. "My grandfather was a cowboy, my grandmother was a cook," Paul said. "I rode horses, motorcycles, went hunting, and went fishing. That was a long time ago." How many people lived there? "They had a bunkhouse, my uncle was a cowboy, they had a family called the Fowlers, and they had a guy named Old Joe, and my grandpa— they were the cowboys. Floyd Smith was the foreman, and my grandma was the cook. Plus, Grandma drove the school bus back into Lompoc. At night she couldn't see the combination lock, so she took me." That was the pretense she'd used to get Paul out of the house, anyway. *Lom-poke*, Paul taught me. "Better get it right when you're there."

I confessed my tentative plan to Paul, some of it, how I wanted to cross his childhood ranch on the rails on my way to San Francisco. "If you keep walking down the tracks, you're going to walk through Hollister, Cojo, Jalama, and the base, and when you get to the base, they're going to arrest you." He meant Vandenberg Air Force Base, which owns the coastline beyond Jalama Beach. I knew about that, too, but hadn't gotten that far in my planning.

"I'm not going to try to get through the base," I said. "But you think I could walk the tracks through those private ranches, during the day? I mean not Hollister, because they're so uptight there . . ."

"Cojo is pretty uptight also. You're liable to get the boot in both places, and that's just from Gaviota to the base," said Paul. "You're going to have to take a different route."

"I'm not going to try to make it through the base, that's for sure."

"Well, you're not going to make it to the base walking the tracks."

"I was thinking about doing it at night," I said.

"That'll work," said Paul, pulling at his beard. "That'll work. Besides the mountain lions, and pigs, and all those things that'll eat you at night, you're fine . . . black bears. It would be a beautiful walk, too. I lived out there, but then I took the train one time so I could see it from another view along the water. Beautiful. All my life I was in the mountains looking at the ocean. So it was kind of fun to get on in L.A. and look the other way.

"For one thing, it's going to be your attitude. If the guards approach you, keep your nice attitude and tell them what you're up to. I wouldn't do it at night, but if you do the night walk, you're going to go right to Jalama Beach. The only way out then is that windy-ass road that goes to 1 that goes to Lompoc.

"Just make sure you don't get stuck in a spot where the train can't go around you. But you'll hear'm. I think you're going to be fine. I know one of the Hollister guards. If you meet a guy named Matt, tell him you met a guy named Paul and describe me, and he's going to be nice. I don't know the rest of them, but I know Matt. Loves to surf, loves to fish.

"One thing they don't like is surfers, because they wrecked it for themselves. When I was little they let'm go out there and go surfing, it's the best surfing around. But they left their crap and their garbage, and their shit. So one day my grandpa and the foreman said, 'No more.' They do have patrol. Hollister, Cojo, and Jalama all have a patrolman for poachers. But you don't got a gun, you don't got a surfboard, you don't got nothing but a laptop. Just tell'm you're doing a historical walk. They don't own the goddamn railroad tracks. But you have to get to the tracks and then get back off it.

"But it gets foggy, buddy, I don't care if there's a moon out there or not. And there's other people on those tracks, there's hoboes out there. That's why you need a stick."

"A stick . . . for the hoboes?" I asked.

"For the hoboes. They used to throw each other off the tracks and we'd see body parts, me and my little sister, all over the place."

"Geez," I said. "You think there are really hoboes out there?"

"No, I'm just kidding . . . this was when I was a little kid. But I do want you to think about the snakes . . . there are big, nasty black rattlers, and they like the warmth of the tracks. You could drag your stick to make some noise. You're going to be at the furthest point west in California, and you'll see the lighthouse. There's a lot of Indian burial grounds out there, but they don't talk about it."

I asked about the chances for fog.

"The way I figure it, right now, at this time, the fog is behind the oil derricks— it's going to take a while to get here. Now if you can't see the oil derricks, it'll be here in two or three hours. That's how I go about it. You can get the high fog, or you can get the fog that's like rain. It looks like it's going to be a high fog night. Or you could get none. And when you get to the Jalama campground, just walk on down and lay down on one of them tables and go to sleep. And when they wake you up, say, 'Oh, thanks.'"

I told Paul I'd do that, and gave him my own thanks for bucking me up so much.

"Well, this figures to be the slowest day in the world," he said before I left. "The kids are going back to school. The old-timers are camping, and they bring everything they need. Until they run out of wine . . . But I brought these stickers in with me today, they were out, and this is a big seller. Everyone wants to know where they been."

IT WAS ABOUT TEN MILES on the tracks to Gaviota, where I pitched my tent with difficulty as an offshore zephyr whipped through the campground and under the towering trestle. The expedition's soldiers managed to shoot a gull here, *una gaviota*, enough excitement to give the beach its name. I-5 turns inland at Gaviota, climbing north into and through the Vaqueros Sands of the Santa Ynez Mountains via a tunnel, and all night the wind ran down this canyon and out to sea like a semi out of control, drubbing my tent and keeping me awake. "At this place," wrote Costansó, "we began to experience cold and violent north winds, and we feared that the effects might be harmful and prejudicial to the health." I slept in as much as possible, shook the blown dust from my things, and packed up in the early afternoon. Then I killed time, finally cracking those walnuts from Brea and carefully noting how often the trains crossed the high trestle. The cashier at the exorbitant Gaviota Beach

Store told me that, a week ago, freight trains had run by every half hour because the inland lines over the Grapevine had been closed due to a fire. That would have been a rough night to attempt the tracks.

My resolve to travel through the Hollister and Cojo-Jalama Ranches had wavered over the last forty-eight hours, but now it was firm. As I thought about it, an all-night walk on the rails seemed more and more appropriate and inevitable. The private coastline of these ranches remains a dark spot, terra incognita, on the map of California in the public imagination. Off-limits to all but a few, this crucial stretch is withheld heritage. It began to seem incumbent on me to shine whatever dim light I could on this corner of the state by traveling through on that slim vein of commerce, the Union Pacific line, which happens to describe Portolá's route.

Hollister Ranch was originally the western end of the Rancho Nuestra Señora del Refugio land grant, but following the ruinous 1864 drought, the Ortegas sold it to the partnership of William Hollister and brothers Thomas and Albert Dibblee. William Hollister had undertaken the first transcontinental sheep drive, starting out from Ohio in 1854 with ten thousand merinos and arriving with a few thousand still bleating. For six months, he fattened them near Goleta before moving north, and for him the Santa Barbara coast became the promised land. During the Civil War, he made a fortune selling wool to the Union for uniforms, so he sold his inland ranch, which became the City of Hollister, and returned to the Santa Barbara Channel, where he bought a half dozen former land grants with the Dibblees—more than one hundred thousand acres in all. When the partnership disintegrated, Hollister retained the three coastal ranches.

One of William Hollister's sons, John, took over the ranch, but the third generation was compelled to sell in 1969, two hundred years after the Portolá expedition. No money in cows anymore, not on these semi-arid seaside lands. It didn't help that unpalatable mustard and other invasives like mallow had swept across the pastures and reduced its profitability. California could have bought the ranch at that moment for a State Park, but instead a subsidiary of the Pennsylvania Railroad swooped in and planned a development of twenty thousand people, one that was only averted when the railroad went bankrupt the following year. The ranch fell into the hands of the mortgage company, which shaped its current existence: 135 parcels of one hundred acres (some of them divided into as many as twelve shared "interests"), with more than eight miles of communal coastline and some of the finest surfing in Southern California.

The Hollister Ranch Owners' Association formed and took control and began to fiercely guard the ranch's privacy and autonomy. It defeated a proposal for a National Seashore along its coast by hiring the right lobbyists. And it has steadfastly battled any proposal to allow public access to its beaches, though the 1972 California Coastal Act requires it. The State has long pursued one potential avenue: in the seventies, the Los Angeles YMCA purchased an adjacent, inland parcel from the Hollister Ranch owners, which included access to the coast at Cuarta Canyon several miles into the ranch. In 1982, the YMCA received a permit to build a camp on its land, as well as modest day facilities along the beach. In return, the State was granted "an easement in perpetuity" to that shore. Soon after, however, the Ranch Owners' Association sued the YMCA and then bought them out. The camp was never built, but the easement nonetheless stands. The Ranch Owners' Association argues that the YMCA didn't have the right to grant it since the YMCA had no beachfront title and its access was via an easement itself. This debate is still twisting and turning in court, with no obvious end in sight, but the Coastal Commission is just now beginning to apply leverage by denying Hollister Ranch owners building permits, as allowed, until the access issue is settled.

Currently the Ranch Owners' Association invites limited numbers of disabled veterans and schoolchildren into the ranch on field trips. It also makes allowances for scientific research, but not, as I learned, humanities projects. If the State has its way, eventually fifty or so people may be shuttled in each day from Gaviota State Park to Cuarta Canyon to lie on the beach and surf the adjacent breaks. But I had arrived at these gates too soon and would have to prowl through the dark.

WHEN ONLY AN ORANGE LINE described the ocean horizon, I stood up from the bluff-top grass and buckled my pack—that waist-strap *click* so focusing, energizing, directional—and wove through the sage to the long bed of clinking ballast. Behind me, over Gaviota Beach, was the Ghost Bridge: the longest trestle between Ventura and San Luis Obispo at 811 feet long. At forty miles per hour, a train covers that distance in fourteen seconds. All day long the looming bridge had conjured thoughts of the two trestles not far into Hollister. On my phone, I had studied them in satellite images, but there wasn't much to see. I only knew that they were long, and I would have to cross them at night.

As I started forward, I felt like a warm train pulling away from a platform, a warm train powered by adrenaline and a Monster energy drink. My pack was heavy with three liters of water and a Red Bull for late night, but it was balanced and I felt fresh. Briskly I stepped from tie to tie, shortening my stride to hit the sleepers, but after a minute I gave up trying to land on them and just strode naturally, embracing the ballast though it made me wobble a little.

The gatehouse, I knew, was about a half mile in, but I wasn't sure how well staffed it would be, or whether it had a view of the tracks. Several people had told me it was set back a distance, but just how far? After about five minutes of walking, up ahead a floodlight poured over the rails, slanting right to left, illuminating the oceanside bank above the tracks. It seemed too soon for the gatehouse, but I was wary. Thirty seconds later, the light went off. Was it motion-sensing? Was a camera relaying a feed to the gatehouse? I began walking toward it again. The light reappeared and I froze, took a knee, and waited. The light vanished again. For five or six minutes, I knelt, watching. If I was going to get caught, it was probably going to be in this first mile or so.

At last I realized the illumination was just headlights from a car whenever one descended the Hollister Ranch Road on the hillside above. Such was my paranoia.

I NEVER SAW THE GUARD station, only the fluorescence it cast through trees and bushes, more incidental than intentional. Probably I could have walked right by standing tall between the rails, but instead I crept like a coyote in the shadow of the cut, bent over and feeling the weight of my pack. Then again, a coyote might have stood tall and trotted down the middle of the rails with its tongue dangling. I watched the sagebrush shadow line opposite me in case my head or humpback silhouette suddenly became noticeable, giving me away, but it never did.

I picked up steam, held a good pace. Chug, chug, chug. No fog, and little wind. In the starlight, the white lines of breakers were barely visible below, pale fans bending and spreading. The Big Dipper hung over a sandstone slope like a child's beach shovel, while the cascading, stilted shapes of eucalypti sometimes interrupted the constellations. I realized I would be out long enough tonight for the stars to rotate noticeably overhead. The starlight was just enough to see my two steel guide-lines. Walking down the middle of the rails turned out to be easier than treading their lumpy shoulders. I had aching shoulders, and the tracks had shoulders, and I was on the warm shoulder of the august continent.

Then a difference in the air, some acceleration: some edge. There was a void ahead, a canyon. I knew because I could see lonely headlights tracing a horseshoe descent and ascent off to my right. The Hollister Ranch Road was once just a dirt ribbon, dubbed the Little Burma Road by the Coast Guard because it was so rustic, often impassable in winter. Now paved, it parallels the coast and the tracks, but veers inland around many arroyos, dipping to a more modest bridge the way Portolá and his horses and mules would have had to weave inland and down before climbing back up to these tablelands. I had come to *Cañada del Agua Caliente*, the first trestle. Finally it emerged from the deep gray. But the bridge was a span to nowhere. I couldn't see the other side.

From the trestles I'd already encountered, I knew there would be several outlets for escape: square platforms, no more than three feet wide, jutting from the track where a maintenance worker or bum could step in the event of a passing train. But they alternated sides and were few and far between. From certain spots on the trestle, you might not make it to one, I thought, if a train was a surprise and traveling with speed. I imagined squeezing onto one of these platforms with my pack as a train barreled by. The force of air would blow off my hat, it would twirl and be gone. Hard against the rushing silver of the train, maybe I would come face to flickering face with a person gazing out a window.

I broke into a jog down the middle of the tracks, my thumbs hooked beneath my shoulder straps, the butt of my pack slapping my lower back. The trestle bed was solid with ballast, thankfully, but it felt like running through empty space. I was eighty-two feet up. The chilly ocean breeze swept up canyon and filled my ears. The span's center was the most worrisome: those few seconds when you entertain the idea, the possibility, of a light up ahead.

The second trestle I came to, at Arroyo de Alegria, was more terrifying because it was longer, 634 feet. That is almost half the circuit of an Olympic running track. After I had jogged it, my T-shirt under my thin jacket was sweaty, not from effort but from the suspense. Yet I had crossed the only trestles of the night, so I steadied myself in the cool breeze and began to relax. To be a train, I said to myself. To be a slow, steady train.

MOONRISE AROUND ELEVEN. AT FIRST it was a glow over a ridge, one I wouldn't have noticed except that I paused for water. It pays to turn around so the moon doesn't sneak up on you. When it rose, it was a great horned owl eye, slanted and austere, no pupil. Half lost to the Earth's shadow, blood-orange red from the smoke of the Rey Fire still burning behind me, beyond the mountains. But enough sun was reflected that the Santa Ynez foothills were revealed, high rounded forms. The rails lit up like fiber-optic cables. Over the stripes of the pale ballast and darker ties, my shadow glided before me like a jailbird.

The waves also came to life, receiving and curling the moon. They were like bright fuses burning in both directions. Then the double boom, crash crash, as they exploded on themselves, and the white noise of the tumble, and the relenting hiss. Alternately the tracks ran through deep cuts in the sandstone hills—cuts that men with mules had dug just before the turn of the twentieth century, when the gap between Goleta and San Luis Obispo was finally closed after a hiatus. These steep, man-made valleys—mule-made—obscured the beach and muffled the surf. I felt most at ease in them, out of sight from everything but the Milky Way overhead, the crickets loud, each stridulating on its individual stem.

Not long before he died, William Hollister granted the Southern Pacific a sixty-foot-wide easement through the ranch. In exchange, the train stopped for the Hollisters anytime. They only had to raise a flag to hail the train, and it would squeal and steam to a halt. Hollister's son, John, brought his new wife to the ranch in the caboose of a work train before the line was complete, so it's said they were the first passengers on this leg of the Southern Pacific. The last bridge, at Arroyo Hondo, was finished on December 30, 1900, and the final rivet was put in about a mile east of Gaviota in Cemeterio. At first trains traveled up the Santa Clara River Valley, following the Portolá expedition's path, and mine, through Santa Paula and Fillmore to Saugus, and then through the congested San Fernando Tunnel to Los Angeles. But by 1904 a shortcut was laid and bored through Simi Valley and the Santa Susana Mountains, which remains the route today.

Often the builders dumped fill from their cuts into adjacent canyons to create level crossings, but the Southern Pacific promised the Hollisters it would trestle over the Santa Anita Canyon that hosted the ranch headquarters. The company betrayed that promise, however, and built one of these enormous berms, marring the drainage and destroying its view. John Hollister relocated the family west to Bulito Canyon, where he built his "Big House" out of redwood and planted a new orchard. As I walked I saw houses not far from the tracks, and others high atop the hills if their pinhead lights were glowing. Most were dark, second or occasional homes with faint outdoor lights left on. In my imagination, they were all fancy, contemporary homes of concrete and glass, but in fact many are low-slung ranch houses. The view, and the privacy, is the main appeal.

EVEN ON THIS REMOTE COAST, my night was defined by the punctuation of light. The moon and stars brought comfort and some detail to the landscape, while electrical lights filled me with anxiety. When headlights suddenly swung through a gap and panned across me, I jumped off the tracks into the fescue and lay there, hiding, for five minutes. Later I paused to assess a lone light up ahead. Even through my binoculars I couldn't decipher what it was: An illuminated window? A porch light? I stood for several minutes before moving forward. It was a bulb not bigger than a golf ball on a railroad shed no bigger than a closet.

Periodically a pulse of warm breeze from the interior swept across my cheek. I began to feel the wear of the shifting ballast on my feet, hips, lower back. All the underappreciated stabilizing muscles of my ankles were working overtime, but after so many days of trekking they were prepared. I tried to maintain a loose stride, to flow over the tracks. To dictate the way your foot falls is to self-impede. Past humming electrical boxes, past sidings where a train could be shunted to allow another to pass. An owl flew from a sign or reflector, its soundless form visible in the stars. Some other, larger creature clambered out of a drainage and over the ballast: a deer, maybe, or a wild boar with ivory tusks, or a bear. A mountain lion would have made no sound.

AS YOU HEAD WEST THROUGH Hollister Ranch, "the mountains once more draw back a bit," as Crespí wrote, and the railroad runs through a sandy plain. One other light appeared: I began to see a diffuse pulse in the distance, the Point Conception lighthouse. It motivated me, pulled me forward, reminded me that I was nearing the great turn toward Northern California.

About three hours from Gaviota, I stopped and cupped my hand around my phone to see where I was. I had just entered the Cojo-Jalama Ranch, which had been a cattle ranch for more than a century, but would, a year after my night excursion, be purchased by the Nature Conservancy as the Jack and Laura Dangermond Preserve. The founders of one of the world's most successful mapping companies, the Dangermonds donated $165 million to purchase the twenty-four thousand acres and so layer a new name on the land, though to what extent Cojo-Jalama will be open to the public remains to be seen.

Not far from Point Conception, Crespí named a village of thirty-eight grass houses *Santa Teresa*, but the soldiers' moniker—*La Ranchería del Cojo*, the Cripple's Village—won out. It may be so named because its chief was disabled, as Costansó claims. But in his field journal, Crespí cites another reason: "A lame mule was left here on our way up, which on our return in January was recovered healthy and fat . . . although still hobbling." Standing on the tracks, peering out at Little Cojo Bay, I felt sure that the expedition and its mules had loitered on this bluff top. That the hurting mule itself had stood in this place and looked out to sea, thinking, *Water*. What must the natives have thought, tending this odd beast, this creature like a deer but not a deer?

I knew if I left the railroad, I would be more vulnerable—I would be trespassing on ranch land—but I couldn't bear the thought of walking all night without touching the beach. It felt like my right as a Californian. So I started down to the shore of Little Cojo Bay on a paved road that crossed the tracks and bent left. Suddenly a bright light flashed up the road. A car, I thought—coming my direction. I bolted back up the pavement, sprinting despite my pack and then turning onto the relative sanctuary of the tracks, where I was trespassing only against Union Pacific. I walked onward into the darkness, but stopped and stood for a few minutes when nothing materialized.

Hesitantly I crept back down the beach road, and about halfway down realized I had been duped by the moon. The ocean's horizon was dark, but the foreground was luminous. The water glimmered white as a gas flame. I stood a minute to gauge whether a large canvas wall tent above Little Cojo Beach might be occupied. But there was no car. Only a grill with a rotisserie, a picnic table, and a rope coiled around a NO TRESPASSING sign to help trespassers descend an eroded chute, but I needed no help. I dropped my pack and glissaded down in my sneakers: the sand so much softer than the railroad's ballast, so forgiving. Mats of kelp sighed and popped as I stepped across them. Come morning, the sand would hold my footprints as evidence, but I'd be long gone.

Little Cojo is finally preserved, but in the seventies and eighties it was the site of a battle over a proposed liquefied natural gas terminal that lasted over a decade. It would have received 127 tankers annually from Alaska and Indonesia. Of course, the Hollister and Cojo-Jalama (then Bixby) Ranches fought this proposal. They got lucky when the seismologists they had hired uncovered a minor fault line at Little Cojo. The Utilities Commission ordered trenching to study the fault, which is when the conflict took another unexpected turn: Chumash traditionalists arrived and occupied the site, arguing that the trenching and, of course, the potential LNG terminal would desecrate Point Conception, a sacred place. "What we are going to do very simply is lay down our lives," one Native spokesperson declared. "If [Point Conception] were destroyed tomorrow, I feel so strongly about it, I would want to die today so that I could pass through the Western Gate." The protesters occupied these grounds for eight months before they were forced to leave by court order, but the delay in seismic trenching helped defeat the project, if only because natural gas soon became readily available in the U.S. No imports were necessary. Strange to imagine something so intrusive as a giant pier with enormous white tanks and a maze of pipe on this otherwise empty elbow of land jutting into the Pacific. Would I rather have no genuine access to this beach, as was the case, or an LNG facility here? The answer was easy.

I SPENT FIVE MINUTES PACING the beach, shaking out my tired body, before I climbed to my pack and the railroad. From this spot, Portolá and his men looked west to a grander curve of cliffs sheltering a bay. "We have a low bare point in sight at about a league or a bit more, going a considerable way out to sea," wrote Crespí, "and we guess it to be Point Conception." The eastern prong of this headland is now known as Government Point, but the western remains Conception: *La Punta de la Limpia Concepción*, Vizcaíno christened it in 1602, on December 8, the feast day of the Immaculate Conception. Cojo Bay, tucked under the arm of Government Point, is indeed a larger version of Little Cojo, with bluffs that appeared in the moonlight like the White Cliffs of Dover. It is a last redoubt before the Santa Barbara Channel cedes to the severe ocean beyond. A lone sailboat, one red light atop its mast, was moored above the bay's quiet swells. They had it to themselves.

Then the track began to curve, long and slow, and with it my journey. The glinting rails turned toward the northwest and then to the north, shortcutting the points, and my body tilted with the banking that cradled the trains. As the bend carried me farther from the shore momentarily, the surf became a quiet simmer. At several ranch gates, I contemplated leaving the tracks, hopping over, and wandering out the point on dusty roads toward the hidden lighthouse. But it was past one in the morning, I had miles to go—at least eight—and it seemed prudent, perhaps, not to get too close to the Western Gate, not to volunteer oneself. Everyone I had talked to had described Point Conception as a place of grave energy, a place sailors fear and others revere. *Humqaq*, it was originally called by the Chumash: "The Raven Comes." Ravens had seemed to shadow me for weeks, and now the night felt something like them. John Harrington, the famous California ethnologist who recorded this eschatology, described how "the soul comes to a place where there are two giant *qaq* perched on each side of the trail, and who each peck out an eye as the soul goes by." The eyes are replaced with poppies and, later, blue mother-of-pearl abalone. For we need only see the path of the dead.

THE LAST SEVERAL HOURS WERE straight and stuporous. My hands grew cold as my body craved sleep, and I began to stumble more on the ballast with clumsiness. For energy, I ate a Clif Bar and several handfuls of almonds. Coyotes howled and yipped and cackled, and I saw the shape and movement of one in a ditch. The black fence posts atop the pale uplifted strata along the tracks looked like small crosses in the moonlight: the West worships fences, too.

Up ahead, like another beacon, was a mountaintop light that I would learn was a listening station in the foggy heights of Vandenberg Air Force Base. The whole night was listening, or trying to. At times my voice, speaking drowsily into my recorder, was lost to the wind, buried in scratchy feedback. I quieted eventually, began to zone out, the world shrinking. The night felt warm, but it might have just been my metabolism churning. I might bonk at the twenty-mile mark, I thought to myself, just like people do running marathons. Finally I opened the energy drink I'd carried and sipped it as I walked. "As I tilt my Red Bull back for the final drops, it takes me up to the stars. Which are fainter now, they've been washed out by the moon. I think . . . is that Cassiopeia? Oh, it looks like the butterfly."

Behind me now, to the south, even in the dark Point Conception did have the profile of a duck's head, as is often said, with its flat bill pointing far west, dabbling toward Japan. The pale funnel of the lighthouse appeared and swung around, and around, and, with more distance, at last the direct shine of the lens revealed itself, every ten seconds or so. There. There. Like souls going out to sea. I had assumed the lighthouse would be high on the point, but actually it was lower on its forehead, seaward, making it difficult for anyone but ships to glimpse. There.

The tracks suddenly emerged to and crossed a hairpin turn on Jalama Road, which I took downhill, a gradual half-mile descent with a whiff of septic on the late breeze and, eventually, lit palms ruffling ahead. At 3:21 I crossed into Jalama Beach Park past the shuttered gatehouse. I found the campsite I had reserved for tomorrow—it was empty—and rather than lie down on a picnic table as Paul had suggested, I pitched my tent on the windswept plot. I'd sleep better this way. A freight train at last hummed by, passing above me on the tracks. It was the first one I'd seen all night.

YOU KNOW I SLEPT IN. Slept until the sun's heat pushed me out of the tent, doughy and fairly gasping like a newborn. Some would say I was in Northern California now. I would say, Not yet. But in Jalama, the air does feel anticipatory, portentous, the ocean rougher, the wind straight and scouring to shore. The coveted campground spots hard on the beach are "tent only" and sheltered behind bushes curled like the waves beyond. Other sites on terraces have immense views. My campsite had neither. It was bare dirt below the final drive and gatehouse, ground too hard for stakes. So I scavenged rocks from underneath the nearly leafless bushes. One of the State Park attendants came around in his golf cart shortly after nine and, studying his clipboard, was surprised to find me. I'd arrived in the early morning, I said—that wasn't really a night's stay, was it?—and still had to register. I planned to spend two more nights at Jalama and get my legs under me again.

Other than trying to stay off my feet, I honestly can't recall much of what I did this day. Except eat several Jalama Burgers, whose reputation precedes them. And I sat at a number of gull-spattered picnic tables. In the evening, I couldn't help but walk the immediate shore and shake out my soreness, get the blood flowing. I watched snowy plovers on the sand. Snowies are a "species of special concern" in California, and once they were "threatened," but I counted forty within fifty feet of me. There were hundreds on the beach, each a fast-walking cobblestone. The fog, the sand, the stone, the water: a snowy plover resembles all of those. It is the apotheosis of coastal California. Hunched, patient, poised, monastic. They skitter forward, then pause. Skitter, skitter, skitter, disappear. Their life is blowing sand and kelp flies on the rotting strand. When a terrier named Elmo ran inland from the shore, twenty or thirty flushed from the ground in front of me, peeping in a pointed flurry of wings. Some had colored bands on a leg: you know a bird is rare, or at least expensive, when it is given that kind of scientific jewelry.

Jalama, I quickly felt and heard from others, is known to shred tents. The wind comes like a wide train onshore or off, and flat-out bends the cattails on Jalama Creek, which Portolá's mules must have drunk from. Above that creek is the rusted trestle across which the actual locomotive runs like a gleaming chime in a vast, rolling clock of hills and waves. You can see the train shining, snaking, to the north on the tablelands as it comes or goes. When it crosses the trestle, it's impossible not to look up and watch. Hello, train-goers, enjoy Santa Barbara, enjoy San Luis. I waved. Red-wing blackbirds sailed up from the marsh's reeds and landed on the RV PARKING ONLY sign, then to the ground, cautiously, to eat scattered bread crumbs, until a Ford F250 with a dog in the rear bed gurgled up and flushed them.

This little creek delta sheltered a Chumash village called *Shilimaqshtush*, no translation, of about 150 people. It was about a hundred yards from the sea, wrote Crespí, probably right under today's trestle. No *tomols* were seen, only a few canoes of bundled tule and "scarcely any fish." Crespí doesn't wonder why, but once you're around Point Conception, the ocean and its risks are greater, profound. He named it *La Concepción de Maria Santísima*, but the soldiers called it *Paraje de la Espada*, Place of the Sword. "Here a heathen from the previous villages stole the sword belonging to one of the corporals, who failed to feel it even though he had it next to his side, but was left only the scabbard. The heathen at once ran off along the shore; while the heathen chiefs belonging to the village here went after him and took it from him, and brought it back all wet, because the thief ran into the sea on seeing himself pursued." I'm almost sorry he didn't get away with it. It would have been a triumph to have returned to his village at Cojo with the blade. As for Jalama, the name comes from a site miles inland, *Xalam*, which means "bundle." It was mainly a stopover between the coast and the interior, a mountain place where people camped temporarily or seasonally with their bundled things.

The fog bank swallowed the oil platforms that evening. Wind sucked sand across the beach. The setting sun was not so different in color from the smoky moon I'd seen at midnight from the middle of Hollister Ranch. People stood in the Jalama surf in waders, fishing rods in hand. Others kicked a lazy soccer ball that jounced over the pitted sand. But the fog was the main show: far to the north, it had shrouded North Point and Arlight, where Space Launch Complex 8 exists, and closer by, it enwrapped the listening station on the peak several miles into Vandenberg—those vaulted lights I'd seen the night before. Fog rolled over those drainages, its fingers pulling back, evaporating, even as they stretched forward. Sluggish and vampiric. But because of the warm inland air pouring over the mountains and down the Jalama Road—it didn't feel so warm, but it was—that fog wouldn't capture the campground. Not tonight.

The aroma of charcoal wafting over my shoulder. When the wind died for a moment I finally felt the goosebumps on the back of my arms from the ocean chill. The sun dropped and lit the fog bank's gauzy upper horizon like a fire burning through sage. Little wonder, I thought, that the Chumash believe in another realm over the ocean. All that glowing, that soft watery apocalypse. I imagined missiles launching through it. Missiles hidden under that moist cotton at Arlight, where I wouldn't try to go for fear of a jail cell. Paul had duly warned me. Even a night walk wouldn't work: they used infrared and would descend on you with a helicopter and searchlights.

IN THE MORNING, MY LEGS felt better and I walked south down the beach without my pack toward Point Conception, which I hadn't quite seen to my satisfaction in the dark. Maybe I would be able to get a proper look at the lighthouse during the day. A few surfers were appraising a break known as Tarantulas. The beach was strewn with globs of tar not yet congealed, and giant sea cucumbers thrown up that resembled that tar. I recalled that, when attacked, sea cucumbers are said to turn themselves inside out, offering up their intestine, which they can regenerate. Saintly sea cucumbers. But now the whole world had been turned inside out for these poor lost sandy pudges.

Still in shadow, the bluffs were eroded sandstone and tilted strata. Early sun and green-and-orange ice plant cascaded through this high-up gentle crenellation. A native succulent of South Africa, ice plant was introduced in the early 1900s to help stabilize railroad beds. Later it was used by Caltrans to shore up road banks, and the California Conservation Corps seeded it, too, in the 1930s. This creeper has been a destabilizing force for dune communities ever since, crowding out native plants and flowers, turning the sandy soil more acidic while hogging its minerals, and even creating erosion because it has shallow roots. Cliffs sometimes collapse under the weight of its sprawling mats. But ice plant is beautiful. It has daisy-like flowers that glow cream, purple, or gold. Its faceted, succulent leaves tinge yellow, orange, and red. Everywhere trailing up hillsides and cliffs, from a distance it can appear nearly as iridescent as the spindrift blown off a dying wave.

Down some of these cuts in the Cojo-Jalama bluffs ran broken culvert pipe or wooden troughs that carried runoff under the train tracks, or once did. Fence posts were silhouetted at the heights with crosspieces askew, harkening to a time when cows were everything here, and in fact, the ranch still runs plenty of cattle. NO TRESPASSING signs high up, too. Piles of talus accumulated below chutes, which even at night had provided triangle views of ghostly surf. You might be able to scramble up one of those gullies to the tracks, but I wasn't about to try it.

The tar blobs looked like car mats, like fresh twisted pretzels, like black mold pancakes, like ruined octopi. Some rocks had spatters on them as if the waves had tossed these bombs. I caught whiffs of what I thought was natural gas and imagined methane bubbling up along with this tar from all those compressed critters and other cells out there, submerged in stone. When I picked up a keyhole limpet shell, it had a feather-like sprig of red algae and a minuscule button of tar that I mushed firm so that it held the lines of my thumbprint.

Soon I was following fresh dog prints. Rounding the remains of a concrete re-taining wall on the beach, some relic of former industry, I saw god's dog itself, coy-ote. It looked at me, hung its snout, and began to trot off, a loose zig. The dog and twenty-nine turkey vultures had been sharing a sea lion carcass, and the vultures settled on the crumbling sidewalls, patiently. They knew they just had to wait. The lion's flippers were stretched out as if still swimming. It grimaced a little, revealed its canines. Would Juana Maria have scavenged slivers of meat from washed-up sea lions on San Nicolas? I touched its whiskers, black and milky white: they were as long and stiff as the quill of a hawk feather, only with a finer point. Flies lifted from the fecal spill that had dried on the sand. From the raspberry cave of its open chest sprawled a mound that also looked like black tar. Intestines. All things come to tar.

I had to climb a minor spur of bluff to get around the rising tide, and I took off my shoes at the top so that I could land shin deep in the waves. The beach continued another five minutes to a cove below the headland, that famous demarcation between north and south, or at least California's farthest point west, the point of no return. Conception.

Even from the beach, it looked like a duck's head, with its bill resting on the ocean. Still I couldn't see the lighthouse, which was disappointing after three or four miles of walking. Only a series of antennas and the green roof of a building, maybe a caretaker's shed. But again, probably it's not the worst thing to miss out on a view of the Western Gate, that threshold to elsewhere. Even if that name is a modern invention. In the sloshing waves were the heads of sea lions like marble buoys. Those eyes, they slay. They are tar. I had read that the waters around Point Conception are extra sharky because of the converging currents and the prominence, and wondered if a great white had hit the lion, but it had wrestled away to bleed out and wash up into these pages.

JALAMA IS DREAMLIKE, MORE SO even than most of the California coast. I could have stayed many days. But the Portolá expedition kept on. They kept along the coast, but I had made no arrangement with the air force and so turned inland on Jalama Road, crossing the tracks toward *Xalam* with my REI bundle on my back. Back at Refugio, Paul had described the road out as a winding deathtrap, a racetrack for surfers. But I had seen worse already, and I would see worse later. To be honest, I was happy to deviate from the sea, so beautiful but mind-numbingly so. Whenever I stay along the coast, after a short while it feels as if my brain has been steeped in brine and preserved in a bell jar, and I have to escape inland to reclaim it.

Nineteen miles to Lompoc. Scrub-jay territory: that particular spread-wing glide into toyon, that sheer blue dive off a telephone wire. Also the *szee* of a gnat-catcher. The *keer* of a flicker lifting, white-rumped, from where it had been pillaging the ants that give fire to its shafts through their carotenoids. The grumpy *chit* of a wrentit, the bright, earnest *tre-dick* of a western tanager migrated from Central America. Elderberry leaves blighted and black, live oak in the swales between the road's turns. *Fuck Cancer*, read a sticker on a yellow reflector. California walnut, leaves turning. Almost September now. Walnuts along the shoulder where they had fallen and tumbled across the road, green and fleshy as apples. Cottonwood appeared farther inland. The potholes were patched with asphalt squares as if tar had been skimmed right off the beach and pressed into them with a roller. Sun-dwarfed poison oak grew through the barbwire that, in form, began to look like the mustard and its bees. Kestrel calling, and a jay imitating it right after. Everything ties together.

This land is not pristine, but it is rich. Cow patties lay just over the Cojo-Jalama fence and in dry creek crossings. Some of the hillsides were laced and tiered with the ruminants' trails. I admired the hammock of their midsections. Their bellies are so low slung, and their spines form troughs that might hold water; they seem bred to sag. Big round tags in their left flicking ears. When two red cars drove by, some cattle all at once decided to trot, away from me, jostling, and the finches feeding behind them—feeding on whatever insects they stirred up—flushed. A Caldera Hay Service truck arrived at the Jalama Ranch with a towering delivery and a forklift to unload. It seemed absurd that they couldn't get their own hay from this place.

The weather does the work of clippers in the chaparral. The gray day started to clear, to lose its coastal influence. Washboard laughter of acorn woodpecker. Windrows of burr in the road shoulder's grass, each like a miniature hay bale with spikes. Along the roadside I found several pretty good chunks of chert, a flintlike rock the Chumash worked to points. I had seen other nodules on the beach, each with an outer layer like the rind on a good cheese, which showed how it had co-alesced in a cliff pocket. Portolá's men had availed themselves of it at their next campsite in Cañada Agua Vida, inside today's Vandenberg: "Here the soldiers came upon a great many very good flint-stones for striking a light, which almost everyone provided himself with, for his weapon." Crespí named it *San Juan Bautista de los Pedernales*—"of the Flintstones." Beyond Arlight lies a Point Pedernales. From the day Europeans stepped foot into what would become Vandenberg, it was a military resource.

I found myself fond of those passing drivers who raised an index finger or a hang-loose or a peace sign, and I had absolutely no thoughts about the others. The UPS man cruised by me both to and from his delivery at the Jalama Beach Store. When I flipped over an Amazon Prime box on the shoulder, it crawled inside with daddy longlegs—must have been thirty of them all together in that shady home, like a few handfuls of clipped hair. But the one consistent item of trash was the empty beer can: people jump-starting their beach vacation or finishing it up. Manzanita grew at the pass, where I imagined *Xalam* might have been, and down the back side were the first lonely examples of tan oak and madrone on this trip, as if a stray bird had dropped a few seeds. So this was Northern California after all.

I tucked into a lima bean field for the night off State Route 1, here called Cabrillo Highway, along Salsipuedes Creek. *Sal si puedes*, leave if you can. The field was maybe an acre and a half—not even as large as a baseball field—hidden by elderberry, coffeeberry, willow, and poison oak. No ranch house in sight. I had walked a quarter mile past the opening, until I decided I wasn't going to make Lompoc. The field seemed a solid bet: there would be space at the edge, out of sight. Anyone but the owner would blast right by the field's entrance before they even knew the plot was there. The beans petered out along the brush line, and I smoothed several empty furrows flat with my sneaker, just enough for my tent. The cup and a quarter of water for my couscous boiled in about one minute. Ate several graham crackers for dessert—a couple at Jalama had given me their s'more leftovers—and watched the darting headlights through the roadside trees, briefest white. The crickets were a shadow traffic in the oaks behind me. The night rustled with rodents in the withered poison oak hedge: lima bean thieves sharpening their knives. A strong scent like store-bought fertilizer, wafting under my tent fly. The plants were breathing and growing.

THE THREE MILES INTO LOMPOC were punctuated by roadkill: my first and last rattlesnake, black, mushed, torn in two. Someone or something had pilfered the rattle. A female California quail with its scaled chest. I had been hearing their clucks and *Chi-ca-go*s in the elderberry brush. A coyote, I think, only its stiff legs revealed and splayed from a shroud of grass. And a hummingbird, an Anna's. I cried out a little "Oh" as I lifted the bird from the curbside. Ants streamed out of its eyes and crawled across my left palm as I turned it. One eye gone, the other a gray sunken disk. White-tipped tail feathers, the rectrices or "governors." Its olive-iridescent back was tinged with orange like smoky moonlight on a green sea. Its forehead was as scaled as the snake's. Slightly decurved bill. I could have packed this animal all the way home and never noticed its weight. I walked into Lompoc with it curled inside my cold left hand, just an empty husk.

The ruins of the first Mission La Purísima are on the south side of town, at the end of the cul-de-sac that is F Street, in a quiet Lompoc neighborhood. RVs are parked in driveways, kayaks are stashed in ruby bottlebrush bushes, and wicker patio furniture sits before windows with lace curtains. At the end of F Street—F for finished, F for fallen, F for Franciscan, F for flowers—you find the church door. It still stands, though the sky is now its head. They say a door frame is the safest place to be during an earthquake, apart from being outside, and this one, having no upper frame, is safe now. Cacti and other thorny succulents adorn the base of one side, and both jambs now seem like memorial pillars. The thorns keep off the climbers the way they keep rogue pickers from the orange groves. The stone is the same I saw in the road cuts traveling from Jalama: sandstone, limestone, and flint. Tiles and brick had been wedged into the masonry to fill chinks or level the stacks, and it's hard for the lay eye to know when these or the concrete mortar date from. It is a conglomeration of conglomerate, a patched-up ruin, and in this way the most authentic thing around.

I crouched in the shade of one of these broken jambs, right where the heavy wooden doors would have hung with their wrought-iron ornaments and ring handles. A scratch card, "Poker Night," was hidden in a chink, folded in half and then in half again—not a winner, I presume—like a secret note or a prayer left in a wishing wall. Playing cards were depicted on it, aces and spades. The railroad tracks run through this neighborhood, too, right where the old south wall of the mission's quadrangle stood. You also can see some of the aqueduct along the railbed's banks; live oaks grow from half-buried stones. People, I observed, had pieces of *Misión Vieja* in their yards, lining their front walkways and flowerbeds. What was left of the mission was disseminating through the neighborhood, slowly.

Serra's successor, Father Lasuén, founded *Misión La Purísima Concepción de María Santísima* on December 8, 1787. It was the eleventh mission in Alta California, and the usual features and faults came along with it. Several thousand Chumash were baptized here, including people from *Xalam* and *Shilimaqshtush*, from which I'd come. The mission's lands stretched almost 470 square miles from the Gaviota coast to the south and to the Santa Maria River to the north, my direction. The Chumash huts had been on the hillside, stretching toward a reservoir filled by an aqueduct from Miguelito Canyon a tad to the west. Their homes were traditional, tule or bulrush bent over willow—"half oranges" as Crespí called them. The neophytes knelt on the church's tiled floor, men on one side, women on the other, as Mass was said. Then they went to the fields along the Santa Ynez River and did real penance with digging sticks in the sun.

ALMOST TWENTY-FIVE YEARS TO THE day after La Purísima's founding, an earthquake, along with aftershocks and a drenching December rain that caused mudslides, devastated the mission. The exposed adobe liquefied before the padres' eyes, and they gave up on it, requesting permission to rebuild on the north side of the valley in a more favorable spot, *La Cañada de los Berros*, the Canyon of the Watercress. More water there, and it would help streamline the El Camino Real. So I walked five miles across town, past a mural that showed the "Last of the Titans" in a roiling blastoff of flame and smoke—intercontinental missiles launched from silos in Vandenberg—and trudged through the sandy, dry, and rutted Santa Ynez River to the new La Purísima. Now a State Park, it has been painstakingly restored and is described as the most authentic of the missions, because it eschews fanciful gardens for ground-squirrel holes and simple period furniture. It's also one of only two missions not owned by the Catholic Church.

Inside the sanctuary, I met a State Park ranger about to finish a long Saturday filled with tourists. There were no pews, true to those early days. A humidifier hummed like a soda machine in one corner, keeping those heavy beams overhead from drying out. The church still had about half its original tile floor, now subsided a great deal. "I keep thinking that they'll open up and swallow me someday when I'm sweeping in here," said the ranger. She was locking up and shooed me out, but, she said, I could probably see most of the buildings if I stayed ahead of her. Rather than a quadrangle, the mission ran in a long line below the hill on Los Berros Canyon's north side. Why they chose this anomalous design isn't clear, but it may have been to reserve the farmland at the mission's doorstep or make its buildings less of a deathtrap in case of another earthquake. It's also possible that by 1813 the padres felt that the threat of an Native attack from without had disappeared.

La Purísima was resurrected in 1934 when the Civilian Conservation Corps, funded by the New Deal, arrived to recreate the crumbled mission in two senses: design and method. They excavated the foundations, mapping its layout and materials. Then they molded adobe from the overburden, dug clay from nearby hills to fashion tiles, and carved and wrought the wood and iron pieces in shops on site with tools like adze and whipsaw. The Union Oil Company had deeded the land to Santa Barbara County in 1933, and La Purísima, still isolated and pastoral, became a state historical monument in 1941. As the architect who oversaw the mission's reconstruction in the thirties, Fred Hageman, observed, "Enthusiasts foresee for La Purísima Concepción not merely a mausoleum of a vanished epoch, but a revivified bit of the past; a tranquil little valley where time has been turned back and shall stand forever still at the most romantic and colorful period of California's history." It is sometimes called "the Williamsburg of the West" for its meticulous and faithful reconstruction, as well as its interpretive actors.

Inside the barracks, a word that comes from the Spanish *barraca* for "soldier's tent," I found two of these volunteers dressed as resident men-at-arms. One them was a *soldado de cuero* as would have accompanied Portolá; the other wore nineteenth-century attire. The leather vest the first man wore was longer than I had imagined, trimmed with red and far thinner than the seven-layer ply Portolá's men wore on their expedition through Alta California. A sword rested on his right hip, a flintlock on his left. His blue coat had red cuffs and gold sleeve stripes that bore rank on the forearm. His hat was broad and brown with a red ribbon band.

Four cots lined the wall with woolen blankets, and above them, on pegs, hung tack and rifles. The barracks also served as their stable, with room for six horses, and as the jail. Whoever was on duty, *soldado* Ron explained, would have to be ready to ride at a moment's notice if a message arrived from Mission Santa Inés, a day's walk east in the valley, or Mission San Luis Obispo, a half day's ride to the north. There was a rack of lances against the wall tied with orange and yellow flagging. Each shaft had a leather thumb loop two-thirds of the way toward its butt, which a soldier could use to hold on, if the lance was tucked under his arm, or to generate power if it was thrown. There were also playing cards on a table, a deck with forty cards, Ron told us, ace through seven and all the face cards, except for the queen. "Sexist jerks," quipped another tourist in the room, a woman. "Sorry," she followed up, with a chuckle. Most of the cards' corners were bent and ripped, which would have gone a long way toward corrupting this particular game.

We were swept out of the barracks by the State Park ranger, the new enforcer. Five o'clock, time to saddle up. Her keys jangled on her belt loop like a bell. "Are you going to load that stuff up in the car?" *soldado* Ron asked the other man in costume, as they packed their rucksacks. "Aren't you supposed to say, 'Are you going to load that up on a horse?'" said that same sharp woman, the feminist. I appreciated her.

TO MY SURPRISE, I ALSO found a gathering of mountain men at La Purísima, an incongruous encounter, I thought, and they outnumbered the mission-era actors. Their camp was around a lofty cottonwood in front of the arcade or *corredor* of the long Padre's Residence, where their bedrolls were laid out and a campfire smoldered. Apparently, twice a year, a dozen or more card-carrying members of the AMM—the American Mountain Men—gathered here at La Purísima, a small "rendezvous" as they go. School groups would visit during the week to see about them and bygone days. Tomorrow these unshaven trappers would disband, back into the woods, so to speak. They wore leather and powder horns, the leg bones of the first bobcat they'd ever snared, beaver teeth, and lord knows what else. All of it had to have existed in the first half of the nineteenth century. The fur trade was mainly farther north and in the Rockies, but it ranged to New Mexico and into California. "A lot of trappers would come down to this mission," said one mountain man named John, who had retired, indeed, to the mountains outside San Diego. "Kit Carson was here during his heyday. They would come to these missions like this, and of course the padres would treat'm pretty good, and they'd trade hides, because they needed them here; and the padres would give'm food and wine, and they could stay for a while and get themselves rested in relative safety, and then they'd head back up into the hills." Nowadays, it occurred to me, someone could make a living, or at least gather many skins, just walking the roads for the animals wrecked and abandoned on its shoulders.

I struck up a conversation with Raul, pronounced Rowl—the towns are not the only anglicized names in California. He had protruding eyes and tended to squint as he talked, drawing crow's-feet under the brim of his felt cap, which was decorated with an upright buck's tail on the forehead. His red flannel tunic didn't make him look as portly as some of the other mountain men. He stood in the corner of the mission's small rear courtyard with his hands rested around the barrel of his black-powder rifle, its butt resting on the red clay tile of the walkway.

Raul wasn't official AMM, but his brother, Art, was fairly zealous. In fact, Art was the other uniformed role player I had just met in the barracks. Raul couldn't stomach dressing up as a Spanish soldier, so he was in the guise of a Native trapper, in my estimation the most palatable of these characters and also the truest outsider. Raul had resisted his brother's encouragement for a long time, thinking dressing up was too hokey. But for a while he had owned a herd of seventy goats and sheep that were hired to clear brush. He and the drove would clip a tangled acre in three or four days. Sometimes he'd spend weeks on a large job. "The sheep I had were the original Spanish sheep. Those things could survive on this"—he swung his arm toward the chaparral beyond the mission wall. "They won't get big, but they'll live." His herd was an ecologically friendly mower, a good means of fuel reduction for fire protection.

"I'd go into the blackberries, and my legs would get so cut up it looked like a hundred cats had scratched them all up. One day I just had this idea, 'Man, these mountain men wore all these things to go through the brush—I wonder if that would work in my job?'" Online, he found a supply company and ordered up some leather pants. In essence, he bought American chaparajos. The duds worked, and he began to order more clothes. "Next thing you know," said Raul, "slowly but surely I got involved with it. But I'm still not really . . . I'm not part of the organization. I do like hunting and trapping and things like that, but I'm a trucker, I own my own truck, so I really don't have a whole lot of time."

In particular he grew interested in the Indian-Mexican trappers, seldom acknowledged, since he has Apache blood and his Mexican grandfather is probably Yaqui, of the Sonoran Desert. "The Mexicans take one look at me and call me '*Indio*,'" said Raul. His grandfather on the other side moved to Lompoc to work for Southern Pacific, and much of the family followed. "I had three uncles laying track, one was working what's called 'bridge gain' . . . painting the bridges and everything . . . and another uncle was working in dispatch." Perhaps a sign of the changing times, Raul had been a trucker since age twenty-two. He gave up shepherding when feral dogs dug into his goat enclosure and killed much of his herd. "I had so much more fun herding," said Raul, "and it was so peaceful and calm."

After he'd lost his sheep and goats—and, I take it, his wife and home, since he had mentioned two daughters—Raul had lived in the hills a few miles out of town for six months. "The main thing is to move often. Don't leave garbage, keep a clean camp. I needed to be near town because I'd drive in every day looking for work. I had a nice chainsaw and I'd work on the fire crews." Raul had been a real mountain man, for a time. Now he mainly runs to Southern California, loads from a cooler into his forty-eight-foot trailer at nightfall as I'd seen truckers do at the Santa Paula lemon plant, and hauls produce to where it's needed, one step closer to your kitchen. "Cabbage, lettuce, squash, strawberries, broccoli, cauliflower . . . those are the big six." He'd worked in the fields as well, picking strawberries and cutting their runners. "A cabbage or a strawberry will go through a lot of hands before it gets to someone's table," said Raul. He marveled they weren't more expensive.

I had thought aloud about pitching my tent off to the side and shooting the breeze or a flintlock with the mountain men around their campfire. Probably I should have done that. But I felt and looked like I didn't belong, and I was ever conscious of the need to keep on and not fall too far behind Portolá. I was taking a long detour from the coast and needed to make time. Raul suggested I walk the Mission Road.

"What road?" I asked.

"The hiking trail," Raul said, pointing behind us, "which goes toward Mission Hills."

It wasn't on my map, but it was the old El Camino, which began at the padres' doorsteps and went up Los Berros Canyon. This remnant had been paved at some earlier time, but now it was returning to dust and sand. Bearded lichen grew in the oak at the meadows' darkening edges. After about a mile the fields ended at the Mission Hills water treatment plant, where fountains aerated the ponds. I bought a beer and two Gatorades at Mission Hills Market, a convenience store. Up Rucker Road I ducked into a scrubby ecological reserve, as the yellow signs declared it. Again the brush filled my pockets with leaves and twigs as I waded through chamise and into manzanita with peeling bark the hue of dried blood, with my hands above my head. In the morning, I buried the hummingbird I'd been carrying in the sand where I had slept, not far from the road.

UP HARRIS GRADE ROAD, THROUGH the Lompoc Oil Field, with Vandenberg's scattered launchpads visible in the distance beyond dumped mattresses and rare bishop pines. I crested the summit of the Purisima Hills and plunged down the back side toward Santa Maria, still far off. "IT'S . . . ALL . . . DOWN . . . HILL," some cyclist had spray-painted along the white stripe. Fire had torn across the road, releasing seeds from the bishop cones, and just down the embankment I found the records of someone's life, as if she had thrown them off the edge or these papers had been stolen and discarded. There was a birth certificate, and snapshots of smiling children, and school portraits, and even a sonogram from the Santa Barbara County Health Department of a fetus with its nose and mouth in profile. "Girl," it said. There was a portrait of a baby, perhaps the same girl a year later, in a Hello Kitty dress with a ball cap tilted on her dark hair. Her rubber-band arms had clenched fists, fierce for life. Her eyes also fierce. A little pugilist. This photo came in various sizes, and was repeated on one sheet, wallet size. Two of eight had been cut out. I wondered who had them now. Who she was, if she was.

I have since read about a legend of the Harris Grade Road, about a woman named Agnes whose car broke down, so she started walking with her baby, only to be hit by a car as she tried to flag it down. She was killed on impact, but the driver had not seen her baby in the darkness. When the police identified her and realized she was a mother, they searched for her child, imagining the terrible scenario. But the baby was never found, if she had been there at all. Agnes, it's said, has since wandered the road looking for her child. Looking at these photos then, and looking at them now, I can't help but think of all the lost people of the road. I can't help but think about the hundreds of roadside crosses I passed on my way to San Francisco, and the others I didn't notice, and of the people buried in the mission cemeteries, and of the people dumped in ditches, both real and metaphorical, and never known. Who are you?

I DESCENDED TO RASPBERRIES IN hoop houses in Harris Canyon. Millions of raspberries and probably dollars. The white hoop houses looked the part of a quarantine in a sci-fi movie, but all they were meant to do was provide warmth, constancy, for an alien species. I ate only one; or honestly, I can't recall. Through fields of broccoli and crushed lettuce, and up the endless grade of Highway 135 past the south entrance to Vandenberg, eventually I reached an overpass where I sat in the shade on the broken half pipe embedded in pavement that carried runoff down the sandy embankment. My feet burned from the uphill trudge in long-dirty socks.

On the guardrail were layers of guano, and when I glanced up, expecting to see pigeons, instead there were the empty *hornos* of cliff swallows, rows of homes. They had built them along the downhill side of the concrete overpass, which is where Route 1 joins 135—I had just returned to the Cabrillo Highway. Here, I thought, were the swallows gone from Capistrano, nesting under one of the state's busiest roads with a view of teal broccoli fields that looked like pools they could dive low over to gather hatching insects. I thought the swallows were all gone, but then I heard a *veep veep* from a nestling, and saw the adult, with its pale "headlight" forehead, in the washed-out blue, flying as if carefree. It seemed to dance, but it had an absolute mission: feed the brood. This bird was the last holdout. I wondered if its first clutch, and maybe its second, had failed and so it had laid again and now was here alone, the others dispersed. I imagined their whitewash falling onto the windshields of the swollen trucks that cause this overhang to echo and roar; and I liked imagining some of those drivers seeing the birds for an instant, noticing them as they dropped from their nests with spread wings, and wondering about them as their rigs blew downhill.

The cars on Route 1 bent toward Orcutt, making a *woosh, woosh . . . woosh* overhead as their tires revolved over a new surface, one scored for traction in the rain or fog. Across 135, a tractor went back and forth pulling a tiller that raked leftover lettuce into the dirt, raising dust. I could see soil pouring over the side behind it like the wake from a boat, burying the lettuce, or was it cabbage, that hadn't made the grade or had been spoiled by insects. On the hill above the flats, vineyards were like contour lines on a strange topographic map; they showed the form of the hill, but masked it, too, as svelte as corduroy. The swallows pilfered their mud from those fields, I thought, from irrigation ditches or the wet puddles between the rows, and then they placed that mouthful just so under this overpass. Probably the State or County will come by and power-wash their nests and they'll have to build their cliff village all over again. They already had: I could see the faint outlines of many former homes, long gone. But they had returned.

Uphill I could see white trucks with blue porta-potties on their trailers in the rolling strawberry fields, the ground-cover plastic just visible in patches. SOLICITAN PISCADORAS, a sign had said at a gate a few miles back. Even on a Sunday, the pickers were squatting in sun hats that could be seen from a half mile off with my naked eye. White buses had passed me on the long descent toward Harris Grade:

ELKHORN PACKHOUSE, said a few, and the others BIP TRANSPORTATION. They had arrived to take everyone back to Santa Maria at the end of the day. I thought then of how Raul said he would sample the strawberries, while picking, to see which tasted "like tuna" and which were sweet as day. I thought of how many I had eaten without a thought in my life.

In drifted the cliff swallow, slow and fluttering, to the only occupied home on the overpass, while its juveniles called with a fast, metronomic ticking. Below were spots on the pavement where droppings had fallen and been worn to a faint spackle by passing tires. Thick on the guardrails, though.

THE SANTA MARIA VALLEY IS one of the great agricultural valleys of California, which means it's one of the great agricultural valleys of the world. To be amid so much flat cropland: your location changes but never seems to. The hills rotate around you as if you were the center, the sun, the god of some universe. A second later you feel smaller than ever, and hungry. My shadow with its big-brimmed hat cast itself on quivering lettuce and broccoli as if it were already inside me, the rotten heads and those useless stems and leaves soon to be churned under in the sharp flash of a tractor. And strawberry, fragrant and lowly strawberry, whose white plastic, in the right light, from a distance, looks like a flooded playa or a mirage.

On my way to Guadalupe Lake, where I would rejoin the Portolá expedition's route, I passed a Waste Management center, and paused in its driveway to watch the machines lift trash into a gigantic bin. Quickly a man strode up and told me I couldn't be where I was without a hard hat. Sure, I said, I was just walking by and would only watch for a minute.

"Yeah, no worries," he said, "just be careful, all right?"

I lingered another minute, and then a woman with a walkie-talkie confronted me.

"Sir, can I help you?"

"Oh, I was just curious, I was just watching the operation," I said.

"Yeah," she replied, "but it's a little dangerous."

"Oh, they already told me, but they said if I just stand right here I'd be okay."

"Okay, yeah ... because we don't allow somebody to walk around or be without a vest around the loaders."

I don't know what came over me, but I asked: "Any chance I could get a tour of the operation if I put on a vest and signed some forms, or something? Do you do that kind of thing?"

"I do . . . I do that kind of thing, if you want to do it . . . uh, and you want to do it right now, right?"

The generosity of people never fails to impress me. Leticia was the plant's supervisor, and she guessed she could spare a few minutes to give me a quick tour, though I might well be a tramp. Short, with black bangs sweeping down her forehead, she wore jeans and a black "WM" T-shirt. Waste Management is an enormous company, one I grew up with in the Bay Area. I recognized its green and yellow, which seems to take its cue from the oak and grass of California. But not really. "We have Waste Management everywhere," said Leticia. Trash is an enormous business. Started in 1893 by a Dutchman who hauled garbage in Chicago for a buck twenty-five a wagon, and now headquartered in Texas and publicly traded, WM has an annual net income of nearly 2 billion. With 26,000 trucks, it services 22 million people and businesses. The glass and aluminum crashing into its trucks' holds is the robin song that wakes you up once a week.

This place was an MRF, Leticia told me, a *merf*, a materials recovery facility: a recycling center. She let me drop my pack in her office and gave me a hard hat that rode high on my head; it was the closest I would come to a soldier's helmet on my journey, I thought. She also gave me clear protective glasses, which I traded for my sunglasses so I could study the warehouse's low-light bowels. Twenty people worked from six to two thirty inside this two-story maze of stairs, platforms, and conveyor belts. It first carried the recycling up to a second level, slowly, like the ascent of a roller-coaster ride, all anticipation and held breath. "In there, it's too loud, so I'll tell you a few things here," said Leticia as we paused out front. "This is our residential pile," she explained. It was an avalanche of debris spilling from the open mouth of a hangar. Commercial was on the other side. The pile was "single-stream," meaning it hit the curb in one blue bin and Waste Management did the rest. Yet what did it mean that this was one of the largest and fastest-flowing streams in the region, as Leticia told me? There was no visible water in the Santa Maria River, or in the Santa Ynez, but here was world-class consumption and sorting.

On the upper level, the stream went through pre-sort, where workers pulled oversized and heavily soiled items, and other immediate discards like plastic bags. Lots of it was sordid, gross with food, unrinsed. "People are lazy, or they forget," I said. "Nah, they don't forget," said Leticia. Red-spattered pasta jars, or tubs with decayed red baby lettuce adhered by its own leakage, all of it gets tossed. Then the cardboard was floated off on finned plates that held it aloft like rafts on waves. The rest sank to another conveyor. Newspaper was siphoned off. Three women were tasked with plastic bottles: the first with clear bottles, the second with colored, the third with milk jugs. All cast into separate pneumatic chutes. "This one here," said Leticia, "you're not going to believe what they become." She pointed to your average clear water or soda bottle, Plastic #1, PETE. She waited for me to guess.

"Clothes?" I offered finally.

"Yes! Anything that is polyester is made out of this. Socks, boxers, jackets." Bath sponges and beer Koozies. Patagonia, North Face—some of my own ware, and my backpack, might have touched your lips before it was turned to pellets and stretched into fiber. Colored plastic becomes playground equipment, Leticia said, and I thought of the dolphin slide in Carpinteria, of the hundreds of slides I had passed in the suburbs of Southern California. Milk jugs are used for freeway plastic, like reflectors. But most plastic is thrown out, or out to sea: less than 9 percent is recycled in the United States.

An electric current whisked aluminum away. Eventually it would be packed in bales weighing nine hundred to a thousand pounds, thirty-two cans to a pound, Leticia said. Which means a bale holds thirty thousand cans. Tin was captured by magnet. Everything was baled by the same packer and stacked outside like giant Legos, waiting for a truck or a tanker that would float it over the ocean. Anheuser-Busch bought the aluminum. China bought all the paper and cardboard. Leticia sent a shipment to port every day. It took three months to cross. "I don't think we have nothing here in the United States that can do what they do over there," said Leticia.

As for the glass, it was shattered in the truck's compactor during pick-up and tinkled musically as it flowed over the conveyor belt, before it was swept off, somehow—I couldn't keep track of everything—into another bin to be sorted by color at another facility. Green, amber, clear.

Some of this scrap might have passed me yesterday or that day on my walk from Lompoc, which was one of the MRF's service areas, along with Vandenberg, Santa Ynez, and Guadalupe. Leticia had me step up on the truck scale, where each load was measured. One hundred sixty, read the red digital screen. I was shocked at the weight I'd lost until she explained it only registered increments of twenty, though probably I had thinned from walking each day: walking past the assorted paper blowing through the grass, and the bottles and cans, which would never decay, bottles and cans filled with sour soda and piss and centipedes. Then a recycling truck pulled up on the scale: 42,280. I shivered to think of the amount of trash and recycling Leticia had laid eyes on as it blurred by on the belts and as California's appetite steadily increased. Santa Maria had boomed, she said. Many strawberry fields have become houses, and they all have fridges and garages rife with containers.

Leticia had started as a sorter, eighteen years ago, and now she was the boss with forty-seven employees. "*¿Que pasó?*" she asked as she passed them on the line. Such fast hands, tough work on your feet. She'd done her part. As we returned to her office, she pointed to a golf cart. "That's my golf cart," she said. It was her only admission of pride. If someone radioed, she'd zip around the plant to help. Before I left, we took a photo together. She hated photos, but was willing. She almost smiled, but didn't. Then she offered me a bottle of water from a bulk carton, Plastic #1.

THE PORTOLÁ EXPEDITION TRAVELED FIVE days on the coast before they reached Guadalupe Lake, and they found that stretch lightly populated. Reading between the lines in Crespí's journal, I sense or imagine some tension between Portolá and his scout Ortega on the second day's march from Jalama. They reached the proposed campsite, and it boasted water but no grass for the animals—all of it had been burnt off. That was as far as Ortega and the scouts had gone. Portolá ordered the whole party to continue on, blindly, over dunes, until at last light—a scenario that sounds familiar to me—they arrived at a hollow with grass but no stream or spring. "A halt was ordered here, as the sun was already setting; . . . [we] managed with a good deal of toil to get a little muddy water for making griddle cakes." They had carried some *agua* from their camp at the stream of the flint stones, luckily. I imagine the soldiers passing the casks or bladder bags with apprehension, though they had been told by their Native escorts that a river lay ahead.

Reaching Ocean Beach the following day, they found that river, the Santa Ynez, which runs west between the San Rafael and the Santa Ynez Mountains. Its headwaters are northeast of Santa Barbara and, after passing through Lompoc, it finally reaches the sea. This river, which Crespí named *El Río de San*

Bernardo y sus Santos Compañeros, defines and drains much of Santa Barbara County; in turn, three reservoirs now define it. Here at its mouth, in 1769, the river was fourteen or sixteen yards wide at its narrowest and "came up to their saddle flaps." Groups from two villages visited them and vied for attention, entreating the Spaniards to come in their direction. "These poor wretches set great store by the beads," Crespí wrote in his next entry, a rare dismissive note and a hint that he was tiring of this daily game, these repetitive exchanges. Among the dancers the next night were two women, a first. "They were dressed in the usual deerskin skirts from the waist downward," recalled Crespí, "with the rest of their bodies heavily painted in all hues, and wearing feather headdresses, so that they looked like so many demons." Costansó's take was quite different: "Two of these excelled the others; they had a bunch of flowers in their hands, and accompanied the dance with various graceful gestures and movements without getting out of time in their songs." The soldiers duly honored the spot as *La Ranchería del Baile,* the Village of the Dance.

Guadalupe Lake, *Laguna Larga,* was their next camp. Today it can be found at a crossroads called Betteravia, after the French word for sugar beets, a onetime company town now evaporated. Betteravia once held 350 people, most of whom worked for the Union Sugar Company and its farm. They were evicted in the sixties, and most moved their homes with them, sold to them for fifty dollars. The refinery building, its rust-streaked silos, and an intimidating furnace stack loom over the vast agricultural plain of Santa Maria, and beneath them I imagined the pale mountains of sugar beets, and the rank odor floating over the fields from them and the wastewater ponds, and the pure crystal loaded into train cars. Thirty percent of the world's sugar still comes from these white tubers.

Now the short-line Santa Maria Railroad, which once did the hauling, has its headquarters and railyard on the dilapidated Union beet factory property, and I strode quickly past the links of spray-painted cars toward the eucalypti of the lakeshore, so as not to be seen or chased out. There was no lake. Down the steep embankment were fields where the lake had been. "The lake here," Crespí wrote, "has very delicious, pure fresh water, and is said by the heathens to be very deep and steep too, having a great deal of tule-rush beds around it, and is fed, or so we understand, by large springs in its midst. There are a great many large ducks in it." The lake was over a mile long, Crespí estimated, and hundreds of yards wide. Why had it dried up? Likely the springs have disappeared as Santa Maria Valley's wells pump water to the vegetables planted to the horizon. Pipes now bring this water down the shelf to the former lake bottom, where they split to either black drip-irrigation tubing or central metal pipes that feed sprinkler heads two feet off the ground.

Across the basin stood a row of cars, with windshields lit like diamonds, where the field hands were working a block. I crashed through the eucalypti, their scythes and shadows, to a road along the empty lake's edge and, walking east a minute, found a cell dammed by a berm: still reedy, wet in places, a remnant. Then I descended to where they labored in the lake's memory. Several men were readying a limp black main-line hose, which would send water to each row. One of them, named Israel, inserted a short length of irrigation tubing into one of the main line's unused pores—those valves in between the rows—folding it in half, crimping it with wire. It seemed a lot of work to create a plug. All the in-between, I thought, is suppressed in commercial agriculture.

On the far side of the lake bed, women hoed surplus young lettuces. Bandannas or collars were stretched over their mouths as the dust rose. They'd cull one, maybe two, of the flickering green shoots with a gentle, efficient sweep but spare the next, leaving about nine inches between plantings: things must be uprooted for things to grow, or so we tend to think. When one woman finished her row and leaned on her implement, I asked about the variety. Romaine? "Not romaine," she said. "*Como una bolita.*" Like a ball. I tried to explain my purpose, how the first Spaniards had camped here, above us, how we were standing underwater in history. "*Fue un lago aquí en el pasado,*" I said haltingly, "*pero ahora hay solamente lechuga.*" We laughed together. My Spanish was poor and sloppy. The lettuce was a lake distilled.

I expected someone to arrive, to drive up in a cloud and tell me to leave, some foreman. No one did. Rancho Laguna was the name of this farm, Israel told me. "Of course," I replied. Another remnant: Guadalupe Lake had once been at the core of Rancho Punta de Laguna, a twenty-six-thousand-acre grant given to yet another Ortega in 1844. As I undid my trespass and returned to Betteravia Road to head west for the ocean, I ate strawberries that had fallen to the clods, big and warm as hearts and almost glowing with a divine and highly engineered love.

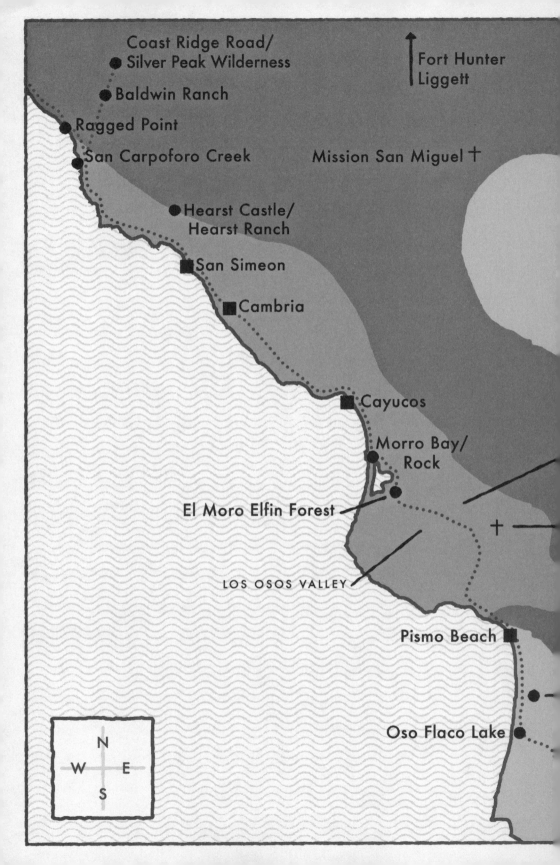

San Luis Obispo County

MORRO MOUNTAINS

Mission San Luis Obispo

Oceano Dunes State
Vehicular Recreation Area

SANTA MARIA VALLEY

I AWOKE IN THE DUNES. The night before, I had walked the road from Guadalupe toward Oso Flaco Lake, but had diverted onto some train tracks to cut a corner—to cut off about a hundred thousand strawberries—and save myself a half mile or so. But the sun plunged into the rolling sand hills over the berries and their runners, time was short, and opportunistically I headed for those dunes and their scrub in search of cover. Pitch a tent on the flats of the Santa Maria Valley and it would be seen for miles. There's not a single tree, unless you count broccoli. I scampered through a ditch where the fields ended shoreward—this was Oso Flaco Creek—and at the tree line stepped through barbwire with one strand cut, enough to squeeze through. Always, it seems, there's one strand cut or snapped somewhere along a fence.

I lifted my pack over after me. In my anxiety, I walked beside the sandy jeep trail instead of on it, past a glen of shooting targets. Then another barbwire fence with another cut wire and a sign, NATIONAL WILDLIFE REFUGE: NO HUNTING, that left me breathing easier. It was illegal to camp here also, but the government wouldn't care. They wouldn't look anyhow. Costs too much. A train passed, the coyotes urging it. In a sedge depression, I tented on a patch of bare ground—there's always one of those, too. Here it was sand. The ocean was vocal but voiceless over the buffy-gray horizon. Stars and pasta, and coyote song.

In the morning, once packed, I wandered the stable hind dunes, empty of all but grasses and sage, rabbit brush and willow copse, red filigreed saxifrage and pink phlox and ankle-biting poison oak, and so not empty at all. I was beckoned forward by the Pacific's white noise until, at the height of one sand swell, there was something like a weather station. A jeep trail service road unspooled from it. I heard beeping in the distance, as if bulldozers instead of wind were moving this sand. To the northwest, bare Saharan pyramids rose, the shoreward parabolic dunes that the Portolá party had negotiated. The road led me to a fence and gate that I scaled back into that endless Santa Maria fertility that only the sand on one side and the mountains on the other had stifled. I was not far from Oso Flaco. No one had missed me while I was lost in the dunes, except maybe Sarah.

In the fields, there is a uniform dictated not only by the sun: a hoodie with a T-shirt over it, a hat underneath that hood, and a bandanna around the mouth. Broccoli dust, broccoli hairs, the squeak of blue latex gloves on rubbery stalks. *Song Hee,* said the boxes that one woman was unfolding from a pallet and popping into shape on a second trailer, one pulled slowly through the field by a tractor on autopilot. It was like a barge drifting on a windswept bay. The crew worked in the glaucous rows beside it. They wore chaps like the hardy bibs of deep-sea fishermen, just one suspender fastened over a shoulder. I could see the glint of their blades— like a barber's razor, with no point—as they pared the leaves and chopped the stem, leaving a nub below the curds. Sometimes they waited until they'd collected three bouquets before tossing them softly onto the trailer with a practiced underhand lob, the crowns suspended an instant before falling to the pile.

The woman packing wore a turquoise hoodie over a pink cap that said *California.* Many of the pickers wear their home squarely on their chests or foreheads: NorCal sweatshirts, ball caps with the Bear Flag. She packed them fast as they came, and firm, stem down, tight so they wouldn't rattle. The wheels of the tractor had broccoli leaves crushed between their swirling treads. The trailer moved forward so slowly you didn't notice at first. The pace of broccoli. The true pace of the food we sweep hurriedly into our carts and mouths. When the trailer that held the full boxes was loaded and cinched, it detached with the tractor, leaving the packing trailer still and alone. The pickers continued to pick and box, the green crowns dwindling until there was nothing left within reach and they could sit in the sun or in the shade under the trailer's wings. The packer tidied by casting the stray florets off to be tilled under, till next time.

OSO FLACO LAKE REMAINS A place of water and bears. *Paraje del Oso Flaco*, the Place of the Lean Bear, was the name the soldiers gave to this spot, though it would seem from Crespí's journal that they did not mean *flaco* in the sense of "thin." Perhaps it also meant "fit." "Through these dunes here," wrote Crespí, "there are a great many tracks of large bears. At the aforesaid small hollow, they [the soldiers] killed one so fearfully and monstrously big that only with a great deal of toil were they able to drag it back to the camp in one piece." They measured its feet: its hind paws were a foot in length. "The toes, soles and forepaws like a human's but with monstrously large digits, the nails alone being not under a good finger thick and three fingers in length. The head, and all of the creature, are a fearful thing to see, with two fangs a finger thick on both sides of its mouth. A bull's head is a small affair beside one belonging to these animals.... God deliver any living creature from their clutches. These huge ones have more meat on them than a large beef has." It was their first encounter with a grizzly.

At the parking lot, a posted flier told me that there were "active" black bears. Another sign warned of cougar. I walked on a wide path into the woods, through a tunnel of trees, past sand-blown fishermen coming off the shore. A pond flowed through a culvert under the trail to the lake, Oso Flaco, held by the dunes, which the soldiers alternately called *Laguna Redonda*; the round blue expanse, which I crossed on a boardwalk, held rafts of algae and tasseled tule, the willows a gyrating wall in the sea breeze. Mallards tipped to forage. Shovelers, cormorants, egrets, herons, coots, terns, marsh wrens, harriers, pied-billed grebes, osprey, and a white pelican that lifted lumbersome as Howard Hughes's *Spruce Goose*, a mere foot above the lake on black primary wing feathers—primaries are often black, because melanin is stronger—before giving up and landing again in a glide.

A boardwalk lets you hover. Lets you levitate. I heard the steps of a family behind me and could tell they had a kid by the exaggerated way the woman said, "Wow, look at those biggg birddds." She asked the boy why he was wearing his cap so low. He couldn't even see the birds; he was in protest. "Just because," he said. "Why are you being a butt-face?" she said. That was a motherly retort I hadn't heard before. But his grandfather was there to lighten the moment. He wore a cycling cap, short running shorts, and had a platinum ponytail. "This is very good skipping material," he said of the boardwalk, "because it's slippery," and off the boy went.

The Portolá party spent a second day at Oso Flaco, resting while the scouts hunted water and a route forward. By this time, they were suffering. Only now does Crespí mention it in his journals. "Ten soldiers have been lame or half crippled in their legs for some days past. Our sergeant, Don Francisco Ortega, fell ill early yesterday morning with stomach pains and an evacuation resembling a fluxus that brought him very low." Scurvy had gripped them, and likely they had nervously awaited the disease's arrival, not just because of the disaster that befell the sailors on their voyage to San Diego earlier in the year, but also because Vizcaíno's account vividly described the affliction.

As we now know, scurvy is the result of a deficiency of vitamin C, which is essential to the enzymes that create and replace collagen, the primary structural protein in our connective tissue. Without vitamin C, this synthetic process falters and stalls, and the body can no longer maintain itself and begins to unglue—"collagen" comes from the Greek for *glue*—from the inside out. The first sign of scurvy is lethargy and then weakness, which becomes aching and swelling. Skin begins to bruise and sores develop, gums soften and bleed, bones grow brittle, teeth loosen and wiggle, one's breath smells of rot. Meanwhile, internal bleeding manifests on the skin as purple blotches. A hemorrhage in the brain or heart is likely to end this misery before the body can fully disintegrate.

In Portolá's day, the common thread of these symptoms and the science behind them wasn't understood. For centuries, scurvy seemed to also "unglue" the knowledge of its remedy whenever it was stumbled upon, a strange societal amnesia. Instead the disease was attributed variously to melancholy, homesickness, fatigue, contagion, seawater or sea air, tobacco, rodents, ancestry, too much or too little exercise, or immorality. Even fresh fruit was inculpated—one of the worst medical opinions of all time. The Portolá expedition pinned their suffering on the fog and cold weather of Northern California, but elsewhere a warm climate has been blamed. It's estimated that scurvy led to the deaths of more than 2 million sailors between the sixteenth and nineteenth centuries. Nations expected that nearly half of all sailors on a long voyage might perish of what Crespí called the Luanda disease. The English Navy was the first to issue lemon juice to all its sailors in 1795, securing a distinct military advantage for a time, and it wasn't until over a century later that the reason for its antiscorbutic property was discovered.

But the cresses the men of the Portolá expedition ate from Oso Flaco Lake staved off the worst, at least temporarily. "Two rainbows came out at sunset last night," Crespí wrote. "We had about two hours of a drizzle." As I walked the board-walk across the lake, an interpretive sign told the story of Rainbow Bridge, an origin myth I'd encountered already on my journey. But here, walking over water, seemed the right place for it: the first Chumash lived on Santa Cruz Island, prop-erly called *Limuw*. But the earth goddess thought that people should also popu-late the great sprawling continent, so she fashioned a rainbow to *Mishopshno*—to Carpinteria—and the islanders began to cross the span, a twenty-four-mile walk through sky. Some reached the coast, but others looked down through the bands of color, and naturally were overwhelmed with vertigo. They lost their balance. They plunged into the ocean. Who knows how long they fell through the air. They be-gan to drown. Their bones must have been broken hopelessly. Yet the goddess took pity on them and transformed them into dolphins. Which is why dolphins are our intelligent ocean shadow; which is why they follow our boats and surf in the lucid bow wakes; and why, it must be, they say nothing about our behavior.

"WE SET OUT AT A half past six in the morning from here at the three lakes of the Holy Martyrs, course northward, through very long, high sand dunes, toward the shore, since it did not allow of taking any other direction without going a long way around. We reached the shore on going about half a league with considerable toil through the dunes, where one kept sinking a good way into the sand." I went as they did from Oso Flaco, except aided by the boardwalk, which continued through the dunes toward the Pacific. Hello again, ocean. How deep are you today, how wide? Gulls shimmied in a rippled creek across the sand, rinsing the salt and drink-ing. It was good to be back after five days in the interior, and I turned up coast, northward, through the wind that pummeled the beach and stripped the sand. I hesitated for a moment because there was a fence across the beach for snowy plovers, but by the water's edge it turned to cable and there was a clear open gate with tire tracks through it. I followed them.

It would have been a lonely few miles except for the Forster's terns, which dove through the lace-curtained green windows of the surf where glinting fish must have appeared. Hundreds of them beating and croaking directly into the wind to steady themselves and this edge of the world. No order to the waves, their staves blown apart and the barrels spilling themselves. Latte to the horizon. Anywhere there are dunes you must often find rough seas. Waves are traveling dunes, and dunes are near-stationary seas. Though I had a chin strap on my gambler hat, I had to tamp it to my head with my hand. Words flew off before they reached the recorder. The foreheadless terns congregated on the sand, ink-masked, with gray Heermann's gulls on the outskirts, all of them staring at the waves as if to confront them. As I approached they lifted en masse, wing tips nearly brushing, a free-form kaleidoscope of near collision, and soon became a coil, a ghost wave, over the shattered breakers. I kept to the highest reaches of wet sand, following the tread marks toward Pismo.

A quarter mile ahead, a red jeep with a pink flag high on a rear antenna drove through another gate and down the beach toward me. The jeep drifted across the beach in front of me and did a U-turn near the high tide mark, and a man leaned out the window, a State Parks decal magnet on his door. "Can you come over here so I can talk to you for a second?" he said. "I'm a contractor with the State Park and, well, you're not allowed to be in here. This is a snowy plover enclosure."

"Oh," I said, "I thought it was okay. A rope was down at the other end and there were tire tracks along the water."

To be honest, I hadn't been sure whether the enclosure was in effect, or not, but I wasn't about to walk any other route, especially, it had seemed, with no one around. As Crespí said about traveling the beach from Oso Flaco, "it did not allow of taking any other direction without going a long way around." Costansó agreed: "There were immense sand dunes along the shore, and on the plain there were creeks, estuaries, and marshes, which formed a labyrinth." Backtracking to circumvent the dunes would have added hours to my day, and traversing the dunes with a pack would have been nearly impossible, a slog for the ages. What's more I had extremely limited water, which made additional miles seem risky.

As the contractor escorted me toward the gate, driving beside me at three miles an hour, I told him about my journey. He told me he monitored plover depredation, had been here some months. I hadn't seen any snowies, I said, but I wasn't looking for them and they would have been farther up the beach. There was no biological or behavioral reason that I shouldn't have been allowed to walk where I had walked, on the wet sand. Snowy plovers don't nest or even typically forage where the tide is a constant boss.

As we neared the gate, two white trucks, these very official looking, drove up with red and blue light bars. "I don't know what's going to happen, partner," the bird monitor said as he peeled off, which did little to reassure me. "All right, man, good luck." It was then that I met Officer Cueto, a State Parks peace officer with a blue uniform and a silver star badge who was, from what I could discern, a dressed-up lifeguard; and Officer Richmond, a blond State Parks officer of the peace in army green with a bulletproof vest under which she tucked her hands to look commanding and keep them out of the biting wind.

"Do you have your car parked over there?" Cueto asked.

"No, I'm walking," I said.

"So where are you walking from?"

"I started in San Diego."

"Oh wow, okay."

"I'm going to San Francisco."

"Did you see the signs on the way in, about the bird enclosure?" he said.

"I saw a rope. I mean, I came from the dunes on the back side of Oso Flaco, but the rope did not extend to the water, so I just walked right by it."

"Did you see the signs that were on the rope?" said Officer Richmond.

"No, I just walked right by."

I was bluffing here, somewhat. I had seen the signs while walking to the beach, but there weren't any signs beside the gate I had passed through. And why would it be left open if the beach were closed?

"Do you have your ID with you?" said Cueto.

Reluctantly I fetched it from my pack, and said, "I didn't veer off the water at all. I didn't go above the mean high tide line, by any means. I know . . . I do know that snowy plovers are in peril, and I know their nesting habits, too, so I was definitely not on the back beach. Nor did I see a snowy plover, but there were tons of terns on the waterline."

Cueto stepped away and left me with Officer Richmond, who was nice enough but glaringly authoritative, a little pumped up behind her vest. But as a woman she no doubt had to be; the macho off-roaders in this area surely gave her hell. "Everything clear and valid with your information?" she asked.

"Sorry, what?" I said, not understanding.

"You don't have any wants or warrants that we need to know about?"

"Oh . . . no."

We stood in silence behind our sunglasses, the wind ripping around us, the sand hissing across our laces.

"So that sound, that bird that was chirping," she said. "That's a tern." It was a nasal ratcheting, somehow melodic.

"Right, I know," I said a bit curtly. "It's not a least tern, though." After a pause, I asked, "Is it usually this windy here?"

"Sometimes."

We were trading perfunctory and ill-tempered replies.

"So how many snowy plovers nest here?" I asked.

"That would be a great question for our resource people. We don't actually have the numbers. I don't have them personally."

"I saw hundreds down in Jalama, just chilling with lots of juvies."

"You sure they were snowy plovers?"

"Hundred percent."

After some silence, I asked, "Do you have a problem with a lot of ATVs going into the bird enclosure?"

"Occasionally," she said. "Most people are pretty good about reading our signs. But occasionally . . . Either a fence will go down, and they'll go in . . . and when that happens, we have to walk the beach making sure there was no damage."

She asked about my walk, and I told her about my project.

"You probably had to cut in from Vandenberg . . . Maybe for Hollister Ranch too . . ."

"I did it in the middle of the night, on the train tracks, which was an experience."

"That is *also* illegal . . ."

"I know."

"Did you almost get hit by a train?"

"No, I saw no train in six hours."

She warned me not to try to walk around Diablo, a nuclear power plant beyond Pismo Beach, though I had already mentioned that I would cut inland to San Luis Obispo. "They have people with very high-power guns that will definitely not allow you to do it, at any time of day or night. I guess you could always try if you want to, but I would highly recommend you not do that. They have their own militia out there. It's kind of crazy, if you talk to them about it.

"What made you decide to do this?" she asked finally.

"I'm a writer . . . I'm writing a book about it. So you'll probably appear in the book."

"Well, it happens. Sometimes I wish it wouldn't be under such horrible circumstances."

"Oh, this isn't so horrible," I said.

"Don't put us in the book," said Cueto as he returned.

"He already said we're going to be in his book."

"*Oh no,*" he pantomimed. "*Officer Cueto gave me a ticket.*"

"Do you have to give me a ticket?" I asked.

"Yeah, I'm afraid we're pretty strict about this enclosure," he said. "In a way, it's to set an example, and in another way, it's to make sure that nobody affects this area."

"In the future," said Officer Richmond, "I would suggest you contact the agencies in the areas in which you're going. It is quite possible that we could have set you up with an escort."

I should have done that, but I hadn't known my route exactly, nor when I would arrive. They didn't know what the ticket would cost me. "It's a fine only," Richmond explained. "San Luis Obispo Court sets the bail amount, so you'll have to work through them. We don't have the bail amount that we can tell you. But you don't have to appear in court . . ."

"I don't think I would, unless I had to," I said.

"Normally you don't tell an officer of the peace that you're not going to show up for something, because they're less inclined to write you a ticket." Instead they arrest you.

"I'll pay the ticket . . ." I said. She had a habit of not listening to the end of your sentences.

I asked Cueto if he knew how many snowy plovers were nesting in the enclosure.

"I don't know. The monitor could give you that info . . ."

They stepped away for a minute and apparently radioed the monitor for an answer: about two hundred this season.

"We just spoke with him," Richmond said, "he said stick close to the waterline on your way out."

I laughed out loud. I had stuck close to the waterline the whole length of the beach. Once again, a reason that so many environmental causes are under siege was made clear. Blind enforcement by people who aren't particularly familiar with the issues or the species they're protecting isn't convincing. Then it seems like someone is just earning a paycheck from a bureaucracy, when actually this sort of conservation work, done right, is crucial. It's something I would walk the whole coast of California for.

"THIS ISN'T NORMAL," A MAN said to me from his plastic lawn chair, with his back to the monstrous wind. He was reading a paperback determinedly. "So you just kind of wait it out, do your best. But everything is fucking covered in sand." His modest pickup and its slide-in camper were just up the beach's slope, diminutive compared to the other RV trailers on the strand. Raptor, Talon, Rager, and Weekend Warrior were just a few of the models close by. Plywood or staked plastic sheeting protected their tires from burial, and their owners had cordoned off their own small enclosures with red rope or flapping caution tape to reserve their territories. Officer Cueto had mentioned that, each weekend, over a thousand RVs flood this beach from the north end, most of those campers here to surf the vast dunes via gasoline: buggies, four-wheelers, jacked-up trucks. Off-highway vehicles, OHVs. Just south of Pismo Beach, Oceano Dunes is a famous State Vehicular Recreation Area: five miles of beach and the dunes behind them, sixteen hundred acres in all. It's the only park in California where you can drive on the beach; thus it attracts recreationalists from all over the county. More than 2 million tourists ride these dunes each year.

On the beach there were trailers to service trailers: trailers with FIREWOOD, $5, and others, like the Banana Cabana, whose ramp gate you walked up to find, inside, a merchandise store with Smashball rackets and Oceano Dunes T-shirts blaring Vegasian sentiments like WHAT HAPPENS IN PISMO, STAYS IN PISMO and SHUT UP & RIDE!

The man reading his paperback in the sand gale told me I could camp on the beach, no problem. "No one checks fucking passes. You could probably just pitch a tent and be good with it. Turn your door backwards."

"Right," I said, "good call. Turn your door backwards."

Otherwise you'd get a face-full of grit before the zipper was halfway down. The wind would billow your tent and rip it out from under you. Something told me that had happened many times at Oceano Beach. Was he an ATVer? "No, not at all," he said. "But this weekend it will be a fucking madhouse. Every Friday and Saturday, it's a madhouse here. Everywhere you look, there's ATVers. And now that this is a three-day weekend, it gets everybody going." He pointed to a big pit he'd dug around his rig, fifteen feet wide and two feet deep. It was filling up again with sand as we spoke. I couldn't tell whether this moat was meant to deter the tide or the ATVers. He didn't say, but no one stops the tide. "It'll be Mad Max city," he said.

I was feeling less than environmental that afternoon, so I decided to join the madhouse and rent a four-wheeler from one of several vendors on the beach. Might as well double down on the day's financial loss, I thought, and see the dunes from their shifting heart. Like officers Cueto and Richmond, this outfitter, Steve's ATV Rentals, asked if my license was suspended. I hadn't used it in seven weeks, so— kind of? I listened to the required informational video, donned a helmet that had a honeycomb breathing vent in its chin, and saddled up on my Honda. A teenage boy turned the thing on for me. Had I ever driven a motorcycle, he asked. No, but I had been on an ATV before. Not in a while though. He showed me how to shift gears, how to use the clutch. And I was off.

Like a boat leaving a wake-free marina, at Oceano Dunes you are allowed to travel only on the back beach and at no more than five miles per hour until, just before Mile Four, the "Open Area" of the dunes materializes in all its raw glory. There I gunned it inland across a sand sheet, a broad expanse where the wind was too strong for dunes to settle. I was letting off steam, leaving those delicate plovers behind. At other places on the beach, incipient dunes begin to build on some wrack or vegetation, soon becoming a long ridgelike foredune that, eventually, might "blow out," crenulating and creating more dunes behind it. But here what are called transgressive dunes rose up, the mythic dunes of desert odyssey and despair: waves of sand slowly traveling inland by as much as thirty feet a year, crescentic or tabular, layered and towering.

I slowed dramatically once I began to climb these. Depending on the light, the crest of one dune blends with the upswell or "stoss" of the dune beyond it, so it was difficult to see a precipice until I was *there*, at the edge of the "slip face": a dune's lee side down which sand avalanches or "slips" at thirty to thirty-five degrees into a trough. From their tire marks, I could see that riders charged up these sheer slip faces and went over their crests. Or they swung up and across the face like a surfer on a wave. But I was afraid of tipping or falling backward. Going too fast or not fast enough, one could easily make a mistake. Hundreds of people are injured at Oceano Dunes every year in vehicle accidents, and a few are killed. All ATVs, buggies, and trucks are required to have an orange flag lofted over their tails, and I understood why now: you can see the flag coming over a beige ridge and avoid collision. One could also get lost, or at least quite turned around. In the troughs, the horizon disappeared, and I found dead ends, unanticipated cul-de-sacs, where the bird enclosure fence met steep dunes. Down the high dunes ran a series of posts numbered 10 through 25, a "sand highway" to help you keep your bearings.

This was a roofless hall of pale, aeolian mirrors: inch-wide ripples on colossal ripples that are hundreds of yards long and fifty or a hundred feet high. The ride was eerily smooth, the sand giving way and cushioning my tires. And while dunes suppress noise, the machine was loud beneath me, lending an industrial soundtrack to the landscape. Riding Oceano was like dropping into a Sahara-by-the-sea, and as I climbed higher and higher the plain of the Pacific became more visible and shining, with the block silhouettes of RVs on the shore. It was easy to imagine them as a colony at the end of society and the world, when petroleum would have to be scavenged from natural seeps. The RVs would become marooned and swamped by winter storms, and people would have to evacuate into the dunes and improvise.

In the twenties and thirties, a bohemian community called the Dunites lived in the more stable, vegetated reaches of the Oceano Dunes. To build their beach shacks, they scavenged wood from a dance hall that, equally whimsically, was built on this flowing sand around the turn of the twentieth century. La Grande Pavilion, it was called. But the well-heeled found it hard to reach this Mission-style club-house and, in 1915, one of its corners was undermined by the wind, collapsing one of its three observation towers like a cupola in an earthquake. It became a ruin. The Dunites gleaned planks from La Grande and, with tar to seal the chinks, built cabins and huts. It was a redoubt from the government and from modernity. They dug wells, burned cow chips, raised modest gardens at the sand's edges, and foraged. The famous Pismo clam, once large and prolific but now undersized and rare, was their primary entrée. To gather them, the Dunites went "dancing for clams," wading in, pushing their heels into the mud and turning them back and forth, drilling down until they felt those clasped shells just underneath. The shallows were their dance hall. They held feasts to foster cerebral conversation, which they called "the

Dune Fire." For a few years, they published *Dune Forum*, an intellectual magazine. Folks like John Steinbeck, Upton Sinclair, and Ansel Adams visited and stayed in a community house that was dubbed Moy Mell, Gaelic for "The Pasture of Honey." It remains a dot on the OHVers' map, but the house is gone.

After Pearl Harbor, the military—an institution entirely antithetical to Dunite philosophy—became a presence in and near Oceano, and when the war ended, a battalion remained stationed to the south at what would become Vandenberg. The dunes themselves began to swallow the Dunite shacks. Then, in the 1960s, vehicles began to drive the beach: the VW, so bohemian now, was to the Dunites an intrusive invention. They were chased out by bigger tires, by a new sound and pace, by renewed scrutiny. But I think of how the Dunites' loss only lightly compares to that of the Chumash, when Portolá's military force first passed through on their own nickering ATVs and the Chumash way of life was soon changed violently. The cycle of colonization and erasure continues its march like sand across the land.

THE PORTOLÁ EXPEDITION WALKED NORTH on the beach, flushing the snowy plovers, and zigged into the dunes to circumvent an inlet that was probably Arroyo Grande Creek. After four hours of walking, they reached a canyon where two streams joined, filled with sycamores and live oaks. This is thought to be Price Canyon in Pismo Beach. Near their camp, Crespí pointed out, was "a middling sized, very swelling knoll some two hundred yards long that consists entirely of tar springs issuing molten out of the ground." Pismo gets its name from the Chumash for tar, *pismu*, which may have also been the name of a village in this canyon where Crespí wrote "a petty king" presided. The soldiers called him *El Buchón*, "the Goiter," for the tumor on his neck "large as a well swollen ox gall." He wore a cape of otter pelts and traveled with an entourage and bodyguards. He doesn't sound so petty from Crespí's description, for he was held in esteem from the Santa Barbara Channel to the Santa Lucia Mountains, much of the Chumash territory. "Great is the fear and awe in which he is held in all the surrounding parts," wrote Crespí. "They designate him by making signs for his tumor." Surrounding villages visited The Goiter and paid tribute. "Whatever seeds they harvest or gather from the fields, whether they slaughter any meat or catch fish, they take it all—or so we understood—to his village, where he receives it and then they take back whatever he tells them to." He was less a petty king than an arbiter of fates, and he is immortalized in the name of Point Buchon to the west of Pismo.

I spent the night in North Beach Campground just south of town, scrounging for enough loose change from my backpack to fill an envelope and slide it into the after-hours payment slot. In the morning, with the firepits still smoldering, I wandered into a eucalyptus grove to which monarch butterflies return each winter and cluster for warmth in hanging wreaths, as if a campfire had accidentally climbed into the resinous leaves. Offshore, thousands of black seabirds, sooty shearwaters I think, streamed to the north in a loose highway. Their advance was endless, and I couldn't tell to where, but at times it seemed some were settling in enormous rafts.

And when I walked out on the Pismo Pier, past the stainless-steel cleaning stations, I found a crowd of about fifty people watching a feeding frenzy. It was more than just birds: humpback whales were rising, lunge-feeding, through bait balls no one could see. They were diving and releasing bubbles to scare and bunch anchovies, if that's what they were, pushing them tighter, denser, a silver revolution. Then the rise, sometimes several whales together, and the open-mouthed burst through the school, water cascading down their heads—their pleated throats expanding with a hundred or a thousand fish swimming inside. Imagine those anchovies darting frantically inside a humpback's dark pouch, colliding with the walls of its throat as it squeezes like a compactor and presses the ocean out its baleen sieve. Humpback whales are sixty feet long and weigh as much as a bus. Their ventral flippers are the longest appendages in the world, up to sixteen feet. They have knobs on their heads called tubercles and a small dorsal fin, not a hump: they're called humpback because of the way they arch their spines as they dive.

Through my binoculars I also could see dolphins in the fray. Other predatory fish were surely in on the action below. One fisherman on the pier, with a long black braid, was hoping the bait would drift in and bring thresher or sevengill sharks. Catching a shark was like winning the lottery. The white steaks cut like pork chop, he said, and he'd boil the fins for broth, let the scales and skin settle out. "The mackerel are going to be out there," he told me. "The sharks are going to be out there. It's an easy meal—all they've got to do is swim with their mouth open, right into the wall." His wife was nursing their four-week-old under a cloth in a camp chair behind him, and she chimed in: "They're basically swimming garbage disposals, that's all they are." Above them the avian world swirled—gulls, terns, pelicans, shearwaters, and more—and dove into the white foam around those prodigious leathery heads and arching backs for the fish stunned or overwhelmed by the uprush. "What's going on in bird form," the angler said, "is going on in fish form underwater."

There was a lone man on his paddleboard in the middle of it all. I almost hated him, my envy was such, and I was also scared for his life. He had paddled farther and farther out, and now he knelt as spouts lifted all around him. He must have felt the mist, the whales' warm exhalations, on his face. Their lobed tails each had a fingerprint of milky blotches underneath, and their dorsals were like fleeting black thorns as they curled. There was a chaos of birds to the right of him, heads and chins emerging. The water boiled as it might have in a tar-sealed basket when a cooking stone was dropped in. One after the next, the pelicans shed their awkwardness in free fall, every last ounce—their strategy and pouch much like a whale's, only aerial. A raised flipper caught the sun and reflected like the flash of a lighthouse. Through it all he knelt on his board or sat with his feet stretched in front of him, his pale back burning. The one iota of terrestrial flesh out there. He disappeared from sight every second or so as a swell passed and he fell into a trough.

A shack in the middle of the pier sold souvenirs and candy and also rented boogie boards. For about ten minutes, I debated renting one and trying to paddle out, closer, as close as need be. My adrenaline pulsed. I could do it. I could leave my pack in the shadow of a pillar under the pier. Probably no one would hassle it. Then I thought of my bare legs dangling in the cold. It was farther than it looked. Let him have that to himself, this experience of a lifetime. In the distance, the shearwaters seemed to stream through him as if his body had become spray. Finally he began to paddle in. I kept an eye on him as I continued to watch the cyclone of birds amid the whale spouts, thinking I could intercept him on the shore and ask him about it. What was it like, this vortex? Then suddenly he was climbing out, I had lost track of time again, and though I hustled off the pier, he was gone.

IT SEEMS I ALSO LOST the Portolá trail that day when I casually stuck to the coast to reach San Luis Obispo, strolling through the arcade storefronts of pastel Pismo and then west through a seaside gauntlet of charming neighborhoods, some named for famous links: Shell Beach, Spindrift, Saint Andrews, Spyglass, Palisades. Seems the scouts and soldiers instead hiked Price Canyon north from Pismo and into a circuitous route of hollows and passes, heading generally northwest, until they reached a lush, boggy plain near the San Luis Obispo airport, where the pools' edges were so soft they had to march on to obtain firm ground so the mules could drink without sinking. From Avila Hot Springs, where I camped, I followed 101 north to San Luis and flew out of the airport for a weekend wedding in New Hampshire, flaunting gravity and the laws of the eighteenth century. Emily and Ed were hitched in a ceremony that would have been unfathomable to Juan Crespí, surrounded by sunflowers. Before I left, I hid my butane and Swiss Army knife in the shaggy grass along a road near the airport so that I could gather them up again—I wasn't checking my pack. When I returned, they were right where I left them.

Heading west from today's San Luis Obispo toward the ocean, the expedition might have traveled down *el Llano de Los Osos* without incident had they refrained from harassing the locals. Crespí's description of this afternoon deserves no interruption:

"The scouts had reported to us that they had come upon a great many large bears in this level. With this in mind, our Captain and five or six soldiers were riding their horses. On coming down to the plain we at once spied some seven of them in two or three different spots. They fired at one, which it took seven or more shots for them to kill, each shot wounding it in the body. They slew it finally, and the rest went galloping off. They attack with more than a bull's strength and ferocity, and truly it is a creature that can well inspire fear in one setting out to hunt it. After the bear they had killed had fallen to the ground, two grown-up puppies that have been coming along with the expedition approached the creature and it caught one of them with each of its forepaws and thrust them beneath itself, paying no attention to them, with the poor little creatures whining and crying, until they shot it again in the head, at last killing it, and it let go the puppies, who were none the worse. In the case of another bear that the men coming up with the pack train fired upon, it was a wonder it did not slay a Christian or two, for on a soldier's shooting at it the bear attacked the man who had fired, caught his mule by the tail and twice made it fall. It was starting to climb onto the mule but when the mule fell over the rider got free. The mule, however, was left badly clawed and with a good-sized wound in one shoulder. . . . As lovely as this level here is, we could plainly tell it is uninhabited by the poor Indians, and the reason can be no other than the vast number of bears inhabiting it, for we saw the places where these creatures had eaten and lain down, and most of this level dug up as much as though it had been plowed, for it is clear the bears must be digging for roots."

A grizzly can run as fast as a steed for a short distance. "When they feel themselves wounded," Costansó observed, "headlong they charge the hunter, who can only escape by swiftness of horse, for the first burst of speed is more rapid than one might expect from the bulk and awkwardness of such brutes." It's estimated that ten thousand once lived in California, often roaming in a pack—a sloth, a maul, a sleuth, as groups of bears are called—along the coast, where they grew larger on the year-round abundance and had no need to hibernate. They preferred precisely the places that the Portolá expedition was scouting: grasslands or valleys with ample water, with anadromous fish like steelhead and salmon, and roots for digging. The best lands to farm. They also ate acorns and overturned logs in oak woodlands for grubs or wandered through the chaparral mosaic, which, along with grasslands, was maintained by the fires set by natives. As fire was suppressed and the landscape was quickly transformed, bears were pushed into more remote and punishing territory, thicker and less fertile. They were ruthlessly pursued by the *vaquero* hunters of Spanish and Mexican California, who challenged themselves to capture the bears with lariats. Grizzlies were then pitted against bulls. The two animals were usually chained together. Often a bear would slay a number of bulls before, weary and wounded, the final bovine would win. Of course, more often grizzlies were gunned down or trapped.

In San Luis Obispo County, in the 1840s, one hunter is said to have killed two hundred grizzlies in a single season. The final recorded grizzly in San Diego County was shot in 1899 near San Mateo Creek, which I had trailed up Cristianitos Canyon after visiting the red font of California's first baptism. What would it have been like to see one of those gargantuan footprints in the dust of a firebreak as I skirted Camp Pendleton? The California grizzly often weighed more than a half ton, unlike today's Yellowstone grizzlies, which are in the four-hundred-pound range. "The Monster of San Mateo" weighed over fourteen hundred. The chief of the U.S. Biological Survey, C. Hart Merriam, personally studied the Monster and named it *Ursus magister*—the master. He and others believed that the California bear was a distinct species, though probably its extra-impressive size was only environmental: the spoils of the California coast were immense and natural selection favored larger bears.

A female griz thought to be the Monster of San Mateo's mate was killed in Trabuco Canyon in 1908, one of the last in Southern California. For the grizzly, Trabuco Canyon was true to its name. In 1924, the last grizzly sighting in California occurred in the high elevations of Sequoia National Park. That we fly this creature on the state flag shows less California's pride in its landscape than its power to master the master, to subjugate and exterminate, to unwild the wild. It is a ghost bear on the flag, a silhouette under a fatal star.

But it is also a real bear: Monarch. His story, too, is emblematic. In 1889, a young publisher by the name of William Randolph Hearst, who owned the *San Francisco Examiner*, decided that it would make for sensational reading to send a journalist to capture one of California's last remaining grizzlies. Hearst wrote a blank check and gave it to Allen Kelly, who found himself in Ventura County, in what's now the Sespe Wilderness to the north of the Santa Clara River, above Santa Paula and Fillmore, with local guides who bullshitted him and were in no hurry to capture a bear when plenty of whiskey and camp time was on hand at Hearst's expense. They built and baited traps that looked like log cabins, so that a grizzly would have to tear through timber to escape. Finally Kelly captured a twelve-hundred-pound bear, though it's rumored that some nearby cowhands actually lassoed it, or that the bear really came from the San Gabriel Mountains. In any event, Monarch was conveyed by train to San Francisco and delivered to the zoo in Golden Gate Park, where Hearst reported that 20,000 people turned out to witness his arrival. Twenty-two years later, Monarch died forgotten in captivity. But just then, in 1911, California finally decided to adopt a state flag, resurrecting and refining the banner of the 1846 Bear Flag Revolt, and Monarch was used as its model. He still lives on, in Golden Gate Park, in the basement of the Academy of Sciences. His snout has been worn clean of its fur, likely from all the passing hands that petted and rubbed him like a worry stone when his taxidermied skin was displayed in the last century.

IT WAS A HUNDRED DEGREES when I headed west the ten miles on Los Osos Valley Road. The corporate strip and auto mall of south San Luis Obispo—Coast Nissan, Coast BMW—eased to farmland. Pumpkins were swelling on the vines. The "great many" oaks and sycamores Crespí notes are primarily gone. Instead, piles of firewood mimicked the isolated buttes on the valley's north side. These were the Nine Sisters, a chain of exposed volcanic plugs that extend from the coast to San Luis: with each one I passed, I leapt forward in time half a million years or so. Crespí doesn't comment on them, but they are striking. They are the solidified cores of volcanoes from which the rest has worn away, formed between 22 and 27 million years ago. Much as with the Hawaiian Islands, a single hot spot likely produced new cones as the continental plates drifted. Traveling toward the coast, my direction, they end with the landmark Morro Rock, the youngest and shapeliest. I started calling them "the teeth" because they looked like the incisors and grinders of a lower mandible buried in the land. Some have raw cliff faces, all have boulder fields, rattler terrain with oases of little-disturbed scrub and oak, only because these are non-arable islands in the sky. The cows stood in the bleached meadows near outcrops that might have been thrown steaming from one or the other of these impressive fossil vents: Morro Rock, Black Hill, Cerro Cabrillo, Hollister Peak, Cerro Romauldo, Chumash Peak, Bishop Peak, Cerro San Luis, Islay Hill. Stretching twenty miles inland, there are many more Morros—*morro* means "a small round hill" in Spanish—but they are worn down like aged molars.

A man with a mustache in a silver van parked on the roadside asked if I needed a ride. "Nah, thanks," I said, "I'm good." I asked him how he was doing. "Good," he said, as I passed him. "Hey," he said, and I turned around. "You asked me how I was doing, and I said 'Good.' You want to know why?" I thought he might be about to proposition me, which had happened a few times on my walk. And I suppose he was. "Because I've got Jesus Christ," he said.

Tiny bleached sagebrush lizards exactly the hue of the roadside sand: I wondered if certain populations had evolved to blend in on the shoulders of our traffic, or if new species might have even emerged that we've compelled, but overlooked. A translucent grocery bag hung like a hammock in a stalk of fennel, and farther off a kestrel landed in some fennel, a devious low perch that bowed under its weight and flicking tail. I realized I couldn't tell my crops from a distance like I could tell my birds, and why not, considering these crops are essential to my being? Meanwhile, amid the wiry mustard there are holes, and in those holes I kept seeing cups: Jamba Juice cups, Big Gulp cups. Cups find their way, like plugs, into rodent holes. Does the wind place them there? I also found a paper on which a kid had written a pretty good story in black ink. Corrections had been made with Wite-Out. *One blooming night on the summer river bank there was a wind, but not just any wind, a powerful wind like a hurricane. Tom was outside, wanting Wind to stop blowing his crops away. Wind whooshed him away. Tom yelled, "You no good wind!" Wind bellowed, "Well that's how you wanna play, eh?" Tom replied, "Why are you saying 'eh'? You're not Canadian."*

On my left, toward the Irish Hills, which hold the valley's south side, I passed a farm with a corn maze. Halloween rituals had begun already. I wanted to try it, imagining that it would give me a sense of the valley that the Spaniards experienced, one in which the grasses weren't shorn but waist- or shoulder-height, and any rustling could belie or mask a bear, either way terrifying. In a marshy valley of grizzlies, it would be easy to understand why there were no *rancherías*. Now instead of brown bears there are brown cows—I counted about fifty Herefords in one pasture. Roughly the same hulk, but not the same quality. Even Crespí made that association and judgment: "They attack with more than a bull's strength and ferocity." It was five minutes to six, closing time at the corn maze, and the ticket vendor wouldn't let me in for even five minutes without paying the fifteen dollars. "It's seven acres," she said, "it's more like a two-hour experience. I have employees who want to go home." I couldn't argue with her. So many things I passed seemed like a two-hour experience I only had five minutes for.

Over the fields, the teeth turned peach, bittersweet orange, pumpkin, end of day. The simmer of the power lines was punctuated by the high squeak alarm of a ground squirrel. I wandered into Los Osos Valley Memorial Park not knowing it was a cemetery. California poppies were planted along the cement path that led to the "Old Glory" memorial at the park's middle: some petals fallen off below long seedpods; others curled up just for the night. At the center of the Old Glory circle was a bread-box-sized bear carved of white stone. Its fur was gestured with crude strokes. Around the sculpture were cremation memorials, flat stones with an embedded canister at their center. Each had a handle to turn to open it, presumably if you had the key. Hermylee S. Godwin and Newt E. Godwin were two of the tenants, born in 1922 and 1923. But the bear seemed to memorialize itself as well. It had bird droppings on its head. A black phoebe would love a stone ear with a view to perch on. Lichen freckled the bear's snout, orange and brown. At the park's edges there was room to grow in the coarse grass that made no sound underfoot. Cutting back to the valley road, I mistook an irrigation valve box for a grave, stepping around it respectfully.

IN LOS OSOS, THE BEARS were large and the trees were Lilliputian. On a sandy dune knoll above Morro Bay, an all-weather boardwalk wound through an elfin forest of live oak. From four to ten feet tall, these oaks are salt-pruned and starved of good soil, and the sand is so porous that it retains little water. But they thrive as pygmies and twist like the silver marsh channels spread before this *pequeñito* reserve and dotted with shining pools of tidewater. Normally oak wouldn't survive on dunes, only behind them, but these are stable relics protected now by new dunes far across the bay, so the oaks have invaded the usual dune chaparral of Morro manzanita, silver lupine, mock heather, black sage, frittered buckwheat. The trees are shortest at the park's top, larger down the north slope where they see less sun and reach more water. For only some minor scratches, you can push inside one of these glens. The branches are so convoluted and altogether domelike that you feel as if you're inside a vegetative brain that has filtered light and time for centuries. Some are four hundred years old—distinguished, for oak.

The spirals of live oak—the way their branches descend to the leaf litter and then, braced, turn upward—are one of California's signatures, from the coast to the Sierra foothills. The script here is quite small, but the trees seem to produce bushels of acorns. That's what's strange, I realized: the trees look like the scrub oak I had seen in San Diego, but the acorns in this elfin forest are the typical live oak size I know from home. Local Chumash bands visited and collected them. Their middens are layered in this and other woodlands nearby. Fragments of shell fleck the red sand and run in paths as if the Chumash ate their clams walking back from the beach, four or five hundred years' worth. The expedition came across a "good-sized village" along Morro Bay, but it had just one house, suggesting it was a seasonal camp—a distinction lost on Crespí, who described them as "poor" for lack of belongings, when probably they were only unencumbered on their summer estate. Had they been poor, odds are they wouldn't have served the expedition a "pinole" of seeds, acorn likely, which Costansó wrote "tasted good to all of us and had the flavor of almonds." The fattiest acorns, coast live oak, were choice. Steatite slabs with an augered hole, so they could be handled with a stick, were heated in a fire and dropped into a bowl or basket of water and leached flour, boiling the mixture instantly. It's said that the boy who gathered the firewood won the right to lick these savory stones, once cooled, while the sloth among the striplings was made to stir the mush as it cooked. It was never served with salt.

Monarchs floated over the pygmy trees. Spotted towhees scratched in the litter and mewed with unseen red eyes and rufous sides. Soon I ran into Don, who was scanning the boardwalk for loose boards and missing screws, and who wore a black sweatshirt with a mural of this place printed on it, *El Moro Elfin Forest, Small Wilderness Area Preservation*. SWAP. I liked that locution: this was a wilderness, though it had a recycled plastic boardwalk and was a mere postage stamp compared to Wilderness with a capital W. Don was not tall, and had silver-and-black eyebrows, and most of all he spoke in a hush like the breeze which struggled to gain purchase on these retired, grown-over dunes. He was a retired environmental toxicology professor. "I did the same thing that you're talking about right now," he said, after I explained myself. "I was employed at the University of California at Irvine, and time came to retire, and I said to myself, 'Well, I got to find some place to live now. I'm not going to stay in Irvine.' I drove all the way from down there all the way up north to Monterey, that area, and through Morro Bay. When I went through Morro Bay, I said, 'You know, this looks pretty nice.'" Perhaps in a sense he was doubly right and I was searching for my home out here on this ancient shore.

Don explained that these old dunes, now hoary with vegetation, were deposited about thirteen thousand years ago at the end of the Ice Age, when the sea was far out to sea. The coast was ten miles west—Morro Rock was landlocked—and a plain of blowing sand stretched inland and deposited just here. It was a larger version of the broad sand sheet I had just driven on my ATV at Oceano to reach the pyramidal dunes. The crown of the elfin forest was 125 feet above sea level, but the layer of pure sand extended double that distance below us, said Don. These stable dunes were what the raw, still-flowing sands of Oceano might become far in the future.

People in Los Osos initially raised $1.6 million to preserve this last strip of elfin forest, which grew at the end of their blocks. Then the State decided to tack on the land just below it on the hill, a successful collaboration that continues. "Well, I got up here," Don recollected about his move, "and now what are you going to do?" He had been a volunteer for the preserve ever since, pacing these trails about twice a week. "This particular hill was bare ground when we took over . . . well, it was fifteen years ago. A lot of native plants were put in, and the rest of the ground was left to seed itself." They had to battle the weeds heavily at first, because their seeds can stay dormant in this dry sand for decades. Now the habitat was under control. Don suggested I follow the boardwalk down and around to a place called Rosa's Grove, where you can walk inside a mature, diminutive, bird-boned grove and sit among its contortions. At my height, I would have to slip my head between two upright branches to enter. It was another kind of Old Glory circle, a memorial to one of the preserve's founders. "She used to call people down there before the boardwalk was built, when they were raising money. She'd have parties down there. But unfortunately she didn't survive that long. You can go in and see what a grove is really like inside. It's enjoyable, I think."

"Oh, it's wonderful," I said. "I love elfin forests."

"Okay," Don said as he turned his eyes back to screws and boards. "Tell your friends."

OVER THE EEL-GRASS MATS, MORRO ROCK was conspicuous to the northwest. Crespí didn't miss it: "A good-sized embayment is formed in front of this spot, and we have quite a high, round island rock in view in the shape of a sort of head." *Un farallón redondo bien alto que forma a modo de morro* were his words. It was only an island at high tide, when Costansó judged it was "a little less than a gunshot" from shore. This marooned cold heart of a volcano is one of the most famous and photographed features of the California coast, and it stands out, at least in my imagination, more like the hump of a grizzly on the coastal plain. Crespí makes no other mention of this landmark, though they must have passed close by the next day. Mainly he was disappointed that the bay had no discernible entrance to make it a worthwhile harbor, just sandbars with breakers washing over. Still, it was a choice site for a mission in his book, harbor or no harbor, bears or no bears.

Today, a cut has been dredged in these bars and many boats are moored in Morro Bay. The breakwalls that protect it are made with stone quarried from the Morro itself. One million two hundred thousand tons of rock were blasted from the Morro from the end of the nineteenth century to 1963, so now only the west side, facing the ocean, is as it was when Juan Cabrillo sailed by in 1542. I can't get over that fact: it would be like blasting Lembert Dome in Yosemite's Tuolumne Meadows or the other Moro Rock, one less *r*, in Sequoia National Park. The causeway to the rock was made this way too, and other jetties in the area as far as Port San Luis in Avila Bay. What you see when you admire Morro Rock isn't the original head, if there is such a thing, but a core of a core, an approximation, accelerated erosion—our disregard.

Thirty surfers were in the water beside the rock that evening when I arrived.

Even at twilight, they stayed out there, black figures in swells that alternately reflected and swallowed that high dying blue of the day. Their van doors sliding in the dark, the gravel under their tires. The rock seemed to whisper, shushing me as it echoed the waves on its north side. On its south side, where a sign warned, DANGER: INTERMITTENT WAVES OF UNUSUAL SIZE AND FORCE, WADING AND SWIMMING UNSAFE, the cliffs threw back the boom of the long, hard breakers. The stone was a jaundiced pink streaked with dark water stains.

Before dusk, I spotted the nearly imperceptible silhouette of a falcon on Morro Rock's crown, which put the 576-foot-tall monolith in perspective. The tiercel took off with a classic *kak kak kak* toward the three smokestacks of a retired power plant in downtown Morro Bay, their red blinking lights intensifying. In one minute it traversed a distance through the air that had taken me about fifteen minutes to stroll. With powerful strokes, a peregrine can accelerate horizontally to 68 miles per hour. Tucking those wings, it can stoop to 240 miles per hour to club a bird and snag its quarry in free fall, in a drift of feathers. Morro is famous for its peregrines. In 1977, at the height of DDT's ravages, the rock supported one of five remaining peregrine pairs in California. Realizing that falcons were crushing the weakened shells of their eggs with their own weight, biologists rappelled the Morro and swapped out eggs for nestlings from captive parents. The original eggs were incubated by biologists, and the resulting chicks were released back into the "wild" once they were ready. Now two falcon pairs nest on the Morro, and in California peregrines have fully recovered.

In the harbor, sea otters swam up to the pylons of a dock and pushed off with somersaults like backstroke specialists hitting the wall, their bodies streamlined through the honey-green evening bay, their fur expanding, filling with warm air, when they surfaced. I took videos of them on my phone that I will never have to watch because I have those movements memorized. I observed one swim into a clump of kelp hardly bigger than its body and wrap itself in the strands, coiling and twisting, for extra buoyancy. Otters doze in kelp rafts off the coast. Another disappeared and resurfaced with a stone on its belly nearly as large as its own head. It slammed a mussel on the rock—some piece of one of the Sisters, of the Morro itself—and teased the orange flesh from the shell before letting the tool sink away. I was reminded of the bedrock mortars I'd seen nearby, where Chumash had pounded acorns into meal with a view across the bay from a prominence and where, along that trail, tremendous whale bones now rest as weathered and gray as the stumps of great trees. The bones were strung together like a necklace with a cable so you couldn't steal them, the kind of bones Juana Maria used to make her shelter on San Nicolas.

The otters ate the broken mussels two-handed as if they were corn on the cob. Both of these behaviors, the pounding and the kelp rafting, I'd read about but never seen in person. They also corkscrewed on the surface of the water constantly, as if simply delighting in their abilities. Likely they do so for lack of eyes in the back of their heads. They swirl and swirl, a nervous tic by evolution.

NEARING CAYUCOS, I CAME ACROSS a woman skinning a shovelnose guitarfish. Her Australian shepherd–blue heeler mix, Jasper, barked at me as I neared and ran up aggressively. She called him off. Ever loyal, he was, with one blue topaz eye. She was kneeling on the beach over the fish, which was about two and a half feet long, with a knife in her right hand. She stood as I walked up. She wore sunglasses and translucent plastic gloves. She had something between a butch and a pixie haircut, reddish and tousled. Black tee, black-and-white board shorts with palms rising over pavement. Bare feet. As for the guitarfish, it is a peculiar and ancient creature, somewhere between a shark and a skate. As a bottom-dweller, its front half is flattened—its pectoral fins form a wide ray-like disk—but it propels itself with its tail and, like a shark, has dorsal, adipose, and caudal fins.

"I think it probably died this morning," Ariana said. "It was at the high-water mark."

"You had a knife handy?"

"Yeah, I carry it with me, because you never know . . . I prayed a couple of weeks ago when I got here. I said, 'Spirit, whatever medicine you want the ocean to give me, I'll receive it.' I had a feeling it would be a mammal. So . . . it's nice. You know, it's a shark, but it's not vicious, not like a gnarly predator shark at all. I'll take that medicine.

"Do you mind if I keep going on this?" she added.

"Oh yeah yeah yeah," I said, "keep going." She clarified that she had happened on the fish walking Jasper earlier and almost ignored it, but then she remembered her prayer. So she returned to her RV for her knife and gloves. She wasn't sure what she would do with the skin. Maybe it would lend itself to some kind of ceremony.

"It'll tell you?" I said.

"Yeah, exactly," she said, sawing. She'd executed the first cut just above the tip of the tail, which peeled up easily. Now she was working the knife along the spine, revealing the white flesh, those segmented muscles that would flake delicately off a fork.

"I have an owl wing," she said. "An owl gifted itself to me up on the Columbia Gorge." It had been roadkill, the fate of so many owls. Blinded, they fly right into windshields and grills. She didn't tell me, but I would bet hers was a barn owl, whose white and tawny upraised wings so often gesture to the traffic from a disheveled clump on the shoulder. In California's Central Valley, on certain stretches, barn owls seem to mark the miles. "I was thinking I'd use this skin to make the handle for the fan, because I'm going to make a smudge fan."

I told her then about my tern wing. I had found it on the beach and now had it at the top of my pack, wrapped in a faded and frayed American flag that had fallen off some car. I unfolded it for her. Jasper stood up to smell it in my hand. The wing was a gray and white dagger for splicing the air and, once tucked, the water. I thought I might mail it home to Sarah, a painter who likes these kinds of objects as much as I do. It was grace succumbed. Maybe a falcon had got it. Maybe hunger or a wrong angle. "That is awesome," Ariana said when I unwrapped it. "Whoa, that's good. That's really good medicine." The ants had gone crazy over it, eating at the shoulder, so a few feathers had fallen out. But she was right, it was a tonic: perfectly suited for its elements, and those elements had turned it into an efficient and aesthetic pleasure.

Ariana offered me a sprinkling of tobacco for the wing and a sprig of wild sage that she'd collected near Lassen or Modoc, she couldn't remember. Two and a half months ago, she had bought an RV and now it was her home. She was glad to be out of Seattle. Originally from Santa Barbara, she had numerous friends on the coast and had parked it in a driveway just up the beach that belonged to a friend's neighbor. Now that parking space was needed again. She'd have to move. "You've just got to go with the flow. It's humbling, it's really humbling."

Jasper shook in his collar and curled up at my feet beside the shovelnose guitarfish. Once he laid his head directly on the fish's back. Its common name is unfortunate: Is it a shovel, or is it a guitar? It's more the former. A guitar is of no use underwater, but these creatures do burrow in with their shovelnose to hide and camouflage, and then erupt from the sand to ambush an unsuspecting fish. During the night, when they themselves are less vulnerable, they cruise the seabed and crunch crabs and shellfish with their knobby teeth. The guitarfish was gnarlier than the tern and its wing, but it was equally honed for its benthic kingdom. It was a pleasure.

"How about you?" she asked. "What's your adventure been like?"

Mine? I told her it had been incredible. I had a month still to go and could hardly imagine experiencing another month, because California was pouring through me. I was seeing so many things I'd never seen before, and at the same time I realized I was seeing everything through my particular lens. I couldn't escape that. But I was trying to be so attentive and present that it was exhausting, and I'd just shut down at the end of the day and then do it all over again. Time was moving slowly, because I was encountering so much. Or maybe it was fast, I didn't know. One of the two.

"Yeah who knows . . . the time-space continuum, I think when you're present it ceases to exist, maybe."

We tried to identify organs as she worked. The liver, the intestines. The heart she held up was a dark mud-red and somehow reminded me of a tongue. She had a quill pen tattooed on her forearm, one that had just written "I love you" in cursive on her skin. Her plastic gloves were slathered in mucus and sand. She kept trying to explain herself though she didn't need to.

"You know, it's one of those things for me. Nature talks to me . . . it sounds crazy to some people, but for me that's how I learn. And I really just believe that the veils are really thin. It's sort of like in string theory in physics. Are you familiar with physics? In string theory . . . I don't know a lot, but essentially there's parallel universes that are these strands and they sort of weave like this"—she motioned with her hands—"and then occasionally they weave into each other. And I just think that they're onto something with that. The veil gets thin."

She was cutting through the veil. And when she came to the fish's low forehead, she struggled. It had raised eyes like a frog's, and behind those are pores called spiracles that pump water to the gills. A guitarfish can't use its mouth to siphon water like the usual fish because it's flush to the sand or buried in it, which would ruin those exquisite gill feathers, the lamellae. Ariana was sweating, but its mask just wouldn't separate. The effort was intense, unsightly, uncomfortable. "I'm just not good at this," she said. Finally she gave up and made one last cut behind its eyes so she could lift a long strip of wet green skin. At home, in her trailer, she'd clean the skin further and add salt. "From a Buddhist perspective," she said, "it can take up to three days for the consciousness to leave a sentient being. So I don't want to dishonor it . . ."

"If your thoughts are good," I offered, "I think you can't dishonor it, even if you make a mess of it."

We laughed at the half-truth of that.

CRESPÍ WROTE THAT THERE WAS "not a tree to be seen in the whole day's march" from Morro Bay. They went north on the beach when possible, on the flat tablelands otherwise. Past Cayucos, in the Estero Bluffs State Park, I could look back and see the whole of Estero Bay, from Montaña de Oro to Cayucos Point. I had to remind myself to take in the southern view. Morro Bay is the harbor set within the much larger Estero Bay, which, if you were to run a line from point to point, is indented into the continent about five miles. But that bracing expanse was just a sliver, a fingernail's worth etched from California. El Morro remained at the center like the dacite hub of a wheel of land and ocean; with ten miles of distance, it was obvious just how much it dwarfed the decommissioned smokestacks where the peregrines also perched.

Estero Bluffs State Park was a pale gem, unassuming and nearly flat, with only easy gullies to dip across. A casual trail followed the lava shore, and 101 streamed a quarter mile inland on the grassy terrace, to my right. In the many nameless coves, the waves sucked and surged around rocks white by nature or with guano, and once with an oystercatcher, light filtering through its orange straw bill. Driving the highway, you can stop at pullouts and walk through gates to find yourself all alone two minutes later at the water's edge. A few people raced down to the short bluffs, turning to capture a selfie with that unbroken heaving behind them. In the covelets, shorebirds and ground squirrels alike probed the algal heaps, knotted and rainbow: green, deep maroon, purple and brown, white, stippled and pustular and slick as oil, sending up a shrapnel of kelp flies. Killdeer, turnstones, willets, and a few I didn't quite recognize. It was a mixed flock, everyone with a slightly different technique or niche, if not purpose.

Along the path, a northern shrike, the first I'd seen in a long time though I remembered them in the fields near my childhood home, was hunting from the cable strung between the waist-high iron posts that, in places, protected the vegetation or kept you from a precarious edge. For a moment, through my binoculars, the bird and Morro Rock were in the same shaking circle. The carnivorous shrike had a gray dome too, flattened by the sweeping wind. It flew low, a foot off the ground, under the radar of grasshoppers and voles, little shadow, until it rose to another swoop of cable, or a dried stalk. When it landed, it rotated straight into the wind or else directly away—rarely sideways.

AT THE CRESCENT BEACH AT Villa Creek north of Cayucos, where the expedition had camped and where I saw a dozen snowy plovers, I cut inland through a minor wetland that forked into two canyons. The Portolá expedition chose left, as did I and the builders of Highway 1, heading northwest along what's now called Ellysly Creek. "Very broad and well beaten trails have been met with at all of these waters," wrote Crespí. "Toward the mountains along the course of these streams, there must be villages." Over a low pass I found a crossroads called Harmony, pop. 18, elev. 175—a former dairy collaborative and company town that today is an even smaller artist community, "the most bypassed town in California."

Soon I was climbing to Cambria, which Crespí named *El pinal de San Benvenuto*, the pine grove of Saint Benvenutus. The padre had wondered, with longing you can almost tell, if it was the Point of Pines the expedition was searching for: "This night the scouts brought back the report that they had come across a stream with a pine grove at it and a wood of the same beyond. Whether this may be the Carmelo already, we cannot tell." Its current name, Cambria, the Latin for Wales, came a hundred years later, but this valley, as Crespí saw and honored it, is home to one of only five native forests of Monterey pine, *Pinus radiata*.

The tree is endemic to California and two Mexican islands. In California, relict groves also exist in its namesake Monterey and, farther north, at Año Nuevo near Santa Cruz, foggy locales all. But this pine has been cultivated to fantastic success and is found around the globe, including in expansive timber plantations where a cultivar has been selected for linearity. We had a small stand of Monterey pine at my childhood home, and occasional red-tailed or sharp-shinned hawks would perch in them. "In the wild" it is a rare and spindly tree, rough barked and fifty to one hundred feet tall with most of its foliage in an umbrella crown. Cones run like armored snails up its branches, a seed bank that extends many years into the past. Its cones are serotinous, meaning their scales remain sealed tight until they encounter the heat of fire and their resin melts, letting the seeds twirl all at once to the enriched floor where now they might have a fighting chance. The pine is neither a fire evader nor resister, but a "fire tolerator": a tree that thrives in mixed-severity fires, surviving low-intensity blazes and regenerating heavily after major burns. Fire suppression over the last century undoubtedly has caused the forest around Cambria to age, with fewer saplings taking hold—less "recruitment"—and now climate change is probably accelerating mortality. Yet the tree has always waxed and waned in response to climate. In the fossil record, the Monterey pine is found as far north as Point Reyes, and carbonized fossil cones have been recovered in the La Brea Tar Pits, washed out of the San Gabriel Mountains. Probably this pine always existed in fragmented populations that expanded in the stretches between warm and glacial periods.

In Cambria the pines have been cut from the valley, but remain on the ridges, tall and straight as masts. Spanish moss sways like rags of cheesecloth from their branches, and the vertical homes seem to take their cue from the trees, rising up with wood decks at the level of the jays and crows in the squiggled limbs. The piney hillsides were too steep to pitch a tent, and the spare understory didn't provide much cover, so I descended to Santa Rosa Creek to hunt for a campsite. Along Rodeo Grounds Road, behind a maintenance facility, I found a brambly scramble down into the creek bed where I set up my shelter on the damp cobble. The creek was fairly lightless, sunken and overhung, as it was even in Crespí's day: "The stream's bed, quite large, is thickly overgrown with a great many trees . . . . This also is a spot having a vast number of bears; going after water, they have seen three or four very large ones in the stream hollow, and between the tall grass clumps there, there are a great many of their lying-down spots and very large beaten trails made by their coming and going." The soldiers called this place *Paraje del Osito*, Place of the Little Bear, because Salinan villagers brought the Spaniards a cub they had caught, "still so young that its hair would bristle whenever any of us came near it." I must say I felt something of that energy in this cavernous creek.

Once set up, I shuffled into town, the historic East Village, filled with scarecrows for its annual festival. There was a gem shop that was the sister to the one I'd known in Yachats, Oregon—the whimsy of these coastal towns attracts gem shops and glassblowing and trinkets, as if these places are still peddling beads like the Portolá expedition. I found a bar in which to grab a burrito and glue myself to the National League Wild Card game between the Giants and the Mets. Journeyman Conor Gillaspie hit a three-run homer for the Giants in the top of the ninth, and Madison Bumgarner dealt three more outs for a complete game, burnishing his legend. In the night, I strode back to my solo dome with orange trim, now a celebration tent, damp and uninviting and pitch black as the *osito* creek was.

SOUTH OF VISTA DEL MAR in San Simeon, on a seaside tableland known as Junge Ranch, I spotted a blue beach chair marooned in the grass. The low chair looked comfortable, with a faded mesh seat and back and a salty aluminum frame. I wiped away a couple of mouse droppings and sat. The land fell gradually away about fifty yards to the bluff and, beyond, the ocean was all glare where kelp beds had quieted the surface and those slick patches were bright with reflection. The last few days, I'd seen great blue herons and egrets perched in the kelp mats as much as a quarter mile out to sea, rising and falling and waiting. Crespí never mentions kelp in his journal, but it was one of "the Signs" by which the Spanish trade galleons returning from the Philippines knew the continent was near and it was time to tack south for Acapulco. Snippets from ship logs before Portolá's time are wonderful: "drifts of vegetation including floating fig-like leaves, similar to [what is] eaten in Japan, that, when boiled with meat, are like collards"; "first Portuguese men-of-war, then frolicking doglets, then knobsticks of 'grass' washed from rivers and more doglets" (these doglets, or *perrillos*, were of course sea otters); "very long stems of seaweed, with leaves broad as those of tobacco and growing in bunches, eighty or a hundred leagues at sea"; "an onion-like weed growing upside down on the water, its stalk long enough to reach from the ship's masthead to deck."

All around were raptors. At one point, I had four white-tailed kites and two northern harriers in view. As advertised, the kites are mainly white, but with a foggy-gray back and black shoulder patches. Eyes the color of vole blood. They hover in place with fast beats as they study the grass and contemplate a pounce. Only about once every fifty hovers do they come away with a rodent. Here their perches were bush lupine, none in flower, some just dead snags. White feathers clung to them, showing how often they were used. I watched a harrier drift as if in slow motion to a perch, touch down briefly, and then let the wind carry it off again. These raptors didn't seem to mind each other, until at last a kite took umbrage and dove on a harrier from above. The harrier swiveled and, in a split second of free fall, parried and grappled upside down with its talons.

That mouse on my chair: What did it think it was doing here?

Brushing my teeth, twice I saw the shape of an owl flicker in the ambient light above my solo dome. The motels of commercial San Simeon were just over the rise. Were the owls interested in my rustling, or were their sallies just coincidence? Maybe owls are everywhere above us as we sleep. This random patch of grassland, former grazing land, possibly held the highest concentration of raptors I'd ever seen. I wondered if they would suppress the rodent population to the point where more shrubs might survive and reappear. At the edges of coyote brush, lupine takes hold and, by fixing nitrogen, leads the way for still other plants, renewing the mosaic.

WHEN I CRAWLED FROM MY dome south of San Simeon, there were more hawks in the sky as well as migrating butterflies. And two zebras across the highway. I double-checked with my binoculars. There they stood, their striped rumps blending with the heat waves between me and a bleached rise, just as they had evolved to do a continent and an ocean away. These wild burros left no doubt that I was nearing Hearst Castle. They were a holdover of William Randolph Hearst's fancy, a remainder of his African menagerie on his California savanna.

Hearst Castle properly sits on the onetime Rancho Piedra Blanca, a name that honored the guano-washed sea stacks, the cormorant rookeries, along the coast. Its grantee, José de Jesús Pico, built his adobe above the creek now named after him, at the northern edge of today's commercial San Simeon, which is where the Portolá expedition hunkered down. Beyond Pico Creek it was about four miles on Highway 1 to the visitor center, and I began to track Hearst's palace on my right, high on a green and buffy foothill of the Santa Lucia Mountains. Tall palms, gaudy spires. The two bell towers of the castle's facade pay homage to a Christian past, but inside they hold tanks for water, the new religion.

I bought a ticket for a Grand Rooms Tour and loaded onto a bus. The glass doors of the depot were etched with the California State grizzly. As we started up the winding drive, once a bridle path, the loudspeaker came alive without a crackle: "Hello everyone, my name is Alex Trebek, and on behalf of California State Parks,

I would like to welcome you to Hearst San Simeon State Historical Monument, better known as Hearst Castle." The host of *Jeopardy* seemed a fitting choice for this fact-filled journey in time up the hill. Answer: sixteen hundred feet. Question: What is the elevation gain on the climb to Hearst Castle, which William Randolph remembered surviving as a boy by "hanging onto the tail of my pony"?

The curve of San Simeon Bay was revealed behind us as we ascended, with its forested point and a long wharf that Hearst rebuilt so steamers could deliver construction supplies and, later, crated antiques. Other exotic ungulates and their shelters stood under live oaks as we wove the five hairpin miles. Hearst had the largest private zoo in the country then, with over one hundred species and a full-time veterinarian. From the bus, the castle flickered in and out of view as it was designed to, making the approach all the more mysterious and cinematic. Hearst loved his movies. We drove past cow patties and the "longest pergola in captivity," as Julia Morgan, his architect, had called it: a one-and-a-quarter-mile path under nearly two thousand grapevines and fruit trees planted besides its columns.

Hearst Castle is one of the coast's most popular attractions. Three-quarters of a million people visit each year. And if there is a lasting symbol of both the fantasy and reality of California, it's this estate. Just like James Flood, who bought the Rancho Santa Margarita that would become Camp Pendleton, George Hearst— William Randolph's father—made his money from Nevada's Comstock silver. He then enriched himself further with equally famous Anaconda copper in Montana and Homestake gold in South Dakota. George Hearst's mining enterprise became the largest private mining company in the United States, and at the time of his death as a U.S. senator in 1891, his fortune was $19 million, or $49 billion at to-day's rate. Like Flood, he parked some of this fortune in vast ranchlands, buying nearly fifty thousand acres of Rancho Piedra Blanca in 1865—Pico had sold the rest already—when Mexican landowners were fairly desperate due to drought and new property taxes that were, in essence, a land grab. Soon he acquired the rest of Piedra Blanca and the adjacent, but smaller Ranchos San Simeon and Santa Rosa.

George Hearst's land and fortune were inherited by his wife, Phoebe, who became an important philanthropist; and when Phoebe died in the 1919 influenza epidemic (she was considerably younger than George, having been just a nineteen-year-old schoolteacher when he briefly returned to Missouri as a Comstock king), it all went to William, their only son. By then William Randolph Hearst had built himself a fortune to rival his father's through a media empire, though only after George gifted the twenty-four-year-old the *San Francisco Examiner*. Eventually William Randolph would own over two dozen newspapers. He would expand into radio, movies, and earliest television. The Hearst Corporation remains a Fortune 500 company (number 24 in 2018) and is headquartered in its Manhattan skyscraper.

George Hearst had taken William Randolph to the ranch as a boy, and William took his kids. They stayed in wall tents on platforms atop "Camp Hill," rode out and watched the roundups, hunted deer and mountain lions. But the very year his mother died, William Randolph, at age fifty-six, contacted pioneering San Francisco architect Julia Morgan. "Miss Morgan," he wrote, "we are tired of camping out in the open at the ranch in San Simeon and I would like to build a little something." This modest proposal became the castle-compound dubbed *La Cuesta Encantada*, The Enchanted Hill, which overlays a certain magic and majesty on rude "Camp Hill" while harkening to the Spanish past relinquished to the Hearsts. The amount of white marble in the Casa Grande, its guesthouses, its terraces and esplanades, and its sculptures would soon give new meaning to Rancho Piedra Blanca. It's rivaled only by the Getty.

"PLEASE TOUCH ONLY THE HANDRAILS of concrete or black iron, and avoid touching or leaning against any other objects," Alex Trebek advised as we arrived. "Chewing gum must be disposed of in the trash containers as you leave the bus. . . . Get ready for your own enchantment to begin." Our in-the-flesh guide, Diane, met us as the bus doors swung open and ushered us up some initial steps to the parasol of a live oak. Hearst, she said, appreciated oaks and had the driveway routed around them to preserve them, which accounts for some of its snaking; he also moved eleven mature live oaks out of the way of his castle, rather than cut them down, which meant pouring a concrete planter around root balls as wide as their canopies. Each weighed six hundred tons—it was like moving a house, foundation and all.

Diane told us how Hearst had said, as he left the castle for the last time, that "The little ranch at San Simeon is only half-finished" (the "big ranch," in Chihuahua, Mexico, was over a million acres). And she told us how Camp Hill was also known as Rattlesnake Hill, but "don't worry, the rattlesnakes only come out on a warm day." She brought up how we would have been greeted and entertained by Marion Davies, Hearst's lover, a movie star thirty-four years his junior and now obscure to generations like mine. Their relationship was labeled "the worst-kept secret in Hollywood." "Now, gentlemen," said Diane, "if you want to, we can do the whole tour talking about how rotten men are. But that's no challenge for me."

Past the Greco-Roman Neptune pool, its colonnade, and its seventeen dressing rooms, where Hearst, ever the animal lover, let his dachshund, Helen, swim. The pool, which Hearst had redone twice before he was satisfied, was empty, drained not because of the drought, as at the Getty, but to repair leaks. "You're just a handful of people who have seen it without water," said Diane, putting a good spin on it. Some of the columns were more than two thousand years old. Past the guesthouses, Casa del Mar, Casa del Monte, and Casa del Sol, named for their respective views, sea, mountain, and sun. They are not mere houses, but lavish residences that total more than eleven thousand square feet. Hearst stayed in Casa del Mar as the main house was built. Past an Egyptian statue of Sekhmet, the female guardian of the sun god Ra, polished diorite with a pink feldspar vein through it so that the statue looks as if it's been broken and mended.

Finally we came around to the Casa Grande. The building is far aslant of Mission style, which Hearst thought "bare and clumsy." The front of the castle is in the image of Renaissance southern Spain, a style that in fact hadn't yet traveled to California in any popular capacity, while the rear aspires to Renaissance Italy. The whole Casa is built of reinforced concrete to withstand earthquakes and fires. Julia Morgan was a groundbreaker for early concrete construction on the West Coast, and I thought about how this castle was the extreme to which adobe had arrived—a whole building as one big poured adobe, with steel for interior support instead of straw. The water tanks in its two bell towers were fed by a spring six miles distant, higher up the ridge, via a 1.5-million-gallon reservoir. The facade is a somewhat spare expression of bas-relief—florets and foliage, angels and mounted knights, and knights' helmets, all of them authentic sixteenth-century Spanish pieces sold at auction to Hearst—with an iron gate at center. Over the door, in a niche, are the Virgin and Child. But as Diane said, "It is in no way, shape, or form a house of worship."

We went through a side door into the Great Room, where we were told to stay on the red velvet runners ("No touching, no touching, remember this is a no-touching tour"), which preserved the floor while alluding to the parade of celebrities, politicians, and Hollywood entertainers that joined Hearst for cocktails in the evening: Joe Kennedy Sr., Doris Duke, Clark Gable, Gary Cooper, Walt Disney,

Jean Paul Getty, to name just a few. Hoagy Carmichael on the piano, maybe. They would train to San Luis and one of Hearst's limos would pick them up and bump past Morro Rock and through the seaside cattle lands to San Simeon for days of riding, pergola strolling, croquet, and more.

Always cocktails. Then dinner in a banquet hall that, like the Great Room, is lined with wooden choir seats extracted from Italy. They made for very fine paneling. There were mustard and ketchup bottles amid the silver on the long skinny table. The paper napkins—because, after all, this was camping—read WRH, with forks set between the letters. Colorful district flags from Siena hung overhead. Oak branches bounced with the light through high clerestory windows.

Hearst began this dream in 1919 and he continued to build for twenty-eight years, with just one hiatus when he courted financial ruin and had to slim and reorganize his empire. To build a house at all atop this remote hill was a grand gesture at the time, even apart from its size. It meant improving the basic infrastructure of the entire county. He had to rebuild the pier at San Simeon Bay for the steamship deliveries, and he was instrumental in bringing electricity to the Central Coast. Though unfinished when he died, the Casa Grande has 165 rooms. He filled the interior with a stunning collection of Mediterranean art, though most of the objets and artifacts were hauled away by the Hearsts when they donated the castle and the 125 hilltop acres around it in 1958. "He was what we call today a 'shopaholic,'" said Diane, and it's hard to say whether his taste was good or bad. It was expensive: Greek vases, statuettes, rare tapestries, and whole church ceilings for his own. The castle was his primary West Coast residence, but he had six estates and thirty homes. He only occupied the Enchanted Hill for a month or two each year. But, Diane told us, Hearst had said he would go riding or swimming every day if could.

Through the parlor we went, where guests could retire after dinner to smoke a cigar and play French carom billiards on a pocketless table in a room with a mille-fleur tapestry of a stag hunt, the kind of hunt that had first entertained the Hearsts at their rustic camp. To finish, we filed into the home theater, a separate building with plush seating for two or three hundred and red velvet on the walls. Marion Davies would very often grace this screen, said Diane, and there was no getting around praising her performance. "If you want an invitation back, you're going to love that film," she said.

Tour adjourned, I wandered the grounds, soaking up the warm drafts that carried the redtails, noticing things I'd missed, like the plank slanting into the marble fountain to let the mice climb out of the lily pads before they drowned. But the best part of Hearst Castle is the panorama beyond the guest houses, through the yucca stalks. The driveway meanders down the ridge to San Simeon Point, set within the gilded, retina-burning Pacific. All of the land you can see once belonged to Hearst, and still belongs to the corporation, though, in 2004, California bought most of the ranch's development rights for $80 million in cash and $15 million in tax credits, while opening most of its thirteen-mile shoreline to the public. This was a win for conservationists, since in 1965 the Hearsts had proposed building a city of sixty-five thousand people, complete with an airport (just around the time that the Hollister Ranch threatened to become a city of similar size). But the Hearsts were able to retain exclusive access to some of the stretch's marquee coves and to San Simeon Point as an amenity for the hotel and twenty-seven houses they are still allowed to build.

Below the guest cottages, gold statues and their dimples of Venus lean toward the ocean, reminding me of what the first Spaniards imagined they'd find here: Amazons, or at least their treasure. Crespí and Serra would have been appalled, I think, by Hearst's opulence, hedonism, and co-option of church architecture, but they also would have been impressed. It was the apex of civilization, wasn't it? I leaned on the railing and stared south down the long way I'd come, remembering Cambria and Cayucos, Gaviota and Ventura, Los Angeles and even San Diego. Then I made my way to a bus, stopping to admire the tennis courts on the roof of the indoor Roman pool. I could almost hear the pop of the ball off the gut of wooden rackets. Translucent bricks in the courts allow light into the lapis-tiled water below.

Beyond the nets and their fences, no longer grown with ivy, stood the seesaw crest of the Santa Lucia Mountains, which were named by Vizcaíno on (or around) December 12, 1602, the eve of the Feast Day of Saint Lucy. Soon I would have to cut inland in that direction, as the Portolá party did, and cross the range. Some near peaks were singed and rusted with swaths of fire retardant dropped during a recent blaze, the Chimney Fire, one that had burned about twenty thousand acres of Hearst land, a quarter of the ranch. The park had been closed for nine days in August due to the smoke. The concrete of the castle was, of course, meant to withstand the flying embers of the inevitable fire that would, that still will, sweep across or around *La Cuesta Encantada*. All those priceless Mediterranean artifacts would stay safe inside even as the glass blew out on account of the heat. Today, a helicopter's bucket might dip into the deep aquamarine pool again and again, if there was water in it, and swing up, dripping, over those Greek columns.

THE NEXT AFTERNOON I REACHED Ragged Point Inn, the beginning of Big Sur and the limits of the Hearst Ranch, where I regrouped and debated my course. The Portolá expedition had labored hard to reach this point, as Costansó emphasized: "The road was frequently interrupted by ditches and gullies (all full of water), and the making of it gave the pioneers much to do—now cutting brush with hatchets and machetes, now opening the way with pickaxes and crowbars." Then they came to the impasse of this steep coastline and were forced to deviate inland up San Carpoforo Creek toward the mountain heights. To follow them, I would have to first trespass over the Hearst Ranch, which owns San Carpoforo Canyon, and then trespass into the Silver Peak Wilderness, which, along with the rest of the Monterey District of the Los Padres National Forest, was closed due to the Soberanes Fire. Many miles to the north, it had been started by an untended illegal campfire and burned across 132,000 acres for more than three months, choking the region with smoke, burning homes, and costing over a quarter billion dollars. At the time it was the most expensive fire in the state's history, but each year might now bring the most expensive fire in the state's history. When I arrived, the Soberanes Fire presented no risk at Big Sur's southern end, but the last thing the region and the Forest Service needed was another accidental blaze, so they had closed the trails. I figured no one would be watching this far edge of the immense Hearst Ranch, and I figured if I entered the Wilderness at an interior edge rather than a normal gate, no one would see me there. But I couldn't be sure of either.

The Spaniards' ascent into the Santa Lucias was a pivotal moment, so I had to undertake it. At the Ragged Point Inn convenience store, I bought overpriced supplies: bread, peanut butter, jelly, pasta, and an extra gallon of Kirkland water that I planned to carry by hand. I wasn't sure if the creeks would be dry. Also Pop-Tarts, which seemed the most calories for the dollar. Near dark I hitchhiked from Ragged Point back to San Carpoforo—I'd already walked it—riding with a family in their SUV (thank you for the ride). They left me where the road bottomed out, and I stepped through a barbwire gate and wove a hundred yards inland, up canyon, through the weedy grass that was rabbit- and deer-chewed near the field's edge. Dew settled even as I set up. Headlights swept the gathering fog as cars descended the horseshoe dip through the canyon.

At 7:30 the next morning I was lost in a milky world, which only spoiled to clear skies as the sun and I climbed the highway south toward the ranch road I'd passed the day before. Crespí also grew acquainted with the mist in this place he named Saint Humiliana: "Most of these last shoreline places are so extremely foggy that there is no sight of the sun all day long." "Impossible to observe the altitude as we did not once see the face of the sun in the entire three days." "We are laying by at this spot while they are opening a road over a ridge of the mountains in order to get up them, and we have not seen the face of the sun once in all the days we have been stopping here, and by day and by night we have felt the cold a good deal." Crespí in particular suffered from the cold of Northern California, and possibly he had a congenital sensitivity to it. On several occasions he reported that shivering fits left him unable to say Mass.

The booming surf dramatized my set-off. A marine layer hung over the ocean. Dark sea stacks were swept with white waves down the scalloped coast. My shins brushed the mustard plants and grew wet from the moisture on their wiry stalks. On the roadside I found a little brown bat folded up, a casualty of a windshield in the fog, wrinkled as an oyster on the half shell, ants crawling from the brine of its belly. When I reached the dirt road that was my turnoff, I hopped its steel gate and pushed the pace for a minute, without glancing back, until I was over the ridge and into the canyon, invisible from the highway. Now I was on Hearst land; the ranch employees might have stock or other concerns back here, but it seemed unlikely I'd see anyone. Still I kept my eyes and ears open, and kept moving, thinking I could beat any cowpoke's car into the interior since I'd left early. Or at least beat it off the road into the poison oak, bush lupine, and coffeeberry, the frittered ferns, bramble, and creeping morning glory. There were a few hanging gardens of scarlet California fuchsia, which the Chumash called *s'akht'utun 'iyukhnuts*, "hummingbird sucks it." Apparitional snowberry and diarrheal cow splats. The creek's gravel and boulders showed through its willows; large boulders on the steep hillsides, too, like glacial erratics. "This stream carries a large flow of water," Crespí wrote, "but there is nothing more than quite a large stream bed with a great deal of stone and sand and all lined with a great deal of trees—live oaks, sycamore, willows, other kinds of trees we could not recognize—along with, to one side and the other, a height of mountains that was fearful to behold." By other standards, these slopes aren't especially tall or fearful—they're no Sierra Nevada—but they are steep.

The expedition walked right up or beside the creek bed, crossing it many times, "following it now on one side and now on the other as the lay of the land permitted," per Costansó. I had chosen the dirt road cut into the hillside above it, thinking I would make better time and be less likely to twist an ankle or confront a dam of poison oak. In the distance, ridges feathered into the canyon. One of those I would have to climb toward the crest of the Silver Peak Wilderness. I came upon three young redwoods—the first I'd seen on my journey that might be native instead of planted. Several streamlets flowed across the road and down its ruts and tire treads, which gave me hope that the mountains would hold water. I wondered if a tractor or truck had been through in the last day or two until I came across a downed tree that looked as if it had lain across the jeep trail for a while.

Fresh and rotting bay nuts were scattered beneath a weeping tree that flared my nostrils. The road fell to the creek where its bed meandered broadly across the canyon. Only a four-wheel-drive vehicle could make the crossing. I found a makeshift pedestrian bridge of lashed branches and sticks, high and dry, and it made me wonder again what kind of bridges the expedition would have fashioned on occasions such as this. The road climbed the ridge again, slightly, as the canyon narrowed, and through sycamore windows the creek filled with stagnant pools. I came to a rope swing in the middle of the road, tied to a bay tree. It was a harbinger of a cabin another fifty feet ahead, a plywood building with a roof of tar-paper shingle. I crept forward warily, silent, but soon saw the cabin was abandoned, and I pushed my way inside.

The cabin was like the one Jack Kerouac had holed up in to the north in Big Sur, only given over to the wood rats. The shag carpets were peeled back as if a sudden gust had pried them up. Dried sycamore leaves and newspaper were scattered about. There was a writing desk and, on it, an unopened pack of cards, bay-nut shells, and several rodent jaws still with their buttery incisors. The drawer had been pulled out, and it spilled with scavenged down and couch material, a rodent's nest. A road atlas in good condition lay open to the California page, and briefly I studied my route, the wandering path that had brought me here to this dreamy mess, this cabin gone to seed. The view through the plate glass windows was down canyon through leaves; mist was flowing over the ridge I'd walked under twenty minutes before. An abalone shell dangling from wire on the ceiling twirled slowly and, when the light was right in the late afternoon, I imagined it would throw rainbows. A Pall Mall carton, empty, the ghost of smoke. The pantry doorknob was covered with bird guano, the top of the door, too—a nighttime roost. But mainly, the rats: they had been into everything, into every single place, every single drawer, generations of rats.

A note over the lidless toilet said, "Use a gallon of water when you flush, it helps it go down." Yet the plumbing was defunct, and outside was a dining chair with a hole cut out of its seat and a mass of toilet paper underneath. Didn't look too old. The flies still hunting it. Down the road I found a padded dirt-bike glove and I wondered if it was trespassers like me that had last used this open-air john. Or marijuana growers.

STRIDERS RINGED THE GREEN WATER. Pinecones were lodged in the alder roots that had also, as they grew, caught boulders, both from the peaks. I crossed San Carpoforo Creek and crossed it again near where Estrada Creek joined it from the northeast. The road turned uphill, north-northeast, loosely following but rising high over San Carpoforo on the west ridge, switchbacking. Portolá had camped at this confluence and then pursued this route after the entire expedition pitched in for a day, padres no exception, with machete and axe to clear a path up. "On merely viewing from below the way by which we must climb, it becomes almost impossible to believe that it can be done," wrote Crespí. "I called this the deep lying, large stream of the Santa Lucia Mountains."

Climbing, my skin began to steam; it was easy to see why the soldiers would have needed to toil for two days to prepare "a road" for the mules up this ridge. The road I and William Randolph Hearst walked, assuming he toured this corner of his ranch, might trace their very path. "I was constantly, while on the way up this grade, remembering Mount Alverna, where Our Lord Jesus Christ imprinted His most sacred wounds upon the body of our Seraphic Father Saint Francis; wishful, as I was, that some spot might be found in the midst of these lofty mountains, good enough for a good sized mission of the Wounds of Our Father." Only two years before his death, while on a forty-day fast in a montane region in Tuscany better known today as La Verna, Saint Francis is said to have been visited by an angel with six wings, crucified. At the vision Francis's heart was filled with conflicting joy and melancholy and he fell to the ground. The marks of the nails then appeared on both sides of his hands and feet, and his side was pierced and seeped blood as if he had been lanced on the cross.

A fall off the road here could be catastrophic. Far below, the creek was filled with charcoal boulders, and in the middle distance was a raw spire at a bend that, from my phone, I understood was called Windy Point. It *was* windy. The bay trees climbing the steep ravine moved like anemones, circulating in all directions at once, the boughs of an identical trunk flowing in disparate directions. The manzanita and coffeeberry along the road were swept inland, trained by an invisible and shaky topiarist. Behind me mist flowed wispy from the ocean, but failed to make my turn and instead unwound up Estrada Creek. "When standing at the top and turning around to look back, it was a very fearful thing to see the depth behind us," Crespí confessed.

I ate lunch hidden off the road in the oak shade of a false summit, making my second peanut butter and jelly sandwich of the day. I had twenty-two slices: 120 calories each, I read on the bag. As I thought about it, that wasn't much for several days' hard walk, but the fare at the Ragged Point Inn convenience store was so expensive I'd opted for the most basic. I pulled out my rain fly and hung it on a branch to dry while I ate. It billowed orange and gray in the breeze. Above me a murder of crows arrived and drifted as if to call attention to me. Farther uphill, the road gave out at a small clearing with a rusted post-and-wire corral, but I followed a faint track up some cattle-grazed meadows, burrs filling my socks. White saxifrage like stars in the grass, and the dried galactic cow swirls. Tiny grasshoppers scattered before my steps. Stock tanks in the shadows. I became a little turned around, but discovered a trail that headed downhill toward the creek—my North Star and mantra always is *Follow the creek*—where another trail materialized and emerged to more meadows and what I thought was the wilderness area's San Carpoforo Campground, though it was rather unofficial. I kept on, crossing the creek, which had plenty of water, and finally found a wooden sign that oriented me with arrows. In a normal year, my paranoia would have evaporated here, or miles back. I was solidly on public land. But because of the fire closure, I stayed wary. The last thing I wanted was another expensive citation.

In these meadows where Dutra Creek joins San Carpoforo, Crespí had envisioned a mountain mission. "The hollows are not very broad but do have good little flats of soil that could be put under irrigation," he wrote. He would be surprised by the religious order that has cropped up. Just up the meadow was the entrance to Baldwin Ranch, a private 485-acre inholding that is now a Buddhist retreat center: not the Wounds of Our Father, but *Shiné* land, the Land of Calm Abiding. Its lama founder, first observing this remote hollow from an airplane, described it as ideal for meditation, "the best of anywhere," with the San Carpoforo, though often dry, running through a "lotus-bowl" valley. He was heeding the words of his teacher: "In such a critical situation, in such an impure world, we create a retreat center. With purity, insight, and order, we can help heal the wounded world." And with wonder. With adventure. With walking.

Wishing to respect the monks' pursuit and privacy, and not knowing how Zen they and their guests, or the center's managers, would really be when confronted with a thru-hiker, I walked the creek, empty again, around the Baldwin Ranch compound, testing my ankles on the cobble. Sycamore leaves fell with a lisping rustle to the rocks under the shadow of my broad hat and swinging gallon. The bright prayer flags fluttered in the oaks and from the central white-and-gold stupa. A bell sounded in the breeze.

The Portolá expedition had camped in the vicinity of Baldwin Ranch for three nights as the men further prepared the route, but I kept on, accelerating into their future—walking as much in one day as the expedition had in a week. I had roads and sometimes trails. I had decent shoes. I had no mules. I wanted to make time because I had limited food, and I still wasn't sure how much water I'd find near or over the crest of the Santa Lucias. Heading up canyon, the expedition mounted the north ridge in the vicinity of a road that now belongs to the Buddhist sanctuary. But because I was already in the creek, I decided to avoid trespass and just follow the San Carpoforo drainage as it snaked into the rugged interior. Soon the creek held water again and was overhung with oaks and, as Crespí wrote, "other trees that look to be (though I do not think that they are) quite tall laurels"—California bays. I paused to step naked into a cold, ideal pool. My scrotum tightening, my shins panging, I scrubbed my legs hoping to shed any poison oak oil.

It was a canyon of calm abiding at first. Then it narrowed and the creek filled with boulders. They grew in size until they were mammoth, the kind of impressive and beautiful rockfall that I had played hide-and-seek in as a kid with my siblings and father below the glacial heights of Yosemite. I was wrong about this route being easier, dead wrong. These stones were the size of the Westfalias camped along the coast. I should have known better, not least because Portolá's soldiers had spent two days preparing another route up a ridge "even longer than the last one." They must have had good cause.

I scrambled forward, though it grew difficult and at times treacherous. There's always that calculus about pushing through versus turning around, but I imagined that reversing course and then climbing the ridge would take even more effort. Plus the high route was unknown. I was banking on the boulders disappearing sooner rather than later. This decision led to hours of arduous clambering, especially with a backpack and an extra gallon of water. I should have just poured it out, but I didn't know how long the creek would last—in California, water can go underground as quickly as it appears. It also seemed a waste of iodine tablets to dump a whole gallon.

You know you're truly in the mountains when you flush a whistling dipper, that monastic water ouzel. Soon I had soaked through my shirt and hat as I made strenuous and delicate moves through boulders, hoisting myself up corners and chimneys, scaling slanted rocks in my worn sneakers. I have always been fairly nimble and confident across rocky terrain, but I'm more of a scrambler than a climber. My strength is in my legs, though I have reach. My pack was burdensome. Once, I lost my grip and the plastic gallon crashed down into a pool, where I retrieved it, noting the irony of saving water from water. Several times I feared I would fall and hurt myself, and no one would quite know where I was. I'd told Sarah I was heading up San Carpoforo Creek, but had said, most vaguely, that I might or might not go over the top of the mountains, depending on what I found at the crest. It would be extremely difficult for anyone to find me in this tumbled, rugged mountain recess in a wilderness off-limits due to fire.

After several hours and not more than a mile—probably less—the boulders finally petered out and the creek returned to gentleness, though the way was bedeviled and slowed by poison oak sprigs. A twig jammed itself under my wedding band and broke off—such was the intensity of this bushwhacking. Dusk crept into the ravine, and I made camp just feet from the trickling creek, scanning with my headlight in the dark to be sure I wouldn't fall into a nest of PO. There was a scat nearby, but it was only black bear. The griz were ghosts, though I could well imagine them here, in this tangle. No light before long. Not a star. This was wilderness, if there ever was such a thing. Probably not. The creek talked and talked and, after some time, said "sleep."

MY USUAL SHIRT HADN'T DRIED overnight on account of the sweat, so for once I put on another one. I followed the morning up the drainage, tracing the abandoned Lottie Potrero Trail, which I'd read about during my last-minute reconnaissance at Ragged Point. The trail, if you could call it that, was overgrown and eroded, with the occasional deadfall. It hardly mattered: just follow the creek. Once through San Carpo's cliffy section, I knew I had to turn left up the third side canyon. I had no GPS and no reception, but I had a map saved on my laptop and my instincts for backcountry travel. Then again, I'd just gambled on following the creek and paid a price for it, when an expedition of seasoned explorers had opted for, or even carved out, a high road.

A bit of faded plastic flagging tied to a toyon urged me on. Someone had marked this trail that was like the tracing of deer, rising over steep and dry chaparral and glancing knolls, through chamise (its showering needles) and manzanita. I stopped to pee on some poison oak, but knew it would have the last laugh. My urine was saffron with overexertion. Yucca put holes through my pants and drew pinholes of blood. Finally I reached one last grassy slope that extended to the sky with stands of pines in view, the trees that delivered those cones to the lower reaches of San Carpoforo. A cairn on a serpentine outcrop reassured me that I had come the right way, and I noticed several sawed branches, though cut at least a decade ago.

Finally the crest: I found a wide dirt road, a firebreak really. Beyond was a trough of endless oak-studded ranges and dust toward the Salinas Valley, not yet in view, but where I needed to go. "A sad outlook for these poor travelers, tired and worn out by the fatigue of the journey," wrote Costansó, "by the task of clearing rough passages and breaking roads through hills, woods, dunes, and swamps." Crespí concurred: "There came into view such vast numbers of extremely high mountain ranges that in comparison this one seemed as nothing, and I imagine that one's view must have reached as far as Cape Mendocino. The country looks from the height as though it must prove untravelable." He had quite the imagination, since Cape Mendocino lies two hundred miles north of San Francisco. It had appeared on maps since 1565 as the northernmost limit of the explored coast, and like Monterey was named after a viceroy, New Spain's first, Antonio de Mendoza. In 1602,

Vizcaíno then pushed the map of California even farther north to Cape Blanco, now over the Oregon border.

I slumped in the shade of a rocky outcrop, scarfed down another PBJ, and contemplated my next move. Beyond this long, convenient fire-road scar lay Fort Hunter Liggett, an army base. I had only realized a few days ago that the base extended this far south and would present a problem, and I had made no effort to reach out to them. Could I slip through these upper reaches to the Gabilan Road that headed toward the fort's center and then Jolon? It seemed likely I would be picked up, and the army might not simply let me go. If I tried to stay off the roads and slip overland, incognito, that would make me look all the more suspicious. I thought of unexploded ordnances, of live fire, of the hunters that were allowed in certain sectors of the fort to pursue wild boar. What's more, I had read that the general area I needed to pass through was currently off-limits for training exercises.

Still I was torn. I thought I could make it, but what if I got into trouble? I kicked myself that I was so cavalier or cowed—which was it? I should have asked for permission to push through two days ago. Going forward, down the range's back side, would be faithful to the expedition's route and a hell of a lot more direct than backtracking to the coast, traveling up Highway 1, and then cutting over on the Nacimiento-Fergusson Road, the fort's one public throughway about twenty miles to the north. I sat by a yellow metal gate, a single bar across the jeep trail that led into the base. There was no signage, no warning; I could argue that I hadn't known. I slipped around the gate and started down the dusty road toward today's Italian Flat, which Crespí had named *Los Piñones*, the Pine Nuts, because of the "great many pine nuts like those in Spain" that some six hundred natives offered them at this campsite.

After a few hundred yards, I halted at a bend of manzanita with a view of that "untravelable" country and resolved to call the fort. I had service here at the crest of the mountains, and I found a number. For a moment I stalled and tried to think through my story; it would be difficult to say that I had hiked in on the wilderness trails, because those were supposed to be closed. I would tell them that I had hiked in from the south and was now, I realized, a little stuck.

The fort's emergency dispatcher was patient and kind enough. He strongly advised that I turn about, that there was live fire in the general area where I wanted to pass through. "It would be terribly inconvenient to turn around," I said, "so if it's not strictly illegal, if I won't be arrested, I would prefer to continue, walking only on paved roads from Salmon Creek." He said he couldn't say for sure and gave me the number of the range controller. I called the controller, who answered. I told him my predicament, asked if I could walk through. He laughed over the phone and said, simply, "No." I must have stammered and sort of repeated my question, double-checking if he meant what he said. "No," he said. "Absolutely not. If you try to go that way, you'll be arrested." In my frustration, I imagined he was a real blockhead. He was. I could tell by his tone. But I didn't deserve the time of day, either. My plan was a farce. "Is there another route I could take through?" I asked. "Yeah, the main one," he said, "Nacimiento-Fergusson." With that, we hung up.

I kicked myself. I was the blockhead. Even if traveling through the base was a ridiculous idea, had I planned better and brought more food, maybe I could have just hiked the Coast Ridge Road north along the crest of the Santa Lucias, keeping my eyes and ears out for a patrolling Forest Service Ranger. I would have reached the Nacimiento-Fergusson Road this way. But my loaf of bread was half gone and it might be two days' walk. Nor was there any water up here. So I turned around, descending the path I'd climbed through dense chamise whose burnt auburn flowers, the color of hot red pepper flakes, crumbled at the touch. It fanned across the hillsides in imitation of the wind-driven fire that eventually would consume it in a bid to jump the plowed break of the Coast Ridge Road.

The downhill was faster, much. I dumped out my water bottles straight off, knowing the creek held plenty, and tied the empty gallon to my pack. No way was I going to negotiate the boulder-strewn gauntlet of San Carpoforo again, and luckily I found the remains of the Lottie Potrero Trail over the sheer heights that rose hundreds of feet above the creek. The trail widened into an old road, and I went through a barbwire gate onto the Baldwin Ranch, the Land of Calm Abiding, unhooking and re-hooking it to a post. I followed a white PVC pipe downhill from the ranch's spring until I hit a twisting road that ran past a few modest cabins with plywood walls painted red and green, and prayer flags waving like the laundry I wished to do. Their doors were open to the evening.

Around a curve suddenly I ran into two monks, a man and a woman, their heads shaved, strolling with their hands behind their backs in their scarlet and saffron and sandals. "Excuse me," I said, not breaking stride. "Good evening," I said. They said nothing, only nodded. It was calm abiding. Rounding the next curve, I glanced back and could see they were looking at me, a probable cannabis farmer and ne'er-do-well, through the bay leaves. I raised a hand to wave.

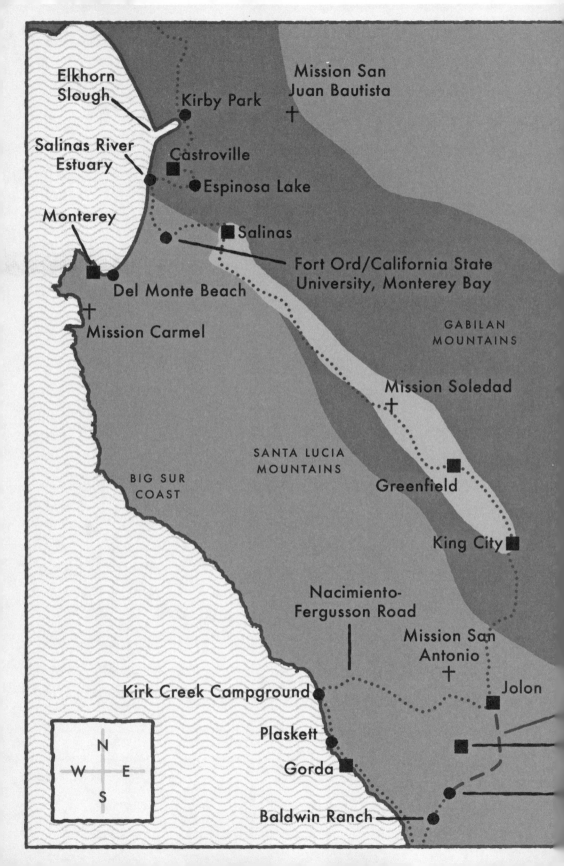

Elkhorn
Slough

Kirby Park

Mission San
Juan Bautista

Salinas River
Estuary

Castroville

Espinosa Lake

Monterey

Salinas

Fort Ord/California State
University, Monterey Bay

Del Monte Beach

Mission Carmel

GABILAN
MOUNTAINS

Mission Soledad

SANTA LUCIA
MOUNTAINS

BIG SUR
COAST

Greenfield

King City

Nacimiento-
Fergusson Road

Mission San
Antonio

Kirk Creek Campground

Jolon

Plaskett

Gorda

Baldwin Ranch

N
W   E
S

Monterey
County

BACK AT THE RAGGED POINT INN the next morning, I devoured another veggie burger, charged up, sent a few emails, let my wife know I was alive, and discovered, with horror, that the Giants had blown a three-run lead in the ninth inning against the Cubs in Game 4, gifting them a ticket to the National League Championship Series. Midafternoon, I roused myself and walked on into *El País Grande del Sur*, though it was *del Norte* for me. What can be said for Big Sur except that it is an almost irresistible coast with a passage that tempts fate? Quickly it seemed a breathtaking death wish to hike this road. I strode against traffic, as I typically do, as seemed a particular imperative here, but it put me on the road's sheer side, the ocean side. My left shin grazed the guardrail and often I preemptively stepped over the rail if a caravan of cars was approaching or if I could hear them around a blind curve. They passed in pulses, bottled up behind Cruise America RVs or other slowpokes. Not much opportunity to pass, not much motivation. Through their glinting windshields, the drivers' eyes were half on the Pacific. I was surprised by how many people in the passenger seats were snoozing, but at this far end of Big Sur, the winding road and heavy dose of the sublime had lulled them to sleep. A keyhole had been smithed in the marine layer and through it, the sun, its reflection, fell on the ocean, a diffuse rectangle to the unending ends of the earth. It looked like crinkled aluminum thrown out someone's window.

Then there was the possibility that the whole hillside would calve away and bury me, as it buried a quarter-mile stretch of road about five months after I passed through, closing Highway 1 for over a year, necessitating a new road over the slide at a cost of $54 million. Five million cubic yards of mountain collapsed and created a new fourteen-acre point jutting into the ocean. While I remained alive, I just enjoyed the invasive pampas grass intercepting the evening light, each a blond mule's tail. The kelp forests far below arrested the water and appeared as oil slicks. The waves rebounded and radiated back across the ocean's edge. I watched a peregrine dive out of sight, out of my life forever, to extinguish some bird. The hills were like old shoulders mottled with freckles and hairs, with chaparral and oak. Hunched shoulders, shrugged shoulders, continental shoulders, old and respectable and destined to slump.

I have to say it was refreshing to know that the Portolá expedition hadn't gone this way, that I could mostly put them out of my mind for a time. I had hoped to get as far as Gorda, about eleven miles down the road, but didn't quite. Instead I saw an opportunity to camp, the opportunity of a lifetime. A horn of land rose up beside the highway, and I figured I should at least climb for the view. I slipped through some barbwire like others before me, dropped my pack, and scouted a loose trail up its rocky spine, hopping boulders to the pinnacle where there was exactly enough flat bare ground for a solo dome. Somehow it had seemed a foregone conclusion, inevitable, that I would find this perfect spot in Big Sur, perhaps the best campsite I'd ever experienced. My choice of gray for a tent color would pay off big: it would look like a rock among rocks. I scrambled down, hauled up my pack. When I pitched my tent it seemed to mirror the pyramidal boulder that crowned the prominence. In every way it fit.

I spent the better part of the next eighteen hours staring into space. The weather was generous; another day I would have been knitted into a wet shawl of fog draped over this edge. From my vantage, I could see 180 degrees along the coast, all the way south to Point Piedras Blancas and its lighthouse, where I'd been five days before. The sun began to obliterate the horizon at exactly 6:34; short days of winter close at hand. Far to sea, a barge passed right through the sun's descent and became an errant Channel Island, drifting ablaze. We were sending materials to China—those massive ingots of crushed paper and containers from the Santa Maria Valley—and they were returning cheap goods and coal particles back over the waves. The kelp beds below were woven mats, mercurial patches. Several swifts chittered above me and at eye level. As darkness fell, the lighthouse began to blip and ray, and on the road trinkets of light wiggled toward me before disappearing, red, in both directions. The road was the ideal human accent, not an intrusion on this remote, sheer shore bridled with white foam. Such a thin paved line. It was the only way to reach here without herculean effort. Prisoners and locals had carved and dynamited the heart of the route through this country's "last frontier" from 1920 to 1938, when the Roosevelt Highway officially opened.

Crickets on the hillside. The chaparral smell that is California. Hoots of a great horned owl far below and, later, a poorwill. The moon rounding toward full. After grueling days in the Santa Lucia interior, this view was calm abiding. I could feel my sore bones healing. The fog or mist moved in and formed a second mountain that embraced the first until it disintegrated. The moon's halo was orange where it filtered through sailing cloud. This pinnacle, this horn, was at the relative center of the descent from either direction into a canyon that dimpled the land, and the headlights swept the mist. A slow-moving car proved a dam to a river of lights as they crawled toward San Simeon or Monterey. I was not at the center of all this, but it was tempting to feel so. The mountains were wings unfurling from my back, and the ocean everywhere before us was beseeching, inviting me and the Santa Lucias to come swim with a tuck like a pelican or an osprey.

I ALMOST STAYED ON MY aerie a second night but wasn't sure I could afford the time, or it felt too indulgent, so I lingered till afternoon, watching the monarchs drift by like leaves turning to ash, and then I hit the sinuous road. The pampas grass marched on, shushing to sea. Its seed had coated everything as if it were snow. I marveled at the sun-blackened coyote scat beside the guardrail—they sauntered even here. The islanded rocks at the base of the cliffs were white with salt or guano and threw off loosely concentric rings as the waves wrapped around them, becoming the middle of a spiral. Egrets rising and falling on their kelp hunting grounds. Suddenly I felt a pain on the outside of my left foot, exacerbated by the crown of the road. Considering the intensity of my scramble up San Carpoforo Creek, I wasn't entirely surprised and thought it might be a bone bruise or even a stress fracture. I wondered what it meant for my expedition, and then I tried not to think about it.

In Gorda, I stopped for lunch at the Whale Watchers Cafe and had the where-withal to ask if there were public laundry machines at the inn. When I dumped my ball of clothes on the washroom counter, leaves and sticks and bay nuts fell out, and I had to sweep this debris into the trash. I imagined all that poison oak oil going down the drain, and later realized I should have washed my shoes. A young woman sat next to me at the long counter below the café's roadside windows. She drew up the shade to look out, and I moved my chair slightly to the right, away from her, to hide in the shadow of the divider between the big panes. The sea was lit tungsten and I had already spent all day staring at it. She also ordered a veggie burger, and she took out a notebook and began to work in it. When I had finished my meal, I asked her if she was sketching or journaling.

"Yes, writing," she said.

"What kind of writing do you do?" I asked. She hesitated. She probably thought I was coming on to her. "I'm a writer," I tried to explain. "I'm actually walking from San Diego to San Francisco right now for a book project."

"Oh wow," she said, but she seemed only semi-convinced. Then she said, "Did you hear about the storm?"

"The storm?"

"Yes, it's supposed to rain for two days."

"Two days!" I exclaimed. "You're kidding. It hasn't rained a drop since I started out."

"The storm's up in Oregon," she replied, "and it's moving this way."

She seemed a little forlorn, maybe not lost but searching, tattoos on her inner forearms and bangs down one side of her face. A writer. She had moved back to California in June, and now she was splitting her time between Northern Califor-nia and Los Angeles, another measure of confusion. I would have guessed, by her caginess, that she was a budder, a migrant worker in the hush marijuana groves of Mendocino County, but she may have just had that Northern California manner of speaking, part soul, part confusion. She described life as "a progress," said we forget to slow down. I tried to say that even when we slow down we usually aren't paying attention, but I'm not sure that made sense. Maybe it does.

Then the whales began to jump. There was a sculpture of breaching humpbacks out front of the Whale Watchers Cafe; there was a whale mosaic at the threshold. It was as advertised. They leaped way out to the sea that poured through the café's windows, a mile or more out, and we would have missed their eruptions except that their back-flop sprays exploded with light and became a dissipating flash. I tried to catch their leaps, these detonations, through my binoculars, but always too slow, I only magnified the impressive slosh that resulted after the whale crashed down and disappeared.

PACIFIC VALLEY 5, MONTEREY 67, SAN FRANCISCO 185. It gave me hope, though my path to the bay would be anything but direct. I passed Treebones, a famous surfing spot, where I videoed riders punching through waves as the week-end swell gathered force. Not long after, a red convertible with a GoPro on its hood passed, videoing me. It was about twelve miles from my dream campsite of the previous night to Plaskett, where I paid my ten dollars for a hike-n-bike spot on the lawn inside the loop. The campground should have smelled of woodsmoke, but no campfires were allowed by order of the Forest Service to avoid more runaway embers. Red tape was stretched across the grills. The hosts, Jim and Natalie, hadn't seen another hiker all season and bent over backward to be kind to me. Jim, who had deep bags under his eyes and curly hair, carried a folding table out to me un-der my Monterey pine, my umbrella, and then returned with a folding chair, too. "Don't worry about bringing it back, because I keep watch out here, and when you leave, I'll just come down and get it," he said.

I told him I planned to go up the Nacimiento-Fergusson Road.

"They have that under tight watch," Jim said. "You're not even supposed to stop along there. On our day off, we drove down to Pismo to party, and then came back up 101, the warm way. We were stopped by the police on Nacimiento-Fergusson, red and blue lights and everything. Of course, when we told him we were the camp hosts down here, he said, 'Oh, go on then, go on.'"

Jim let me settle in, but he was back five minutes later as I was rummaging through my pack in the late dusk. "Here's some high-energy food to help you," he said. "Canned salmon, from Costco."

"Oh, you're too nice," I said, "but really, I'm fine, you keep them." I didn't say that I was a vegetarian.

"You take them," he said, "you'll need them. Do you have a can opener?"

I did. I tried to accept just one, but Jim insisted, saying, "No, no, one for tomorrow, too." As he disappeared in the near darkness, under my headlamp I opened that can with my Swiss Army knife and, with the last few ragged cuts through the tin, the salty brine squirted on my jacket and into my eye. I ate the salmon on saltines with Monterey Jack cheese. Monterey was close. Ate every last morsel, and drank the brine too, and I already looked forward to the next can.

Natalie came by in the morning as I was rolling up my dome. "You shouldn't step one foot on the Nacimiento-Fergusson Road," she said. "They're giving out tickets." I was pretty sure it was fine to walk the road, but I thanked her. That was probably sound advice, but I was the numbskull already hiking swervy Highway 1 through Big Sur.

It's true, though, that I was faced with a conundrum: I could certainly walk and find a place to camp in the National Forest where no one would see me, maybe in the thirsty bed of the Nacimiento River as Jim suggested. But if the same ranger or policeman saw me on the road on two consecutive days, they would deduce that I had ignored the closure order and tented somewhere. Fifteen miles down the road, on the other side of the mountains, meanwhile, was Fort Hunter Liggett, the army base, and I couldn't camp there either. I might end up in a stockade. The road through the fort was maybe another ten or fifteen miles. Thus I would have to hike over the mountains and through the fort in one day: about thirty miles, in sum, to Jolon. That would be a *massive* day, especially going over the mountains in poor weather; it was about ten miles farther than I'd walked any day of my journey, or ever, though on the Pacific Crest Trail some people build up to walking that distance every single day.

I decided it would be not only wise, but fair, to hitchhike to the summit and walk from there, saving six miles and twenty-five hundred feet. My guilt about bumming a ride to the top was tempered by the fact that I had already summited the Santa Lucias up San Carpoforo Creek.

JIM HAD TOLD ME ABOUT a nearby Jade Cove and piqued my interest by reaching into his truck to reveal a huge slice of black jade. "Everyone here has jade in their pocket," he said, "because this mountain is made of jade." I went across the highway in search of the cove, but found Sand Dollar Beach instead. The tide was in, the jade drowned. Cole and Aaron, a couple of surfers, were sitting on the rail looking out at the growing swells, twelve or fifteen feet. The water was so messy, so smashed and foamed, it wasn't worth it. They would take waves on the head in chop like this; the risk-reward calculus didn't add up. "For us to go out there right now, those waves would have to have a barrel big enough to drive a car through," said Cole. He had bed head like me and wore a satiny Padres-Chargers jacket he'd bought for a dollar at Salvation Army, and he smoked a cig. He'd spent the summer teaching surfing in Montauk and only recently come back home. Reticent Aaron, from Florida, had a dirty backward cap, blond hair to his shoulders, and bright blue eyes. About the only thing he said was, "You probably don't want to hear this, but there's something called an 'atmospheric river' coming our way."

"I didn't want to hear that," I said, as a light drizzle began to fall. "What's an atmospheric river?"

He explained, gesticulating softly with a rising and falling hand, that a typhoon had sputtered or spun out in the northern Pacific and become a heavy flow heading south. Atmospheric rivers account for most of the rain California receives.

"Man," I said, "you just went full weatherman on us." Surfers are some of the best weathermen.

I left them ogling the cove, taking videos of the tantalizing slop, and walked a few miles until I reached Nacimiento-Fergusson, an inconspicuous turnoff that zigged sharply uphill. There I was confronted with fair warning: THROUGH TRAFFIC ONLY, NO CAMPING. As I sat beside the Forest Service closure sign, waiting for a compassionate passerby, I studied the bees gathering pollen from the florets of the lean mustard along the asphalt. The bees were silent as they worked, as if gathering that gold furiously before the storm. A flock of band-tailed pigeons clapped out of the hillside, the pale band at their tails' edges visible, but the iridescent purple-green on their napes, you just had to know that was there. After two hours, I cut my losses. I was determined to walk down the back side of the mountains and through the fort after hitchhiking to the top, but my window of opportunity had more or less closed for the afternoon unless I wanted to hitch all the way through. So I hoisted my pack and crossed the road to Kirk Creek Campground, a stone's throw from the junction. It was my father's name, a good omen. LOVE was written in spray paint on the concrete bridge over the creek.

To my surprise, the camp host was a man I'd met on Mill Creek Beach just down the way, picking up trash. "Oh, it's you," I said. "Is there a hike-bike site with some tree cover?" Relentless rain was increasingly on my mind. He directed me to 23 E in a chaotic eucalyptus grove at the bluff's edge. Surf battered the sable rocks beyond. The campground, he said, gave water to hikers and bikers for free, since no potable water was available. If I needed a shower, however, there was the rushing creek. "I do need a shower," I said. Way too cold, though. I surveyed the mosaic of crescentic, minty leaves for flat ground that would drain and, not finding much, pitched my tent. Finally I was camping below the eucalyptus that had kept me company the whole coast. Trees that would have been the railroad ties I'd stepped on for days, if only they'd grow straight and firm instead of just tall and detrital. The atmospheric river began to flow, to rise, and I crawled inside my dome for good. Even as large drops began to pepper my fly, I could hear the Anna's hummingbirds jiving with each other in the high branches.

I thought it had begun to pour, but it was only the acceleration of drops from the eucalypti, which, like redwoods, sieve the mist and funnel the clouds to their roots. The rivulets snaking across my translucent rain fly were steeped in resin, tinted brown. The pounding surf made even a drizzle feel like a hurricane. The pounding surf, the surf, confused and lodged in my brain, the surf, an anthem of this place. In the evening, I boiled pasta just beyond my veranda, peeling my wet fly back so that it stuck to itself and reaching my long arm into the drip to dial back the heat when the pot bubbled over onto the leaves. Steam began to billow inside my dome, and I strained the hot water just out the door. I dumped a can of raw tomatoes with diced green chili over these noodles—can't remember if it was Ortega, but surprisingly spicy—and sliced more Monterey Jack into the bowl. Drank the remaining pasta water, thinking the soup would at least have a few calories. Decided the pot could be cleaned in the morning.

When I stepped outside to pee, my tent fly was lathered with eucalypt suds. The first rain in a long time washes the oil off both the trees and the roads. Well, this ought to put the fire out in the mountains, I thought. At Plaskett, Jim had said that after two days of rain the fire ban would be lifted, but it was too late for me. It was Saturday night. The Forest Service wouldn't end the closure over a weekend. The drum of droplets on the taut snare of my ceiling played on.

"I learn how fastidious I am when it rains," I said into my recorder. "I take such pains not to get anything wet, try to keep everything tidy, that I end up expending much more energy than seems necessary. And it's an impossible battle, anyway. The water seeps in at the sides. I just brushed my teeth out the door and spat into the leaves in the little space between my shoes and my pack, and then insisted on washing my toothbrush with water from the canteen. I suppose I should have just not bothered brushing my teeth. On the other hand, these little rituals are nice. Why give them up? Easy enough."

THE RAIN EASED BY MIDMORNING, but my gut was ruined. Green chili in my pasta was a terrible choice. I felt nauseous and weak and had to scramble to the vault toilet several times through the drizzle. Probably I should have stayed at Kirk Creek Campground another night, but I was worried about losing time—I wanted to reach the San Francisco Bay on November 4, as the expedition had—and I was still three weeks away.

I waited three hours for a ride in an on-and-off sifting rain. The THROUGH TRAFFIC ONLY, NO CAMPING sign on the road had soaked through at its staples, wet blossoming under the laminate. Three guys hoping to go off-roading on the crest's Coast Ridge Road were nonplussed to discover the closure, especially since they'd driven all the way from San Francisco. They gave up and loaded a dirt bike into their pickup so they could travel all together and head to a brewery. I felt like doing the same. But I sat back down. Then three cars turned up the hill all at once; it seemed like a critical mass, my best chance thus far. A middle-aged man stepped out of the first truck to study the closure information. I reported what I could and asked for a ride. He seemed open to it, but his wife, with short dyed hair, shut him down, grim lines appearing on her face as she shook her head and looked straight through the windshield, saying, "We don't have space." Clearly they did have space. But I understood her reaction. I was a tall, wet derelict.

The next car, a black BMW, held a youthful pair, my age, and "Sure," they said, to my immense relief, as I hoisted my pack into their trunk. Isabel and Todd were from Brooklyn and had flown out to join this small caravan for a memorial ceremony, I learned with some dismay, a funeral gathering, at the crest. That helped explain that woman's sour mood, her slightly shell-shocked or locked-down face. I felt terrible about intruding, but Todd and Isabel didn't mind. They were glad for the diversion. She was from California, and had thick mascara on her lashes as she peered at me through the rearview mirror. Her family, she explained, had started bringing ashes to a grove just off the road at the summit decades ago, when one of her uncles plunged off a cliff near here. "That's a sketchy way to die," she said, but they had been hippies. Maybe it wasn't a suicide, but an acid trip gone awry. Other family members had since been scattered in the same spot. It took them about ten years to finally bring her grandmother's ashes here and scatter them. Now they were delivering her grandfather.

The rental BMW smelled of new leather, felt like a cocktail lounge, played electronic music. Isabel and Todd wore the subdued clothes of city-dwellers and mourners. He was a man of few words, but he asked if I wanted a hit off his silver pipe as we climbed the uncoiling road. "Nah, I should probably not," I said, "I have a long walk ahead of me." I understood their need, though. They passed the Mary Jane to each other as we rose into the wan fog, past redwoods in the hairpin clefts and the writhing madrones, some burned black and somber in the mist. The ascent was extreme, 2,780 feet. "I'm so glad I don't have to walk this," I said, though that was only half true. "When it's clear," Isabel replied, "the views are just unbelievable. You can see so far out into the ocean." They pulled off at the summit. "Okay, we're going to set up a tent," she said, as her family milled in the drizzle. Her father had stayed below to direct a few more cars to the top, to reassure them they had made the right turn toward the sky. "Have a nice ceremony," I said, as I backed down the sword-fern-grown Nacimiento-Fergusson Road and then turned and picked up speed. I imagined the old man's ashes mixing with the droplets to feed the redwoods and run into the sea.

EVEN BEYOND THE CREST, WHERE the redwoods disappear, the Santa Lucias were a cloud forest on this day, all drips. Golden maples, yucca, and purpling poison oak on the road's banks. Steller's jays laughing harshly on fanned dark-cobalt wings. Steller's jays plummeting downslope like black rocks cast through the pall. The ridges fell in and out of definition and faded to white. Madrone and oak on the north-facing slopes, chaparral on the south. At times, the road seemed to loop in nearly a full circle so that you could look directly across a ravine to the same road and wish for a rainbow bridge. I had gone about three miles when a Forest Service truck came up behind me and pulled over. It was a technician I'd met while I had been waiting on the coast; he had been driving in the opposite direction, but had stopped to check on the signage before driving on to . . . well, it was a little difficult to understand him through his thick mustache. "To check on some more bears?" I had asked. "No, *barricades*," he had said. He was one of the wizards behind the fire closure, the guy who would replace vandalized signs or pick up traffic cones that had been knocked over by joyriders. At the base of the hill, he had said that if I was still waiting when he returned, maybe he would give me a ride. Now he offered again, and I decided to take him up on it to the gate of the fort. Ten miles through Hunter Liggett was probably all I could manage with the energy and remaining daylight I had.

Because he was hard to understand, Bill, with a vigorous beard and chops, had something of a Popeye effect. His lower lip overlapped his upper. Sixteen years he'd worked for the Forest Service. Enough to retire, but not enough to get much out of it. He cleared out his passenger seat for me gruffly, picking up scattered NO FIRE and FOREST CLOSED laminated 8.5 x 11s and tidying them, tossing empty soda cans into the pickup bed. The cab's heat was turned all the way up, and quickly I was toasty. As we drove east, the road bottomed out and began to roll, and Bill told me how he once had been hitchhiking toward Eureka when he threw out his back. No one would pick him up. He could hardly walk, let alone carry any weight, so he started jettisoning his belongings from his duffel: all his nice clothes, his food. He just couldn't hump it. I suppose that's why he took pity on me, though he wasn't supposed to give rides. All these years he had remembered that episode. He knew the plight of the hitchhiker. When I asked him to let me off at the Hunter Liggett gate, in the middle of nowhere, he could hardly believe it. "Then why am I doing this?" he said with exasperation. "Well, at least my seat is clean." I just had to walk it, I explained. For my project. Had to make the effort. And I wanted to.

THE WALK THROUGH THE FORT was a gorgeous misery. Still feeling sick, I was drained of energy, but the road marched through a savanna of valley oak, the largest oak species in North America, monumental, twisting, fast growing: twenty feet tall after five years, forty after ten, sixty after twenty. These were as much as a hundred feet in height, I gauged. They had found a sanctuary in this military base, which so often double as preserves; training exercises and occasional scorched earth are far preferable, for natural communities, to agriculture or suburbia. Their bark was deeply corrugated, cracked like mud. You could use these handholds to climb into their girthy crotches as if into the saddle of an elephant. But on the trunks nearest the road, red-white-and-blue shield placards read, U.S. PROPERTY, NO TRESPASS-ING. Their glossy acorns were the length of rifle bullets, and when one hit me on the shoulder, it stung. Their empty casings had been scattered by the Belding's ground squirrels, which, every mile or so, also lay on the road with their teeth bared and bloody. But I should not use metaphors of war. It's bullets that look like acorns, even down to the striations. October is the harvest month. Coastal villages of tribes like the Salinan and Esselen would have crossed over the Santa Lucias to gather them. "All the trees were loaded with acorns, as yet unripe," Costansó wrote of this area. "The crop would be so great that many herds of swine could be maintained."

These grasslands hadn't been wet in a long while. Soon green would part the flaxen; already it was emerging on a swath that had been burnt from the road to the near foothills from a stray cigarette or bullet. The low ranges beyond the grass were forested and sometimes ruddy with chamise. I stepped off the road only to piss. Few cars passed, and most of those were white pickups with orange ball caps on the dash, out hunting. I found a boar tusk on the shoulder. And when a bald eagle flushed across the road, I discovered the whole animal: an enormous sow boar, excremental spatter on its rump, bristled, marvelous. The silence in the fort's savanna was complete aside from the manias of acorn woodpeckers and the ground-squirrel alarms. It was an immense relief to have no surf in my ear, a relief I didn't know I needed. Because the fort's airspace is restricted, I heard no plane traffic either. Only the birds simmering hidden. The San Antonio Valley, held here between the Santa Lucia Mountains and the Salinas Valley, has the highest density of oak savanna avian species in North America. These deciduous oaks were called *robles*, rather than *encinos*, the evergreens; due east is the city of Paso Robles, the pass through which El Camino was eventually threaded to avoid the steep Santa Lucias.

My rain jacket was bad, worn out. The drizzle soaked through at the seams, especially at the shoulders, and then the rain picked up more. Water dripped steadily from the right side of my hat brim. I had to suddenly dash off the road and use one of these elegant trees, but hardly bothered to hide. A rainbow over the range, and finally I reached the Nacimiento River, dry, which Portolá's soldiers had named *el Río de las Truchas* farther downstream for its "considerable" schools of trout darting silver. The bridge's weight limit was twenty tons, but an alternate road went *through* the river, which made me think about the weight of those army vehicles.

BEYOND THE RIVER, I PASSED the turn for Mission San Antonio de Padua, which I would have liked to have seen because I've heard it's one of the more authentic. Crespí sensed this corridor would be important, naming it after his guiding light: the canyon of the white oaks (*de los robles*) of the Wounds of our Seraphic Father Saint Francis. In 1771, Junípero Serra and two other missionaries then rode the eighty-five miles from Monterey down the Salinas Valley to this Santa Lucia dale, a five-day excursion. Their guard of soldiers hung a new bell in a standout oak, and as soon as it was suspended, Serra began to ring it fervently, shouting, "Come, you pagans, come, come, to the Holy Church; come, come to receive the faith of Jesus Christ." The magpies and finches must have flushed for a mile around. One of the other padres lamented that it was a "waste of time to ring the bell," since no one but them was around. They had seen no indigenes. But Serra replied that his spontaneous first act was an expression of his joy and that he hoped the bell would resound "throughout the world." A single Salinan man attended the initial Mass. Four boys were baptized that first summer; three of them soon died. It wasn't until nearly two years later that the first adult was baptized.

But the mission museum was about to close for the day and I needed to keep going to exit the fort by nightfall. The red roofs, tan walls, and white hangars of the base appeared on my right. At five o'clock, taps played on the speakers, an excited and mournful trumpet drifting across the grass. A USAA insurance banner: IN MILITARY LIFE, THE ONE CONSTANT IS CHANGE. In the walking life, too. In the life of forests. In history and its interpretation. On the last mile or so toward the entrance gate and guardhouse, I passed signs for, in sequence, LOYALTY, DUTY, RESPECT, SELFLESS SERVICE, HONOR, INTEGRITY, PERSONAL COURAGE. Beyond the barbwire, in the scraggy oaks, there were nets and hurdles and in the distance a giant tower, like a wildlife blind out of control, with ropes leading to it. For practicing the siege. This whole journey, I thought, had been one big obstacle course. ELK CROSSING, NEXT THREE MILES. Yellow-billed magpies sat on the telephone lines and shimmied the rain from their iridescent tails. FOLLOW US ON FACEBOOK flashed the sign beside the checkpoint entrance. Even the military has been colonized.

I sat for a moment in the glass bus stop beyond the gate, across from a retired army tank, and let my shoulders go slack. The Salinas Express did not come. I had thought Jolon would have services, at least a gas station with hot coffee and a frozen burrito, or even a motel, but there was nothing but a few houses and a white Baptist church, where I took water from a spigot. Had I tried to walk to Jolon from the Silver Peak Wilderness, I would have been in trouble even if I hadn't been arrested; I would have had to approach the base for food, or else ride out to King

City. There was a campground in the oaks just inside the gate, but when I asked a man in an idling truck, he said it was "military only." The military, it seems to me, is often in the business of protecting its own. I trudged up Jolon Road as darkness itself began to spit, and I began to feel desperate. Cold and wet, I decided I would hitchhike to King City in the Salinas Valley, a day's walk, for a hot shower and hitch back tomorrow to pick up where I'd left off. That's what happens when you give in to hitchhiking: the dam breaks, a habit forms.

No one stopped in the fading light and rain. I was again a sketchy figure of the blue hour. After ten minutes, I gave up. I would have stayed at the Dutton Hotel across the street, except it was a ruin, an adobe first built in 1849 and now with ornate poison oak braided ruby across its mounds. The hotel had been the center of a thriving town that vanished when the railroad was strung through the Salinas Valley, deciding the fate of the region's commerce. In 1925, Hearst bought the hotel, along with the entire 153,000-acre Milpitas Ranch, adding it to his already enormous coastal estate and pushing its total acreage to 250,000. Near Mission San Antonio, he had Julia Morgan design and build a refined yet rustic hacienda as a base of operations for the Milpitas Ranch and so that unshrinking, saddle-ready Hearst Castle guests could now ride the way of the Portolá expedition and arrive at comfortable digs, "cowboy rooms." Deeply in debt, Hearst then sold the Milpitas Ranch in 1940 to the army, and the hacienda became an officers' club. The Dutton Hotel became a bivouac. You still can rent a room in Hacienda Milpitas, but even the high roof built over the old Dutton Hotel to preserve its adobe is now a ruin, its remaining boards sagging like ribs. All structures eventually become a trellis for poison oak.

So I dove into the roadside ditch, into my one true friend, coyote brush. Its flowers shone white as fresh popcorn. But the muddy patch of ground I found reeked of death: the bones of deer, either hit by cars or thrown there by hunters, were all around me. As the rain continued, as I choked down three Fig Newtons and some saltines and cheese for dinner, as gradually I went from numb and clammy to warm in my bag, I smelled them, rising through my dome's screens. At nine, taps played again. Must have been from the entrance gate. This time the coyotes joined.

ALL THE NEXT DAY, I walked the Jolon Road—the former El Camino—sometimes through rain and dribble, finally rejoining the Portolá party's route as it headed northeast through foothills. Twenty miles later, I would reach the Salinas

Valley. Coming down a grade, on the road shoulder I found a flattened young mountain lion, not long out of its spots, its body arresting oak leaves that covered it like a blanket half torn and thrown off, its muzzle mushed into an artificial grin. It was hardly bigger than a bobcat, but had the identifying long tail, the creamy chest and tawny coat. I kept on, remembering my encounter in the dark of Mission Viejo in Orange County, months before, hearing that loud *Zoe*. I have still never seen a living cougar, though I have seen their signs, heard a female growling in heat in a buckeye and willow arroyo, found their raw kills half-scraped with leaves and grasses.

After the pass, the canyon became a valley that widened until it gave way to the plains of the famous Salinas and its benchland vineyards. Highway 101 and the deciduous mess of the river bottom came into view. "Very much overgrown with trees," Crespí wrote, "white cottonwoods, black cottonwoods, live oaks, pines, willows, and other trees; whether or not this be the Carmelo River, we cannot tell for sure. The sea, it is supposed, may be six leagues away or more." He noted that the valley trended southeast to northwest between two mountain ranges, the Santa Lucias and, to the east, the lower Gabilan Mountains, as they're called today. The natives pointed out where, the next day, the expedition could ford the river. "Everywhere else it is standing in large deep pools where the water is over a man's head," Crespí wrote. The soldiers thought they spied fish of eight or ten pounds. The description of water this far down the Salinas Valley is startling, because today the Salinas is notoriously dry except during flood and is known as "the upside-down river" because it flows mainly unseen through its bed's porous gravels.

After ten days of camping, I found a room at a Days Inn, and I put my stinking clothes in a washer and hung my wet tent, sleeping bag, and jackets from the shower rod, the room's curtain rods, and from all the chairs. My instant coffee had burst open, on the one day my things were wet, staining my sleeping bag, but it rinsed out. More than anything, my feet were in trouble. I had foolishly ignored the signs and not bothered to change my socks after my sneakers had soaked through. The final few miles into King City, it felt as if I had sand bunched between my toes, but it was irritated skin. Now I had "hot spots," loose areas of pallid flesh, emergent blisters. I cursed myself. I've never been prone to blisters, but a bad case could derail my trip. What if these hot spots suppurated and popped overnight, and I had to walk on duct-taped sores the rest of the way? Would continuing even be possible?

It was a rookie mistake and possibly a grave one, but I didn't feel like a rookie any-more, nine weeks into my trek. Which made it inexcusable.

THE NEXT MORNING, MY FEET were only slightly tender. It was a minor miracle. Gingerly I started off through downtown King City, named for its founder, Charles King, who, in 1884, bought thirteen thousand acres of Rancho San Lorenzo and put about half of it under wheat, which the Southern Pacific carried north when it was strung through two years later. This was Steinbeck country, the place where many of his novels are set. John Steinbeck's father was among King City's first set-tlers, selling flour for the S. P. Milling Company. Those were boom times, but now the town felt less royal. Main Street was lined with vacant storefronts whose dim glare threw back my humped reflection. I was surprised to see how long my hair had grown; it had begun to flare over my ears from under my ball cap, "my wings" as some friends like to say, marking the season. Between the *tiendas* and *joyerías*, local schools had taped up artwork inside these dark windows: still lifes of fruit and Ethernet outlets in colored pencil; Halloween cityscapes that doubled, in these environs, as knowing commentary. Studies in perspective.

I walked the tracks out of town, past warehouses and agricultural equipment repair shops, and signs for YES ON Z, PROTECT OUR WATER, and NO ON Z, STOP THE OIL AND GAS SHUTDOWN, Z being a proposition to ban fracking in the county. Both signs were green and white—as if either decision would be environmentally friendly (the small print on the latter: "Paid for by the Chevron Corporation"). Past a car wash that overflowed with the silt of this rich valley, dark clods thrown to the edges of the cinder-block stalls and piled up in plastic buck-ets. Over the sound wall along the tracks, backyard fruit trees shared their yield with me: persimmons, oranges, quinces, firm delicious pears. FRESH HEARTS OF ROMAINE boxes lay limp along the ties. Abruptly King City gave way to the fields that marched, endlessly it seemed, toward Monterey Bay with a brown range on either side. "I remember that the Gabilan Mountains to the east of the valley were light gay mountains full of sun and loveliness and a kind of invitation, so that you wanted to climb into their warm foothills almost as you want to climb into the lap of a beloved mother," Steinbeck wrote in the opening pages of *East of Eden*. "The Santa Lucias stood up against the sky to the west and kept the valley from the open sea, and they were dark and brooding—unfriendly and dangerous."

The Spanish crossed the river upon entering the valley and remained on its east side, I think, the whole way to the Pacific. I stayed on the tracks while they shadowed Metz Road near Portolá's path, the valley's eastern edge. "There was not, nor could we desire, a better road," Costansó wrote of the Salinas. Past fields of baby lettuce, electric when backlit, shivering and shimmering like the water they were, maroon and emerald. Eighty percent of the lettuce grown in the United States emerges from the Salinas Valley, which inspired a nickname from promoters: "the Salad Bowl of the World." Tractors rattled and inspired dust off the rows. Highway 101 in the western distance, heading up a rise. Turning my back to the wind, I couldn't feel it, only the sun's warmth. But when I walked north again, the wind was steady. It swept across the bridge of my nose and cupped my cheeks, and it did the same to every one of those lettuce leaves, wicking.

For three long days I would walk north through this air rushing south from the Pacific, and I marveled at the breadth of this funnel, the Salinas Valley. "The hollow's width here at this spot may be a league and a half from range to range," wrote Crespí, "with the bed of this river running along about in the midst. All along its banks this river makes a low bottomland, pretty wide, with a vast lushness of brambles, countless rose bushes . . . so that all this soil could be placed under irrigation with very little trouble. Beyond it on both sides there comes a steep bank of earth, not very high, and after this comes the plain reaching to the aforesaid ranges." He was dead right about this soil being placed under irrigation; and he felt this portion of the valley was "a grand place for a very good large mission . . . wherefore I named this spot the hollow of Saint Elzear, his day being tomorrow." I felt like I was back in the Santa Clara River Valley, in the Santa Maria Valley, and much of California is relative déjà vu, as I suppose any one state or region tends to be. The hills, they start to appear the same and merge in memory. The degrees of difference are hard to discern at a walking pace. You have to slow down even more, or maybe speed up. You have to live there to understand them or find a guide.

AN HOUR OUT OF KING CITY, I came upon some onions, at least a quarter million. They glowed like grounded paper lanterns in their long rows where they'd been turned up and left to cure. The wind shook their skins and stalks, whisking parchment scraps to a fallow field to the south. What a bowl of soup you could make from these, I thought. The field was like a ballroom floor strewn with marbles. It begged and begged for metaphor. Kelp looked like onions to early sailors and, in turn, these onions reminded me of those wreaths and their bulbs hurled onto the beach, knotted heaps, knotted comparisons, in need of untangling. Or each row was a mountain range like the one beyond it sweeping north, which itself was a braided rope, folds of tan and green, south and north slope, dry and less dry. The whole world could be seen in these onions or a single one.

This many onions just lying out in the sun as if for the taking, with no indication of the work or the water or what had been cleared, _was_ the California promise. And all that skin and those blemished or gashed bulbs would be folded back in, become more onions, or something else: worms and beetles and redtails and the tumbleweed that, as if out of a Western, literally rolled down the tracks past me toward King City like a skeletal bowling ball between long steel bumpers.

The smell, it wasn't as overpowering as you might imagine. The wind carried it from the nostrils. Each onion shining. I wondered if I had ever eaten an onion from this field, and I wondered what I had paid for it. Inexplicably, there was one red onion among these pearls. Certifiably red, which more actually means purple. Then I saw another, several rows in. Was it a genetic anomaly or a stray seed?

The hollow whistle of the wind around telephone poles. The telephone poles stretching north to the ridge where it jutted into the valley and the tracks disappeared into a tunnel. I would instead climb Metz Road over this shoulder of the Gabilan foothills hard on the river, not risking the darkness and the Coast Starlight train. This may be the same prominence that Crespí and Portolá climbed: "We came to a low little range, went over a knoll, and down once again to the same level and river."

When I reached that knoll top, I could look back on the day across the vegetables to King City's warehouses. God rays, splintered light, fell through the notches of the intermediate Santa Lucia peaks, to the west, and I realized it was near time to find a campsite. At my shins was a roadside cross and a mug of nylon flowers for Chilo Peña, who was born the year I was born, 1984, and had died earlier in the year, in May 2016, presumably in a crash on this hill and its sharp bend. "Chico," I thought it said at first glance. In the grass a few paces away, I found a dead northern shrike among the white conical paper cups from the fields' water coolers. Like hawks, shrikes use their sickled bills to tear flesh from the mice and other birds they hang from thorns or barbwire, caching them for later. What to make of this? Not much light left. I descended to the upside-down river.

AS IF THROUGH STAINED GLASS, the sun penetrated the year's final leaves of the poison oak that provided my cover, throwing crimson ovals, blotches, on my rain fly. I had wandered sandy jeep trails in the Salinas River bed before finding my place in space for the night, not far from where Chalone Creek enters the river from the east, which is where Portolá likely camped in a cottonwood grove. The signs let me know that I had trespassed on Topo Ranch, and I tipped my cap to them. Cold morning in the bottomlands. I Jetboiled water for instant coffee and stood drinking it in the grass and mostly leafless scrub, bouncing for warmth. To the northeast, beyond the valley, was a large notched mountain I had been tracking since King City; now I realized it was Pinnacles National Monument. Through my binoculars, I could see rock spires. Pinnacles is a famous climbing destination. Seemed too far to detour, but I was hopeful I might spot a condor, which nest there above the Salinas Valley.

I backtracked to Elm Ave and headed east toward Greenfield, with the goal of making it to Mission Soledad by afternoon. This direction was a divergence from Portolá's route; I was meandering like the river itself, side to side in the valley. Along the shoulder of Elm, a spill of blue rubber bands had occurred, printed with PRODUCE OF THE USA #4060 and cracked now. Greenfield has an apt name considering the agriculture that surrounds it, but actually the name honors an early settler. It is also known as the "Broccoli Capital of the World," and true to form, broccoli also was strewn up and down Elm Ave like the footprints of the Green Giant I saw on cardboard scraps along the same road. Broccoli is especially spongy when stepped on, soothing.

Right on Second Street, left on Apple Ave: suddenly I was in suburbia, on a street with adolescent sycamores and modern stuccoed houses with two-bay garages, all of it shades of beige and yellowish-brown. NO ON Z, YES ON Z. Halloween ghosts and witches suspended from doorways and balconies like the plastic bags I'd seen on road shoulders and barbwire fences my whole walk. I passed Cesar Chavez Elementary School—RETAKES ON TUESDAY, OCTOBER 25—and imagined those kids with their wandering eyes, inopportune blinking, and braces. They'd grown up in a sea of agriculture, but you wouldn't know it from these streets. I hadn't been in a suburb in several weeks, so I enjoyed this oasis. Just over 101, I found myself in Burger King, logging on to Whopper Wi-Fi and eating a value bag of onion rings, each ring no more than two inches wide and impossibly savory. How did they find onions so tiny? The uncountable ones I'd seen the day before were enormous by comparison. Did they discard the outer layers in favor of a more succulent interior?

ACROSS ARROYO SECO, A TRIBUTARY of the Salinas that is an ample boulevard of cobble flowing, motionless, from the Santa Lucias, I spent a half day walking north on Los Coches Road, a country route that climbed from the floodplain to the upper bench through vineyards and past a prickly pear cultivation that seemed a nightmare maze. The light had the flatness of autumn. Once lettuce pickers erupted into cheers on the plateau above the river, honking and shouting, and I wondered what it was about: how seldom we learn the true nature of the triumphs and sorrows of those we pass by.

The bird guns boomed. Starlings rose from the vineyards, leaf and wing alike rustling emphatically in the wind. The flock expanded and contracted en masse—becoming a basket funnel, tightening to a ball, spreading into a blanket—until it sank back into the grapes where the birds would plunge their stylus beaks into the pulp once more. Hundreds, maybe thousands. One on every single post. Other vineyards had tied flashing to every fourth post, each length shining and blowing southward. I gleaned culled bunches off the earth, pinot noir, rich purple, and ate around the powdery mildew, the grit, the leakage. A mile down the road I wondered about pesticides and, with a whiff of hypochondria, began to feel sick. I had seen and would see signs along the fields with a skull-and-crossbones pesticides warning. But then I remembered the recent rains and felt better, and probably these vines were only sprayed with sulfur anyway. At one vineyard, a picking machine drove over each row like a zipper, shaking the canes furiously to harvest the clusters, the whole trellis rattling whenever the Zamboni-like vehicle passed and pounded the steel posts. It was economical, but it was undiscerning and would produce inferior wine. It was a way around hiring field hands, who are both hard to find and expensive, though by California's standards often they're barely paid a living wage.

The Portolá expedition saw bands of antelope as they marched up the Salinas, "of all hues, just as they were scattered flocks of goats." "Everything has been burnt off by heathens," Crespí wrote, "so that because of this hardly enough grass can be found for our mounts. A great many large beaten paths made by the heathens are met with, but we have not come across any village, nor heathens either, beyond two who have accompanied us from the Saint Elzear place." As in Los Osos Valley, one wonders whether the bears deterred the Salinans from living on the plain. Or maybe it was the relentless wind.

The vineyards became lettuce fields as the road angled toward Soledad, two-thirds of the way up the valley. Bus after white bus, trailing porta-potties and their berry-cherry fragrance, carried the *piscadoras* home past me. Rather than crossing the river, I turned onto Fort Romie Road toward the mission that lent Soledad its name. Modest houses were isolated in the fields. An eerie sound emanating from one, I realized, was a recording of a peregrine falcon, another bird deterrent, and on another driveway a NO ON Z pro-fracking sign stood beside an ORGANIC sign, emphasizing that many farmers go organic for the money, not on principle: there's nothing organic about pumping chemicals into the ground to dissolve hidden rock and extract natural gas. But one's livelihood is the bottom line. I understand that.

MISSION SOLEDAD GREW LIKE A lone vegetable in the Salinas fields, a purple onion. I reached it around 6:15, my pace quickening as the long ramps of light through the Santa Lucias' gaps levered into the stratosphere on the crest's fulcrum. You might mistake the mission for just another farmhouse, except for the olive orchard beside it rather than an ensemble of tractors and equipment. The old adobe remains were covered by a sheet-metal roof, and a newer mission building stood behind it. Ice plant out front beside the closed gate: SMILE, read a sign, YOU'RE ON CAMERA. It was after hours, but I was in need of a campsite, so I walked the north perimeter, which wasn't fenced, only planted with trees. I wondered if anyone would mind if I slept on the rotting olives or pitched my tent in a weeping willow. But when I reached the rear of the property and saw a caretaker's house, I thought better of it, though in retrospect it's hard to imagine them refusing a pilgrim like me enough ground to pitch a tent for the night.

I stood by the mission gate and considered the river, which lay across a quarter mile of miscellaneous fields, planted or unsown, with houses on spur roads to either side. Scanning the wash's tree line with my binoculars, I saw a fence, at least in places, to keep the deer or other marauders out of the vegetables. I started toward the nearest offshoot road, one that would take me past two houses before I could dash for the riparian cover. It seemed equally brazen to just light out through the fields, where there would be no hiding.

But a woman in a white sedan turned into the lane and parked in the driveway of the first house. She then pulled out and backed in, awkwardly, like she had never done it before. She turned her headlights off but remained in the car, and I understood she was watching me from behind the windshield. After weeks of surreptitious behavior, I recognized it in others. So I aborted my plan and kept walking, nonchalantly following the road's curve toward the far ridge that rose into the Santa Lucias, but soon pausing to study a satellite map on my phone. There was a strip of scrub against those far bluffs, and a public road beside it. I didn't know if that ground was flat, but feeling desperate in the dusk, I headed for it, about a half mile away.

"Shortly after we stopped we heard a great deal of shouting and uproar from some heathens not very far off in the thick woods along the river," wrote Crespí near here, "woods that in places must be four hundred yards and more through. We thought it must have been some village that had been encamped among the woods. They [the soldiers] went to approach where all the shouting and uproar was heard from, and a great many heathens were seen all of whom had their bows and arrows, seemingly hunting; for we had been guessing that they perhaps had noticed us and had become upset, but it was seen this was not the case, but instead they were so intent on their hunting they had not noticed us. Along with our officers I myself so approached them, and it was clear to see how they had not heard us but then caught sight of us and stopped their shouting. They were signaled to with a white cloth to come over, but they commenced to throw handfuls of earth into the air and play on a pipe. Our Captain [Rivera] said they were not in the mood . . . Not one of them came over nor even approached, and these are the only people whom we have observed such behavior along the whole way since San Diego."

To make time, I decided to cut through the fields on a dirt access road between blocks, just as a white truck drove by. I assumed the driver was just passing by and wouldn't care. But he turned onto the road parallel to mine and started to drive my pace. These neighbors were watchful. "Cut me some slack," I said aloud in the wind. When I reached the end of some lettuce, I veered on a diagonal, directly through an empty field, to avoid tromping right past another house and unsettling any dogs.

My feet sank surprisingly far into the freshly tilled soil. My tracks would be obvious tomorrow. If any lettuce sprouted in these prints, those heads would be eight inches shorter than the rest. Another white truck—all trucks in the Salinas and in agricultural valleys everywhere are white, to reflect the heat—slowed on Foothill Road where I was headed, probably also studying me, but it didn't stop. Scrambling up to the road, I saw my goal, what looked like a shrubby terrace on the other side. In fact, it was a berm that hid a trough filled with chamise and desiccated fennel. Going over the top I felt something like a soldier finding cover in a trench. This would do. If no one had seen me climb over. I stomped a clearing for my tent in the dry fennel, cracking and sweeping away the canes with my feet before bedding down to dream of starlings.

LA MISIÓN DE MARÍA SANTÍSIMA *Nuestra Señora Dolorosísima de la Soledad* was founded in 1791 by Father Lasuén at the site of an Esselen village called *Chuttusgelis*. The Esselen were a small, linguistically distinct population of about five hundred to fifteen hundred people, whose territory was mainly the rugged Santa Lucia Mountains. They moved up and down the drainages to harvest from both the seashore and the acorn interior. The archaeology of the mission's "neophyte plaza," around which dormitories with a total of forty-four rooms eventually housed the natives, uncovered hearths and lithic shards on the packed clay surface of the original village. It was hidden a foot underground and showed the village's gradual assimilation, with manos and metates appearing for grinding corn and other evidence of European presence and trade.

Mission Soledad remained a lonely and difficult outpost, and it experienced a revolving door of padres, thirty-three in all. Most couldn't handle its stresses and requested transfers. Perhaps above all, the mission wasn't endowed with a reliable water source. Even after 1795, when a five-mile aqueduct was built, enough water for irrigation or bathing was likely seasonal. The zanja ran from southeast to northwest parallel to the El Camino, both now disappeared. At the mission, the ditch separated El Camino from the neophyte plaza, likely an intentional design by the padres to help keep the neophytes from European diseases and other meddlesome or tempting intrusions walking or riding by. At its peak in 1804, over six hundred neophytes lived at the mission, not many compared to other missions, but impressive considering Soledad's conditions. Many of its neophytes were "recruited" from the Chalon and Yokuts because the local populations—the Rumsen, Salinan, and Esselen—were relatively small, and two other missions already existed: San Carlos and San Antonio, the second and third oldest missions in Alta California.

The narrow chapel that stands today was rebuilt on its original footprint from its own disintegrated adobe in 1954 by the Native Daughters of the Golden West. Its hand-hewn planks and beams are painted cerulean, the color of the real Salinas sky on a clear day, with accents of yellow and red, offering a sense of the mission's original hues. In fact, this chapel was first built to be a storehouse. It was only converted to a chapel in 1832, just three years before secularization, after repeated floods destroyed the original church. This conversion and downsizing were a sign of both persistence and defeat.

The residence wing that was the quadrangle's western side was rebuilt in 1963 and now houses the mission's museum and offices. Outside, around a corner—past a statue of Junípero Serra set in lavender, bees humming in the scent—is the exposed footprint of the original church, which made up the quadrangle's south side, just fragments of floor tile and foundation cobble and stone. A sign there says PLEASE HONOR THE REQUEST OF THE NATIVE AMERICANS AND DO NOT PICK UP OR MOVE ANY BONES. José Joaquín de Arrillaga, twice the governor of Alta California, is buried in the old church floor, his grave now under a concrete pad in the bare dirt. He died in 1814 while visiting, and he may have come for precisely that reason: to pass on in the company and care of his friend Father Ibáñez, the mission's longest-standing padre of fifteen years, who is buried not far from him under another concrete rectangle, his brown Franciscan habit now burrowed through. Beyond them I saw a field of broccoli with a hundred sprinklers moving in arcs, several barns, and the mountains. With nothing but agriculture in all directions, including vineyards striating the western hills, Mission Soledad may paint the most accurate picture of the cultivation that would have surrounded each mission. Five thousand vines were still planted here when the mission dissolved in 1835. But the sprinklers, the groundwater pumping—those are miracles that would have made the padres and neophytes drop to their knees.

The eastern side of the quadrangle is a melted adobe ruin, now under a high sheet-metal roof, that once held an agricultural loft and workshops. I stood thinking of the similar ruins I had seen marking the ghost of the El Camino, most recently in Jolon and, long ago, at the beginning of my walk, at Las Flores in Camp Pendleton. Then I walked by the courtyard's central fountain that, unlike some of the wealthier missions such as San Juan Capistrano and San Buenaventura, was an abominable but fertile cascade of algae teeming with grazing snails—one snail floating along in the water, upside down, to eat the particles trapped in the surface film, a behavior I had never seen or imagined.

IT WAS THEN THAT I saw three men on the driveway, which was lined with a riotous grapevine. Their white pickup held a pair of hundred-gallon totes, so I surmised what they were up to and headed for them. A man named Tom greeted me and seemed a little relieved to hear that I was just a curious visitor, not an authority. "I saw you guys were harvesting," I said, "so I thought I'd come check it out."

"Absolutely," Tom said. "These are like one-hundred-twenty-year-old Mission vines. They're about ten times bigger than any other vines we work with."

Canes and tendrils sprawled out onto the driveway and rose into the sky like my cowlicked hair. The main trunks were a good foot in diameter, with a gray and shaggy bark that swirled upward, while the vines' branches seemed to consume the rusty wire that supported them. Underneath this unruly foliage were caves of green that I could have slept in. The actual grapes, meanwhile, were larger than any other wine grape I had seen, big as marbles. "These are prehistoric-sized clusters," Tom said. "I've never seen clusters like this before." He held up one bunch by its stem, for a photo in front of the Santa Lucias, and it was as if he was hoisting a trophy fish. It wasn't clear if anyone had pruned in the last decade, but probably that was fine. Mission grapes are known for hardiness, longevity. "If it isn't broke, don't fix it," said Tom. "For how old it is, there are so many grapes."

Tom and his colleagues had driven an hour and a half from the Picchetti Winery in Cupertino on the San Francisco Peninsula to harvest this single row. "It's real special," said Tom. "At one point, this was the only grape grown in California, the Mission varietal. And now it's almost extinct." Only about five hundred acres of Mission grape still exist in California, and this row at Mission Soledad is one of the oldest examples. This year was the first year Picchetti had harvested here, but for fifteen years they had been making a fortified dessert wine called Mission Angelica from legacy Mission vines. "It's got lots of sugar, and lots of alcohol, about nineteen percent," said Tom. Between this haul and one other from another source, they hoped to produce about a hundred gallons, or roughly a thousand half bottles (375 milliliters). Each would sell for twenty dollars from their tasting room at their historic winery on an open space preserve above Stevens Creek Reservoir. They serve it with ice and a lemon twist, the traditional way. Every year they sell out.

"We'll get as much as we can," said Tom. As they harvested, they discarded excessively damaged clusters. "There's not too much mildew on these, though," said Tom. "It's more like bird damage. I wonder if the birds are going to be upset because we're taking all their food?" The starlings wouldn't mind. The Salinas Valley is awash with grapes.

About a decade ago, the Mission grape's origin was genetically traced to an obscure Spanish varietal called Listán Prieto. Also known as Palomino, Listán is a white variety grown for sherry, and Prieto means "dark or black." The name hints at a quirk of the Mission vine: both white and red grapes occur within individual clusters, which was plainly seen as these men clipped the bunches and let them plop into a five-gallon orange Home Depot bucket (LET'S DO THIS on its side). Listán Prieto is rare now in Spain—likely it was devastated centuries ago by a louse epidemic. But the variety was cultivated extensively in the Canary Islands, Tom explained, a key stopover for the Spanish on their voyages to the New World. The padres carried seeds or cuttings to the Americas, planting them at missions to produce sacramental and table wines, and from the first mission vineyards, cuttings were grafted all over California.

Mission Soledad was letting Picchetti Winery harvest them for free in exchange for a few cases of Angelica, a fantastic deal for the winery. Back in Cupertino, the totes' spoils would be forklifted right into a pneumatic press: a large stainless-steel drum with an inflating bladder that, over the course of three hours, would squeeze the grapes dry. "All the nasty shit will just be left in the press," said Tom, the skins, seeds, and stems. Dust and other particles settle out within twenty-four hours, and the juice is siphoned into barrels to ferment. Finally the wine is fortified. "We use high-proof brandy to arrest the fermentation, keep it sweet, and increase the alcohol," said Tom. "It also prevents spoilage organisms from attacking the wine. With that level of alcohol, it's a completely food-safe beverage, so it can survive a donkey ride in the hot blazing sun of California without spreading botulism. If you make wine the wrong way, you can just start spreading diseases." Botulism: a word I hadn't heard in a while.

When the visible grapes were gone, Tom and his colleagues crawled under this behemoth into the filtered green light, where they discovered more glowing clusters. As they knelt and reached out with their red clippers, they were like surfers grazing the inside of a slow-motion barrel, one of the last waves of Mission grape. "I can't believe how many grapes are down here," said Tom. "When you're up inside, looking out, you see a lot more. There's a lot on that side of the vine, too, but we can't get over there. That's, like, priceless artifacts over there."

Beyond the vine were the rubble foundations of the mission's original blacksmith shop and gristmill. The millstone lay on a pile of other rocks and was angled toward the sun like a sacrificial altar, its once-round shape chipped now, worn rectangular. HERE GRAIN WAS GROUND INTO MEAL AND LATER PREPARED AND SERVED TO THE MISSION INDIANS AS PART OF THEIR DAILY DIET, read the wooden sign. It did not mention that the Esselen themselves had done the grinding and serving; that they were the stone that made this place turn; that they had harvested and pressed the grapes from the many rows of vine that once stretched out from Mission Soledad.

DOWN THE ROAD, I FELT some of those Mission grapes being pressed in my own stomach. The shadow of a butterfly crossed my trail. Yellow-rumped warblers pounced in the grass below a row of pines that, along with eucalypts, typify the windbreaks that are so necessary in the Salinas Valley. Not much breeze today, the sun stronger, trade-offs. Retired tractor tires painted white were buried in front of the irrigation wells along the vineyards, to protect them. The drip of a thousand perforations in the irrigation lines in the southern light was silver, was art.

By a fallow field, I came to an abandoned barn and detoured off the road to step inside and see if there were any owls. The doors were thrown off and, inside, the slatted walls were cast with hundreds of bright ovals and slants from missing roof shingles, reminding me of how brilliant the stars had been here in the Salinas Valley, an inherent agricultural dark sky reserve. In one corner, coils of poison oak grew toward the gaps in a horse stall, where an old, curvy Studebaker, or something quite like it, was rusted out with its shield hood thrown open as if someone had just stepped away from tinkering with its engine block, fifty years ago. In another corner, a spindly oak tree my height grew. Its serrated leaves—and everything in the barn—were covered in a film of dust swept down the valley. Through the barn's glaring mouth, beyond a grandmother oak, the tractors that had replaced the horses that had once lived in this stable raised more dust. Slow and fast, the surface layer of this whole valley was blowing to the south while the upside-down river ran north with phantom sepia floods.

There were no owls, but it did seem they sometimes roosted inside this ramshackle barn despite the revolving constellations of daylight. I found a rodent skull upside down on the earth, its stained incisors pointing toward the roof as if they had gnawed all those holes. There were owl pellets and piles of rat droppings side by side: the rodents moving in as if to keep their enemies too close for a full-throttle swoop. Out the back door, an orange tanker truck roared past on the road, its job to pump the porta-potties that migrate throughout the Salinas. As I stood inside this wooden planetarium of the imagination, I was carried back to when these shrunken planks would have been new lumber, these walls stacked high with alfalfa. And as I walked on, I thought about how, except for the holes and the lack of pews, there wasn't much separating this barn from the chapel at Mission Soledad, which had also been a storeroom.

THE STATE PRISON ROSE FAR over the vineyards, massive and pale beyond the gray scruff of the Salinas River, amid the blue-green fields of lettuce and broccoli, in front of the moving dashed line of Highway 101 and its semis. "Two mountain ranges have been keeping with us during all of these marches," wrote Crespí. "The very high mountains grown over with live oaks, on the west; a high range also on the north, with only a few patches of pine trees here and there." These mountains began to taper toward the sea and "the country became more open," as Crespí observed. On the shoulder, I found the Platinum Wells Fargo debit card of Irma Salas Escobar. A hundred meters on, I found her Costco Wholesale Executive Member Club card, nontransferable, but, on the reverse, saw that Irma was a man: his photo in gray, a ball cap just like mine. On this stretch, I encountered the first buckeyes of my journey. "Wild chestnuts, the fruit of which has a bitter taste," said Costansó. They had dropped their large five-point leaves, now shriveled and curled on the ground; their branches were drooped with the year's nuts, the largest seed of any temperate tree. I've always felt buckeyes properly should be called "buckballs," since the pods are so scrotal. The husks are stiff and leathery. The rusty seed inside is smooth, shiny, and soapy, almost reflective, with a distinctive green smell. Hold the naked seed in your hand and the name makes sense: buckeye staring up at me, poisonous. California natives crushed them and dumped them into rivers to subdue fish, which could then be collected off the surface, still alive but paralyzed. I worried this buckeye in my hands for miles like a rosary. And I talked to myself in the past tense of the present that was hardly a minute old:

"Then I found a screech owl that could only have been killed last night because, as I moved its wings, its feet, they were still completely mobile, completely fluid, could open its claws all the way. I could move its wing at the shoulder joint in the silence that it would have enjoyed, would have needed, in life. One eye seemed to have been eaten out already, the eye that was exposed. The other was shut. When I put my finger up to its claw, its talons barely wrapped around my middle finger. How petite it was. Its tail so much shorter than its wings. A beautiful gray-brown-white pattern and, um, very small 'ears.'

"I examined it and took some photos. Then I decided I shouldn't leave it in the sand, in front of that block of vineyard hard on the road. So I saw a buckeye tree on the other side of a skinny little patch of vineyard on the other side of the road, took it up there, climbed up there over the black old buckeyes of years past, and left it right at the base. And I took two of the wing feathers, I guess just to remember it by and have a record of what a screech owl feather looks like. . . . Maybe it had sat in that buckeye at some point in its life. Maybe it sat on that buckeye just before it flew and got confused in the light and hit some hard air. Smelled faintly sulfurous. There was one dead yellow jacket I noticed next to it, maybe killed off by another yellow jacket . . . maybe just coincidence. . . . I suppose I could have tossed it into the vineyard and then someone would have had owl in their wine."

ONE MORE NIGHT IN THE dry river. Dirt bikes startled me at last light. Their headlights guttered like a candle flame carried down a hallway, through the arundo and fennel, as they revved and whined across the soft silt from the Santa Lucias. There's something so menacing about a sudden motor in a feral space, in particular when you're all alone. Silence is good news.

The next day, as the mountains began to fall behind me, I crossed the river near Spreckels, named for a "Sugar King." A few miles south of Salinas, once Spreckels hosted the world's largest sugar beet factory: it processed three thousand tons of beets each day and consumed a river of groundwater and sweet-smelling air. John Steinbeck worked for a stint in the refinery out of college and later set part of *Tortilla*

Flat in this company town. The retired stacks and silos rose up over the river's cottonwoods. Soon I crossed the intersection, Confederate Corners (now Springtown), where the Portolá expedition approximately camped. There was a pumpkin patch and farm equipment center: NEW, DEPENDABLE FARM EQUIPMENT. RENT THE BRANDS YOU TRUST. I kept walking into Steinbeck's hometown, Salinas, on Main Street with my stilted shadow in the broccoli heads. Crespí wrote: "In the distance in between two points of mountains, a great amount of trees appears to be in sight, and with more assurance now we suppose this to be the Carmelo River, and the trees in sight perhaps to be the point of pines, and Monte Rey to be not far off now." He could hear the sea, but I only heard cars. The air was tinged with salt.

"No village nor a single heathen has been met with in today's march," Crespí recorded, as they neared the valley's end, "though a great many large beaten paths made by the heathens crossing between one mountain range and the other have been, as well as a great many narrow paths that we think belong to the great many antelopes and bears found throughout these lands." All of California was drawn with these cross-hatchings, now paved over or overgrown or plowed under, the grizzlies and the antelope gone. Their trails and scents linger in the natural imagination only. And where there were no obvious villages—quite possibly because of the bears—now there is Salinas, the Monterey County seat.

Salinas is a place where a Morgan Stanley stands across from vegetable rows to the horizon. Where succulents grow in wine barrels at the local smog check station, Valley Center Car Care, and sea otters are painted on electrical boxes. The downtown, with its Victorian and Art Deco buildings, is a time capsule with fabric stores, tailor shops (rows of gleaming Singers, SUITS CUSTOM MADE ON PREMISES), and even a camera store that still sells and processes film, probably one of the last in the world. One hundred fifty thousand people live in Salinas, but it had the feel of a town half that size, which it was until recently. Salinas draws its name from the salt marshes that occupied much of the plain at the valley's head, marshes long ago filled and made field. In 1795, a Spanish concession was given for a seventeen-thousand-acre ranch, dubbed Las Salinas, which included today's town and stretched to the Pacific. After the American acquisition, the town finally boomed when the railroad went through in 1867. Always the same story: the railroad made kings of outliers. By 1924 Salinas had the highest income per capita of any town in the United States. That is no longer the case, though the valley still supports a $2-billion agricultural industry. This "green gold" is concentrated into the hands of fewer and fewer, and many of the farmhands barely earn a living wage. Thirty percent of agricultural workers in the Salinas Valley live below the poverty line, and ironically the valley is known for its food deserts: places where it's difficult to find a grocery store with fresh and healthy food.

THE EXPEDITION MOVED ONLY A short distance on its next leg, just a league downstream, and they ended up camping there for six nights. Crespí and some others climbed a low prominence close to the shore, but it's difficult to say exactly which rise that is—perhaps a stable dune? They were in search of confirmation that this was Monterey; they yearned for a celebratory vista. Crespí tells: "And the better to assure ourselves, Captain Don Fernando de Rivera, Engineer Don Miguel Costansó, five soldiers and myself went off to a small hill that lay a good league off close to the shore, and stood there, having a clear view of the two points and of a very large bight that begins from the aforesaid point of Pines and extends across to the other point, Point Año Nuevo, upon the coast. We were, however, greatly confounded by the sight of high sea with no shelter or harbor in view anywhere— instead only embayment and high sea, which we thought could be no less than twelve leagues, or more, in a straight line from one point to the other, whereas according to the histories, this embayment was where the harbor of Monte Rey ought to lie . . ." Had they come all this way only to find a non-harbor, a gigantic and rough and breathtaking bay? They refused to believe it.

Captain Rivera and nine or ten soldiers crossed the Salinas River then and headed west to scout the Monterey Peninsula, because there must have been some mistake; and I followed these scouts, leaving my shadow company, the main expedition, behind for a spell. From Salinas, Blanco Road took me directly toward a fog bank that lorded over the point of pines I knew was there but couldn't quite see, past a bedraggled field of cauliflower and a field of lettuce picked over and ready for the disk. So much greenery remains after the harvest to be churned under—more green than is collected. The fields were at every stage: a grand array of growth and recycling, a kaleidoscope of brown and blue-green that the gulls had the best view of. Turquoise plastic flats rose in stacks out of the strawberry forests like Jetsonian cities. A yellow road reflector, like the one I'd collected from Highway 1 in Big Sur—the rockfall plow truck rips them up by the dozen—caught my eye in a barren furrow. It would tumble for years in that soil, surfacing occasionally to shine like an arrowhead. No one would pick it up.

The traffic to and from Monterey was brisk on this Friday evening. The wind gathered force, and the fog descended over the low Santa Lucia hills as they lapsed into the Pacific. My hat blew off and rolled twenty feet. Still, the pickers' cars lined the roads. When finally I walked under the fog, I stopped to pull on my lime-green micro-down jacket. My nose began to drip with the cold, but looking back the way I'd come, the city of Salinas was bathed in sun under powder-blue skies. Blanco Road shepherded me over the Salinas River. At last it held water: ponded with duckweed confetti in patches, pinched like an hourglass with tule and cattail. Banks of willow, bramble, and cottonwood. Arundo reached up to the overpass guardrail, but otherwise it seemed like what Portolá might have experienced, the general impression at least. A thriving corridor for egrets, steelhead, and rambling grizzlies.

Near this crossing at Blanco Road, Crespí described the river as full and beholden to the ocean: "There is a vast amount of water here in the river, but it is not flowing, because of a large inlet that shoots into it at the shore, making the river here a bit brackish at high tide by holding back its flow." During Portolá's time, the Salinas River traveled to the shore and then apparently jogged northeast behind the humped dunes of Monterey Bay, emptying about nine miles to the north into Elkhorn Slough. The town of Moss Landing is built on its old bed, and out to sea is a submarine canyon that is one of the deepest in the world at more than twelve thousand feet, a trench befitting a river the size of the Colorado or the Mississippi. It leads geologists to suspect that Elkhorn Slough once was the outlet of a much larger river at the latitude of Los Angeles, before this chunk of earth's crust began its tectonic creep north. Like many of the world's most fertile valleys, the head of the Salinas is in essence a vast delta, now largely relic. Mid-eighteenth-century accounts describe water spilling the banks and sheeting a mile wide across this alluvial plain. Early settlers began to fill in those flood-prone areas, and then the earthquake of 1906 caused the Salinas to jump channels entirely and flow more directly into Monterey Bay. What I saw before me was in truth a vastly different riparian corridor from what Crespí and Portolá encountered.

As the light faded I went up a hill into the former Fort Ord, which was established during World War I and hosted fifty thousand troops during Vietnam. It was decommissioned in 1994, and afterward California State University, Monterey Bay, was chartered on its ground. Their mascot is the Otters. As I walked the campus and its periphery, the difference between dorms and barracks seemed one of degree, lending the hillside, in the fog, a twilight eeriness. Not far from CSUMB's student center, I slipped off Imjin Road and down a network of sandy jeep trails once pounded by soldiers in training, until I found a scrub oak grove like those I'd seen along Morro Bay. From the outside, the grove was a fortress of prickly leaves, but once I bore the scratches and pushed inside, it was spacious, cranial, private, only the poison oak sprigs giving me second thought. I ignored them. In the morning I awoke to a *chit-chit-chit* and the twitchy, monstrous shadow of a wrentit and its cocked tail playing across my dome as though I was confined, as I was, inside Plato's cave.

THE KELP FOREST TANK INSIDE the Monterey Bay Aquarium, on Cannery Row, is one of the wonders of built California. The twenty-eight-foot-tall acrylic windows submerge the visitor in effect, turning spectators into sudden divers. The tank holds three hundred thousand gallons. Two thousand gallons are pushed through each minute from the bay via a piston that, outside, nods up and down much like a pump jack. Inside the tank, the honey-olive strands of kelp sway from their holdfasts with blades that ripple and wave asynchronously. All of the other algae varieties, maroon and green, arrived by spore. During the day, the aquarium filters this kelp forest for clarity but, at night, when the visitors have gone out like a tide, the water is allowed to pour in with all the life of the bay. When I arrived at the Kelp Forest tank, however, its contents were a murky green. "The 'soup' you see is full of tiny plants called plankton," a temporary sign explained. "When they multiply like this, it's called a plankton bloom.... We're sorry the view is clouded, but the plants and animals are eating it up!" The filters couldn't filter it all, and the bloom had even bloomed inside the tank.

Finally I could see the covert world I had walked past for day upon day, only seeing the kelp slick, the herons rising and falling on its bulbous stems as they waited for baitfish to rise and forget themselves in this floating canopy. Leopard sharks, one of the more common sharks in California, pushed by the windows with tapered tails, their spots dark and prominent along their pale bellies but as subtle as damp stains on their shadowy backs. Bass drifted slack-jawed and nearly motionless, only their pectoral fins treading.

As I sat on a bench and stared up at this swaying tableau, a group led by a docent filled in around me. They wore headsets so they could hear the guide's words directly from a microphone on his lapel amid the aquarium's din and hum. I leaned in, listened. "Otters are what's known as a keystone species," he said. There were no otters in the Kelp Forest tank, but there were five somersaulting in an exhibit near the aquarium's front, where parents lift their kids to the acrylic as the svelte bodies glide by, trailing bubbles. "They are a part of the ecological system that supports the whole food web. Think of the wolves in Yellowstone, the way they were almost hunted completely out and when they were reintroduced, it balanced the landscape by keeping the elk and deer in check. The way otters serve the niche out here is . . . Well, I mentioned that otters eat sea urchins? The favorite food of urchins is all kinds of algae. Young urchins eat small sea scums that cover the rocks, but as they get older they get more voracious, and they come out from between the rocks and crevasses and munch down, literally like little lawn mowers, and take out whole kelp forests."

This creates what's called an "urchin barren," he went on to say, which, particularly in Southern California, is now common. There are no otters to eat the urchins. Ironically, the lack of kelp likely makes it difficult for otters to survive even where there are plenty of urchins to devour. Without cover, they get picked off by sharks. "There wasn't a kelp forest in the Monterey Bay in the late eighteen hundreds or early nineteen hundreds," said the guide. "This"—he gestured toward the grand tank, its golden understory and canopy teeming at every level with different species of fish and invertebrates—"just wasn't there." It was thought that otters had gone extinct due to the fur trade until a population of fifty was discovered near Bixby Canyon in Big Sur in 1938. Now about three thousand live off the coast, an incredible recovery. With the return of otters, a forest burgeons again in Monterey Bay and Northern California. But the coast's natural carrying capacity might be three times that number, or once was.

In the tank's clerestory windows there were also anchovies, held in an ongoing and finely tuned twist of fate. They swirled, pieces of a broken mirror. "Why do they do this tornado thing?" said a woman, watching. Because there's safety in numbers. There were sardines, too, which are slightly larger and tend to school forward rather than revolve and tighten into a bait ball. They swam with their mouths open, their cheek slits flaring red as they filtered phytoplankton through the delicate rakers of their gills.

Without sardines, there would have been no Cannery Row, made culturally famous by Steinbeck's novel about its characters and underbelly of bordellos and crime. Monterey was a boom town just like any other. At its peak, nineteen sardine canneries operated night and day. Redwood "hoppers" floated in the bay, mega tanks where the purse-seiners dumped their living tons for processing. They were siphoned through a tube into the factory at a rate of ten tons per minute in some cases. Inside, assembly lines, mainly of women, sorted and placed the fish belly-down in slots on a conveyor that fed the machines. Automated, whirling blades gutted the fish and trimmed their heads and tails. They were steamed in the open can. Oil, mustard, or tomato sauce were added. Then the sardines were sealed and packed into the "retorts," where the cans were pressure-cooked at 240 degrees for sterilization, ninety minutes per load. Narrow sky bridges running across the street conveyed the fish, in their new silver form, to the warehouses for loading onto Southern Pacific cars at the rear.

At the end of the row, the Hovden Cannery was the largest factory and, in 1973, the last to close. Its flagship brand was Portola Sardines. Fittingly, the aquarium bought and remodeled the Hovden building for its use, transforming a space of reckless misuse to one of stewardship. The aquarium now displays this earlier history in its lobby beside the shiny boilers that powered the machines and cooked the fish. Gaspar himself graces the labels and crates on exhibit, in a red cloak and a hat with a plume. Debonair but placid, he sports a white beard, suddenly in his golden years it seems, which would place him back in Spain. And in one of the many black-and-white photos that depict Portola Sardines, a female employee stands next to a display of tins with their foil lids half-peeled away. She wears a white apron and a hat with *Portola* embroidered on it. TRY OUR PORTOLA SARDINES (THE SUPREME IN QUALITY), says the table sign beside her. PEELED AND BONELESS 15 ¢, GARNISHED 15 ¢, FRENCH STYLE 15 ¢, IN WINE SAUCE 15 ¢, MACKEREL SLICED AND SOUSED 25 ¢. And another sign: TRY OUR HEARTS OF CELERY, HEALTHFUL AND DELICIOUS, PROVIDES IRON FOR YOUR SYSTEM, 50 ¢. A vegetable from the Salinas Valley, for balance.

That celery was more expensive than this fish reveals how immense Cannery Row's haul once was. Soon the canneries began mincing the scraps and selling them as fertilizer and animal fare. It would go to the fields of the Salinas, and far beyond, to enrich crops and lay muscle on cattle. Before long, more sardines were being sold in bags than in tins, and the fish were being pressed into oil, paint, soap, and more. A quarter million tons of sardine were processed a year on average during the decade that straddled World War II, when the fisheries in Europe were closed, generating new demand. By the mid-forties, however, the fishery in and around Monterey Bay had declined dramatically. It collapsed entirely in the fifties. Within a period of five years, the catch plummeted by 90 percent and the boisterous, ceaseless Row emptied out until the aquarium and other touristy diversions that now fill the old cannery buildings—the taffy, the Ghirardelli, the Bubba Gump Shrimp Company—moved in. The sardines returned, too, but recently the fishery was halted again, this time by regulators: over the past decade the sardine population has fallen by 97 percent due to natural fluctuations exacerbated by overfishing. Sardines are an essential strand in the food web, providing for animals like seals, pelicans, and predatory fish, and they remain a way of life for a modest fleet of fishers. Their dwindling is serious.

Out there in Monterey Bay, and in the aquarium's whopping tank, the fish hang in the sway or sway themselves, and cut the darkness. Sunlight surges through the kelp as if through the shutters of a dusty room. The sardines wind around these lengths and slants, breaking apart and coming back together in the same instant.

I WANDERED BACK THROUGH CANNERY ROW, through Steinbeck Plaza, to a "recreation trail" that aimed me toward historic downtown Monterey. The scuba divers who had been training in the impossible murk of the algae bloom off San Carlos Beach had departed for long, hot showers. Along the bike path, on the retaining wall, was a mural of an oak overhanging a creek and lush hills pillowing beyond it to a coniferous ridge. It was a vision of Monterey before it was Monterey, but strangely no Rumsen, the local Ohlone group, were depicted, only tule elk grazing among the wildflowers near the shore's edge.

When Sebastian Vizcaíno and his men visited the bay in 1602 and gave it its name, they anchored and came ashore for several weeks. Right away, Vizcaíno had a hut constructed under a prominent oak just above the beach to serve as a chapel. Under this tree the first Mass in California was said. When Portolá and Crespí made their second expedition to Monterey in 1770 to at last found the presidio and mission, they had been reminded of this particular oak. It remained in their minds as a landmark, helping them finally identify the bay, which they had no trouble recognizing this go-around. "We turned our eyes upon this fine and handsome shore," Crespí recounted. "[W]e saw thousands of sea lions seeming like a cobblestone pavement, and two whales close together that must have been about a hundred yards from land. We saw the closing-in made by the mainland with the Point of Pines, and with a single voice all three of us broke out, 'This is Monte-Rey Harbor!'"

A week later, on May 31, 1770, Junípero Serra arrived on the *San Antonio*. The next morning he landed at what's thought to be the mouth of the creek now named for him, and he followed it a short distance uphill to Vizcaíno's oak, whose branches dipped into the creek's pools. Several days later, another important Mass and ceremony were conducted under this respected tree. Serra headed a procession from the landing, and Portolá led another from their camp. They converged at the oak, where again a makeshift altar had been arranged holding a painting of the Virgin. Serra sang and recited scripture as the rest knelt, a *Te Deum* thanksgiving service. A wooden cross was erected. "Long live the Faith!" the men shouted. "Long live the King!" Bells that had been hung in the branches were rung, muskets were fired. Portolá went through the motions of taking possession of the territory for Spain by, as Serra described, "waving once more the royal flag, pulling grass, moving stones and other formalities according to law." A soldier who had died aboard the *San Antonio* was buried beneath the cross, which, more than pulling up grass, perhaps begins to lay claim to a place.

An elderly, twisting oak with limbs bowed to the earth does form a natural chapel, calling out for marriage and for burial. This one became known as the Vizcaíno-Serra Oak, or the Junípero Oak, or the Charter Oak, or the "Plymouth Rock of the West Coast." The tree stood for another 125 years, surviving a lightning strike in 1840, but it died in 1903 when work on a culvert diverted too much water in its direction. One day the dead snag disappeared. It had been cut down, ironically to clear ground for a Junípero Serra monument. Legend has it that when the local priest, Ramon Mestres, discovered that this tree had been thrown into the bay, he enlisted local fishermen to help retrieve it and they found the tree floating twelve miles away. Mestres had the sacred trunk propped up behind the presidio chapel, slathering it with creosote and filling its rotted holes with concrete. Eventually the tree deteriorated and collapsed—I imagine acorn woodpeckers drilling into it and transforming it into a brine-soaked granary—but relic pieces still can be found around Monterey, including at the presidio chapel and at Mission Carmel.

I left the recreation trail and circled around to the site where this oak had stood, roughly at the base of Artillery Street below the Monterey Presidio. Beside a little lawn, a pallid egg-shaped rock was nestled in a bush not far from a large dark granite cross, both historical markers. There were young oaks, and I wondered if they were related to the original. In the mulch was a trail of oyster and limpet shells scattered up narrow Serra Creek by a fat raccoon, or so was my hunch. The plastic clamshell of a Trader Joe's spicy Thai-inspired salad lay open in the grass, too. I walked up Artillery Street a short distance to the presidio's terrace and surveyed the harbor and Fisherman's Wharf. The cove where Serra and maybe Vizcaíno came ashore no longer exists: it was filled to allow the road and the railroad into Cannery Row to pick up all those sardines. Serra Creek now spurts from an outfall onto a sliver of riprapped beach.

I KEPT GOING, HEADING EAST, light fading, back toward my campsite in the scrub oak of retired Fort Ord. But I was in search of another marker. When Portolá and Crespí returned to Monterey Bay in 1770, they first went to find a cross that they had raised the year before as a sign to others that they had explored the area. They had left a cross on the Carmel shore as well, with a note buried below it detailing their efforts, so that a ship cruising the coast might glimpse the cross and learn of them. On the Monterey cross, meanwhile, they had etched a message: "The land expedition is returning to San Diego for lack of provisions today, December 9, 1769." Now, six months later, Portolá and Crespí visited this cross immediately in case the ship carrying Junípero Serra had arrived already and left some message. "We found the cross all surrounded by arrows, and wands with a great many feathers on them," wrote Crespí, "all driven into the ground, set there by the heathens, with a string of still half-fresh sardines hanging on a staff beside the cross, another staff with a slice of meat on it, and a small heap of mussels at the cross's foot." The Rumsen clearly conceived of the cross as something worthy of respect if not veneration, a reminder of a spectral visitation they did not expect to become a mortal occupancy.

Two hundred years later to the day, on December 9, 1969, a twenty-foot redwood cross was planted in the dunes above the Del Monte Beach in Monterey to commemorate the original one that Portolá and Crespí had propped up and returned to, though its original site is in reality unknown. This commemorative cross was sturdy enough to last a century, but in 2009 it was cut down in the middle of the night: a cross is a symbol of faith to some, of tyranny and demise to others. A debate ensued about whether it should be restored. Though the cross was a historical monument, it promoted Christianity on public land and thus stoked the same timeless church-and-state controversy that beset even the earliest days of the Spanish in California, when padres and military officers butted heads over who should control operations, resources, and ultimately the local "heathens."

I had read that eventually the cross was raised again, so I trundled past the wharf toward the beach, strolling the bottom curve of Monterey Bay. In the cypress along the bike path, three or four tents of the homeless were tucked into the alleys between dunelets despite NO CAMPING advisories. The waves shone a muddy amber and then, as the low light poured through them, wine-red. They lifted and rolled and sloshed, their foam gathering in and spilling from the beach's mangled bull kelp. Far across the bay was Point Año Nuevo, and in between was a single sailboat like a white feather that a swallow might swoop up and use to pad its nest.

Back toward Cannery Row, Point Pinos was still, 250 years later, a brooding mass of pine and other conifers, though now those trees lifted above neighborhoods. Over and over, a man ran a set of stairs up a dune for a workout. Others catapulted tennis balls for their pooches from orange Chuckits. I strolled past condominiums. Past a family barbeque and a pizza party. Past the black shards of the season's bonfires. A flock of twenty or thirty western sandpipers swung in and out of the onrushing waves like marionettes beholden to the froth's lead. They surged downslope to bunch in the creases and Vs of the retreating waves, where they put their heads down for a half second to probe, to siphon hidden worms, before they were compelled upslope again by the swash. They skittered and peeped past me into the rose and peach reflection on the sand.

As dusk came on, I began to ask beachgoers: "You haven't seen a cross around here, have you?" Mainly people shook their heads, but one man nodded, told me he thought I should continue on. So I stayed the course, walking past the sunset as it flamed out, as we all snapped photos of it a few minutes too late, past its full glory.

Past the Monterey Tides hotel, which dominates the beach, but will be protected only a while longer by its seawall. Soon it was past twilight, but I kept on, hopping across runnels of seawater trapped on the beach and scrambling up the tideline's short, steep, crumbling plateau, the scarp. Finally, I saw the cross in the dunes, in the faint remaining light, and I swung toward it. But it was a telephone pole.

I turned back. Past dark now, and the bright floodlights on the Monterey Tides illuminated the surf for its patrons on their balconies. In the night, roadway signs, anything tall, became a cross in my imagination. I climbed into the dunes beyond the hotel and found the recreation trail again, following it back toward Monterey as it snaked above the Cabrillo Highway, and above Roberts Lake and Del Monte Lake, in the vicinity of which the Portolá expedition had camped on their return to San Diego in 1769. I felt, in the black sea breeze, as lost as they. They were searching for a phantom harbor. I was searching for a phantom cross in memory of the one they had erected. Only later, sitting defeated but full in an In-N-Out, did I learn that the commemorative cross had been moved from the beach to a nearby cemetery.

IN THE COURTYARD OF Mission San Carlos Borromeo del Río Carmelo, better known as Mission Carmel, a circle of children stood around the plashy fountain in their Sunday dress, reciting Hail Marys, their parents standing beside or behind them. They passed the microphone counterclockwise. "Hail Mary, full of Grace, the Lord is with thee," each child began, their voices high, yet also flat and sleepy. They blurred or skipped words though they must have said them often. They were only eight or nine years old, some younger. Several girls snuck up to the fountain and with their elbows pushed themselves up onto its brick rim so that their ballet flats dangled, and a mother soon followed and patted them on the behind to shoo them off. "Blessed art thou among women, and blessed is the fruit of thy womb, Jesus." Each time the whole circle joined in to finish: "Holy Mary, Mother of God, pray for us sinners now, and at the hour of our death. Amen."

The city of Carmel, which means "Garden" in Hebrew, owes its name to the Carmelite friars on Vizcaíno's voyage. *El Río del Carmelo*, they named the river on the south side of the Point of Pines in honor of Israel's Mount Carmel, where their order began in the twelfth century near a spring associated with the prophet Elijah. I had caught a bus at the CSU Monterey Bay student center and ridden it over the ridge; unlike the expedition's scouts, I had no horse and felt an acute need to save my legs. But from downtown Carmel, I walked a mile or so through affluent, numberless bungalows to the mission at the estuary's edge, not far from the beach, with Point Lobos to the south. The sea breeze pushed the fountain's spray east toward the hills so that it rained askew on its flower-shaped basin. Strands of wispy cloud glided over the cypresses and the olive trees and the lemons. There was also a small farmers' market set up in the courtyard, just a few stands, and two girls walked by eating strawberries from a clear bag, eating them and throwing the leafy whirls and severed fruit crowns under a holly tree. When a man read the Lord's Prayer, saying the words "Forgive us our trespasses, as we forgive those who trespass against us," I thought of all the times I'd cut through fields and leapt fences and walked the tracks, and of all the people and neighborhoods I'd studied as I passed by; and I thought also of coming here, to this mission, as a nonbeliever: forgive me.

The bell began to toll—Mission Carmel still has its original bell—calling us to the eleven o'clock Mass, and everyone began to move toward the church. It is the most Moorish of California's missions, with an off-center bell tower and a central star-shaped window. The baptistery is steeply vaulted, so much so that, inside, I felt as if I were in the belly of a whale: its pale rib-rafters, its organs like golden chandeliers, its mouth open to Christ hanging on the wall in a blue window. After secularization, the stone church fell to ruin, much of its roof collapsing, but it has been impeccably restored since the 1880s. In 1960, Pope John XXIII named this chapel a minor basilica. I left my pack leaning against the wall in an anteroom and shuffled to a pew on the gospel side, below the pulpit, as the church filled with parishioners.

There was a loud knocking on the door as Mass began. It was the unbaptized and candidates for confirmation seeking entry. Everyone stood as they were let in and marched to the front. Many of them were children. "What do you ask of us, the community at Carmel Mission?" intoned the priest. "What do you ask of God today?" I couldn't hear their answers, but soon he moved to each catechumen and candidate and, with his thumb, drew in the air before them, speaking of each sense: "Receive the sign of the cross on your ears, that you may hear the voice of the Lord. Receive the sign of the cross on your eyes, that you may see the glory of the Lord. Receive the sign of the cross on your lips, that you may respond to the word of God. Receive the sign of the cross on your heart, so that Christ may dwell there by faith. Receive the sign of the cross on your shoulders, that you may bear the gentle yoke of Christ. Receive the sign of the cross on your hands, that Christ may be known in the work which you do. Receive the sign of the cross on your feet, that you may walk in the ways of Christ."

It was the children that Serra and Crespí reached first at Mission Carmel, just as at the other missions. Once the kids were captivated, eventually their parents followed, or at least that was the hope. In their first year in Monterey, the padres baptized just twenty Rumsen, all children, luring them with beads and blankets, exotic tongue and rituals. It was a difficult year. Serra called it another "novitiate": a period of monastic isolation, intense prayer, and study that Catholic clergy must undergo to see if they are truly devoted to this lifelong vocation. He and Crespí discovered just how foggy and cold Monterey is, even in summer. Their first agricultural plot came to nothing. They planted seeds in a fenced garden, but the soil beside the presidio was too salty—"fit for nothing but reeds and nettles," Serra wrote, though both plants are edible and nutritious. Nothing grew, which didn't help win any converts. The natives saw that living at the mission would mean giving up the stability, or even plenty, of subsistence foraging for famine.

The Monterey presidio and mission were established side by side, but Serra quickly felt the arrangement was untenable. Serra and the presidio's commander, Pedro Fages, who had led the volunteer soldiers on both of Portolá's expeditions to Monterey, found each other overbearing. Both wanted power. Serra was monomaniacal about rapidly expanding the mission system: only two weeks after landing in Monterey, he wrote to the Franciscan college in Mexico asking for more padres so he could found new missions. Fages was concerned with building a secure and lasting fort, and he was wary of stretching their limited resources too thin. He also forbade Serra to punish neophytes without his permission, less it foment unrest, a decree that Serra felt hindered his ability to instruct. In his eyes, it was the undisciplined and predatory soldiers who made winning the trust of the locals so difficult.

A year after their arrival, the *San Antonio* returned with supplies and ten additional padres. In his zeal, Serra wrote again, immediately, about the need for even more padres, touting a chain of missions between San Diego and Monterey that would let his Franciscans "sleep at least every third day in a mission belonging to the College." His superior in Mexico told him he was rushing, but Serra wasn't deterred, and his vision was eventually realized after his death. He shipped six of those padres back south to found Missions Buenaventura and San Gabriel and to support

Mission San Diego. The next day, he left with two padres to walk the Salinas Valley and found Mission San Antonio de Padua. When he returned to Monterey, he moved its mission over the ridge to Carmel and spent half a year there as the only Spaniard in what another padre, Francisco Palóu, his friend and biographer, called a "hermit's life." Crespí joined Serra in Carmel in December 1771.

Unfortunately, the supply ships did not return in 1772—lost again, they turned about for Mexico. The Spaniards in Monterey and Carmel were stretched to their limits. Serra and Crespí lived on cow's milk, rudimentary vegetables, and the offerings of natives—which must have been particularly galling to Serra. In August, he and Pedro Fages put their differences aside temporarily and journeyed overland to San Diego in search of help, founding Mission San Luis Obispo, California's fifth mission, en route. Serra would be gone for nearly two years, because he traveled all the way to Mexico City to make his case personally to the viceroy for more supplies, more skilled craftsmen, and more autonomy. He received everything he wanted, and it would allow Serra to firmly establish his chain of missions, many of which would prosper, by his standards, at least for a time. He brought back to Carmel a hundred blankets, more than nine hundred large bushels of corn, generous portions of meat and chocolate, and over four hundred strands of beads to hand out to the natives. "The whole extent of the territory which, but recently, was weighed down with melancholy and suffering, is filled with happiness," he wrote, and the natives "three times a day eat from our hands."

MISSION CARMEL BECAME THE HEADQUARTERS of Alta California, but in truth it wasn't highly successful. Its birthrate never outpaced its mortality. Its population peaked at 876 in 1795. Its practices were harsh. One of the most telling descriptions comes from a French captain named Lapérouse who visited Mission Carmel in 1786. To his eye, and ear, the mission held unsettling similarities to the Caribbean's slave colonies: "The color of these Indians, which is that of the negroes; the house of the Missionaries; their storehouses, which are built of brick and plastered; the appearance of the ground on which the grain is trodden out; the cattle, the horses—everything in short—brought to our recollection a plantation at Santo Domingo or any other West Indian Island. The men and women are collected by the sound of a bell; a Missionary leads them to work, to the church, and to all their exercises. We observed with concern that the resemblance is so perfect that we have seen both men and women in irons, and others in stocks. Lastly the noise of the whip might have struck our ears, the punishment also being administered, though with little severity."

California's padres sent soldiers and other loyal neophytes after "fugitive" Indians who had been baptized but then thought better of being "yoked"—Serra's word—to God and the missions. Serra himself set a precedent of recapturing and punishing defectors. "Last Friday I sent out eleven adults with the servant Cypriano," he wrote in 1775 to Fernando Rivera y Moncada, Fages's successor as governor and yet another familiar officer from the Portolá expedition. "They were to go to the mountains to search for my lost sheep. . . . I am sending them to you so that a period of exile, and two or three whippings which Your Lordship may order applied to them on different days may serve, for them and for the rest, for a warning, may be of spiritual benefit to all; and this last is the prime motive of our work." Serra offered to send extra shackles should the governor need them. The neophytes were subhuman in his eyes, chattel, "my lost sheep," dull animals whose skin could be shorn or whipped to illustrate a point. In some cases, the padres did the lashing themselves.

In the Mission Carmel basilica, as I listened to a reading from the Book of Sirach ("The Lord is a God of justice, who knows no favorites"), and a reading from the second letter of Saint Paul to Timothy, and the Gospel according to Saint Luke; and as Psalm 34 was sung, and as *Alleluia*s rose up in acclamation, I finally realized what the towering altar, olive and gold, reminded me of: it was a view like the one I had seen at the aquarium the day before through those great, thick windows. If you only squinted, it was a kelp forest rising toward the ceiling, ornate strands and columns housing figures, each in their niche with their arms outstretched like fins, hiding and waiting, predator and prey.

And when the organs and the chorus quieted and Mass was over, I stood below this glowing altar at the front of the basilica and considered the white marble grave markers inset in the tile floor. Serra died in 1784 and is buried in the church beside Crespí and Lasuén. They were exhumed in 1882 and reinterred two years later, when the church's restoration began. Through the glass of an ornate reliquary I saw wood allegedly from Serra's coffin, plank fragments bundled like a Christmas present in a thin gold ribbon. A painted portrait of the bald saint looking severe was propped on the altar steps above his gravestone. Crespí lies to his left, Lasuén to his right. "*Compañero de Serra*," reads Crespí's marker. It's true, they were companions and partners. But much like Pedro Fages, Crespí felt that Serra was domineering. He requested transfer to another mission, citing the cold, but didn't receive his wish. Serra thought Crespí was weak and hard to please, despite the fact that Crespí had twice walked from San Diego to Monterey. In one moment of tension, Serra suggested Crespí pare down his official revision of his Portolá expedition journal by cutting the "minutiae," to which Crespí replied, "Then you do not want me tell things just as they are, or as I saw them?" For all his limitations, Crespí was arguably California's first writer, though by no means its first or best storyteller. He died two years before Serra, in 1782. I lingered in front of his stone, visiting with the voice that had accompanied me for months now and had told me, roughly, where to go.

Outside, in the shadow of the basilica's north wall, were other graves: ovals of beach cobble and abalone shell, cracked and bleached white on bare dirt. A small wooden cross like those found along roadsides was planted above each grave with another abalone shell hanging like a hat from it. These weren't in fact specific resting places, only gestures: THESE SYMBOLIC GRAVE SITES, ADORNED WITH ABALONE SHELLS, REPRESENT THE MANY HUNDREDS OF INDIGENOUS PEO-PLE BURIED IN THIS GRAVEYARD AND BEYOND. The sign hung on an olive tree, whose shadows lanced this text and the earth below it.

Standing there, I thought about how these symbolic graves were tucked off to the side rather than set prominently along the church's front walkway and lush garden. A garden where, four days after Junípero Serra's canonization by Pope Francis in 2015, his likeness was toppled by vandals or activists, who wrote "Saint of Genocide" on the statue's base. I thought about how the natives and neophytes might have instead, or also, been represented by a white marble stone in the chapel's tile floor beside the padres. I thought about how abalone, which Crespí described as "a sort of limpets" and which the natives traded as mother-of-pearl, are now difficult to come by on the West Coast, at least sizable ones, because they've been so poached. And I thought about how, to accurately symbolize the losses of early California, these prismatic shells would have to ring the mission for miles around and far beyond.

THE BUS DROPPED ME OFF later that afternoon in Marina, near my scrub-oak campsite, and I found my pack where I'd stashed it and headed downhill toward the bay's dune shore, hoping to gain some ground and reunite with the ghost of the Portolá expedition. All told, they had camped for six nights near Blanco Road, on the eastern side of the Salinas River, while the scouts probed in both directions and found only the underwhelming, but eventually important, bay at Carmel. They wondered if Vizcaíno's Port of Monterey was tucked somewhere along the sheer coast of the Santa Lucia Mountains, which they had made a long road around. But possibly it was still ahead.

The decision as to whether to push forward or concede defeat and turn back was put to a vote among the officers and padres, a testimony to Portolá's fair-mindedness and diplomacy. Costansó recalled the governor's words: "He drew attention to the scarcity of provisions that confronted us; to the large number of sick we had among us (there were seventeen men half-crippled and unfit for work); to the season, already far advanced; and to the great sufferings of the men who remained well, on account of the unlimited work required in looking after the horses, and watching them at night, in guarding the camp, and in the continual excursions for exploration and reconnaissance."

They voted unanimously to walk on. "And, if God willed that in the search for Monterey we should all perish," Costansó wrote, "we would have performed our duty towards God and man, laboring together until death for the success of the undertaking upon which we had been sent."

THE TRAIN TRACKS AND THEIR sister bike path took me east, where Marina ended abruptly in low scrub and fields of strawberry, the white plastic of future rows like a seaside snow in the distance. Fingers of ice plant tinged with red reminded me of the changing season, and the sandy-blue sky was blotchy, herringbone. A line of RVs in the distance caught my eye, and when finally I turned onto Lapis Road, I saw that many of them had been parked there for a long time. They were streaked with grime and covered with tarps, and some of their tires were flat. Dutchmen, Allegro Bay, Bounder (with a kangaroo for a logo), Pace Arrow: it was another Campland on the Bay, but more desperate. Marina had banned oversized vehicles from parking overnight on its streets, dismissing these people to this county road named for a semiprecious stone. A utility cord ran from a generator in a pickup bed to a camper set on the ground, and I imagined this person driving off each day and leaving his home on stilts. The RVs had reflective sun shades under their windshields, which flashed like sardines, and cardboard in other windows for privacy. As I passed by an orange San Francisco Giants blanket hung inside a driver's window, it stirred: its inhabitant assessing me. Did they think I might be a plainclothes cop as Ulysses had thought back near Ventura? The view from here was faded lapis across Highway 1, both luminescent and blotchy gray, quintessential California, and these RVs and their residents were part of the picture. Veterans and retirees and transplants, they couldn't find or afford the housing they needed.

Just where the cars trickled out was a driveway toward the shore: the entrance to a Cemex plant. Cemex is a massive Mexican-owned cement and concrete company, and here it dredged sand from a lagoon to sell to golf courses and more, a controversial operation slated to be shut down in part because it was contributing to substantial coastal erosion. The Cemex road went under the highway in the distance, but just inside its yellow metal gate, at a pullout, was a silver VW van. A man in a red flannel shirt was sitting near it on a stool. Perhaps another vagrant, someone who wanted some space from the crowd before he pulled back into line for the night.

Then I spotted a large bird on the ground next to him. As I walked up, I thought the falcon was on a leash, but it was only toying with a homemade lure, a halved tennis ball at the end of a rope. The falconer, David, told me he had fed her from a tennis-ball hemisphere when she was young, because it made a perfect little dish. Now that she associated that lime-green fuzz and rubber with food, he swung a halved ball around on the rope whenever he wished for her to return from the upper levels of the air. "She's obsessed with it," he said in a smooth baritone voice. "I've got food right here, a nice little quail breast, and she's like, 'No, I want my lure, and you can't have it.'" Her wings were partially outstretched over the lure, a possessive posture, a shield—"mantling," the behavior is called. Rust-orange and gray, she was an aplomado falcon, of Peruvian descent but bred in Los Angeles. Her name, Mora, means "little fruit," often specifically "blackberry": when she was young, David had a job flying her over blueberry fields to keep the frugivores away. *Aplomado* in Spanish means "lead-colored," plumbeous, which refers to the shading on her wings, back, crown, and prominent cheek stripes. It looked as if she were wearing a medieval helmet, a barbute. Her chest was cinnamon. Her feet a lemon yellow. Her talons were as curved as a suture needle in the steady hands of a surgeon. Aplomados range today from Mexico through South America, and they've recently been reintroduced, with mixed success, to southernmost Texas and New Mexico, where they once lived and bred until habitat loss extirpated them in the 1950s.

David looked a little like the poet Robinson Jeffers, with a broad straight nose, severe smile lines, and striking baby-blue eyes over periorbital bags. Or maybe it was only this sand country, the fierce quiet bird, and his rock voice that lent him such a countenance. One thinks of a line from Jeffers's poem "The Cruel Falcon": "Pure action would make a good life, let it be sharp— / Set between the throat and the knife." David had been flying hawks almost every afternoon for seven years. His son had gotten him into it. "When he was fourteen, he was a little listless, and I said, 'Do something, do sports.' He told me he wanted to fly hawks. When he was in the fifth grade, you know, they came to the school with birds, an educational program, and there was a golden eagle. He came home and said, 'I want to have a golden eagle.'" His son didn't forget that dream, and once they were introduced to falconry, David was hooked too.

They had to apprentice themselves for two years to another falconer before receiving their licenses. "His whole high school years, after school, we would be out flying birds together." In addition to Mora, David had a Harris's hawk and took care of his son's hawk, now that his son was off at college in the Bay Area. He had bought a female aplomado because they're hardy and, since she is slightly larger than a male, can handle a Cooper's hawk when one flies in for a confrontation. Often he was hired to fly his raptors for the purposes of "bird abatement," keeping them off crops or out of landfills. Recently he'd worked at CSU Monterey Bay, where they were tearing down more dilapidated military buildings: I'd seen those low-slung empty barracks and homes, sometimes door- and windowless, row after row behind chain-link with their yards overgrown. "They had issues with swallows nesting while it was happening," said David, "and that would stop the construction—the deconstruction—so we flew our birds for six months at the campus."

Mora weighed ten and a half ounces, less than the pigeons David sometimes released for her to catch. She'd never caught a wild bird. "The hungrier they are, the better they'll hunt," he explained, and she was well provided for. She wore a mini leather backpack around her wings and, before flight, David would snap a GPS unit to it so he could track her if need be. "I can pinpoint right where she is." If she catches a released pigeon, for instance, she can't carry it back and instead will commence plucking feathers wherever she and her quarry tumble, locked together, out of the sky. So David has to go to her. "Once she was chasing redtails," David told me, "and the redtails will catch a thermal and she will just go up and up and up and disappear. You can't see her. We were up the Carmel Valley, and she went a mile away, and it was over valleys and ridges, and I thought, 'Oh, how is she going to find her way back?'" He and a friend were ready for a wild-goose chase when the dot on David's GPS began to move back in his direction.

I asked him if he came out here a lot, to Lapis Road. "I do," David said. "There are not that many fields to fly in anymore. But I need to change up fields, because she likes these fence posts. She goes and sits and waits because she knows she's going to eat eventually." I asked him about the campers strung like a necklace back toward Marina. "It's just turned into an RV park now," he replied. "It didn't used to be this way. I mean, some of these RVs, big ones, they've got flat tires. I've seen the sheriffs, they just make sure they're registered. The worst part is that some of them pull away and leave trash."

I told him about the falcons I'd seen, the many kestrels and the peregrines angled low along the sea rocks to flush and pin the shorebirds, and of course, I mentioned the peregrine on Morro Rock and the smokestacks. "There's a lot of falconers that really wished the state would allow them to start raising peregrines again," said David. He pointed out that it was falconers who were in no small part responsible for their comeback, including at Morro Rock. "I think she'll step up on a glove if you want to hold her," said David. He gave me a black rubber and neoprene glove to slip on, warning me that I might feel her talons anyway, and had me place my hand just next to his. "Step up," he said to her. "Step up." She fell back a little as she tried. "Oh, slippery," David said, as she finally managed it. He wrapped her tether around my fingers and asked me to close my fist. Then I held her, visualizing her circling up in one of those thermals over the Cemex sandpit, and the new houses at the edge of Marina, and the plastic snowfields of the strawberry plains, the mottled rows of lettuce, the cutlass of the magnificent bay the Portolá expedition left San Diego in search of and found, in October 1769, though they did not know it.

ARTICHOKE COUNTRY: A LONG TICKER tape of purple "artichoke" PLU stickers—product look-up stickers, the kind stuck to every fruit and vegetable in a grocery store—led me along the road, for a moment, toward Espinosa Lake, where the Portolá party bivouacked to the north of Salinas. A field of these prehistoric-looking plants, gentrified and bulked-up thistles with names like Green Globe, Big Heart, and Imperial Star, swept down toward the shoreline of the mud-green lake. Likely descended from a wild cardoon of North Africa and Sicily, the artichoke made its way to the American colonies by the 1700s. In California, Italian immigrants began cultivating it in the late nineteenth century, and early planters could easily barter a sack of them for other coastal delicacies such as abalone and apricot. Three-quarters of the state's and nation's artichokes are now grown in Monterey County. The nutty, edible interior is the flower bud, and of course the bracts that sheathe it also have edible nubs, pieces of the heart as they're torn away, for dipping in butter or mayo. The plants are perennial and thrive for up to a decade, but are cut back to the ground each year to spur growth. Since the buds mature asynchronously, a field has to be harvested by hand in two-week intervals over the course of a season, making artichokes especially labor intensive. Pickers slash the stem below the bud and toss the globes over their shoulders into backpacks, each doomed flower floating for a split second.

Artichokes waved before me like an intricate William Morris wallpaper extending to the slope of the lake. Redtail floating in a slate sky. Only one patch of blue visible beyond Spreckels and above the humped Santa Lucias, those mountains I was slowly leaving behind. Espinosa Lake is now locked in fields; on its west side, lettuce grows on an old lake bed almost to the lapping water. There are reeds around the rest, a commercial nursery on the north bank. This lake is more or less the last one standing in the area, but the environs of Salinas were once something of a lake district. "We passed four good-sized lakes that could be gotten around only with a great deal of toil, after preparing some very miry crossing," Crespí wrote of this day's march. The country was so rife with water that a serious proposal was made to connect Salinas and Moss Landing with a twenty-mile canal for barging grain, which would have threaded the lakes and sloughs together. But the railroad ended that idea, and now the lakes are gone, "reclaimed" for artichokes and lettuce.

Crespí christened the lake *Santa Brígida*, but the soldiers gave it the name *Laguna de Las Grullas*, Crane Lake, on account of the fowl. Three white pelicans wheeled and settled on the water, which was divided, as if with a fishing weir, by a barbwire fence. Maybe the lake vanished altogether on occasion. Several dried and shriveled artichoke heads had rolled across the lane and come to rest in the clods where I sat to gaze and eat lunch, a pan dulce from a Marina bakery. The disked road was so saturated with irrigation drainage that my sneakers became coated with an inch of gumbo mud, weighing me down. Beyond the lettuce, pickers were harvesting brussels sprouts. Roberto's Catering Truck #4 was parked at the field's end, with its silver hatches propped open like a plumber's truck, only with snacks and hot lunches.

As I walked into Castroville, "the Artichoke Capital of the World," the killdeer flew up calling when the tractor came disking back down the rows. They had been feeding on exposed worms. It was still a week before Halloween, but a pair of jack-o'-lanterns had already melted on someone's concrete threshold. Was it the fog? I stopped in to the Giant Artichoke, a restaurant which boasted, in its frontage, exactly that: an artichoke large enough to live on or in for years, if only it were real. I bought a half order of artichoke fritters and an artichoke cupcake, both to go, and hustled on, crossing one of the first tendrils of Elkhorn Slough and past the North Monterey County High School, "Home of the Condors." The cross-country team jogged by and filled me with a nostalgia for the season and its scent of musty oak leaves. The championship races were coming up. The qualifiers would gather in Fresno to toe the line. The gun would sound. But I was happy with my artichoke fritters.

"AFTER MASS BEING SAID, AND the viaticum and holy oils being administered to two dangerously ill buffcoat soldiers out of the eleven of them who have become almost entirely crippled by Luanda sickness, we set out at about eight o'clock in the forenoon from this spot"—from Espinosa Lake and its eventual artichokes—"and headed into the range among higher knolls and hollows than before so as to be able to get around a throng of lakes and inlets that because of a greater number of bogs allowed no way through them anywhere." The expedition had come to Elkhorn Slough, the primary stem of which winds inland seven miles, curling to the northeast with spurs of channel and marsh unfurling in every direction. Aside from the Bay Area's remaining wetlands, Elkhorn is the most extensive swath of tidal marsh in California. At the slough's head, the Moss Landing Power Plant now rises with twin stacks: stag horns that we've imposed on the totality of Monterey Bay, though it's possible this natural gas plant will be decommissioned soon and the stacks will fall. For now, on a clear day, you can easily see these pale prongs from either Monterey or Santa Cruz; from them electrical lines dip inland on towers toward San Jose, retracing the El Camino.

I took Elkhorn Road around the slough's back side, its eastern edge; the sinuous road wove in and out of steep draws that tumbled to the brackish water, for a time traveling past farmsteads of goats and sheep and vibrant shorn grass. Easy to see how this section of Portolá's walk would have been maddening to the expedition, it was so up and down. "In every depression of the land there was a pond of greater or lesser extent," Costansó quietly complained. They, and in particular the scouts, would have had to guess their way around these inlets and pools, not knowing where the next would appear. The sun, I could tell, was about to drop from the clouds and turn the slough into a shining, irregular blade. In the distance, rays found a slit in the marine clouds beside the smokestacks, making the power plant look like an abandoned castle in a sparsely populated kingdom.

I came to the headquarters for the Elkhorn Slough National Estuarine Research Reserve. The center and its acreage were closed, but a biologist pulled up to me on the road a moment later, having seen me peer through the gate. He was heading home for the day, and he told me if I wanted to see the slough I could visit Kirby Park. Furthermore, no one would be looking if I camped on the knoll above it—he'd gotten married up there with a view of the landscape he studies. I took unfair advantage of his generosity of spirit and soon stepped over some downed barbwire to cut downhill to the research reserve's cinder trails, which traced the lobed shoreline. The light intensified under the thin wool clouds at the coast, and the silty estuary glowed a sallow blue-green. Stands of eucalyptus stood queerly at its margins, and oaks seemed to mimic the waterway's branching. Most things, when you zoom in or out, come to look dendritic. Elk horn. Peering through the trees to the slough, I felt hidden and removed, out of time. I had the after-hours preserve to myself and experienced, I imagined, what it might have felt like to Portolá: wide, watery country and the trails of a people you did not know and never would.

Where the reserve and its peninsula ended at Strawberry Canyon, I stepped onto a curving railroad causeway through islets of pickleweed. Portolá and Crespí would have praised the Lord if they'd been able to cross the slough like this rather than negotiate the hills. The white mud prints of an otter or raccoon walked the rails with me. I almost heard those wet nighttime footfalls, that padded step, that gnashing of crab and minnow. The rail's ballast was laden with fishy scat. A snowy egret slunk off, its ivory hackles ruffling in the breeze over the shallows. Daisy-yellow feet. Avocets and stilts crying on the wing. Then I emerged at Kirby Park, which was just a launch and a concrete lot where men were loitering by their cars.

"You surprised us by coming up from the tracks," said an older man in a jean jacket, as I arrived.

"I try not to do it too much," I replied, "but it's the scenic option. It's more direct than any road, and it's quieter and safer, too."

"A lot quicker, too," he said.

"Quicker to jail, probably," I replied.

"Technically, it is trespassing," said a younger man with a buzzed head. "I got busted once for pissing on the tracks. And I wasn't even drinking that night . . ."

These guys were members of the "Kirby Club," the sole obligation of which was drinking and shooting the shit, sometimes with fishing on the side, though evidently not tonight. But it was a real enough institution, and someone must have paid dues, because I saw official stickers and a T-shirt with a leopard-shark logo. The C in "club" was spelled with a fishing hook. After some pleasantries and their jokes about sex with prostitutes in the nearby bushes, I explained my journey.

"The missions and shit?" said the young buzzed man.

"Before the missions actually, but yeah."

"Hell yeah, hell yeah," said the one Latino among them, slapping the hood of his car with pride.

"Get the fuck out of here with that shit," the buzzed man quipped. "I thought you were Mexican?"

"I don't care . . . I'm sometimes Spanish, bro," he said.

Still another young man and club member kindly offered me a sandwich from his sedan, which I tried to refuse.

"Are you sure? It's fucking baller, dude."

"You know, I really can't," I said. "I've already got one. I've got a Subway right here." In addition to my fritters, I had picked up a Veggie Delight in Castroville, across the street from the Giant Artichoke.

"You know what," he said. "You don't want the sandwich? Feed it to the fuck-ing animals."

This statement was somehow more playful than belligerent, and I laughed. He'd sized me up pretty well as a nature boy who might feed the birds. "I really am thankful," I said. I accepted a Gatorade instead, from the man with Spanish pride, and he also offered me a clean pair of socks, brand new, which I sorely needed but reflexively declined.

"Take the sandwich, too, and feed it to the fucking animals if you want," reiterated the sandwich owner.

"Feed it to your dog, if you want," I said, with a laugh.

He looked down at his mutt with obvious affection and said, "Fuck this fucking slow bastard."

I sipped that Gatorade's maraschino as I made for the knoll, its nuptial view, nighttime's fucking animals, the mice and voles stirring the parched grass.

THE PAJARO RIVER IS THE division between Monterey and Santa Cruz Counties and between the towns of Pajaro and Watsonville. The expedition left Espinosa Lake, circumvented Elkhorn Slough, and arrived at this stream: slender, Crespí reports, but with "a very large bed and a great many sand banks, showing it must carry a great many floods." Two days earlier, the scouts had found an Ohlone village of about five hundred at this spot, and apparently these "souls" were unnerved and bothered by their arrival—must have been that they had received no forewarning from neighboring villages. Costansó heard that "some ran for their weapons, others shouted and yelled, and the women burst into tears." Crespí relayed that the village was "so exceedingly ill-behaved that it cost them [the scouts] a great deal of trouble to pacify them and give them to understand we were coming in peace and not in order to harm them." We now know that these Ohlone were right to be concerned and agitated, though there is probably nothing they could have done to change or even slow the course of history.

When Crespí and the main expedition arrived the next day, to everyone's surprise this village had been vacated and torched. "A great many upright poles, surrounded by many arrows, have been found, with a great quantity of their seeds scattered on the ground at the foot of them after they had burned and abandoned the village. We found half the body of a black bird hanging with the same poles, with two wings brought together; these when spread out measured from tip to tip thirteen quarter yards." Quite possibly it was an eagle. But if Crespí's *vara* or yard was the standard thirty-three inches, the bird's wingspan measured eight feet eleven inches. At that size it could only have been a condor, North America's largest bird, the famed carrion eater. Crespí named the river the *Santa Ana*, but the soldiers of course provided its abiding name: *El Río del Pájaro.*

The bird might have seemed an ominous or at least gloomy sign, but Crespí makes no interpretation, and he was right to withhold judgment. The Ohlone's specific treatment of the condor is little known, but in California the bird was involved especially with mourning and renewal ceremonies, and a ritual sacrifice of a condor was thought to convey its powers of movement and eyesight. The best-documented ceremony involved the Luiseño, who held an annual *Panes* (bird) festival in which condors raised from the time they were chicks were sacrificed by pressing on their hearts. The flesh was immolated, the feathers and skin incorporated into revered items. Whether the Portolá expedition interrupted an ongoing ceremony is unknown, but there's no suggestion of it in the journals; neither Crespí nor Costansó write of the scouts seeing anything of the sort. Rather it seems possible that this Ohlone village felt they had encountered visitors from the land of the dead, or some other frightful omen, and so burnt their village and left these offerings, this bird and these seeds, to assuage and cleanse.

Beneath the overpass that carried Porter Drive into Watsonville, the river was much as Crespí described: more the size of a creek, it was four to six feet wide, manifesting brown and languid from a knitted tunnel of willow to flow under the concrete. Yet there was a ruddy layer of silt on the cresses and grasses on its lowest banks, showing that not long ago the river had been several feet higher and that it was, yes, prone to floods. Knots of debris from these torrents hung in the crotches of saplings like birds' nests, while the overpass's piers were, as usual, most colorfully tagged. *iTrap-aholic*, was one of the graffiti. *Dang*, read another.

Higher up the bank, trash was everywhere, including three black bags someone had either collected from the creek or dumped from the bridge. A lime-green plastic Nerf gun rested on top like a weapon surrendered. There was a peanut butter jar and three empty cans of beef stew, and the old tepee and defecations they had turned into. One scrap of litter was a handwashing advisory from Driscoll's, "*Lave sus manos al menos durante 20 segundos,*" with illustrations (hands rubbing) of each step, a bid to avoid berry recalls: "*Palma con palma; palma con dorso; palma con dorso dedos entrelazados; dedo pulgar; punta de los dedos y líneas de la palma.*" Don't forget those fingertips. Like a fool, I picked up a bright tissue thinking it was a napkin I'd dropped from my pocket, but someone else had used it as toilet paper. I wanted to rinse my own hands in the creek, but the water looked no cleaner.

Most striking was a bike that had been hung off the bridge from a rope—dangling, twisting slowly, its handlebars wide. Instantly it associated in my mind with the black bird that the Portolá party had discovered. Whose bike was this? Why was it strung up? Its rear tire reached down to the thirty-five-foot mark on the measuring stick painted onto the pier. The Pajaro could roar. Then all this trash would be swept into the Pacific to join the ever-widening gyres of plastic. Other things were hanging, too: on my way out, I studied an enormous spider, black-and-brown checkered, with its own eight-legged molt caught beside it in the web.

Back on the road, just before the overpass into Santa Cruz County, was a weathered sandstone boulder with a bench in front of it that said, "Rest and think it over." The rock had an old plaque affixed to it: HERE CAME THE FIRST WHITE MAN WITH PORTOLA AND FR. CRESPI, OCTOBER 9, 1769. THIS RIVER THEY CALLED RIO DEL PAJARO. MARKED 1909 BY THE WOMEN OF WATSONVILLE. So this boulder had been in place over a hundred years. There was a cross above these words on the plaque and a bird flying below them, like that condor resurrected. A more modern memorial was only a few paces off: a painted electrical box, orange, purple, and green, which mentioned the Ohlone, later called the Costanoan or "coast people," by name. I sat and thought it over, studying the scraps of a mandarin peel at my feet and the ants exploring them. I couldn't get the phrase *palma con palma* out of my mind.

Waddell Creek

SANTA CRUZ
MOUNTAINS

Mission Santa Cruz

Davenport

Red White
& Blue Beach

Wilder Ranch
State Park

San Lorenzo River/
Santa Cruz Beach Boardwalk

N
W E
S

Santa Cruz County

Soquel

Aptos

Corralitos Lagoon/
Freedom Lake

Interlaken

Sunny Cove

MONTEREY BAY

Watsonville/Pajaro
River Crossing

BEYOND THE WATSONVILLE TOWN SQUARE where once bulls and bears fought each other in the dust; where now a dozen *abuelos*, some in cowboy hats, sat on benches across from one another, listening to *ranchera* from a little red radio; where Taqueria La Fuente was flooded with high schoolers on their lunch hour in skinny jeans and Santa Cruz-brand hoodies; beyond all that, I turned right on East Lake Road and came upon Gurnee Freze-Dri Taxidermy. OPEN, COME IN, read the door's sign. Red geraniums grew below the shade-drawn windows of a small beige building with an eave of warped shingles. The cowbell hanging from the handle clanked and settled as I entered. Black linoleum, wood paneling, fluorescent lights: the room hadn't changed since the sixties. Animals everywhere, a dry and quiet ark. Dust coated everything. A table of ducks lined the left wall, and another with snakes filled the center of the room like an island hibernaculum: western rattlesnake, eastern diamondback, coral snake, copperhead, Boyle's king snake, boa constrictor, and more. PLEASE DO NOT TOUCH, said a cardboard sign printed decades ago, but I was not about to. Their coiled poses raised my instinctual hackles. Stacks of Styrofoam coolers were pushed up against the wall, the sort that might deliver oysters or ham hock as holiday cheer, but these vessels had delivered specimens overnight.

"Oh, hello," said a tall and thin white-haired man, stepping suddenly from the back room. Mr. Gurnee, I presumed. He wore spectacles and a full khaki uniform as if on safari.

"Oh, how you doing?" I said, startled.

"Okay, okay," he replied, breathlessly. His upper teeth shone as he smiled weakly. His mouth hung open a touch.

"I was just . . . I've never been into a taxidermist shop before," I said, still taking in the room. There was a jumbled pile of branches pressed into and warping the slats of the front windows' blinds along the floor. There was a beautiful piece of wood peppered with holes in one corner, an empty acorn woodpecker granary awaiting its woodpecker. Above a vitrine, on the wall, flew a northern shoveler with its evergreen head and goldenrod eye, and a handsome male wood duck in its mating regalia was also perched there beside a giant relief map of California, "the Golden State."

"Well, this is freeze-dried . . ." he said. "This is not taxidermy, this is freeze-drying. I dehydrate them from a frozen state. So, it's not taxidermy. I can do caterpillars and all sorts of things that I can freeze-dry without shrinking them." His distinction was befuddling for a moment since the shop's exterior boldly declared "taxidermy." But he hewed close to the word's root: *taxis* and *derma*, an "arrangement" of "skin." Richard Gurnee removed no skins, only the moisture within them. I noticed there were mushrooms, even, among his sample collection, some of them under bell jars like clappers never rung. Freeze-drying worked with some fungus, Richard said, not all.

He explained the process: "I get'm frozen, then I thaw them out, then I position them the way they look while alive, get the eyes into them—I make artificial eyes for them—and then when I get the eyes in and the thing looks just like it's . . . right . . . then I put several of them in a freeze-drying chamber which evaporates the ice out of them. It's like an outer-space vacuum type of chamber." My own eyes widened. "I maintain a vacuum pump . . . you can hear it now . . . I maintain a vacuum of maybe, oh gosh, a hundred thousand, maybe two hundred thousand, feet of altitude."

"Whoa," I said, in all seriousness. I could indeed hear the humming, the pulsing. It sounded like an engine deep in the hull of an ocean liner. It was transforming the bodies of the creatures inside it, taking them to another state. Some of these models were forty years old, he said, and they hadn't budged.

"It's a very rarefied air," Richard continued, "so that the water vapor coming off the animals can condense on a coil in there at a minus-four temperature, while it's plus five in the specimen tank. That difference causes the ice to transfer by diffusion to the condenser inside the chamber." In other words, the reduced pressure in the tank is such that, when the animal body's temperature is lifted above freezing, the ice within its cells sublimates, turning directly into a gas that leaves its skin. There isn't enough pressure for a liquid to even form.

Richard had the class of old-timey accent fit for radio, a massaging or stretching out of vowels. It sounded almost midwestern to my untrained ear, but he was born and raised in Watsonville, so it was just rural or rustic. He leaned back on his hips with his hands in his beige pockets and shied away in his gaze, blinking. He really didn't want to look me in the eyes and deflected his head to the right instead. Despite my efforts to see otherwise, he seemed to live up to the popular image, the stereotype, of morticians and other artisans of the beyond. And then there was the homophone inherent in his name, Gurnee, the faint creak of a stretcher.

Richard's career began with the Boy Scouts: his first merit badge was for taxidermy. "After that I did a lot of ducks," he said, alluding to his high school days. "There were a lot of hunters then in Watsonville." Like the delta region of the Salinas, the Pajaro Valley once abounded with water. At Humboldt State University, while pursuing zoology (*zoe-ology*, he pronounced it), he learned you could freeze-dry tissues to preserve them, and he wondered if maybe he could preserve a complete animal this way. So he pioneered the field. "I developed the freeze-drying technique and went on from there, because museums wanted to have things done." After graduate work at UC Berkeley, for six years he worked for the Smithsonian before returning to Watsonville as a freelance freeze-drier. His clients include museums and nature centers around the country. If you've admired dioramas at a natural history museum in the West, likely you've seen one of Gurnee's animals and looked into his handmade epoxy eyes.

He drew the line at dogs and cats. "It's too anthropomorphic, and it's not for scientific reasons," said Gurnee. "It's for emotional reasons, and I don't want to do that. It's part of the family, you know." He's done just about everything else, though smaller animals are most practical. The tank is only so big, and larger animals, by the basic surface-area-to-mass equation, require a long time to freeze-dry. No deer or elk busts. The largest creature in his shop was a coyote on its haunches, its narrow snout extending under black eyes. This was the creature I had heard from my sleeping bag so many nights, had seen at the fringe of Irvine howling at that immense orange rotting into the Pacific. It sat beside a gray fox. I asked him if he had any favorite critters to dry. "Ah, there's no favorites . . . all it has to be is fresh. It needs to be a good animal. I can rescue things that have gone too far, but it's always better to get them when they are freshest. So those are the favorites."

Could I take a look in back, I asked, or was it top secret? "Well, I'm getting kind of busy now," Richard said, but I followed him back anyhow, into a windowless shop, a den fit for a bear. He was working on a couple of coachwhip snakes, which are known for slithering at fifteen miles per hour and periscoping their heads for a vantage over rocks and grass. These were for a museum in Ridgecrest, California. Richard slid back a sound-dampening plywood board to reveal the silver tank, his outer space, about eight feet long and thirty inches in diameter. Old and beat as an oil drum tumbled off a truck. He would ready a number of specimens over the course of days or weeks and then freeze-dry them all at once, like a potter firing his ware after weeks of throwing bowls. He arranged about one animal a day and did finishing work on others. "It takes a little while to get'm to look right. I can fire them up and get'm into position, but then it takes a while to make them look right." *Taxis.* By "fire them up" he meant thaw them. On a table was a gray squirrel in progress for "a private party" that had gleaned it from a road. The pose was classic: an arched back, tail curled, a brown acorn between its paws at its twitchless lips. Wires extended from its elbows and wrists and toes and were pinned temporarily to a board. Richard slid this armature *into* the animals for positioning. They were like silver veins. Some of them he drew out once the animal was done.

A colorful plastic fishing tackle box of resinous eyes sat on his desk like a tailor's button collection, hundreds of black pupils staring up through dust from irises red yellow orange brown olive turquoise white, all shades, a subdued and uncanny rainbow. He always made duplicates for future specimens while he was at it. "The most common is a brown eye, for birds," he said. Behind his desk was a row of field guides with one splayed open to those coachwhips. But he received fresh specimens often enough that for most animals he had examined their eyes still glistening. Almost all were roadkill, shipped frozen overnight.

I thought of the hundreds of animals I'd seen destroyed on California's macadam: the fox disintegrating in the white oleander off the highway north of Ventura; the mountain lion cub flat in the leaves, like a grease-stained pizza box thrown out a window; the little brown bat near Ragged Point; wrens and sparrows and owls and insects by the handful; so many animals that I noted but haven't written of, and so many more I did not record or even see. On his desk was an Anna's humming-bird, its wiry black claws grasping a branch, a white tag around its neck. Suddenly I was compelled to mention the Anna's I had carried for two days through San Luis Obispo before I buried it in the manzanita sands when it began to off-gas and reek. "Oh, it was a fresh hit then," said Richard. He pointed out that only a pedestrian was likely to find a roadkill hummer.

Finally, I brought up the condor that the Portolá party had found strung up and stuffed, with its wings folded. It was taxidermy, the first record of it in Cali-fornia, but unlike the creatures populating his shop, it was overtly symbolic, with a meaning that they couldn't quite interpret. "Oh yeah yeah yeah," said Richard, implying he well knew the origin story of Pajaro Valley's name. "I did a condor once for the Pacific Grove Natural History Museum. A four-year-old bird. It died down in Ventura, and the museum acquired it. There were very few of them at the time." I should have asked him how he posed it, with its wings outstretched nine feet—wire running down its long airy bones—or folded behind its back like a magistrate.

"Well, I should let you go," I said.

"Yeah, I've got to get back to work," said Richard.

"Do you have a website?" I asked. It was a dopey question.

"No," he said.

"Why bother," I said.

"Why bother, that's right."

Back in the main room, I lifted my backpack and asked one last question: "It's always a new challenge for you? It doesn't seem old hat, even though you've done all these animals?"

"Oh, no," he said. "Every one is a new thing. Everything's different. There might be repetitions of waterfowl, and things like that, but you've got the whole reptile kingdom—the whole animal kingdom!" With that, he bade me adieu— "Well, ohhkay, I'm glad to meet you"—and disappeared. Surely I would be the only visitor-interloper Richard would receive all day. The radio started up in the back room, loudly; Richard was a little hard of hearing, probably from all those years beside that thrumming tank. I saddled up, cinched myself tight, and looked around at "all my friends," as I had put it to Richard: the bobcat, the mourning doves, the monarch in its glass case, the California quail, the Belding's ground squirrel. Their souls, or whatever had lived inside them, were long gone but their bodies were still mysterious and beautiful. This place was a strange account of California.

I reached for the door, but had a thought: I should have taken a picture of him. I stalled, worked up the nerve, dropped my pack, and walked into the back room again with a little trepidation. He was at his desk with a paintbrush in hand, repeating, "The future, the fuuuuturee," back at his radio. The second time I spoke his name, he looked up.

"Oh yes, hello!" he said.

"May I take one photo of you, for my memory?" I said. "Of the master at work?"

"Sure, sure," he said, holding stock still with his mouth agape, his palette resting on his lap atop a striped beach towel. "Got it?" he asked.

THE EXPEDITION WAS GROWING A little desperate to find Monterey Bay, though in fact they had already found it. While camped on *El Río del Pájaro*, the scouts ventured downstream to the shore, hoping to meet a harbor, but only discovered a large "inlet"; and they scouted to the northwest across the valley to what appeared to be a large "point of pines" fingering into the sea, today's Aptos Hills. They found these trees weren't pines at all, but "very straight, very thick trees, quite tall, with a very short slight leaf." "Some said they were savins," wrote Crespí, "however, they are not so to my understanding, since the wood is red." A savin is a European juniper, but what they had found, of course, were coast redwoods, *Sequoia sempervirens*, soon called *palos colorados* by the Spanish.

The whole group set out in roughly that direction, some of the men so afflicted with scurvy that they began to slip off their mules. Crespí describes passing a cluster of six lakes, now the Interlaken area slightly east of Watsonville, which runs from the southeast to the northwest: Lake Tynan, Drew Lake, Kelly Lake, College Lake, Pinto Lake, and finally, the Corralitos Lagoon. The Spaniards camped at one of these spring-fed waters, where there was "a good deal of the aforesaid sort of tall thick savin grove." Now just a handful of redwoods are found on the ridge between Kelly and Drew that is threaded with cottages and fine houses. College Lake, which

I surveyed from the St. Francis Cemetery, was dry amid encroaching fields and glossy white rows of raspberry hoop houses. An osprey nest was perched atop a telephone pole above its vaporized shore.

Rather than camping I kept on north as the Spaniards did on their next leg. I wasn't sick with the "Luanda disease," so I made better time than they. The season was shifting, pivoting toward its final stretch and mine. Men were taking down plastic on the hoop houses along the road, rolling and tying it at eye level like a sail on a boom, and the raspberry clippings lay between the rows. *¿Quieres trabajo piscadores de fresas y moras? Llame 750-5394.* Then the country became orchards with windfall Pink Ladies and Granny Smiths rotting in droves beneath the vener-able scabbed and burl-swollen trees. On this leg, the expedition saw herd animals, which by many accounts were once superabundant along with the redwoods in the Pajaro Valley plains, including some beasts the soldiers described as "buffalo," through Crespí seems doubtful. They also saw herds of a "stout deer or elk" with large antlers "like two of the latter which I saw cast off on the ground along the way on this march and that the soldiers picked up and brought along as a curiosity." Like me, the Spaniards felt the urge to collect—I wonder how far they carried those elk antlers. Crespí himself confesses to examining scat. "Tracks and droppings have been seen like those of a mule-like creature . . . long-eared like mules and with a short broad tail." This is the first European description of the ubiquitous mule deer, no friend of suburban flowers and perennially frozen in headlights with a cool blue stare.

In the Pajaro Valley, the mule deer must now eat from the millions of fallen apples. I was poking my head into a brimming bin by a warehouse, marveling at the fruit, when a man hailed me from the yellow loading dock. "How's it going?" he called out. "Where you headed?" Jake Mann was one of the few who could discern, at a glance, that I was a backpacker, not a threat. His grandfather had owned this orchard, and he and his father now harvested about a hundred acres, some of it belonging to his uncles. Jake invited me to climb up on the dock, which I did with a groan, my legs sore from a long, slow day, and we slipped through the heavy clear vinyl curtains into the cold storage. As at the lemon plant in the Santa Clara River Valley, the perfume nearly bowled me over. Giant plywood totes, weathered and with rusty hardware, were stacked to the high flu-orescent ceiling with the season's haul. It was a good year, Jake said, and the totes were overflowing. The windfall I'd seen from the road also attested to that. From a hundred acres, they would harvest thousands of bins, about four trees to a bin, Jake estimated. The crews picked the limbs and then gleaned those knocked down in the process, along with the windfalls, which isn't the harvesters' favorite chore: harder on the back, a different labor entirely. Pink Ladies, Braeburn, Red Delicious (not terribly delicious, if my elementary memory serves), Granny Smith. Some would chill for a half year until they were needed. The Manns stored apples for neighbors, too, so with a forklift Jake was building a careful jigsaw puzzle of totes to make sure apples would be accessible at the right time. Most of these apples would be bought and pressed by the famous Watsonville-based Martinelli's, the sparkling of choice for nondrinkers and kids everywhere, golden bubbles rising in party cups like the spirits of apples on their way to heaven. But Jake wanted to deliver more of their harvest to hard cider makers, a still-burgeoning market on the heels of the microbrewery explosion.

I asked Jake what it was like growing up in the Pajaro groves. "It was pretty great," he said. "Rotten apples are good for bomb-throwing. You can get a medium-rotten one on a stick and throw it. And apple bins are perfect for forts. The sound of tractors is also pretty nice . . . That is the sound of my childhood." That rumble and clickity-clack, I would argue, is a fundamental California sound; it's the surf of the inland valleys, of fossil fuel enabling fields far beyond the old human scale. But these distinguished orchards seemed of a different, more hands-on era.

Jake invited me to his folks' farmhouse for barley soup. They would be glad to meet me, he said, and his father would yak my ear off. I should have taken him up on such hospitality, but my weariness got the best of me again. He even offered to let me camp in their orchard, under those sweet-smelling fruits. But I didn't want to surprise anyone—or maybe I just wanted to watch some baseball, World Series Game 1—so I gave him my thanks and walked on to my lagoon, Corralitos, where the Spaniards had camped for several days. "As we had some eleven sick men here, with a few people to do the work, they made a pen up against the lake in front of us in order for a single soldier to be able to keep in the mounts at night, so that this spot has been dubbed among the soldiers *el Paraje del Corral.*" Today it's better known as Freedom Lake and is blanketed with the invasive jade of water hyacinth. I pitched my tent in the nettle beside the lagoon's duckweed edge, and then backtracked a distance farther than I remembered to El Azteca Mexican at the crossroads to catch a few innings, tottering back in the dark two Modelos and one burrito deep.

FOG OF MORNING, FOG OF history. A female mallard dabbling in the duckweed margins feet from my tent, cresses dripping from her mouth, was hardly fazed when I tossed back my wet fly. The sky was spitting as I left Sunflower Lane at the head of the lagoon. "Indeed, most days the sun is scarcely seen," wrote Crespí. The expedition spent four days at *el Paraje del Corral* while scouts looked ahead. Each man was given three mules as remounts. Meanwhile, the scurvy-ridden soldiers rested. Crespí logged that "measures are being taken to contrive a sort of saddle with back rests, to see whether they can ride more comfortably, as the sick men are entirely unable to shift for themselves or do anything requiring use of their legs—it takes two or three men between them to get them onto their mounts." I thought of how I had walked for days through the orange and lemon groves of the Santa Clara River Valley.

Where exactly the expedition went over the Aptos Hills is slightly unclear from the journals. They may have continued to the end of Pleasant Valley and into the Valencia Creek drainage, but I chose the more direct pass over Freedom Boulevard, climbing through redwoods. Their finials were a chiffon gray in the moisture. Redwoods seem to invite mist wherever they are, which is wherever the mist is, and they catch it the way the cirri of barnacles, those feathery arms, sift plankton. All these forms, textures, and organisms tendril together, tighter and tighter. The Anna's hummingbirds throwing off the cloud droplets just as fast as they come. Periwinkle coiling with poison oak. A Steller's jay's black wings spreading in a copse like a lacquered fan. Poppies and mustard pushing through the artificial turf of a neglected putting green. Quail flushing, clucking, from the roadside rounds of a downed oak into bramble, hunting for seed or bugs in the new grass of winter, whose cold I could feel in my carpals.

I stopped to examine a young redwood three feet in diameter and feel its soft bark. Hammocks of spiderweb were strung between its fibrous ridges. The lower branches were dead to about ten feet up, and lichen or some other algal film grew on the limb's upper surfaces, where it met sufficient light. Each needle of a redwood has fifteen or twenty symmetrical leaflets, and each year's growth emerges lime-green at each needle's tip. But the thing about redwoods and mountains and a months-long journey is that if you're close enough to see any of this detail, you're too close to see the whole, the full structure.

Two semis of apples passed with their plywood crates, trailing an intoxicating smell, wine-sweet. Not long after, I came upon a skunk minced to the consistency of ground chuck. I had five or six apples in my pack, a few from Jake and several others that I had pilfered from the ground beforehand, not realizing the growers harvested those, too. I did not mean to steal. At the crest of Freedom Boulevard, near Redwood Heights, the fog began to dissipate. Surf and skim boards started to appear beside mailboxes as street number signs, and the roadside trash now included items like a Ball jar carton, the detritus of canning: Santa Cruz was nearer and nearer.

Crespí wrote, "In coming down the hills it is necessary to stop every moment to fix the contraptions," the saddles on which the scorbutic men suffered. They halted for the day at the Valencia Lagoon, now hard on Highway 1, but I kept going, turning right onto Soquel Drive. Around the bend, in "downtown" Aptos, the first NO SKATEBOARDING sign appeared. Shops overhung the redwood creek, the understory maples gone yellow. In Soquel, I followed the creek, "quite sunken in and deep" as Crespí put it, toward the ocean with the sun hot on my face. Aptos, Soquel—these town and street names are the echoes of the first people on this coast. Soquel was the chief of the Uypi, the Ohlone tribe that lived in and around today's Santa Cruz and were the first to be baptized at the mission. A man "serious, reserved, and of a melancholy disposition" according to one Spanish sergeant, Soquel died at the mission five years after its founding. Just to the east, the Aptos tribe was the Uypi's main rival, with a territory that extended into the Pajaro Valley. At the mission, these rivals were forced to become allies and live side by side.

From Capitola and its fancy bric-a-brac, I crossed the outlet of Soquel Creek. Straight down in pea-soup water, an American coot swam with feet of astounding size, the lobed skin of its toes streamlining as it drew each leg to its chest and unfolding again on the downstroke, a sudden paddle, a model of energy efficiency. In the far distance, the Moss Landing Power Plant towered like the axle pin of the Monterey Bay environs. Up the hill the road became Portola Drive, and I half imagined the expedition walking down its middle past the baby-blue and peach bungalows, their hooves clapping the pavement. The soldiers' jaws would have dropped at the density. The surfers' jaws would have dropped too. Instead, a bicyclist pedaled by with the same relative motion as a coot. He had a radio tied to his frame that crooned a Doppler "And I love you."

PORTOLA WAS THE COASTAL BIKE route, but it wasn't the scenic route, so I turned toward famous Cliff Drive. Surfers were stripping off their neoprene layers and booties on their tailgates. The stop signs' versos were a nebula of fading stickers: CALIFORNIA GROWN. I BARK, THEREFORE I AM. BUILD RAMPS, NOT BOMBS. ALWAYS REMEMBER MARIA BOISA. She went missing in Big Sur. She was a surfer. Here, forty or so were floating off The Hook and as many off Pleasure Point. The day was superb, but the surf lacked luster. "It's terrible," said one man. "It's mushy," said another. "It looks pretty good," said a third, an optimist or a rookie. A dripping twelve-year-old told me that he'd just finished his fourth session of the day: out at 5:30 a.m., in for breakfast, out again, and again. Soon I passed the cliffside home of wetsuit baron Jack O'Neill. Though not especially glitzy, it is one of the few houses on Cliff Drive's ocean side. The closest to a saint that Santa Cruz has, O'Neill then had less than a year to live. After his death, thousands would parade to his home with their boards over their heads for the largest-ever "paddle out": everyone floating, splashing in praise, holding hands in unity, tossing white orchids, some wearing an honorary patch over their right eye. He had lost his at The Hook. O'Neill was testing a prototype for a surf leash when his board whipped back into his face. But the leash transformed surfing.

Then came Sunny Cove, where as a child I had spent many days boogie boarding and watching the sand crabs burrow furiously into the slick, like fingernails, as the waves and our own hands dug them out again with little compunction. Afterward we would stroll back down the street to peel off our gritty wetsuits under the outdoor shower. Along with another family, mine rented a house a stone's throw away, 103 Sixteenth Avenue, for a week each summer. The tradition seemed to last forever; actually it was just three or four years. Sunny Cove is horseshoe shaped with modest sandstone cliffs draped in ice plant. Now the hind beach was temporarily a lagoon, the remainder of inundation from the storm I'd experienced down in Big Sur.

I descended the stairs carved into the bluff and lingered on Sunny Cove's bridge of sand, watching the skimboarders finesse minor peaks and foamy rails. "Is this a good spot for it?" I asked one young man who seemed fairly expert. "Not really," he replied. "But it's the only spot working right now." He slathered sand onto the bottom of his board to counter the wind by adding weight. Then he sprinted, perceiving some seam I couldn't see, and slid his shield-shaped board onto the glass as it withdrew into the chop, weightless in his temporary playground. Childhood goes so fast in the end, and yet it never finishes. I spotted otters in the surf, just where I had so often encountered them while floating on my own board a dozen feet away. It was reassuring to see them still here eating the clams and crabs and urchins and eyeing the neoprene beings that once had killed them indiscriminately and now bobbed beside them. Everything and nothing had changed, in this one cove. I wondered if Portolá's scouts had come to it and quietly steered their horses around it. It was a mere scratch on the coast, a tally.

DURING OUR WEEK-LONG VACATION EACH year, we would venture one evening to the Santa Cruz Beach Boardwalk and hold tight on the Giant Dipper, a wooden roller coaster decorated with bare bulbs. And we would hold tight on the final wet descent of Logger's Revenge, which we simply called the log ride. Though I never thought about it as a kid, the log ride is a regional legacy: all those Santa Cruz redwoods carried out by the San Lorenzo River or by mules. California rode those trees to wealth and cities; on the log ride, we ride a synthetic version of this history. The San Lorenzo's outlet is at the boardwalk's east end, and during the log ride's calm sluice prior to its final splashdown, I would always study the wide, calm river. Downtown, the "great many cottonwoods and sycamores" Crespí saw have vanished, as has the "thicket that covered the river-bottom" that tested the trailblazers and their machetes, according to Costansó. Now the banks are riprapped and grass-grown, the mallards settled on driftwood. Crespí named this river *el río de San Lorenzo*, and a stream joining it *el arroyo de la Santísima Cruz*, "one of the best spots for a very large mission that have been come across upon the entire journey." He was especially taken with the headlong creek, which, with the help of ditches, he believed could water the tablelands above the river and make them bloom.

I strolled the bike path along the San Lorenzo toward downtown, the lights of the Ocean Gate Inn, the Del Monte Court, and Budget Inn on the flat water, sparrows flitting through its tule at dusk, Torch Lite Inn, Best Value Inn & Suites, Super 8, the coots sinking away through these reflections. "Not in my house, fool!" shouted a basketball player blocking a shot on a riverside court. Their game was just one-on-one. Skateboarders clicked across the sidewalk as they left their dug-out park. The dark water of which Crespí wrote was serene and off-limits: SAN LORENZO RIVER AREA TEMPORARILY CLOSED, PERSONS WHO ENTER THIS AREA WILL BE CITED FOR VIOLATING SANTA CRUZ MUNICIPAL CODE. Was it pollution? Were too many people sleeping by the river in grimy sleeping bags and frayed blankets? Downtown's main drag, Pacific Avenue, was bustling and incandescent in the early night. I bought a pizza slice and a book of poetry, and I put down my pen for the day when a shirtless man, homeless or addled or maybe a visionary, walked up to a motorcyclist and his gleaming hog and said, "I can jump a skateboard over that chickenshit thing."

SERRA'S SUCCESSOR, FATHER LASUÉN, RAISED the cross for *La Misión de la Exaltación de la Santa Cruz* along the San Lorenzo River, but when the location flooded that first year, in 1791, the padres moved it a short distance uphill, to a plateau now called Mission Hill. Once it must have had an uninterrupted view of the river's willowy meanders and outlet, but now it overlooks rooftops to the roller coasters and the bay. The only original building that remains is a neophyte dormitory built in 1824, the oldest edifice in Santa Cruz. When I visited, drips fell from the eaves of the corridors of this long white stuccoed dorm, their beams hand hewn, crossed with branches, laid with straw, and stuffed with mud. The quarters were dim, with just one window punched through several feet of adobe. DOES A SMALL, CROWDED ROOM BOTHER YOU? an interpretive sign asked. Teasel hung on the wall to suggest how wool from the mission's sheep—a herd of five thousand in 1806—would have been carded before it was spun into yarn and woven into a blue-striped cloth for trade. A redwood pole ladder slanted to a loft, its rungs fastened with stiff leather. A fire circle was staged at the room's center with clam and abalone shells and a skillet of three stale tortillas. Nearby, beside a woven mat for kneeling, were a metate and mano to grind the corn. I searched for the tally marks the Native residents apparently had notched on the wall, but in the meager light I couldn't find them.

In the last room, an elementary school group was weaving tule mats under the guidance of a State Park ranger. Mats to kneel and sleep on, to roll across willow frames as a refined thatching, to cradle an infant on one's back. "Now we're going to take our second piece of tule, and we're going to place it in here," the ranger explained, demonstrating how to entwine a spray of loose ends. "Then we're going to tie just one simple knot." I asked her where the tule was from, and she didn't know, but it still thrives along the San Lorenzo. Outside, other children were cooking tortillas on a propane griddle and dipping nascent candles into a vat of hot wax. The Ohlone neophytes would have immersed their wicks in tallow rendered from cattle, but the motion was the same. Pale and narrow, the students' candles looked like gourmet heirloom carrots.

"I'm the fastest candle maker," said one kid. "Am I the fastest candle maker you've ever seen?"

"I would say probably yes," replied an adult chaperone. "Now come stand right here so that we know you're ready to go to tule mats."

"What's tule mats?"

"That's where you're going next."

These activities were educational enough, but I'm not sure it occurred to the teachers, let alone the kids, that they were playing at exploitation, at the daily life of the oppressed.

Mission Santa Cruz also was never particularly large. Its population peaked at roughly five hundred neophytes in the late 1700s, even less than in Carmel. During the first twenty years, the mission recruited from the surrounding Ohlone tribes on the western side of the Santa Cruz Mountains, mainly Uypi, Cotoni, Sayanta, Achistaca, and Aptos; afterward Yokuts from the San Joaquin Valley were brought to the mission to replace the many who had died or been relocated, and they came to make up four-fifths of the mission's population. The Spaniards had a strategy of extracting natives from their homelands and shepherding them to more distant missions, thus thwarting their local knowledge and alliances and making escape more difficult.

Mission Santa Cruz's struggles are also attributed to the pueblo that New Spain established across the river in 1797. Called Branciforte, it was named after the viceroy at the time. In the eyes of the padres, these colonists of mixed and hence dubious ethnicity were riffraff and miscreants—those were the only people that Spain could convince to attempt the journey. They were rounded up in Guadalajara and shipped from San Blas. A bridge was built over the San Lorenzo to allow the pueblo's citizens to venture across for Mass, but the pueblo tempted the neophytes in the opposite direction and, the padres argued, set a less-than-industrious or -pious example. A year after the pueblo was founded, one of the mission's padres,

Manuel Fernandez, confessed that "Everything was in a bad way": most of the neophytes had abandoned the mission, leaving only thirty or forty natives to keep its operations afloat; livestock were dying; and furthermore, a spoiled whale carcass had lured swarms of wolves and bears to the beach. The icing on the cake, when it came to Branciforte? In 1818, hearing that Monterey had been raided by pirates, Mission Santa Cruz's fathers retreated with their neophytes over the Santa Cruz Mountains, often just called the Coast Range, to Mission Santa Clara. Rather than watch over the mission, the settlers of Branciforte looted it themselves.

MISSION SANTA CRUZ IS ALSO renowned for the murder of a padre, Andrés Quintana, committed in retribution for the severe punishments he administered. He was the only padre slain in Northern California (several were poisoned in Southern California), and his killing was a relatively rare example of uprising by California's natives, while the violence and atrocities perpetrated against them were extensive and commonplace. Most of what we know about this intrigue comes from an 1877 interview with Lorenzo Asisara, a native who was born at the mission in 1820 and heard the tale from his father, who was one of the first to be baptized and personally witnessed the assassination. Fourteen men gathered at the house of a gardener to plot the deed, among them a young man named Lino who was the padre's assistant and, apparently, a frequent target of beatings. They set the conspiracy in motion the next night, knowing that on the following day Quintana planned to publicly demonstrate a new whip tipped with iron wire. He had boasted of it.

The gardener, Julian, pretended to be gravely ill at the suggestion of his wife, Yaquenonsat, and after dark she summoned Padre Quintana to visit him and perform last rites. Meanwhile, several of the plotters hid behind trees. Twice they couldn't bring themselves to go through with the ambush, but Yaquenonsat threatened to tell of their scheme if they didn't muster the resolve. For a third time, she asked the padre to attend to her dying husband. He obliged, walking with Lino and two other pages to the neophyte residence, where he prayed over the supposedly unconscious gardener. "Now your husband is prepared to live or die," Padre Quintana said, according to Lorenzo's narrative. "Don't come to look for me again."

This time, the conspirators confronted the padre on his path back to his residence. Lino gripped him from behind, made him turn. The other men emerged from their hiding places. As Asisara tells it, Padre Quintana said to Lino, "Oh, my son, what are you going to do to me?"

"Your assassins will tell you," Lino answered.

"What have I done to you children, for which you would kill me?" Quintana said.

"Because you have made an iron whip," a neophyte answered him.

"Oh, children, leave me, so that I can go from here now, at this moment."

They asked him then why he had fashioned this novel whip, and Quintana responded that it was only for "transgressors."

"Well, you are in the hands of those evil ones," someone shouted. "Make your peace with God."

They strangled Quintana with his own robe and quite sensationally extracted one of his testicles, probably so that he would bleed out and show no bruises. They carried him back to his room, dressed him in his nightclothes, and arranged him in bed, making it seem as if he had died in his sleep. Then they stole his keys to the dormitories. Each mission had a *monjerío* and a *jayunte*, dormitories for unmarried women and men, respectively. The *monjerío* was often located across the quadrangle from the padres' quarters so they could monitor its door. Thus the padres served, indeed, as overbearing "fathers," not just the spiritual kind. By their orders, older Spanish or reliable neophyte women also held lock and key to the virgins' quarters, and these women, called *llavera*s, would usher the women in and out, watch over them as they bathed, raise eyebrows, and sometimes administer punishment. The *monjeríos*, which had high windows with bars, were a means of assimilation and indoctrination, dividing families and isolating impressionable girls, though they were allowed to visit their families during the day. Likely these bunk rooms were less than sanitary and contributed to the waves of disease that swept through the missions. They were also tacitly acknowledged as a means of keeping the Spanish soldiers from the Native women, at least those at the missions, further burdening these spaces: they were a colonial cell couched as a redoubt from the very same imperial force. There were stocks and shackles in the *monjeríos* to punish "transgressions" and "evil intercourse," as one padre wrote. These punishments were out of sight to all but the others meant to be intimidated, and these girls slept with the constant threat of being disciplined.

As Asisara tells the story, after Padre Quintana had been dispatched and the dormitories had been unlocked at Mission Santa Cruz, all the men and women immediately rendezvoused in the orchard and embraced each other, revealing the depths of the sexual repression imposed by the missionaries. Partway through the night, Quintana apparently began to revive—he had only passed out. They "crushed" his other testicle and he finally died. According to Asisara, one of the men who had been whipped by Quintana paced the room with these seminal trophies in hand, saying, "I shall bury these in the outdoor privy." It would seem no accident that they emasculated this man who had treated them as children and asexuals. It may also suggest that the padre had sexually abused some of them. Or it may be myth, a sensational and resonant addition to the story.

Arguably the assassination was neither an anti-colonial nor anti-Catholic act; it was the removal of a particularly sadistic padre who had destabilized the mission community. He had horsewhipped several neophytes to near death; he would have done it again. According to Asisara, Lino well articulated a rationale for why this execution was justified: Padre Quintana's violent punishments did not live up to his preaching or the word of God, and since he held power and was their leader, he was accountable. It was almost a year later that the conspirators were caught when someone overheard two women mentioning the deed. Four men were convicted of murder and sentenced to ten years' imprisonment and hard labor; three other accomplices were sentenced to six years; and a fourth to two years. All of these men were given a *novenano* of flogging—fifty lashes per day for nine days in a row. This punishment likely contributed to some of their deaths: four of them died in the San Francisco presidio before their sentences were confirmed by the powers in Mexico. Three others died in the Santa Barbara Presidio.

The military governor of Las Californias at the time defended the Franciscans, denying that they sometimes abused their neophytes. Missionaries and the military had little affection for one another, so likely this charitable report was due to the fact that the soldiers at Mission Santa Cruz had been negligent in letting Padre Quintana leave his compound at night unguarded. There's little doubt that the mission system persisted, at least in part, because of the padres' harsh practices. But these same abuses also helped doom the missions, because they were repressive and hypocritical, and thus ultimately counterproductive. Lorenzo Asisara finishes his narrative of Quintana's murder with this: "The Spanish Padres were very cruel toward the Indians. They abused them very much, they had bad food, bad clothing, and they made them work like slaves. I also was subjected to that cruel life. The Padres did not practice what they preached in the pulpit."

I WALKED WEST, ONCE MORE following Cliff Drive, this time to Natural Bridges State Beach where the pillars of its prominent stone arch were swallowed by the rising tide. It was an *arc de triomphe* weathered and fallen into the sea, with UC Santa Cruz students playing Frisbee on the beach. The Spanish had named their next campsite *Las Puentes*, too, The Bridges, since they were forced to lay logs across many ravines west of Santa Cruz and cover them with "fascines"—bundles of limbs—to let the mules cross. Past the Homeless Garden Project I went, where those people who had slept under the concrete bridges of the San Lorenzo could find work growing herbs and vegetables, new roots and a new life. As I left town, fields of brussels sprouts appeared on the plateau to the left of Highway 1, between me and the ocean, and I stopped to watch the sprouts pour into a tote from a trimming and cleaning facility, a mobile trailer, like coins from a green slot machine. Inside, the workers hunted for and discarded sprouts speckled with mold or the black holes of *gusanos*. In the fields, they cut only the ready sprouts from the top of each stalk and left the rest to grow larger, returning in waves to collect them.

Then I came to Wilder Ranch State Park, seven thousand acres with thirty-four miles of trails, which was once part of the mission's agricultural lands and later, by 1835, Rancho Refugio. Mr. Wilder established his dairy farm in 1871 and made a breakthrough when he decided to employ a Pelton water wheel, which moves by the push of water rather than the weight of it, to spin his separators and part the fatty, lighter cream from the heavier milk through centrifugal force. His was the first ranch on this stretch of coast to generate electricity—an "artificial sunrise," as one San Francisco newspaper called it, in the shadow of Ben Lomond Mountain and its evergreen canyons. "We departed from the handsome savin trees," wrote Crespí as they left Santa Cruz, "although in the mountains a great deal of country still runs on much overgrown with what I thought must have been the same sort of timber, but the scouts told me it was pine-nut-bearing pine groves." The canyons are thick with Douglas fir.

Just before Majors Creek, where the expedition likely spent the night and which Crespí named the Arroyo of Saint Luke, I studied my phone for a camping prospect. Finally, I crossed the highway, hopped a gate, and climbed an old road into the far west end of the Wilder Ranch State Park, this portion off-limits to the public. But in truth I had been trekking for so long that I had started to feel as if I were no longer a member of the public, but an outsider, a person slipped between the cracks or the pages, and the distinctions between public and private had become more fluid. I was a traveler passing through in his own world in order to study our one world. On a grassy knoll, I laid out and set up my tent: the sea before me, the stipples of pumpkin in one direction like a piece of the sunset cast up and atomized, and the brussels sprout plains.

Rain in the night. In the morning, my sneakers were quickly wet as they brushed through the new shoots and clover. The fruit of these first fall showers was germinating through the dry gray grass, replacing it. I ambled downhill to the patch I had seen, Rodoni Farms. It also had a corn maze off to one side with muddy trails of stalks flattened by a four-wheeler. I wandered into the labyrinth for a moment and imagined it was quite like what the Portolá expedition would have felt while traveling down the Oso Valley, or other wet drainages, on the bear trails. The horizon all but disappeared. The corn rustling in the ocean breeze. Raven and harrier flying over old silk.

Some of the pumpkins were ornate, streaked like candy cane and blistered, while others were bone white or a pale green. All were edible, the stand's employee, Eve, told me, but some were choice. "These orange-red ones," she said, pointing to an ordinary pie pumpkin, "the flesh is, like, so bright orange." She wore a trucker's hat, and only worked the patch on Saturdays, since the owner was a friend; primarily she made salsa and sold it at the farmers' market in Santa Cruz. "It doesn't look like something that you'd want to *get in there* and it would be all, like, supple and delightful. But pop it in the oven . . . it doesn't take that long, like thirty minutes. Cut and steam it, you know . . . *get in there*. People are like, what, you're going to eat this pumpkin? *Dude*, do you know how long this pumpkin has been thought about? Like, it's been seeded, planted . . . it's been chilling for months to get that big. Then all the hands that touched it, to picking it, to trucking it, to carting it . . . it's, like, dude—it's a *vegetable*."

JUST DOWN THE ROAD, I arrived at Majors Creek, really quite minor though it decants from a striking cleft in the Coast Range; and here I swerved toward the ocean briefly on a little horseshoe lane, Scaroni Road. It swung downhill past another modest pumpkin patch, went on a wooden bridge over the clear, willowed stream not wider than an arm span, and then trudged back up to the highway past a farmhouse, white with a robin's-egg trim around its windows. As I passed, a teenage girl exited a car in the driveway. She was startled to see me, and I said, "Hello," to try to reassure her as she walked toward the house. A dog bounded past her, barking, and rushed to the road to stare after me and bark some more. A minute later, when I looked over my shoulder, a white truck was backing out slowly. I assumed right away that its driver was following me. I saluted the man with a flat wave as he rolled past. But he slowed and paused at the highway, ostensibly to check the mailbox and thumb through envelopes and catalogs. "How you doing, sir?" I said.

"Good, how are you?" he said enthusiastically. He had dark hair, a curved nose, and vibrant green eyes. He wore a black T-shirt and jeans.

"Pretty good," I said. "What a beautiful house you have."

"Yeah, this is all private property around here."

"Oh, I know," I said, though I was pretty sure the road was public. "I was just passing through . . ." I told him about my long walk. "Have you ever heard of the Portolá expedition?" I asked.

"Nope."

"Apparently they camped right here. This is Majors Creek, right?"

It was, Roland acknowledged. There was an emergency "call box" at the intersection with Highway 1, a yellow phone and its solar panel. Humble fields of strawberries and other crops grew along the highway and beef cattle roamed the hillside beyond. Directly across the road was the yawning mouth of Majors Creek canyon where it opened onto the coastal bluff. Low boulderish cliffs were exposed above the chaparral. Mist hung in the fir and redwood spires about a quarter mile in. Two telephone wires strung across the canyon's opening and a steel gate on one side were the only indication that this drainage had entered the twentieth century.

A Farmers Insurance envelope sat atop the mail stack in Roland's lap. His fingers had the slightly swollen and mashed appearance of someone who'd worked hard with his hands for a long time, and his left index finger had a crooked tip, I noticed, as he gestured to emphasize, eventually, one of his many points. As I disclosed more about my expedition, he grew increasingly at ease. Soon he told me about how he'd met a man right here who had been walking for more than five thousand miles. Roland thought he was about to trespass, but, learning the guy was a vet on a journey, he offered him a place to camp. "What about you?" he said. I wasn't sure if he was offering, but I think he was.

"Oh, I'm just passing through . . ."

"Yeah, we saw you yesterday. I looked at you . . . because we have a problem with transients . . . but I looked at you, and I go, 'He's not a transient, man, he's just looking for a place to sleep.'" I had been staring at my phone on the roadside, scanning a map for possibilities, relying on any number of satellites.

Roland owned a 175-acre ranch passed down from his father, and from his grandfather before that. The property stretched about a mile down the western flank of Majors Creek to a private cove, one the public can only reach by sea. For over thirty years, his father operated a nudist colony here at the Red White & Blue Beach, which earned its name from the colors on their Route 1 mailbox—the only indication of the colony's existence. In the 1970s, entry was two dollars a day for a family, two dollars for a single man, and one dollar for a couple. Single women and children under twelve were free. The colony closed in 2006 when Roland's father died.

Roland leaned out the window with his truck idling and bemoaned his trouble with drifters, something Santa Cruz County invites more generally because of its liberal temperament and temperate weather. He had stories. An older man had camped on Majors Creek on his property for two years, and Roland had felt sorry for him so let him be. "I could hear him coughing in the winter, because he was cold. Floyd was his name. He rode the bus with my kids." But when Roland discovered the two tons of trash that Floyd had dumped, he confronted Floyd and asked him to move on. Floyd blew up at him. "I've got a gun in my backpack," he threatened. Roland flipped him upside down and dumped out his pack. There was no gun, but he wasn't about to take any chances. Another man had threatened Roland with a Glock and a SWAT team had to remove him from the creek. Tweakers had stolen a truck in the East Bay, cut through his gate, and abandoned it by the creek after stripping it for parts. "The sheriff's department calls it the Wild Wild West out here," said Roland. Often he caught folks going over his fences. His insurance company—Farmers Insurance, I'd wager—had threatened to raise his rates because of the liability, so he had become more vigilant. The canyon mouth was only four or five hundred feet wide, but that was fairly impressive by the coast's standards, and too bad, said Roland, because it attracted more attention.

What's more, until recently cars and RVs had been lining up on Highway 1 like I had seen on Lapis Road in Marina near Monterey. "Fifteen-hundred-dollar rat-infested piles of crap," Roland called them. They came from all over the state in search of leniency. But overnight camping in Big Sur had become illegal, Marin had followed suit, and finally Santa Cruz County had passed an ordinance, each county passing the buck in turn. The new ordinance had helped, but the problem hadn't gone away. "I've surfed along this coast for fifty-two years," said Roland, "and I can see what's going on, and it puts a tear in my eye."

"You mean people are living harder?" I asked.

"Yeah that, and the way they treat the land. They're Okies, they're slobs. They have no respect for the environment, or anything. You don't know how many tons of trash I've taken out of my property."

Roland had no love for the State Parks, either. As far as he was concerned, California had purposely raised taxes on coastal ranchers—the taxes on the ocean side of the highway were three times those directly across it, he said—forcing owners to sell, usually to the state, which then mismanaged the land and let the public run roughshod over it. "People don't see it like I saw it, as a kid . . . how well preserved it was. I used to catch eight-pound steelhead with a stick, three-pound test line, and a worm, with Mr. Wilder, for dinner, behind the barn. There's nothing in there anymore. It's all dead." He blamed the silt runoff from overrun and unauthorized trails, but of course any number of degradations have plagued steelhead. "State Parks have ruined this coast," Roland argued, "all the way to San Francisco. They've ruined them! The beaches, when I was kid growing up, they were so cool. Now you go there, there's not a stitch of driftwood, there's not a rock, there's not a shell, there's no abalone. There's nothing, because the public has carted it all home."

"I'm so lucky to grow up here when that highway was a little teeny two-lane road, and the sagebrush would grow in the road so you'd have to go in the other lane. Look at this road . . ." It is two lanes still, but paved, now, and a veritable raceway for tourists and San Francisco day-trippers. "When I was a kid you could stand right out there with your thumb out for two days, and the only ride you'd get was because a rancher came by and recognized you. I walked all the way back from Santa Cruz High when I missed the bus, because there was no traffic. The population of Santa Cruz was forty-eight hundred. I see what's going on now and it's just like, 'Holy shit, are you kidding me?' In three years, I'll probably be gone. 'Cause

I can't take it anymore. I'm selling the ranch, and I'm going to move up to Bonny Doon. I've had it up to here with . . . all the BS."

In recent years Roland had started renting his private beach for weddings and hosting pricey dinners on the sand. "The people that come in here . . . they're a different class of people," Roland said. Individuals had paid two thousand dollars a day to have the beach to themselves. "This is my first new truck in thirty years," said Roland, patting his dash. "I've been land rich and money poor my whole life." But now he was hoping for something different. He was hoping to entice a buyer who would drop an enormous sum for the property, yet treat it sparingly and sustainably. "It can be developed in a manner where the public can use it. But not in the sense of a State Park."

Post Ranch, an iconic and sustainable Big Sur getaway with rooms that are thousands of dollars a night, was his model, so his definition of the public was, it seems, a narrow one. He mistrusted the local land trust, believing it would simply hand the ranch to the State Parks. "Eighty percent of the California coast is public," Roland said. "The little twenty percent that's left . . . There's a guy that lives in a ranch in Southern California. He's a Patagonia guy. Well, now they want to open it up, the lower part of Bixby, to the freaking public. And this guy's into preservation. And the ranch is preserved, because they don't open it up to the public. Why can't that little twenty percent be left alone?" I didn't tell him that I'd trespassed through Hollister Ranch, where Patagonia guy Yvon Chouinard and other celebrities have their homes and, not surprisingly, make the same argument: that private ownership is better conservation. There's some truth to it, but only some. Fundamentally the argument seems self-serving. With proper funding, there's no reason that a public beach couldn't be impeccably cared for.

A year after I shook hands with Roland at his mailbox, RWB Ranch had been rebranded as Coastside Ranch and placed on the market by Sotheby's for $35 million: "a billionaire's paradise," as the brokers described it, a Silicon Valley retreat of the highest order. The land trust offered $18 million. Roland and his siblings declined. The asking price has since fallen to an easy twenty-eight.

ALONG THE TRACKS INTO DAVENPORT, escaped calla lilies swayed on the hillsides and chestnut-backed chickadees hung in the willows, where the hollows of the homeless were also beside the rails, much as Roland had claimed: a radio playing, a blue tent, sleeping bags, piles of cans and plastic bottles, a bike to pedal the ties into town. There was a tent on Davenport Beach, and another behind a bush on the bluff, this one Hello Kitty, pink with white polka dots. Its faded fly whipped in the zephyr, and a doormat was out front in the dirt for cleanliness. This coast was a harbor to the dispossessed, but the Pacific currents soon would tear these shelters to shreds, I thought. Winter was nigh. A storm was forecast to let loose a half inch of rain that very night, and all day I was looking ahead to my unknown campsite, where I would cinch my guidelines and cocoon.

The expedition marched up and down "profound hollows," but I only noticed these drainages from above as I walked smoothly across them on Highway 1. Beyond Davenport, at Scott Creek, the Spaniards came upon an abundance of live oaks and "a village of a few grass houses here in this hollow, abandoned, with well beaten paths all about the spot." Maybe these Ohlone had heard the Spanish were coming and made themselves scarce. More likely the season had brought them inland to harvest. In a beach viewing area along the highway, the sand had nearly swallowed three benches like a vision of an archaeological future, of rising seas disregarding our infrastructure. Just the dedication was visible on one bench: IN LOVING MEMORY OF ROBERT "MOOSE" MITCHELL. HE LOGGED LOCALLY OVER FORTY YEARS WITH PRIDE AND CARE WHILE PRESERVING HIS BELOVED REDWOODS. 1932-1995. The concrete span over Scott Creek framed, as if with graffiti curtains, a lagoon of yellowing tule and, beyond it, a patchwork of conifer and buffy hillsides that climbed lumpish into the Coast Range. Fall had arrived wholeheartedly.

Costansó wrote of having to use "the force of the pick" to open a route north from Scott Creek, and Crespí wrote that "people had been preparing the road for about two hours in order to get up the mountains here, there being no way through by the shore as it was very cliffy upon the sea." As I went up the steep but perfectly gradual road cut through that cliffy mass, I thought about how we had used the force of the pick, of the shoveler and dynamite, to blast a route along the once impassable shore. Now you can travel at fifty or sixty-five miles per hour along this "backbone of a chain of broken hills," as Costansó described it, or three miles per hour if you're walking like me. Cars flew down the long descent, bush lupine flouncing in the wind off the shoulder with gray seed pods. The sun showed itself in advance of the rain front visible miles out to sea, and suddenly the light was hot on my face, both direct and off the ocean. My shadow reached across both lanes of the highway. The cars drove through it. "We went up over quite a high pass in these mountains," wrote Crespí, "and then on over very big and high yet quite rolling ranges of knolls and tablelands out from the same mountains—themselves quite high and white colored from a fine white gravel." This portion of the Coast Range is pale with Santa Cruz mudstone, lifted ocean floor, which explains names like Chalk Mountain; but that Crespí thought it so prominent may be a sign of the extent to which the grasslands were burnt by the Ohlone.

BEFORE LONG I COULD SEE Año Nuevo up ahead, which the expedition correctly identified based on Vizcaíno's description. The road, cut as it was across and often through the hillside, was a long train of windows to the Pacific, none with the same view, not quite. As I passed one roadside pullout, I lingered to photograph the polished distance, and a man standing by his white truck said, "You should go over there and look over the edge, and you'll get some vertigo." So I did, and he was not wrong. No person in their right mind would look, for long, over this crumbling ladder. A crow soared by and tucked its coal wings, dipping along the cliffs. The waves seemed to lap at my worn sneakers, lace on laces, hundreds of feet below. It was easy to forget how tall these cliffs were, how impassable this stretch before modern roads and cars.

"You're not hitching?" the man said as I returned to the highway. "No, only walking," I replied. Standing beside his truck, he wore a royal-blue ball cap, a sage-green shirt tucked into his beltless jeans, and leather sandals. There was a gap between his upper front teeth. His beard was full but trimmed, graying on either side of his chin. Crow's-feet stretched out from his eyes like the lines of erosion down the bluffs. "If you need a place to stay, if you get out where they can't see ya, you can stay there," he said. Those were the truest, wisest words I'd heard on my whole journey. If you can get where they can't see ya, you can stay there. You can stay there.

I asked if he was out to enjoy the sunset. "No, I live out here," he said. "In my car." For three years, Jim told me, he'd been sleeping in his truck and spending his days at the lot of Grayhound Rock County Park a mile up the road, where he listened to the radio and made sure nobody's car got broken into. "There's a bathroom and a garbage can, and that's the main thing," he said. "I'm sixty-seven, I'm on social security, I get a thousand bucks a month. I'm not going to get a house."

He was, and he wasn't, the kind of itinerant that Roland, just a couple of hours back, had had enough of. Jim felt this was his only option, so he seemed careful and responsible, realizing that loafing on the roadside was, in the eyes of the state, a privilege he couldn't take for granted. He kept a tight ship. Didn't cause problems.

"The cops don't run you off?" I asked.

"They get their little thing going," he replied. "It'll last for a night, and after that, they're gone." Whenever he was confronted by the police, he offered this argument: "You want me to be the guy scaring people under the bridge in Santa Cruz? Because if you fuck with my car, if you take it, that's what I'm gonna be."

Mainly the cops were trying to do away with the rundown RVs that people shuttle to and from each day. Said Jim, "They've found people out here who put their toilet discard hose over the edge into the ocean, and it's like, 'You freaking assholes.'" Also true words. And when those RVs finally shove out, they leave piles of garbage. "The raccoons come out at night, rip them bags open, and the wind out here blows it everywhere and makes a big mess." I told him about the dead raccoons I'd just seen. Two of them, side by side, down by the Cemex plant (yet another one) in Davenport. "I saw that big one when I went," he said, nodding. "I was down there for ice this morning. Fucking buggers. They were my buddies. Raccoons and skunks! I've been cooking on my tailgate and think, 'What's that on my foot?' And there's a big old freaking skunk. And it's like, 'Okay.' I grab some of the meat out, bend down and give it to him, and he walks away with it. Skunks are my buddies."

It had taken Jim six months to realize what he truly needed in his truck. The rest he gave away or tossed. He cooked on his tailgate on a portable stove much like mine. Eggs and bacon for breakfast. Dinner tonight would be macaroni salad with tuna fish. The farthest he'd ranged was Lucia in Big Sur, to the Nacimiento-Fergusson Road. Did I know it?

"I sure do," I said.

"I stayed there for six months during the winter," Jim recalled. He was parked on a turnout in the National Forest, one I had probably walked right by. I could only imagine how rainy, dripping, mossy, moody, funereal his time there must have been, waves of moisture billowing off the ocean through the living and burnt madrone and redwood, the hills full of chants and spirits. "The ranger came out and said, 'You only got fourteen days to be here.' And I said, 'Why is that?' The ranger said, 'Because other people want to stay here.' I said, 'How many other people are in here?' He goes, 'No one. Stay as long as you want.'"

Jim grew up in Menlo Park and had lived in Palo Alto and Redwood City. He couldn't afford it now. Most of his life he'd labored as a carpenter, plumber, and electrician, an honest-to-goodness handyman, but the contractor who had employed him had folded in the wake of the 2008 crash. Afterward, he worked under the table for a number of years. "That's why I only get a thousand bucks a month on social security. Because I worked under the table too much."

Three years seemed a long time. Jim replied that he was going to be here, in his truck, until he died. He couldn't get another job; he could barely stand for twenty minutes at a time, his knees were so shot. I imagined him aging until he could no longer climb into his cab, and what then? Would someone eventually find him in the back of his own truck, tucked in, with the Pacific soft in his bristled ears? "If you go to Greyhound Rock," Jim told me, "there's like five people who have been living there for eight years. Yeah, there's no other place to go. Every place else is either too cold or too hot, you know? That's what it is."

The truck bed was six feet long. Jim was six foot one, so he had to sleep diagonally. He had parked at the ideal angle, so that his head wouldn't press against his tailgate and his feet would be ever so slightly downhill. This pullout wasn't his usual, but someone else had grabbed that one tonight. He preferred the other spot because he could park behind a berm. "In other places, people start sliding off the fucking road, right next to you, and you go, 'Holy fucking shit!'" I'd thought about that, I replied: camping too close to a roadside, at any moment a car could barrel off for no reason, or a good reason, and run you over in your sleeping bag. I asked if he heard the traffic at night, if it bothered him. He was used to it, he said, and plus, "It's supposed to rain tonight, and that'll put me to sleep real quick."

"I get to see every sunset of the year," Jim reflected, looking toward the ocean. "If it rains, I go to Davenport and get something to eat. It's supposed to be pouring tomorrow, and I got to go to town"—to Santa Cruz—"so that means Target. If I open the top of the hatch and it's raining, all that water pours right into the car. I can't do Safeway if it's raining."

"Well, soak it up," I said, before I left. "I hope it's a good sunset."

He popped the tab of a Budweiser in a red Las Vegas Koozie and said, "Yeah, I know. I love it."

THAT NIGHT I MADE CAMP south of Waddell Creek on the needle under some Monterey pines, thinking this ground would drain nicely if the torrential rain I'd been hearing about was realized. Last year's rattlesnake grass quaked in the breeze and fiddleheads were nosing up. Around my tent were shell fragments, the scatterings of an Ohlone midden. This intimate slope would have been a fine site for a village, I thought, sheltered as it was by a small steep ridge to seaward, but with a view of the tule estuary and the steep north ridge across Waddell Creek. Crespí noted this "large inlet" between "very cliffy mountains."

It rained lightly during the night and then unleashed for several hours in the morning. I lay half-conscious in the dim orange light of the tent and thought about the syncopations this sustained cloudburst would make on Jim's pickup. The Portolá expedition stayed here two extra nights on account of heavy rain, and it was eerie to experience a deluge of rain just as they had, as if it was the presence of the Spaniards drumming my tent. "We came to the stream here with some of our sick men very ill of Luanda sickness, especially three or four of them who had already been anointed," wrote Crespí. They had been prepared to die. "Yet, after a good soaking that they got from heavy showers, when we were expecting that two or three of them would waken only into eternity, instead, these ones and the others all woke up in the morning much improved." As a result, Crespí named it *el arroyo de San Luis Beltrán y de la Salud*, the canyon "of health." In the very next sentence of his journal, he mentions "at this stream the soldiers found madrones laden with ripe fruit, though very small ones, like the beads on our rosaries." Crespí doesn't make the connection, but it's these fruits, fiery in their hue but mild tasting—with the gentle flavor of melon, slightly granular in the mouth, chalky—that likely explain their recovery. Berries are rich in vitamin C. Madrone was their miracle.

My rains did not last as long as theirs. Midmorning, portals of blue appeared in the mist across the dell. "The men were wet and wearied from want of sleep, as they had no tents, and it was necessary to let them rest today," Costansó wrote. Only the officers, padres, and other specialists like Costansó slept under canvas. "We delayed here today as well, in order to dry out whatever had been soaked," Crespí reported. I also packed up loosely and, after a short walk, hung up my sopping tent on the picnic tables that overlooked the thicketed creek near the terminus of the Skyline-to-the-Sea Trail that slaloms down from Big Basin, California's first State Park. Canada de la Salud, as it's still known, had been dubbed Rancho del Oso by Theodore Hoover, brother to the president and head of the Stanford University School of Engineering, when he bought much of the valley in 1912. Grizzlies persisted late into the nineteenth century here, and the creek's namesake, William Waddell, who logged these redwood drainages, lost his arm to one of those bears in 1875. He died a few days later.

The park's nature center was closed, but as I looked through its dark glass, into the former home of one of Hoover's daughters—what a good end for a home and a life, to become a nature center—I saw the humped form of a taxidermied brown bear. Below the center I followed a trail through blackberry, poison oak, and swampy willow across narrow plank bridges to Waddell Creek, which was about twenty-five feet wide and the opacity of black tea. Until 1995 there were native coho in the creek, a final stronghold, modest as it was, for salmon in the San Francisco region. It still had the hush of bear country and felt like it.

This was also the wet heart of logging country and still is, though most people in the Bay Area probably don't know it. Waddell hauled redwoods out of the drainage to a wharf he built on the beach, and then he built another in the crook of Año Nuevo, a mile north, after the ocean battered his first one to smithereens. The redwoods he cut helped fill out post-gold-rush San Francisco before they were incinerated in the inferno that followed the 1906 earthquake. Now, just to the south of Waddell Creek is the Big Creek Lumber lot and sawmill; I had seen imposing stacks of boards from the road as I walked by. After World War II, Big Creek was started with seventy-five hundred dollars and modified surplus military equipment that still can be found rusted and abandoned in these hills on Air Force tires. Big Creek purchased rights to some of upper Rancho del Oso from Hoover and, within a decade, its mill—dubbed "the Termite"—was chewing around the edges of thirty-five thousand board feet a day. Today Big Creek churns out one hundred thousand board feet a day and owns five retail yards in Northern and Central California.

As I left Waddell Beach, I saw two backpackers—a couple who had just completed the drippy trek over the Santa Cruz Mountains on the Skyline-to-the-Sea Trail—rubbing each other's legs at the bus stop. I envied them, just for a moment. What a different experience it would have been to have made this journey with a partner. But my pace and direction were mine alone, or mine and the Spaniards'. The highway ran under steep cliffs with a rockfall guard below them: a reinforced chain-link fence bowed toward the road, evidence that it was needed. Up ahead was a sign I had been anticipating for months, though I had never really thought about it: SAN MATEO COUNTY. One more week to walk.

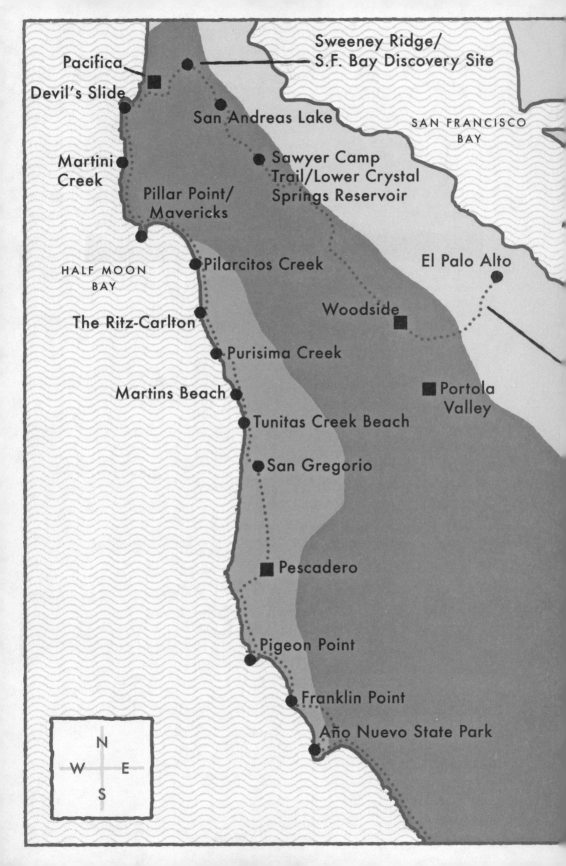

San Mateo County

† Mission Santa Clara

San Francisquito Creek

SANTA CRUZ MOUNTAINS

THE FINAL MILES TO AÑO NUEVO were marked by the bass of a foghorn. I didn't arrive until almost four o'clock. Where the cliffs tapered, a forgotten lane took me over Año Nuevo Creek and I found myself at the State Park's old dairy farm head-quarters. The beams in the barn had been salvaged from the seven-hundred-foot wharf that William Waddell built in the shelter of the point; he had used wooden rails, in the era before steel, to pull his redwood timber to it via horsepower below the bluffs I had just skirted underneath on Highway 1. Waddell's wharf was the small center of activity at Año Nuevo until it was destroyed in 1880. Three years later, a family named the Steeles moved their creamery off the bluffs to its current location. One of the earliest dairy families in California, they had first leased, then bought Rancho Año Nuevo, where they ran over a thousand head of cattle and cultured a renowned cheese. This included, in 1864, a thirty-eight-hundred-pound round as a fundraiser for the Union Army. It was displayed in the center of a dome pavilion at the Industrial Fair of the Mechanics Institute of San Francisco. Samuel Clemens, who would become Mark Twain, reported on this Año Nuevo novelty: "It is the contribution of two whole hearted brothers, and it is worth twenty-five cents to look upon such a monument of kindly Christian charity." It was determined that the cheese was too delicate to tour the country, so instead San Franciscans took home and savored slices at fifty cents a pound. But a bite did eventually reach President Lincoln.

Some of the walking trails to the point were under construction and closed, but I made my way nonetheless. Poison oak swept up taller than me. The dovish foghorn sounded on the island off the point, which held a deserted lighthouse building. I came upon a trail crew spreading decomposed granite, "DG," on the new path they had built on a raised bed of rock that would allow the yearly flooding to pass underneath: now we painstakingly engineer trails that pretend to be natural, as if the Ohlone had worn them. The foreman had seen me on the road the night before, and after hearing my story, he radioed ahead to let the crew know that I had permission to pass through.

Soon I had an exclusive view of Año Nuevo's terminus, only animal prints in the rain-bespattered sand, coyote and cottontail and mouse. The beach was sulfurous with decaying kelp, sea grass, and a few seal carcasses. Ravens were working some body on the wrack line. The glare on the choppy expanse between me and the nine-acre island was near blinding, the wind stiff. In Portolá's day, the island was actually a peninsula, but the flow of sand to counter erosion is no longer as strong as it was. Today cormorants roost in the forsaken buildings of the light station, its roof green with algae, its five silhouetted chimneys somewhat sinister in profile. Sea lions have moved in, too, and, even before the station closed in 1948, the turgid herds had invaded its grounds and blocked its doorsteps. Fences kept them out of the garden. Now they trample the auklet burrows. The modern foghorn and the bugle of elephant seals were together mournful, sparse, Pacific; inland the Steeles' dairy barn was guano-white against the stern conifer beyond the cliffs.

For ten minutes, I stood alone. Then, walking north around a corner, I found a huddle of female seals and an interpreter, Ryan, who all day had been posted like a soldier at this viewing platform, even during the morning's downpour when I was warm in my tent. About three times a month, he drove over from San Jose to talk pinnipeds. He'd become keen on these elephant seals after, as he described, he "fell in love with the idea of a reserve." Año Nuevo had been "left alone" for the last fifty years, Ryan pointed out, and it can still be imagined to be the way Portolá saw it, and earlier Vizcaíno, when he sailed around the point on January 3, 1603, and gave name to it.

Portolá and Crespí didn't mention any elephant seals, however; the idea that this landscape still looks much as it did is in large part myth, and not just because of the grazing and logging, and the end of the Native burns. Along with Piedras Blancas near San Simeon, Año Nuevo is one of the most famous and most trafficked elephant seal colonies in the world, yet it wasn't until 1965 that males began hauling out to defend these territories. The first pup didn't arrive in an amniotic rush until 1975. As Ryan told me, elephant seals didn't breed at all on the continent until grizzly bears were exterminated and we stopped hunting the seals for their blubber. Vizcaíno had seen bears swarming whale carcasses on the beaches of California. The northern elephant seal only survived us because a colony persisted on Mexico's Guadalupe Island to repopulate the Pacific.

Male elephant seals can grow to be more than five thousand pounds, outmuscling that famous Steele cheese wheel. Their eponymous proboscis not only steers sexual selection, but also contains moisture-retaining folds that are critical as the seals hold the beach for months without eating. With each breath, they conserve water. Apart from these breeding months and an additional month-long midsummer haul out for molting, the males undertake a vast circuit north to the Aleutians. They dive up to five thousand feet for more than one hundred minutes in search of prey like bioluminescent fish and squid. Ninety percent of their time at sea is spent underwater; their heart rate slows by half as they dive, conserving energy. They go under without air in their lungs, which collapse under the water pressure anyway, relying instead on an enormous volume of blood.

The corpulent bulls hadn't arrived at Año Nuevo yet. The first arrivals were about a month out, just leaving Alaska. "The first scouts will be here right about Thanksgiving," said Ryan. "I call them the bar strategies: You can arrive as soon as the doors open. You can arrive at happy hour. Or you can wait in the parking lot because she has to leave eventually." The "battle class" males would arrive in January to stake their beach claims and secure a harem, and by the last week of January, over four thousand seals would reside at Año Nuevo, and the sharks would loiter offshore, turning circles around the island. The largest bulls are rippling monuments of muscle and fat as they worm forward to assess each other. Sometimes they rear chest to chest, lifting their proboscises to the fog with their mouths agape. It looks as if they're smiling. If neither male stands down, if they are evenly matched, their patience occasionally breaks, testosterone overflows. Then they whip their punching-glove noses onto their opponent's neck with jaws wide, slashing with large upper canines. The throat of a bull elephant seal is tough and scarred. A fight can last from a minute to a half hour. But for now, the beach was quiet, nightfall in the waves, the scouts plying the cold waters south, the sky flush with color.

I CAMPED ON WHITEHOUSE CREEK, where the Portolá expedition likely settled for the night beyond Point Año Nuevo. Either there or Gazos Creek. A momentary squall swept in over the ocean not long after I slipped into my tent having just brushed my teeth, the sound of it at first like the sandman gently sifting the fine contents of his pockets on my tent, but then becoming a bucket of marbles. There is nothing more comforting than lying in a tent, in a sleeping bag, when it rains: nowhere to escape to, and no need to escape. When I stepped out to pee hours later, the headlights along Highway 1 swept through the mist rising after the rain, their beams extending far down the road: each invisible droplet illuminated, refracting, rays beaming through cypress.

Picking a campsite, usually I would try for a spot between the highway and the waves, so that neither was too loud. The traffic on Highway 1 tended to drown out the surf until nine or ten at night, depending on the wind and tide, and then the ocean would clarify in the ear. Around six in the morning the traffic would accelerate again. I had fallen into a routine of shutting my eyes about nine, but often I would wake up in the middle of the night and think about the day before lapsing back to sleep, so I rarely left my dome early in the morning. "It's eight o'clock now," I mumbled into my recorder. "I feel really groggy. I've been dreaming really wildly. Like, fragments of dreams about people I know ... I dream more in this tent than I ever remember dreaming. I think it's all just light dependent ... The wrentit is trilling ..."

"The village here," wrote Crespí, "had a very large round house like a half orange, grass-roofed, which, by what we saw inside it, would hold the entire village." *La Casa Grande*, the soldiers called the *ranchería*, before William Randolph Hearst stole the name and gave a less communal meaning to it. "Around the large house they had many small houses made of upright split sticks." I wonder: What would it be like to be in one of these grass houses during a rain? Would the sound be different? These villagers presented the expedition with acorn pies, and a delegation from another nearby village offered four feathered, red-painted staffs to Sergeant Ortega, the chief scout, whom they had met once already. These Ohlone wore "wreaths made of green branches" and spoke of two harbors at a distance of three days' march, sunrise to sunset. In his field journal, Crespí prayed that it be Monterey at last: "Divine Providence grant it is so, and that we reach there as soon as can be!"

In the morning I jumped across Whitehouse Creek on two stones and followed the shoreline toward Franklin Point, also called *Punto Año Nuevo Falso*. Sitting on a rock fire ring, I ate a two-day-old muffin from Davenport as the turnstones stayed ahead of the surf and the gulls snapped kelp flies off the gelatinous wrack. White water funneled through the chutes between islanded outcrops and the ten-foot bluffs, each surge washing over then receding; and over those same rocks, waves shot up as if punched in the gut and cascaded like a fountain of milk or, as the trickle slowed, like cream down chocolate. Above the bluffs stood low dune hummocks of wind-shorn coyote brush, willow, and sage, and here and there sandstone boulders were worn with natural hieroglyphs. From an unannounced observation deck on Franklin Point I looked across the churning bay to Pigeon Point and its lighthouse hostel. Pigeon Point is so named because, before the fog station on Año Nuevo Island, a ship called the *Carrier Pigeon* wrecked off the point and lost all that it carried. Now, each incoming foamed breaker was like a serrated ring on a scallop shell, rings radiating from an umbo, some hinge far out on the Pacific. "I feel worn down like those blocks," I said into my recorder, "those rocks, that are taking wave after wave. At this point in my journey . . . this point, so beautiful . . . it's just like another wave hitting me."

BY LATE AFTERNOON I ARRIVED in Pescadero, having followed Bean Hollow Road over *El Arroyo de Los Frijoles* and its natural lake, which Crespí mentions. Which now is dammed. It was a gradual climb and a steep descent on hairpins to the Pescadero Marsh. From the crest, looking inland toward San Jose, the view was a quintessential Coast Range mélange. What's the right word for buttons of chaparral, for wind-nibbled spherical canopies of coyote brush, some of them white with tasseled flower, some of them not? I wondered then, fancifully, if the "white range" Crespí observed this whole stretch had not been this shrub in bloom, California's October snow. There were runaway eucalyptus windbreaks and far ridges of Doug fir and redwood. My shadow was thrown sixty feet across the barbwire and the hillside softening with each rain. Looking out, I thought about how all of this might be the territory of just one mountain lion, also a shadow. California is a tawny shadow.

In the valley, I pitched my tent along Butano Creek where the road crosses it, just past the fire station and about fifty feet into a buffer of woods. I had to tamp down the fragile plants for lack of a better option and whispered my apologies as the aroma of crushed herb lifted into the damp air. If it rains, I thought, I might well be flooded in the night, and what a disaster that would be. Mosquitoes in the alder shadows, and I was so preoccupied with scanning for poison oak, though it prefers full sun, I didn't see the nettle until my bare legs began to kindle and burn.

My dome in place, I walked the half mile or so to the coast. Not to admire the breakers, though I did watch them for a moment, and the god rays splitting the clouds, but to wander the marsh on the east side of Highway 1. I had visited the Pescadero Marsh on a field trip as a kid and it had always stuck with me, becoming my archetypal wetland. Only a few hundred acres, it's the largest coastal marsh remaining on the San Francisco Peninsula. Down the Butano Creek Trail, a kayak and a metal canoe were chained to an aluminum pedestrian bridge. I dropped my pack—why I didn't just leave it in my tent, I'm not sure—and crossed to a levee path that wound through sky and water and reflection. Harriers low, spotted towhee. The ducks panicking, lifting in a dash, when I suddenly popped into view. It began to drizzle. There's nothing like being in an overcast marsh on Halloween, a dreariness full of life. Common yellowthroat in the bramble. Northern shovelers. Ducks I didn't quite recognize. Ducks whistle-whirring in vital caution. As I retreated, the sun wedged through and a rainbow fragment appeared, a trick if I ever saw one. I made a recording of the marsh wrens in a levee hedge. Can you hear their chatter?

Then I plodded a half hour into town past the kids in their sheets and rubber masks, holding their flashlights and their jack-o'-lantern baskets. Pescadero is a town with one blinking red light, and I took a left to Duarte's Tavern, where locals had come out of the hills for a few pints in a dark paneled hall dating back half as far as the Portolá expedition. Like a redwood, the saloon had survived a fire that destroyed much of the town in 1920. I picked off a tick as I sat on my stool, smooshed it, and let it fall to the floor. I'm not ashamed to bring a tick into a bar. I ate a bowl of artichoke soup and a fried calamari sandwich, one big translucent cut as good as anything I'd ever tasted. And I threw it all up on the roadside on the way out, either one beer too many after three months of walking or a reaction to the seafood, which I rarely indulge in. A man I met at the bar, a Silicon Valley type who now lived in an old farmhouse near the beach—I thought of Roland's property, soon for sale, back near Santa Cruz—gave me a ride in his sports car the mile to my dank creek, where I waded blindly through the nettle and couldn't sleep, for a time, on account of the stinging that brightened like a dawn.

IT HAD THE FEEL OF the morning after a storm as I walked back through Pescadero on the first day of November. People hauling down the decorations: the cotton spiderwebs, the cutout skeletons and witches. The pastures were flooded, killdeer churring along the pondage, but I had managed to stay dry overnight on my nettle bank. In fact, the expedition didn't stop in the Pescadero Valley, but passing through they saw two empty villages. The Ohlone escorting them these miles signed that these people were higher in the hills, where they mostly lived. So I was out of step with the Spaniards in time and space, but at this point, it felt right for our journeys to be layered. This was a different time, and I was just one person.

I followed Stage Road north from town, past some piglets I will never forget, and over a pass to San Gregorio, a valley much the same as Pescadero, only narrower. Crespí named it *Santo Domingo*. "Very lush brambles are plentiful throughout these spots, greatly hindering travel," wrote Crespí. Stage Road left me at a general store, one of the few buildings at this crossing. I knew this road, since it was the most direct route to the coast from my home, but not the fastest, because it was windy as hell. As the crow flies, I was no more than twenty miles from the expedition's finish, but they didn't cross the range just yet. They spent two extra days in San Gregorio because the mules were exhausted, increasingly frail, and Captain Rivera and others were sick. "Somewhat indisposed," Crespí wrote. "Diarrhea," Costansó clarified. Members of a nearby village brought black mush pies, chia seed, which the soldiers recommended. They had run out of peas, Crespí noted dryly. These Ohlone men wore a pale upper-body wrap or tippet that covered both neck and waist, but let everything else hang free. Finally he comes right out and says it: "Indeed, all the men everywhere go totally naked with however much nature gave them in plain view."

My sister and brother, Lucy and Simon, made the drive over from the bay and met me at San Gregorio State Beach in the early afternoon with sandwiches from our childhood grocery store, Robert's. An Italian sub on Dutch Crunch is my comfort food. Their arrival felt like the beginning of the end, a final tour, the last mile of a marathon when a friend or family member jumps over the barricades to jog with you in solidarity. They were fit and hiked fast, and as we went up the first rise on Highway 1, I was more nervous than I had been the whole journey as the cars roared fast downhill past them, around semi-blind turns. It gave me perspective on the risk I had assumed just by walking the roadsides. They laughed as I spoke crazily of irrelevant details into my recorder: of the silver hubcap levitating like a UFO in an orbit of leafless poison oak, the holes of its rim like windows to a woody universe. Of the psalm on the back of a "smart" phone case: *God is within her. She will not fail.* Of the ocean fuzzy on the horizon with an indecisive fog, as fuzzy as every description is at heart.

We descended to Tunitas Creek, crossed, and ignored a few concrete barriers set below a line of pines to reach the tableland above the creek's striking sandstone cliffs. To the north suddenly we could see Half Moon Bay and the bulbous white radome of the Pillar Point Air Force Station. To the south, the surf along Tunitas Creek Beach was broken and beautiful, a plastron necklace laid out for wearing. Whose spectacular land, about to collapse into the sea, was this, we wondered. When we came to the cliffs, Simon said, "If you lived out here, you might limit how much you came to this edge." Or as Jim, the man who lived in his truck, had said, "If there's an earthquake tonight, I'm doomed. This whole fucking thing is going in, with me with it." Tunitas Creek Beach was until recently one of the best-kept secrets on the peninsula, only accessible to those in the know via unofficial trails. Now it's slated to become a county park, safer and cleaner but ruined in another sense, Roland would argue. Below us, the waves echoed as they pounded two crescent sea caves, which showed how eventually these cliffs would calve away with a crash the whales might hear. Cormorants roosted just below a knobby ledge over the caves. They faced into the rock, staring at their shadows like two-headed Hydras above white streaks of guano. They had no room to turn around, but swiveled their heads 180 degrees to survey the ocean, their mother and maker, past, present, and future.

Soon after, Simon pointed out Martins Beach, which I would have passed right by. Martins has long been a favorite of smelt fishers and surfers, but in recent years has been a source of public outcry and attention after a billionaire, Vinod Khosla, bought the surrounding fifty-three acres and locked the gate across the beach road, even going so far as to post armed guards for a time. It seemed to flaunt the 1976 California Coastal Act, which bars developments and homes from blocking beach access. Khosla won a suit in the San Mateo County Superior Court when a judge ruled that, since his land had been part of an original rancho, *Rancho Cañada de Verde and Arroyo de la Purísima*, his right to privacy superseded the California Constitution. The original land claim had been upheld by the U.S. Supreme Court in 1859, and it made no mention of an easement. This ruling, which from a conservative judicial stance is defensible, has severe implications for public access and more. However, the Surfrider Foundation won a second lawsuit on more limited grounds, arguing that to lock a gate Khosla needed to apply for a permit from the Coastal Commission because the act qualifies as "development." The Coastal Commission of course would be unlikely to grant such a permit without continued public access. This ruling stood through rounds of appeals, and the U.S. Supreme Court declined to hear the case. But after a decade of contention the ultimate outcome at Martins Beach remains unsettled.

The infamous gate was locked when we strode up, low and junky, only waist height. One side of it was automatic. Signs on its metal frame read, PRIVATE PROPERTY: NO TRESPASSING and RIGHT TO PASS BY PERMISSION AND SUBJECT TO CONTROL OF OWNER. I had come this far, though. I stepped over the gate and went down the lane, while Lucy and Simon waited. Martins Beach Road was straight and narrow, unassuming. The shadows of fence posts slanted across the pavement toward a white corral fence under the pines at the edge of Khosla's yard. Quail flushed, scurried. The road turned sharply left to switchback downhill to a community of pastel bungalows above the beach: Khosla owned that, too, but tolerated his tenants. I couldn't see it, but there was a retaining wall below them, holding back the sea but also accelerating coastal erosion.

Instead of turning downhill, I stepped off the road onto a vacant lot, newly green on the bluff top, where I probably could have been arrested but now had a view of the beach's sea-bound Pelican Rock, better known as the "Shark's Fin" for its triangular jut. Surfers ride the break beside it. The pampas grass gathered the day, swaying. On the next bluff over, beyond the creek, was a Hollywood-esque sign of huge cutout letters that, through my binoculars, asked, WILL YOU MARRY ME? It was decorated with clear white bulbs. It seemed the right sentiment for this place, not closure, not litigation, not billions. Just this. The one and only. I imagined her reaction, or his, on the beach at dusk. Or was it past dark? Was it years ago? Someone plugged in the extension cord. Someone looked up to discover the sign, each bulb an incandescent "yes." The light was like that this evening.

I LEFT MY DEAR SIMON and Lucy at the intersection of Verde and Purisima Creek Roads to hitchhike back to their car, and in need of a quick campsite, took the drastic approach of climbing a steep hill. On account of the poison oak, I stopped to slide my rain pants on before pushing straight through chaparral, a handy technique I had used several times before. In the morning, the ocean fell through my nylon curtains. I sauntered down to the road feeling none of the anxiety of the campsite rush, crossed the highway, and cut through a fallow brussels sprout field to a portion of the California Coastal Trail, a crushed granite path along the bluffs. It took me down into and across Purisima Creek, which seemed impenetrable with willow. Hoping for a path to the beach, I climbed the other side, where Portolá and Crespí had found an empty village. But the bluffs were sheer, so I backtracked to the arroyo and found an inconspicuous deer trail of a path into the knitted creek. There I left my pack and traded my sneakers for flip-flops so I could splash right down the middle of the stair-stepped Purisima, first called *San Ivon* by Crespí. The creek was no wider than a sidewalk. My ankles tingled, and I clenched my toes to prevent my sandals from floating off as I ducked under overhanging branches. The narrow corridor made a sharp bend through the cliffs. Up ahead was a jagged blue V of ocean and horizon. I wondered if the soldiers also had followed the creek to the shore after making camp; certainly the Ohlone had many times.

At Purisima Creek's mouth, I discovered large potholes in the soft bedrock and a shallow infinity pool. The glassy water braided off a ledge of bright aquatic plants, and cascaded left, south, to the beach down a last hump of cliff. All around I began to notice fossilized mollusks emerging from the mudstone and shale, which in fact is here known as the Purisima Formation: rock about 2.5 to 7 million years old. Mostly clams, the fossils were like half-moons gradually waxing toward full. I imagined these hard-soft creatures suddenly buried or uplifted in the fault rupture that destined them to become stone. Some of these stone bivalves now had been released and lay dry beside the pools and the waterfall, where I could pick them up, turn them over in my hands. Others flickered under the rivulets that, in each instant, excavated them, grain by grain. Some had mineralized, become hard, polished stone. Others were hearts of sandstone between the clams' original shells. All of them seemed portents from a world where Portolá and all that has ensued would matter only a smidge, though it is everything to us. Bubbles circling past. On the beach was a Frappuccino bottle and a pair of swim goggles so scuffed that the lenses were like a frosted glass. I held them up to my eyes, saw only brightness. These would fall out of the cliffs in a million years.

No one would find me at this concealed waterfall, not for weeks or months, so I stripped down and bent my head under the cascade—I hadn't showered in five days—and air-dried in the wind and November sun with my hands on my sore hips and however much nature gave me in plain view. Seals bobbed in the surf only feet from the beach in the sandy foam and undertow, and I wondered what they were eating, whether it might be living clams, the descendants of the ones unlocking from the cliffs, their polished stone eyes watching.

THE COASTAL TRAIL WASN'T ACTUALLY open, to my surprise, and I had to hop a gate on the way out. It's only open weekends and holidays, the opposite of normal business hours. An unofficial trail, on the other hand, is always open, and I took one, rutted and nearer to the edge and more charismatic, toward the Ritz-Carlton Half Moon Bay and its golf course, which together are designed to look something like Saint Andrews in Scotland, with dune grass along fairways leading toward a castle of a building. I walked holes sixteen through eighteen, halting to let golfers tee off—that ringing of plastic off titanium—and staying clear of their sight lines while they putted. What would Portolá think of links? Would he wonder why he had gone through the trouble of opening this territory so that we could waddle these lawns and smack a dimpled ball, or would he trade in his lance and yell "fore" with the best of them? "How'd your shot go?" I asked one golfer. "Well, it didn't go into the water," he replied. His cart whined off, but I caught his foursome at the green, where I narrated their putts and chips, whispering into my recorder like a tournament broadcaster. "Hit the pin!" said the man to his ball, but the ball disobeyed and ran eight feet past.

Natural gas was flaming in the pits on the Ritz's oceanside patios, though it was three o'clock and warm. A woman sat in a white bathrobe on an Adirondack chair drinking a glass of chardonnay, though it was three o'clock and warm. A man in a suit paced with a cell phone, and I heard him say, "our strategy on Cape Cod," though we were in Half Moon Bay. A dapper eared grebe caught my eye for several minutes, though it floated on a clubhouse pond. But what I remember most is the cross I encountered near hole sixteen: *this*, I realized, was what I had really been after as I had searched aimlessly on the Del Monte Beach for the memorial replica of Portolá and Crespí's original cross, the one on which they'd carved, "The land expedition is returning to San Diego for lack of provisions today, December 9, 1769." Six months later, on the Spaniards' return to Monterey, they found it surrounded with arrows and feathered staffs, with mussels and sardines. The locals had made it more representative of the land and put it in conversation with their own beliefs.

The cross near the Ritz was just a metal post with a driftwood two-by-four lashed across it. Barbwire was wrapped around it like a crown of thorns, one that we'd designed and strung throughout the West; and tucked under this tetanoid strand or glued to the crosspiece, right where the nails would have been, were pieces or relics of California: jingle shells, limpets, mussels, driftwood bored by worms and burnt by fires. Blue glass, the rarest. Amber, the most common and hoppy. A buckwheat sprig, a rainbow bracelet of beads, a golf tee, turban snails, a dime with patina on its ribbed edge, a finger of still-living ice plant, a bottle opener, a lichened stick, feathers. The cross had become a living collage, a work of found communal art that brought together disparate worlds and meant no one thing. There was also an aluminum token imprinted with the Serenity Prayer: "God grant me the serenity to accept the things I cannot change, courage to change the things I can, and wisdom to know the difference." I had gathered what I could these long months, and that would not change, and I had to find the courage to write it up the best I could so that others could at least glimpse the California I had seen and loved even as it had betrayed so many.

I SPENT THE EVENING AT the San Benito House bar in downtown Half Moon Bay watching the Cleveland Indians tie up Game 7 of the World Series with a dramatic eighth-inning home run. Two innings later, the Cubs finally broke their drought and won for the first time in 108 years, not quite half the span since the Portolá expedition. Too bad, I thought, that we'll all be dead before the Cubs win again. Too, too bad. I walked back to the State Beach needing no flashlight, stars out, elated to have a sanctioned plot for my dome for the first time since Kirk Creek Campground in Big Sur more than two weeks ago. The expedition camped at Pilarcitos Creek, which borders the Half Moon Bay State Beach and flows south from the crest of the Coast Range to entwine with east-west Highway 92 below the pass. The men's scurvy continued to dissipate, but they were short on food. "We had our men reduced to the simple daily ration of five tortillas made of flour and bran," Costansó wrote. Five tortillas doesn't exactly compensate for leagues of marching. They had agreed to begin butchering the mules, but postponed it—they would do this on the way back, eating one every third day, arriving in San Diego "smelling frightfully of mules." Here they were buoyed by some ducks they shot and more black pies offered by a village near Pillar Point. Crespí highlighted this headland: "The coast and mainland at about a league from this stream form a very long point of land reaching far out to sea, and a great deal of flats running along its tip, with many large rocks seeming from afar to be island rocks." These rocks are the local pillars and *pilarcitos*, named in land grants as early as 1836.

When I arrived home to my tent that night, something silver on the ground caught my eye, and I switched on my headlamp. It was the aluminum underside of my Blue Diamond Almonds carton. It had been inside my backpack, inside my tent. My stomach sank. Raccoons must have ripped into my dome and torn open my pack. Then I noticed the tent had been unzipped. My pack was intact too. Dexterous scoundrels! They had fished out the container through a drawstring opening and, furthermore, unzipped a side pocket to snatch a Ziploc baggie with several tea bags. That was a loss, because I had carried those tea bags all the miles from San Diego and grown fond of them. Sure enough, I saw three forms in the darkness twenty feet off and shone my light: young raccoons. I ran toward them, and they padded, not too quickly, across the grass to a neighboring cypress and slunk up its dense interior. The shine of their eyes, their stripes. But if that was the worst theft and wildlife encounter I would experience all trip, then I had immeasurable luck.

The ocean woke ultramarine, deep and lucid to the horizon with a brisk offshore wind coming over the Half Moon Bay pass, an unusual occurrence. No creeping fog today, only clarity. I sheltered my stove with my body for instant coffee. My tent fly was completely dry, another rare occurrence. The easterly wind caused the waves to rise limpid and break perfect and clean, a surfer's holiday, spindrift rising off their crests, an opalescent veil. "It's awesome, man," said a videographer studying a few surfers before he stretched his hood over his noggin and headed for the water. "We haven't had this in quite a while." He fought the surging breakers gripping an aquatic camera in one hand.

Dozens of snowy plovers in their nonbreeding beige were hunkered in the footprints of beachgoers, no ranger in sight to protect them, some of them color banded. They seemed testy and territorial, chasing each other from divot to divot. A peregrine falcon, a large female, was perched inconspicuously on a low foredune, biding her time and blending with the tapering Santa Cruz Mountains behind her. The range was scabby with chaparral, eucalyptus, and a few pines as dark as the falcon's sideburns, the redwoods long since cut or simply left behind to the south: Crespí mentions a dearth of firewood surrounding Pilarcitos Creek.

I strolled the beach and then the bike path north toward Pillar Point to rendezvous with Sarah after five weeks apart. She was going to walk a couple of these final days with me. My father drove her over on Highway 92, and they spotted me by the jetty that borders Surfers Beach. I can't remember what was said, but there wasn't much time for hugs and sweet nothings because we heard an Australian accent say through a bullhorn, "When you're digging, think about how hard it would be for a mommy turtle to do this!" School kids from Los Altos were excavating nests with rubber flippers on their hands. They'd been split into pairs and were readying for a second race. The goal was to beat their previous depth. "Flipper check!" shouted the woman with the amplifier. Turns out she was their PE teacher, so she was used to a megaphone and starting races. "On your marks! Get set! Go!" One member of the team crawled to the nest site, where the flippers were handed off to their partner, who dug. "Go, go, go," shouted the kids. "Ellie, watch your eyes, sweetie!" said the coach as sand flew up. At other stations, their classmates were learning how riprap can accelerate erosion and filtering the sand to see just how much microplastic is in the mix. It reminded me of the excursions I had taken in school in the Bay Area, only these activities were more creative and current. When the final countdown ended, the "turtles" laid their red Wiffle golf balls into each depression and swept sand over the top. The winners had dug sixteen centimeters—the PE coach measured with a ruler—besting their previous effort. The team raised their arms and bounced up and down. This wasn't the eighty-two-centimeter average that a leatherback accomplishes, but a real turtle does have all night.

AFTER LUNCH AT BARBARA'S FISHTRAP with my father, Sarah and I walked through a neighborhood to the beach below Pillar Point, an uplifted ocean terrace that Crespí named *la punta de los Ángeles Custodios* for the twin honed rocks that stood out among the pillars off the headland. They looked like wings, I imagine. Most of Pillar Point is now occupied by an Air Force tracking station, one of our guardian angels. The famous surf spot, Mavericks, lies about a quarter mile off the end of the point. There waves swell to as high as twenty-four feet, which means fifty-foot faces from crest to trough. The underwater topography of Mavericks converges wave "rays," or paths of wave energy, up a gradual bedrock ramp that lifts the breakers to these freakish heights. Its name immortalizes a white-haired German shepherd, Maverick, who in 1967 swam out to his owner as he and several friends tried to surf the point's peripheral waves. Legend has it this lionheart of a canine often surfed with his owner, but these waves were too dangerous, so he was paddled back to the beach and tied up.

But "Mavericks" naturally also alludes to those who are audacious enough to surf here. In the early seventies, a kid named Jeff Clark scrutinized these mammoth waves beyond Pillar Point from his hillside vantage at Half Moon Bay High School several miles away. At age seventeen, he paddled out, by himself, to surf these titans. One of his friends remained on the beach, reassuring Clark that he would "call the Coast Guard and tell them where I last saw you." Clark surfed Mavericks alone for seventeen years, becoming ambidextrous so he could stand up on the enormous "right" while facing into the wave (the left break at Mavericks is even more dangerous and incendiary, seldom ridden). Other big wave surfers finally found the courage to join him in 1990. A contest was initiated in 1999: if the conditions become right between November and March, twenty-four exceptional surfers are given twenty-four hours' notice. The competition is on.

The first major swell of winter was building when Sarah and I arrived. Past the harbor and its lazy raft of bufflehead ducks, we rounded a corner and hit a startling blast of wind below cliffs 175 feet tall. The ocean crashed and sloshed into the stone, prohibiting any further passage around the point. Out front was a shallow, frothy, chaotic cauldron. Black rocks were silhouetted in a blinding wave field—what's left of those tall *ángeles* that inspired Crespí a quarter millennium ago. They were "shaped like toy tops," he wrote. And past those rocks, we saw at last a dozen or so surfers, waiting. They were farther out than you might think to look, far past the obvious waves. Through my binoculars, they vanished into troughs and rose again into view—some prostrate, others astride their boards with arms crossed, uniform in their neoprene, a floating sculpture garden, Rodins of the sea. The swells come from the west, born of storms off Japan. They arrive parallel to the headland's southern face. To the east of this isolated flotilla was a Jet Ski: not strictly legal in the Monterey Bay National Marine Sanctuary except, in winter, on declared "High Surf" days. But mostly they are tolerated, because they save lives. Two world-class surfers have died at Mavericks.

Several surfers arrived and began to pull their wetsuits over their inflatable vests, which made their chests look extra burly. They zipped each other up from behind. Rip cords hung from their shoulders: one pull, and carbon dioxide would fill those vests and lift them to the surface.

"How do you guys swim out?" I asked one of them.

"Well, you could go this way," he said, pointing to the right. "Or you could go that way," he said, pointing to the left. "We'll probably try that way." Left it was: the longer but safer route around the pillars.

"You need a vest?" I asked.

"Always. Once you have one . . . It's cheaper to go without one, but it's kind of lame." This invention has made big wave surfing considerably safer, but lowered the average level of expertise at a place like Mavericks, a trend dangerous in and of itself.

In a good year, when the storms and currents align, these men might surf Mavericks ten times. "The swell is coming," said the surfer, "it's just not here yet." It might bring fifteen-foot waves, he guessed, thirty-foot faces. "This is really awesome conditions. Rarely do you get them when it's hot . . . it's usually cold fronts." He and his buddy waxed up in sync. "Stay safe," I said, and he returned a thumbs-up. "I'll try to do that." They Velcroed their leashes to their ankles and dove in, paddling unhurriedly, conserving energy, lifting their chests to let the first waves slide between them and their boards. They stroked far left, circumventing the rocks; it would take them twenty minutes to reach the group.

Sarah and I turned about. The buffleheads in the calm, windless harbor now seemed to convey a certain judiciousness. Then we scaled the neck of Pillar Point on a jeep trail. The multistory radome looked like a giant's golf ball teed up and ready to be driven, *ping*, into the ocean; inside was a forty-four-foot telemetry dish that receives signals from aircraft, including missiles launched from Vandenberg down the coast. The military always seems to claim the most prominent land as if to broadcast its ascendancy. Was there a reason the Air Force needed to situate this radar on this prominent coastal point, instead of a trifle inland? The army obtained Pillar Point in 1940, when no one could argue.

Once we were north of the point, we could better see Mavericks' swells in the distance from the bluff-top trail, see their impressive contours and the pinhead surfers on the glaze. One dude managed to catch a modest colossus, and he rode its triangle form, its dark translucence, until they both suddenly disappeared into the cliffs, swallowed by the sandstone, a trick of perspective. Overhead a stunt airplane began to loop-the-loop; we heard its engine sputter and stall and restart in free fall. I wondered if the surfers were watching this display as they waited on their boards. Maybe they saw themselves in these acrobatics. Meanwhile the bushtits tumbled from a ceanothus in every direction, even falling out from underneath, peeping and trickling, their entire lives like sand through an hourglass. They were the ultimate scouting party. I was relieved whenever I saw them.

SARAH AND I MADE IT another four or five miles, dawdling for a time at the Fitzgerald Marine Reserve, which looms large in my tidal imagination for its portals of anemone and sea star and chiton, an edge I experienced as a child on field trips and later returned to as a teenager. We made it as far as Montara State Beach, where Martini Creek enters and the Portolá party camped, Crespí naming it *el arroyo hondo del Almejar*, or "the deep stream at the Mussel Bed," on account of the shellfish the soldiers discovered—one of the few times he granted a place a secular name without a grudge. Concerned about the lack of trees, they had carried firewood on this leg of the journey, and from the sound of it they lit a big pot.

Here an embayment begins, Crespí wrote, defined to the north by a point, "one called in the histories *punta de los Reyes*, having consequently *el puerto de San Francisco* close to it." Point Reyes was named by Vizcaíno, and San Francisco was the original name given in 1595 by Sebastián Rodríguez Cermeño, a Portuguese who likewise mapped the coast, to what's now Drake's Bay in the point's southern shelter. You can hear the impatience in Crespí's final draft: "Everything that can be viewed of the embayment here is entirely as depicted by Cabrera Bueno: and thus there can be no slightest doubt of that harbor's lying in this district." The harbor he's referring to is the original San Francisco Bay, now Drake's Bay. "However, even with all of these lights, many still will have it that the Santa Lucia Mountains, and consequently Monte-Rey, lie ahead."

We took a car back to a motel across from the Pillar Point Harbor as darkness fell. As when Sarah visited Los Angeles, I wasn't about to drag her into poaching a campsite in a one-person tent. The next morning, November 4, we returned to where we left off, destined for Pacifica. From a culvert, Martini Creek rippled in an S on the sand below the conglomerate bluffs. Crespí reported with barely suppressed horror that the creek was flea ridden and "that anyone who went into it, even without pausing there, would come out teeming and reddening with them." But we felt none. I thought I saw another falcon or osprey atop the bluffs, but then the bird's head moved: it was an iPhone in the hand of a woman preserving the view. "March," said Sarah. We crossed the highway and on a trail traversed the hillside of lower Montara Mountain, where I had once forayed with my father on a wildflower identification trip. The path was lined with fragrant sage, shining coffeeberry, a purple aster much like fleabane, sticky monkey flower, and on our left shoulder, the Pacific, its endless corolla.

Crespí's journal suggests the expedition trailed up Montara Mountain's western flank, not up Martini Creek, heading "northwestward," "all of it very close to the shore," before descending to today's San Pedro Creek and Pacifica. Instead of continuing up the hillside to a saddle, however, we dropped back to the highway, lured by the sight of a bunker on a prominence just before the twin mouths of the Devil's Slide Tunnels. The graffitied concrete shelter was perched on a pedestal of granite, as if the earth all around it had eroded away while the bunker's foundation had protected the stone underneath it. Actually the property's previous owner had excavated the ground around the bunker, leveling the site for development, but his plans fell through. The bunker, once flush to the ground, was left hanging. It was one of several "fire control stations" from which soldiers scanned the horizon in search of Japanese ships and submarines, ready to help triangulate coordinates so that batteries on the Marin Headlands or at Fort Funston, on either side of the Golden Gate, could do their damage. Dark slit windows opened to the ocean, and we imagined the glint of spyglass lenses scouring the horizon. Ice plant hung over the top, as if for camouflage: the army also propagated ice plant for cover. The bunker was another reminder of the coast's long militarization from Portolá onward, of a surveillance that is subtler now, more inconspicuous, but still omnipresent, up in the sky via satellites. In every cell phone.

We walked the Devil's Slide pedestrian trail, a section of the coast highway that was abandoned after too many rockfalls, landslides, and cracks—too much folded shale and conglomerate sheeting off the underlying granite—in favor of new tunnels through San Pedro Mountain. A few hundred yards off the retired high-way's sheer edge was Egg Rock with its rookery of common murres. The sea vista was smudgy, a purple rung of moisture between us and Point Reyes. The pale cliffs of Point Reyes appeared as an island, just as Crespí described them; the cape's low-lying middle was lost to me and to him entirely. The Farallon Islands, "six or seven white island rocks," were all but obscured. Only the peak of the largest was visible through the ocean vapors, a tanker in the foreground. Notorious for their currents and great white sharks, noteworthy for their seabird colonies, the Farallones are twenty-six miles from the Golden Gate and among California's rawest places. Cre-spí believed, wrongly, that they lay inside the bight between Pillar Point and Point Reyes, which is now known as the Gulf of the Farallones. But Crespí was impressed with and optimistic about this "bay." "All the navies of Spain could fit within it," he wrote. "There are three white gorges seen from afar, at one of which appears to be a cove to give shelter from the open quarter." Likely this is Bolinas Bay and the sands of Stinson Beach.

WE DESCENDED THROUGH A EUCALYPTUS forest to Pacifica, eucalyptus be-ing the best approximation I know of what it's like to be submerged in a kelp forest, birds fluting high in the canopy, garibaldi swimming in the imagination, the dapple-gray light itself like a revolution of anchovies. There's a gentle beach in Pacifica that receives San Pedro Creek, there's a bowling alley, Sea Bowl, and there's a patinated cubist statue of Portolá given to the city in 1988 by the Generalitat of Catalonia, where Gaspar was born. His hat looks like an upside-down steam iron. There are the Portola Shores Condos, and a Crespi Center commercial building with a Fog City Java. One of the main roads into the scrub-suburban hills is Crespi Drive, which joins Fassler Avenue, which is the route that Sarah and I—and, it's believed, the Spaniards—followed to reach the crest of the ridge.

When the expedition reached this valley on October 31, they followed the San Pedro Creek toward the ocean and encamped. "A village of very fine, well-behaved heathens was hereabouts, and they came over at once to the camp, bringing a good many black pies made of their seeds." How I wish to try one of these famous black pies. For the next three days, the men waited while Sergeant Ortega and eight soldiers reconnoitered. A pulse of drama or even foreboding creeps into Crespí's hand as he waits, writing of November 2, "At night on All Souls' day so strong a north wind blew here that it tore down everything that was standing and tossed quite large firebrands into the air." I picture the men sitting around a campfire with these sparks flying into the night, all of them wondering what the scouting party would encounter, whether they would find Monterey, and if they would live to see San Diego again.

On November 3, the patrol returned: "Friday at night they came back from scouting; they fired off their guns on arriving, to tell that they had come upon a sea arm that reaches many leagues inland, and had gotten near to one extremity, and there had met with about seven villages in a short distance; that there are large plains, many lakes with enormous number of geese, ducks, cranes, and other fowl, and very large tall live-oak groves . . . We are all very joyful; though having, in the midst of this, a good deal of suspicion that Monte Rey may have been left behind us." Despite this last frustration, the journals give the sense that this discovery promises something major for their journey and perhaps for their personal and national prosperity.

The incline was steep but we were motivated. Along Fassler Avenue was the same nature that had accompanied me much of the trip: crisped mustard, flowering fennel, the toyon of Hollywood with its scarlet and graying berries, and empty liquor nips in the weeds. The streetlights' glass caught the lowering sun and glowed. Poison oak in liminal colors: light pink, green, yellow, mottled, speckled, luscious. Cars pushing forty uphill in a twenty-five-mile-per-hour zone. We couldn't quite see the Golden Gate: the coastline blended as one curve of haze and land mass. We passed a SeaCrest development across from a Driftwood Circle, and came to the intersection of Crespi and Fassler, continuing on past a NOT A THRU STREET sign. This steep cul-de-sac was lined with houses. Three tennis balls were lodged in the shallow gutter, the property of a golden retriever.

My family and several friends met us at the yellow gate to the Baquiano Trail, which heads up to Sweeney Ridge. Our friend Byron jumped out of his car dressed as a mountain man, in a buckskin shirt and coon hat, and shorts. Half-dressed. It brought me back to the men in costume at Mission La Purísima, to the pair of raccoons lumped on the road near Davenport, to Halloween in Pescadero just a few days before. Patches, my dog, leapt from the car and was so excited to see me that she attacked my brother's Lab in a senseless act of fealty. We started up, zig-zagging past several water tanks and stands of pampas grass. I brought up the rear. Drums and horns began to drift up to us from the San Pedro Valley below, and as we climbed I spotted the marching band on a field down in the vale, their lines passing through each other, their brass and steel rims shining. I swear I could hear a cowbell ringing. Clouds of gnats like embers above coyote brush. The air seemed washed with a silver particle, and I wondered if the view at the ridgetop would be clear. Wondered and hoped.

As we climbed, the Farallones were revealed over our shoulders: either the moisture layer was evaporating or we were rising above it. The towers of the Golden Gate Bridge appeared in their shade of "International Orange." Now we could see the whole of Point Reyes, and to the south the glaring sun poured over Pedro Point, where the coast highway's curve vanished into San Pedro Mountain via the nostrils of those $425-million tunnels. We began to hear a periodic roar from over the rise, an engine roar that Portolá and company wouldn't have understood, a roar louder than surf, louder than tractors, louder and loftier than highways. Mount Tamalpais dark to the north. The inky lines of telephone wires swung through the view as if relaying the trills of the wrentits between drainages. Blackberry shoots, notes of sparrow, thistles and whistles. Grass marching out onto the adobe trail, trying to reclaim it. The grass below the chaparral was close-cropped by the rabbits who rely on its cover. Evaporating puddles. The outsized rattle of a single motorcycle resounded, as if through the whole Bay Area. I wondered if the Portolá expedition had stepped foot on any point of this ground that we were walking. Had they come up this exact ridge? How long had this fire road been a path? Had it originally been maintained by fire?

I WAS BRINGING UP THE rear, but as the ridge crowned, the rest of the party slowed and waited, and let me pass so that I could reach the summit first. "There it is," I said, as the bay rolled over the top, "the inland ocean. This is it." It was revealed seamlessly, a curtain smoothly lifted: the Berkeley Hills in a band of smog, the densely built East Bay, then the shadowed blue of *el Puerto*. San Francisco International Airport on the near side of the bay and its roaring planes, which left the ground miraculously at a thirty-degree angle every thirty seconds on land that was once marsh. Directly below us was San Andreas Lake, a reservoir that helps supply drinking water to San Francisco. I swung my pack off my sweaty shoulders and rested it against the Discovery Site's historical marker. "Hope that's not too irreverent," I said. It was a serpentine block with a polished and inscribed face, mottled with orange lichen and streaked with bird droppings: FROM THIS RIDGE, THE PORTOLÁ EXPEDITION DISCOVERED SAN FRANCISCO BAY.

When the expedition crested, they would have seen smoke columns rising from dozens or hundreds of villages along the bay's edges and in the folds of its canyons. Seventeen thousand Ohlone, Miwok, and in the far north bay, Wappo lived in the Bay Area. It was already a metropolis by the standards of California at the time. Now 7 million people live around the Bay, nearly a 450-fold increase. Now the Bay Area has traffic that is officially worse than in Los Angeles, and "super commutes" of over ninety minutes are common. Now "low income," in San Francisco and San Mateo County, is a family of four that makes one hundred and ten thousand dollars a year, and now a prospective buyer needs to make more than a third of a million a year to buy in these counties. Now three and a half new jobs are created for every new housing unit. Now, and since 1902, the dead are no longer buried within the city limits of San Francisco for lack of space. Now some people pay four hundred dollars a month to rent a dilapidated RV in a driveway or illegally parked on the street. Now the region holds forty-eight of the top one hundred most expensive zip codes in the country. Eighty-two of them are in California.

Still, we celebrated. Our walk up Fassler and the Sweeney Ridge Trail had been a little more arduous on account of the prosecco. The discovery of the Bay isn't necessarily something to celebrate, certainly not without reflecting on what became of the people who lived here, how they died of disease and murder and marginalization, and how the environment has been forever altered, damaged, overrun, though so much is still reserved as open space, including these heights. But after twelve weeks of walking, bubbly seemed in order. Sarah had packed a bottle from a grocery outlet in Pacifica, and my family had brought one, too, along with plastic cups. My father set out cheese, crackers, and a clamshell of strawberries from Monterey. I wondered if I'd passed the field they had ripened in.

When I popped the cork, it launched like a plane from SFO into the blue evening and landed, lost, in the chaparral, a missile of Italian origin. "I lugged something else up here for everyone," I said.

"Artifacts?" asked Byron.

"Maybe . . . but everyone needs to turn away for a moment."

They all faced the ocean or the bay, or toward Mount Tam, or south down Sweeney Ridge—the view was full circle—while I rummaged through my backpack for a bundled T-shirt. "Can we turn back?" my mother asked.

"In a sec . . ." I said. "All right."

I explained, then, that after Lucy and Simon had taken me to Purisima Creek, the next morning I'd visited the creek's mouth and discovered scores of fossilized clams that had fallen out of the mudstone and shale. "So I brought a little hammock of rock clams," I said. "I wanted everyone to have one. I carried them the last few days."

"So they've never been opened?" said Byron. "This is like finding a sixteen-hundred or seventeen-hundred Bordeaux or something. You can get in there and have an old clam!"

When the prosecco was finished and the sky began to drain, everyone readied to leave me, even Sarah. I needed to set up my tent. My journey wasn't quite done. "So where are you going to camp?" my brother asked.

"Oh, I don't know, those trees over there . . ." I said, gesturing toward the bay-side slope about a hundred feet away.

They laughed. They left me some of their water, said their goodbyes, and headed downhill as the air began to chill. That grove was, it's true, where I pitched my tent, beneath a giant pine that had created a flat spot uphill of its trunk, the side that caught the tree's own debris.

BUT FOR A WHILE STILL I paced back and forth at the Discovery Site as if in search of something. It might have looked to other hikers as if I were searching for my lost car keys and becoming increasingly desperate. This was it. The view. The inland sea and the real one. The Farallones were laid bare at last, silhouetted, a light flashing on the southeast island—the 1855 lighthouse. Mount Tamalpais turned slate blue in Marin. Wispy cirrus on the horizon held the sun a little longer as it descended over the curve of the earth, though really it was me, us, North America, revolving east at a thousand miles per hour.

In the other direction, the sunset transmuted the windows of Oakland into burning pearls, Mount Diablo far beyond. A red army of taillights sedately marched north past Oyster Point, with a counterforce of white mobilizing in the other direction. These colors were reversed as I swung my gaze to the south near Coyote Point. UNITED AIRLINES glowed on one of the airport's behemoth hangars. All along, and until about eleven that night, the avalanche rumble of the planes filled my eardrums: a stylized Inuit on one tail, Alaska; a golden crane on another, Lufthansa. I studied them like birds through my binoculars. Nearly 2.5 million people a year board planes at SFO.

And the moths flying between the moon and Montara, their flickering shadow bodies. And antennas blinking in every direction. I was rotating the way the second historical marker at the Discovery Site, a black granite cylinder, teaches you all of the Bay Area's major mountains at once as you walk around it and study their outlines. I was like one of Crespí's "toy tops." I was trying to keep the day alive, then and in memory. But it was nearing nautical twilight. It dawned on me that I was leaving the ocean, that I was turning toward the bay for these final days. In fact, I was leaving the ocean behind for some time. I would have to crawl into my tent, in the morning I would descend, a president would soon be elected, I would go back to Idaho, I would within a year have a daughter, which would make another expedition of this nature all but inconceivable, and undesirable.

"From up here, it's impossible," I said to myself, though I was really talking to these pages. "You want to look two ways at once. Several times I've started to head toward my campsite. 6:25 now, but I linger, I linger. Through the chaparral bushes, over the top, all the Farallones are framed briefly as I walk back toward the ocean side. A barge that had seemed stationary now creeping toward the Farallones, and it will pass in front of them, and maybe even merge with them, or just below . . . hanging in the ocean. A streak of contrail where the sun disappeared—the last slit, little nick, of brightness. And Jupiter, the first non-moon celestial object to the southeast . . . the southwest, sorry.

"In my tent now . . . The glow of the Bay coming through the long wall, as if to keep me company. It's like there's a light on the tent. I can see the wrinkles of the mesh, of the screen, wrinkled to the seam . . . like waves . . . Thinking about how earlier I couldn't find my Swiss Army knife. Maybe I've lost it . . . fallen out of a pocket. The trouble of forgetting to zip and then walking. And so I used a tent stake to undo the teeth of a cap on an Anchor Steam lager, which I enjoyed—a San Francisco beer, Sarah's idea—looking out at the bay, sitting on a log with a plastic bag under me to keep the wetness off my bum. Sat there long enough to get pretty chilled so now I'm in the tent to warm up before the night . . ." The recording ends there.

MORNING WAS CLEAR, BUT BEYOND the folds of the San Bruno hills, fog had slid through the Golden Gate over to Berkeley as it so often does. And even before I had broken down the tent, fog claimed Sweeney Ridge, too, sweeping over it like so much cobweb through the chaparral brooms and stripping the pine under which I slept to a gray skeleton. When I pushed out of the bushes into the Discovery Site clearing, two men in Lycra were alternately posing for a photo with the serpentine marker. Their mountain bikes were leaned against it. "It was two hundred fifty years ago today," said one. "Well, two hundred forty-seven years ago," his friend corrected. On my phone, I'd seen a "Portola Road" that continued south from the ridgeline trail, and I speculated this was close to the expedition's approximate route southward. A San Francisco Water Department gate blocked my path. Not feeling especially confrontational, I backtracked. At the Discovery Site, a group led by a ranger had suddenly materialized to mill around the marker. Wondering if their hike was in honor of the anniversary, I asked the ranger, and it was, so I told him my secret, that I'd walked from San Diego in the expedition's footsteps.

"You did?" he said. "You're kidding." He asked if I'd say something to the remaining crowd. "Hey guys, ladies and gentlemen, we've got something that I've never seen before . . . I'm going to have this gentleman talk to you briefly about his experience. This man claims to be telling the truth . . ."

We all laughed. "Will you swear on a Bible?" said a woman.

"So I, last night, reached this point having left San Diego on July 14 retracing the Portolá expedition . . ." They gasped or exclaimed and then gave me an ovation, which lent me the energy to finish this walk to Menlo Park. "There was a view then," I said, as the fog swirled around us, "which was quite satisfying." We talked for five or six minutes, and they were patient with my half-fumbling answers. "Anyways, congrats on making it here yourself," I said. Which goes, of course, for anyone who ever visits this ridge and its misty, enduring view across open and contested space.

SNEATH LANE, NAMED FOR THE dairyman who later owned Sweeney Ridge, carried me out of the fog and the Golden Gate National Recreation Area. Soon I was on Skyline Boulevard and then plodding the bike path along the San Andreas Lake, now a reservoir. The famous fault runs directly below it. "We . . . had now changed course to the southward," wrote Crespí, "at which we went down from the hill we had been on, to a hollow running between high grassy knolls upon this side of the inlet"—San Francisco Bay—"and a mountain range, very green with low woods, that kept with us upon our right. At the two leagues, we made camp at the foot of this mountain range, close to a lake where there were countless ducks, cranes, geese and other fowl." The expedition traveled this rift valley to today's Woodside, and this corridor is still "very green with low woods," as anyone who has driven scenic Highway 280 south from San Francisco knows. It's a fifty-square-mile wildlife corridor: the San Francisco Water Department's twenty-three-thousand acre reserve, county and open space district parks, and private lands. Crespí gave this long valley the name *Cañada de San Francisco*, but when the bay was explored again in 1774, Padre Francisco Palóu renamed it *de San Andreas* on the Saint's feast day. The map of California rippled for a long time with linguistic aftershocks. As for the lake by which the expedition camped, once it was a "sag pond," a pond formed in the depression of a seismic fault. This is something not uncommon in California. In 1868 a dam was built across the valley to supply water to San Francisco. Over the reservoir's chain-link, mule deer nibbled or bedded down, their ears a relaxed V. "The scouts aver that when they explored here they succeeded in counting a band of fifty deer together," wrote Crespí. Beyond the fence, these deer had little to worry about in broad daylight. At night they would worry about mountain lions.

Strange to be heading south. I had to apply sunscreen to the neglected side of my face. The light felt different, too, more direct, though the sun was buried in drifting clouds or shining through only as bright as the moon. The trail sidled up against Highway 280 and arrived at the top of Hillcrest Boulevard. I crossed under the highway briefly to survey "the inlet." West of 280 is preserved; east of 280 is all houses, the land enveloped to the shoreline. The airport's runways extend into the bay like springboards, which they essentially are. About two hundred thousand acres of marsh ringed the bay when Portolá arrived: mudflat transitioning to salt-excreting cordgrass, salt grass, and pickleweed, transitioning to brackish tule and cattail, all these habitats tied to sea level. Ninety-five percent of it has been filled or diked, including the 350 acres under SFO. The airport is subsiding by a half inch a year, while the bay is rising, and by 2100, half of those runways and taxiways will be submerged. But one of the world's largest restoration projects is ongoing in the Bay Area, so maybe the airport has a chance. Myriad agencies and municipalities are restoring salt marsh, gradually breaching dikes to recreate the natural buffer the metropolis will need in this era of climate change, of floods and high seas, the next chapter of history.

SAWYER CAMP TRAIL IS ONE I know well. In high school and afterward when I returned home during college, I ran many miles on it training for cross-country and track races. Not once did I consider that Portolá and his men had marched roughly this same path. At the top of Hillcrest Boulevard, Sawyer Camp Trail begins next to another serpentine marker, this one even more hulking and turquoise, which memorializes the expedition's first camp after Sweeney Ridge. A jogger's black glove rested on it, dropped by someone, but this rock was a lost and found in more ways than one, since this and their next campsite are flooded. Their exact route lies below a chain of three reservoirs in this valley: the San Andreas Lake, dammed in 1868; the Upper Crystal Springs Reservoir in 1878; and the Lower Crystal Springs Reservoir in 1890. It made me wonder how many of our historical sites are poised to go underwater as the oceans rise.

The access road along the reservoirs closed to public traffic in the late 1970s to protect San Francisco's water, and it became this paved recreation path, Sawyer Camp Trail, instead. The trail snakes through an intermittent tunnel of oak, bay, and madrone, opening to broad "lake" views and Crespí's "very green" hills. There are half-mile markers, which I used while running to track my pace and time my splits. "On your left," said a biker. *Chup chup*, said a hermit thrush in the flooded willows. A bench looking out on the water held a small plaque: CANDLE OF MY LIFE, WE ARE ONE FOREVER. *JE T'AIME*. RICH AND ENDLESS LOVE, TRANSCENDING TIME AND SPACE. The western overhang of trees and their Spanish moss were reflected like paint pressed between the pages of a book.

In between San Andreas Lake and Lower Crystal Springs Reservoir, a man named Leander Sawyer lived near a notable bay tree along the onetime stagecoach route. He sold goods to picnickers and passersby, and let his cattle ramble. This tree, named the Jepson Laurel after California's most famous botanist, is thought to be the state's oldest living bay tree. Its rival to the north, along the Russian River near

Cloverdale, was felled for casting too much shade on a hayfield. Crespí cataloged the diversity of trees in the San Andreas Valley and noted one kind in particular: "A great many *madroños*, small and large, have been met with during these two days' march, laden with fruits the size of so many beads off our rosaries." A tree that is smooth and sinuous, with ruddy, often peeling bark as thin as crepe. A tree that, in the fall, boasts drooping clusters of vermilion berries below glossy leaves, boat-shaped and yellowing.

Some years ago now, I first encountered Crespí's expedition journals while looking into how the madrone got its name. I was following my nose, far from California, on a trail of nomenclature and perhaps nostalgia. I knew this tree well as a kid. We called it the "refrigerator tree," because its trunk is cool to the touch, even in summer: cold sap courses just below its nearly translucent russet skin. Crespí, I learned, was the first to write of this tree, comparing it to a closely related species in Spain, *el madroño*, the strawberry tree we now have in our parks and city streets and mission gardens. California has a Mediterranean climate—or perhaps it's the Mediterranean that has a Californian climate—and so the plants were more recognizable, the names more transplantable, than they otherwise might have been.

When I read about the origin of the madrone's name, I looked up from my page and wondered: What else had the Crespí and Portolá expedition given name to? What else had they seen? In that moment, this walk somehow seemed inevitable. Now, on Sawyer Camp Trail, on the penultimate day of my own three-month expedition, I picked a bunch of madrone berries and rubbed them between my dirty fingers, popping them from their stems into my mouth as I strolled, crunchy and fresh, and tasting something like an unripe strawberry, only less tart. It was the first time I had tried them, though I had lived among madrones much of my life. As I ate them, I felt the scurvy of my tiredness drop away.

WHEN SAWYER CAMP TRAIL ENDED, and I stepped back onto Skyline Boulevard, I discovered that the road over the San Mateo Creek Dam was closed, blocking my path. "Seismic instability" was cited. This dam created the Lower Crystal Springs Reservoir in 1890, drawing engineers from all over the world to study the feat, and deservedly so since the 1906 earthquake did the dam no harm. Finally it needed retrofitting.

I thought about crashing into San Mateo Creek just below the dam and scrambling up the other side, but there is a power station and other infrastructure to contend with. So I made a long detour. To reach my high school, many days I exited Highway 280 just up the road, drove across this trusty dam, and turned down Crystal Springs Road as now I was forced to do, slaloming past maples and bay laurel, rushing like a February spillover so as not to be late for the bell. Not too late. But I had never absorbed the creek as I did walking past it this day, with my backpack. At last, I saw the value of an easy pace.

Not long after, before the light ran out, I climbed above Polhemus Creek and its road in Baywood Park. The dogs across the ravine barked as they heard me in the leaf litter of the steep slope. This was no deer. They knew better. A few golf balls were nestled like eggs in the duff, probably from a swing across the canyon. Where the slope leveled, I pitched my tent under a grand live oak with its girthy limbs arched to the ground, an exemplary specimen, a California icon. The remaining boards of someone's childhood tree house hung above my fly. I emptied my pockets, placing my recorder in my ball cap beside my inflatable travel pillow, as usual. Everything in its place. Sleep took me and then, after a few hours, didn't.

"COMING AWAKE IN THE TENT, my whole body humming in the sleeping bag, which is a little too warm for what still feels like a summer night.

"The crickets, these crickets, are classic ... *churr churr.* Summery crickets. A few cars, and then the coyotes, which at first sound like teenagers, simply calling out, *ouooooo,* and then they sort of disintegrate into what sounds like a flock of geese, on distant ridges across the way. Sounds like it could be a hundred coyotes in this greater area, but it's probably only four or five. They're their own echo chambers ...

"I have limited water, but I'll get more at the gas station in the morning. This might be my last night in a tent. My legs out of the sleeping bag. I've got my sleeping bag liner ...

"Listen to the coyotes. I wish I could record them. But it would never come out, using this instrument. Story of this whole journey, in some ways. The crickets won't come out. The coyotes, they won't come out ...

"Felt the side of the tent, feel the moisture level ... it's very dry. The smell that fills the tent is of decomposing oak leaf. I'm underneath the broken ceiling of an old platform tree house, which also feels fitting. How could I not camp here once I came up the ridge and discovered it?

"My pad ... semi-deflated. But the leaves are so soft underneath you can't really tell. It's the end of daylight savings tonight, and we all have an extra hour of sleep that the rest of the world doesn't have. The coyotes don't have ... the crickets don't have. That we don't really have.

"My feet are still radiating heat. The rest of my body, I can feel the patches of coolness where my hips ... where my hips are most prominent, my shoulders ... I know I'll probably be back in the sleeping bag before long.

"When the coyotes sounded while I was falling asleep, I wondered how close they'd get, wondered what I'd do if they circled my little tent. But not tonight, and not this whole journey, though they came close at Portola Springs, Tomato Springs, in Irvine ... what a long time ago.

"That smell of wet oak leaves. That smell of oak leaves is California. Musty, organic. It's the smell of agriculture, too.

"It was 1:59 when I flipped on my phone just now. And now it's one o'clock. That faint sound of the plane, high in the clouds, so different from it taking off ... softer."

IN THE MORNING, I SHOOK a cricket out of my tent and tried to take a self-portrait with my solo dome by balancing my phone in a neighboring tree and scurrying back like a wood rat to my nest. Several times, I tried, before I stuffed my dome into its sack for a final time. I crashed back down the ridge ankle deep in oak leaves and walked uphill to the Chevron, just as I surmised, for coffee and the restroom, for water. He gave me free coffee. Nice guy, even after I spilled water all over the floor trying to fill up my Gatorade bottle. "Just put us in your book," he said.

I crossed Highway 92 and kept walking through Belmont's highlands, past Christian Drive, past VOTE HERE signs, past a smashed pumpkin, until I found the turn and path to my high school cross-country race course, known as Hallmark. From the back of the first loop, I could see the finish-line sign, and the hut where course records are posted, and the plastic flagging of the chute where racers often stagger and hold their hands on their heads to open their lungs. When I hoisted my pack again, I found myself shaking out my legs just as I had before a race.

Below Hallmark and beyond Highway 280, Upper Crystal Springs Reservoir reflected the fog ceiling that had settled halfway down evergreen Skyline Ridge. A trail carried me under the highway to Cañada Road, again into the trough of the San Andreas Valley. The madrones stood out red with berries across the hillside near the Filoli estate and garden: a real bumper crop, this year, berries for all the birds. This portion of Cañada is more or less the Portolá expedition's line, and on weekends, they close the road to cars so that fluorescent cyclists can fly by in pairs or pelotons, along with the occasional Rollerblader. Just snippets of banter as they pass: "The value of your vote really diminishes when your voting population is more than, like, ten," said one to his partner. "The ones that are, like, working the system . . . I don't get it . . . even, like, the farmers . . ." said another cyclist. "Watch out for those fast cyclists, like the group that just went by us," said a father to his son.

Of their walk on November 6, Crespí writes of marching south down the San Andreas Valley with "high knoll ranges of sheer soil and grass" between them and the bay to the east, and a "green mountain range," the Santa Cruz Mountains, to the west. Before long, the valley began to close, steering the Spaniards toward the bay. As Costansó observed, "We arrived at the end of the canyon where the hilly country, which extended to our left and lay between us and the estuary, terminated. At the same time the hills on our right turned towards the east." As I walked Whiskey Hill Road from Woodside, I saw the impasse they described up ahead, first Jasper Ridge, which is half a Stanford University biological preserve and half within my hometown, Portola Valley, and beyond it some foothills that belong to Palo Alto. And I considered whether the expedition had walked through my hometown, which officially took Portolá's name in 1964, before turning east, or if they had turned toward the bay beforehand. My hunch is the latter: they must have followed San Francisquito Creek, shooting the gap between Jasper Ridge and what's now Sharon Heights in West Menlo Park. They must have walked roughly on today's Sand Hill Road toward the plains of Palo Alto. So I turned up Sand Hill and made a beeline for the bay.

"We went up a knoll and once again saw the inlet still continuing on down southeastward and southward, the same course that we had been bearing. It was all level land, seemingly of many leagues' extent, the entire plain much grown over with a great many large white oaks and live oaks." Stanford's National Accelerator Laboratory, still known to locals as SLAC, was on my right now, running at the foot of Jasper Ridge like a stationary freight train just where Portolá might have passed, those subatomic particles inside hurtling, on occasion, at incomprehensible speeds to help us understand physics, cosmology, the nature of time, who knows. It's a two-mile-long building that was once billed as "the straightest object in the world." Incidentally, SLAC also hosted the first World Wide Web servers in the United States. The hills around it are dotted with craggy oaks, and I recalled often watching white-tailed kites hover over them, a flicker the color of salt flats, and once hopping the barbwire fences along the road to photograph those unruly limbs at dusk.

Grasshoppers from grass to pavement and back again. Toyons as highway ornament. I crossed 280. SAN FRANCISCO NORTH ⇒, MENLO PARK ⇑, read a forest-green sign. My two best childhood friends and I had scavenged an enormous MENLO PARK highway sign just here that had been knocked down by a car; it continues to lean up against a redwood in the hills, pointing the way. Sand Hill Road has been called the Main Street of Venture Capitalism, or the Wall Street of the West, both tawdry labels, both perhaps accurate. But you would never know it hiking its cracked and root-humped sidewalk past buckeyes and yellow-jacket traps and ground-squirrel holes and low-slung edifices. It is the most expensive street in the United States on which to rent office space, outdoing Fifth Avenue in Manhattan.

Down the long slide of Sand Hill toward Stanford University. The Hayward Ridge was illumined beyond the bay, clouds mounded over its buff and oak. I was feeling the day's long walk in my hips, but was buoyed by the prospect, the likelihood, of finishing my journey. Past Sharon Park Drive, where my grandparents used to live, and the shopping center that held the bakery from which my grandfather used to bring us pastries some mornings in a perfect white box, and the gas station where I ran out of gas twenty feet from the pump and had to push the open door with the attendant to roll the rest of the way. The red trim of Stanford University's buildings appeared down Sand Hill. There was a sign for Stanford Hospital, where I was born. Through the intersection with Santa Cruz Avenue, I met the Stanford Golf Course. A woman on the fourth tee, a par three, carved a hefty divot with her first swing, a mulligan. On her second attempt, she shot her ball into the San Francisquito Creek, which is nothing to be ashamed of, and I was well reminded of doing the same and of collecting hundreds of golf balls, of all stripe and color and sponsorship, from the brush and flowing creek while playing the rare round with my dad. Finding those pointless things was as exciting, for me, as the actual play.

I LEFT SAND HILL AND its heavy traffic then, choosing to stay on the west side of the San Francisquito Creek. For some reason, this decision felt right and important, as if the Portolá expedition would have been unlikely to have crossed the creek, too much work. I strolled down Oak Avenue in Menlo Park, relaxing into a dense and leafy neighborhood with modest three- and four-bedroom homes that have at least doubled in price in the last ten years and, in some cases, decupled—a tenfold increase—over the last twenty, selling now for north of $1.5 million.

The first house on the street was 1985 Oak Avenue, with a red terra-cotta roof and a cotton ghost still lingering, floating, in a tree. 1985: the year after I was born.

Next was 1975 Oak Ave: the year twenty thousand Vietnamese refugees were relocated to Camp Pendleton as the war ended, where they resided in tents. And 1965, a rugged front yard with a sprawling Monterey pine that had sifted down a mess of needles: the year Marquette Frye was pulled over in Watts and riots ensued.

I passed 1955, with a lovely rose garden along the driveway: Disneyland opened its gates this year. 1945: the year the United Nations was established in San Francisco. 1935, a basketball hoop with lichen flourishing on its backboard's lower edge: the year San Diego held the California Pacific International Exposition, the year Amelia Earhart flew from Hawaii to California, and one year before the San Francisco–Oakland Bay Bridge opened.

Past 1925: the year after the population of Los Angeles reached a million. 1915, an octopoid succulent set in rocks: the year the Hetch Hetchy Railroad was begun so that the dam could be built and the reservoir could supply San Francisco, though it would inundate a glacial valley comparable to Yosemite, and the year a transcontinental call was made by Alexander Graham Bell in New York to Thomas Watson in San Francisco. 1905: the year before the earthquake and its firestorm, and the year the *San Francisco Chronicle* published a baseless series accusing Japanese immigrants of debauchery, crime, and economic disease, which inspired a Japanese and Korean Exclusion League that grew to eighty thousand members.

1895, a GMC Yukon XL hogging most of the drive: the year the state's Bureau of Highways was created, a bureau that shortly determined that "the conditions of highways in California today is the result of generations of neglect and apathy." 1885: the year three Hawaiian student-princes had seventeen-foot-long boards hewn, in a royal shape, of redwood and rode them at the mouth of the San Lorenzo River in Santa Cruz, the first surfing in California. 1875, a Japanese maple, a scattering of red-orange star-shaped leaves: the year the Cahuilla tribe of the Coachella Valley was relocated to a reservation in the town of Anza in Riverside County.

1865: the Civil War ended; seventeen thousand Californians had joined the Union Army, the most per capita of any state. 1855, the rapid chipping or trill of a dark-eyed junco, which nests in cups of grass low to the ground: the year the first tourists visited Yosemite, and the year the state legislature outlawed the sale of firearms and ammunition to Native Americans while white settlers waged a "war of extermination" against them in Humboldt County; also the year that William Mulholland was born. 1825, an old-fashioned letter box hanging by the door: four years after Mexican independence, San Diego became the unofficial capital of Alta and Baja California on the whim of Governor José María Echeandía, even as the institution of its presidio began to crumble.

1815, a newspaper on the driveway with the headline of "A Case of Bullying" legible through its diaphanous sack, and a swarm of gnats over a hedge: epic rains flooded the pueblo of Los Angeles, forcing it to relocate to higher ground, and the Los Angeles River jumped its channel and found a new outlet to the ocean twenty miles to the west. 1805, a San Jose Sharks hockey decal on a Nissan sedan: the year the Lewis and Clark Expedition reached the Pacific.

1795, pink oleander petals: more than two hundred Costanoan made a mass escape from Mission Dolores in San Francisco. 1785, a picket fence, a man dutifully organizing his garage: the year the medicine woman Toypurina launched a foiled revolt at Mission San Gabriel in protest against a ban on Native ceremonies, among other cruelties. 1775, a pile of ornamental pumpkins by the threshold: the year the Kumeyaay at Mission San Diego revolted, burning the mission and slaying one of its padres, and so delaying the founding of Mission San Juan Capistrano for a year. In the interim, its bells were buried on the spot for safekeeping.

1765, its house number backlit beside a red door: the year ambitious José de Gálvez, the "second Hernán Cortés," arrived in New Spain as the visitor general, setting in motion Portolá's journey into Alta California four years later.

All of this history, or a history just like it, lies behind the average neighborhood.

ONTO OLIVE STREET, ONTO Bay Laurel Drive, onto Oak Creek Drive, which shadowed the San Francisquito. The creek was dry cobble and chunks of concrete. Bay laurel sprouted from its embankments, and California walnut and young redwood, buckeye and invasive mimosa, eucalyptus: all the characters. In places a guardrail kept you from falling off the earthen banks, and here and there sandbags were piled to shore up the creek's edge. Houses and driveways lined the street's other side just as on Oak Avenue, only slightly grander. Costansó wrote that this creek "flowed precipitously" from the mountains, but all I could see, since the wet season had only just begun, were the first emergent puddles: the water table beginning to rise.

The San Francisquito Creek drains approximately ten miles of the eastern ridge of the Santa Cruz Mountains from the heights of Portola Valley to just north of Woodside. Bozzo Gulch, Neils Gulch, and Bull Run Creek run into Sausal Creek, one of the streams I know best in this world. Sausal joins Corte Madera Creek, Alambique Creek, and Westridge Creek in Searsville Lake, a reservoir in the Jasper Ridge Biological Preserve. Which joins Dry Creek to form the San Francisquito, which I walked down into now, stepping around a guardrail, since its bed was mostly empty.

The Portolá expedition camped along the San Francisquito Creek for five nights, from November 6 through 10, 1769, about a league from the bay according to Crespí. "The white oaks here have a great many large ripe acorns," he wrote, "now fallen, of which everyone has gathered a good deal, being, as we are, now in considerable want of provision, so that for days past the soldiers have been getting by on no more than a griddle cake." So many acorns lay for the taking, Crespí reported, that "the ground could not be seen." What he doesn't share, Costansó does: "Our men, being without meat or seeds, tried the acorns, but most of them suffered great injury to their health, [and had] indigestion and fever." You have to leach the toxic tannins from acorns, as everyone else in California at the time knew. An intimidating amount of nutty bear scat was also seen. On November 7, Sergeant Ortega and his scouts were dispatched to the south, given four days' time to round the bay and explore the far side of this formidable "inlet." The rest of the expedition cooled its heels, and some of the other soldiers apparently headed toward the bay and probed its vast marshes etched with lakes, lagoons, and tidal channels, and dotted with "countless fowl, ducks, geese, cranes, and other kinds; while the miriness of the aforesaid lakes and small inlets makes getting past them very toilsome."

Scrub jay: intruder, intruder! Willows hemmed the channel, which had the feel of a sunken, single-lane road. Several road reflectors were even strewn on the cobble, like those from the shoulders of Highway 1 in Big Sur. An empty gallon water bottle, much like the one I had carried needlessly up San Carpoforo Creek, was suspended in poison oak. I found a bike with no tires, just the frame, victimized. Someone had told me on my trip, and I can't remember who or where, that the homeless were a "problem" in the San Francisquito Creek near Palo Alto and it might be unsafe to camp there. Those words had wormed into my head. But this looked doable, though buggy. There was no horizon. All I could see were banks, trees, the sky; banks held by concrete, by chicken wire over riprap, and by English ivy.

A yellow-rumped warbler landed on the rim of a culvert and drank from its mouth, as the cylinder made tympanic sounds from the vibrations of cars where a road crossed it, I thought, and carried the faint calls and laughter of children and even of birds from its other opening, who knows where. Up ahead I heard the rumble and whistle of a Caltrans train, so I knew I was nearing the park I wanted to find. I climbed out on the convenient ladder of the culvert's poured concrete, and as I climbed, I came face to face with two banana slugs on the bank's humus, hermaphrodites together in a mating circle: a yin-yang, all of one slimy cadmium yellow, their heads sweeping back and forth as they caressed and nipped each other.

It was three o'clock in the afternoon. A person was sleeping behind a log between the creek and the bike path, half in a sleeping bag. Tepee nearby, old boots. A Macy's Men's Store across the street in the Stanford Shopping Center. I had surfaced to the final hundred yards of Sand Hill, and a minute later I was standing at the intersection of Sand Hill and El Camino Real, the royal road of the missions. *Walk, walk, walk,* said the crossing sign, so I did, over El Camino to a short diagonal spur of Palo Alto Avenue, which quickly becomes Alma Street, just blocks from downtown. *Alma* means "soul" in Spanish. The railroad crossing started to flash and ring like the bells in a church tower swinging in the sun, and the bar came down between me and the tracks as the engine left the station an eighth of a mile off. Purple and silver, the commuter rail, Caltrans, accelerated with its passengers seated in both directions. Through the tinted windows, some were watching the landscape recede like time itself as they sped toward San Francisco. When the bars raised, I stepped across the tracks, turned left on a bike path, and found myself below an ancient but unassuming redwood tree. You can walk right up to it.

EL PALO ALTO, "THE TALL TREE," is the redwood that the Portolá expedition is said to have made camp below when they arrived on November 6, 1769. It's debatable, and I believe unlikely, that the expedition actually camped or convened under, or even beside, this particular *Sequoia sempervirens*. The diaries make no mention of a redwood or "savin-like" tree, only that they camped along San Francisquito "in the plain of white oaks." Padres Francisco Palóu and Pedro Font, in their respective diaries of 1770 and 1776, do mention a soaring redwood on this creek, but they make no mention of it having a twin trunk—a second tree of equal size sprouting from its base—which today's El Palo Alto did have until 1886, when a storm and high creek waters toppled it. In 1770, Font wrote, "I beheld in the distance a tree of immense stature rising above the plain of oaks like a grand tower." According to his and other early accounts, you could see this redwood from hills as far north as Belmont or possibly San Bruno, a distance I had walked over the course of two days. Meanwhile, Palóu describes a singular redwood a hundred paces downstream from a grove of them. So there were numerous, with one rising above the rest. At just over 110 feet tall, however, our El Palo Alto doesn't threaten any records: coast redwoods are often more than 300 feet tall. On Font's 1776 map, the earliest map drawn of the Bay Area, El Palo Alto is illustrated as a landmark, but once again it's a solo mast, not a pair.

Nonetheless, the El Palo Alto that stands off Alma Street is an old, handsome specimen and a rugged survivor, one that has shouldered the weight of these associations for well over a century. Palóu erected a wooden cross under his Palo Alto about a day's ride from San Francisco, where he thought a mission should be. Juan Bautista de Anza located this cross, but ultimately thought the creek was too unreliable in summer, so he moved the planned mission south to Santa Clara. The 1769 expedition did camp just about here on the creek, and they would have seen and admired the standout redwood that these other padres later wrote of. Crespí himself wrote that the camp at San Francisquito was "a grand spot, this, for a very large plenteous mission." So I wanted to see this Palo Alto, to imagine that Portolá, Crespí, and Costansó had spotted this tree, or one just like it, from afar and then placed their hands on it and felt something powerful if not divine.

I put my hand on El Palo Alto and felt its soft-scratchiness. Its rufous bark was airy as fiberglass insulation. Had I come all this way for this single tree, a legend I had never seen before though I grew up less than ten miles from it? Is this how one discovers one's own home, by starting at a great distance and then slowly returning, spiraling in? The tree's folds ran upward like taffy stretched thin as the bole tapered and disappeared into radial, persistent green. Two jumbo branches, thick hulking granddaddies, emerged at right angles about fifteen feet overhead. They were the sort of limb a marbled murrelet might nest on if only they had more moss and forest around them instead of a metropolis. From these limbs, girthy offshoots rose vertically, one of them about eighteen inches in diameter—a tree in its own right. Two hundred fifty years after the Portolá expedition, this tree is now 1079 years old. Dendrochronological cores show it was a seedling in the year 940.

That this El Palo Alto and other redwoods grew here at all, in these clayey and warm bay lands, seems a miracle, or at least a low-odds propagation. Redwoods love canyons laced with fog, not inland flatlands that reach ninety degrees in summertime, as Palo Alto does. Crespí himself complained of a sudden heat: "On reaching this spot we noted the days as being all very clear, without the fogs that we had had most days on the coast; here we had some sunshine so hot it could not be borne." But the climate, in general, was cooler a quarter millennium ago during the "Little Ice Age." And redwood cones still swirl down from the mountains on the San Francisquito's tributaries. I'd like to think that this particular cone fell off a redwood near my family's home in Portola Valley and caromed into Sausal Creek, into the San Francisquito, from which it eventually sloshed over this bank and sprouted under an umbrella of other plants. Then it overtook them. Its genes were suited for the outlier conditions of this place, a place we now called Palo Alto thanks to those genes. I would like to think that the origin of Palo Alto, and all that's arisen from it since, existed in a teensy seed, in a cone, just over a millennium ago out my back door.

The tree is California State Landmark No. 2. (No. 1 is an 1827 Mexican Custom House in Monterey.) In 1850, it was used to help route the official El Camino.

A quarter century later, Leland Stanford named his ranch the Palo Alto Stock Farm. After the tree's twin fell, he ordered the remaining trunk propped up with a bulkhead. He valued it, at least as a symbol. When Stanford turned his farm into a university in honor of his son, who died too young, the redwood became the school's emblem, a stately and shaggy sign of aspiration. Once first-year students competed to see who could place a flag at the tree's top; sometimes they had to be rescued. When I attended Stanford basketball games as a kid, the tree mascot danced wildly on the court, spinning and kicking during time-outs as the school's irreverent band blared, the student underneath this costume often shirtless and sweating because of the weight of his (or in later years, her) scaffold of PVC and fabric.

I circled the tree. On its "back side," facing the creek, was the stump of another lost bole, a third trunk, smaller and adjoining. It appeared cleanly cut or tidied, perhaps by the Southern Pacific. Leland Stanford's railroad is only a few paces off. THERE IS HELP, read a sign beyond the fence to dissuade troubled high schoolers from stepping onto the tracks. A residue of green graffiti can be seen on this stump: NAIL-GUN, the vandals wrote, which haunts me. But any trace of this faded spray paint will be worn off soon. A banana-slug trail meandered glistening around the corrugated bark of the main tree, and about twelve feet up I found a railroad spike embedded in the trunk. This seemed perfectly natural, necessary even: the history of this tree and its location beside Leland Stanford's tracks are inseparable.

A black irrigation pipe also runs up the tree's back side to misters at its apex, which provide El Palo Alto with a simulated fog, a daily municipal bath. By the early 1900s, a century and a half after Portolá camped near it, El Palo Alto had become rather imperiled: wells outcompeted its shallow roots, and passing trains billowed soot onto its needles. Its canopy grew sickly and died back significantly. Yet the tree lived. It lived to see cleaner trains and, at least locally, wiser water use, and its canopy has returned. The City of Palo Alto very much values and babies this tree now. In recent years its trunk has been scanned with radar in search of rot, and an "air spade" has pumped compressed air through its soil, unpacking the earth around its roots. The tree has been treated for termites; its base has been enriched with mulch; dead or dying wood, including its crown, has been trimmed so that the rest will thrive. The tree is fifty-two feet shorter than it was in 1814.

On the night of November 10, Sergeant Ortega and his scouts reappeared and offered their report to Portolá: they had followed the bay all the way south and there discovered "a full-flowing river," the Guadalupe, so difficult to cross they had to use a downed tree for a bridge while the mules swam. Since the whole bay was skirted with lakes and sloughs, it was, Crespí relayed with understatement, "hard going because of the great miriness." What's more, Ortega finally had encountered some resistance from the East Bay's Miwok, the first they had experienced, really, in all of California. "The folk upon the other side of the inlet seemed wild and would pay no attention to anything," Crespí wrote, "and that they [the scouts] had spent about an hour stopping with one single heathen, in order to pacify him." Costansó put it more bluntly: "They said the whole country which they had gone over to the northeast and north was impassable . . . more than all, because of the fierceness and evil disposition of these people, who received them very badly and tried to prevent them from going on."

From the crest of the San Leandro or Berkeley Hills, which rise above the bay's eastern shore, the scouts had seen San Pablo Bay to the north and looked inland to Suisun Bay and the Sacramento River Delta, all of which made them speculate, rightly, that it would take weeks to circumvent such a waterway, if it was even possible. The next morning, Governor Portolá circulated a formal, written request for an officers' meeting about "what decision to take in view of the report given by the scouts." The padres were again invited to attend and advise. The officers voted in writing, Costansó details, "and resolved to return in search of the port of Monterey which they knew . . . must lie behind them." That very afternoon the expedition began to retrace its path, moving camp two leagues back along their trail to the vicinity, I would venture, of Jasper Ridge or Woodside. Right back up Wall Street.

But I had only just arrived. For another angle on this famous redwood, I walked onto the pedestrian bridge across San Francisquito, which unites the two halves of Alma. A man with a tawny greyhound, its ears erect and pointed, crossed and strolled through the parklet without glancing at the totemic tree. Their usual afternoon walk? I thought of the generations of insects, spiders, avians, and humans who had used this redwood, or just ignored it. The bank and the tree, and especially the train trestle, were supported by a gently curved and slanted concrete retaining wall streaked with algae. Its foundation was piled with redwood needle that had slid down its side. PALO ALTO, 1908 was imprinted in the concrete. On the downstream cobble lay the obligatory shopping cart as well as a neon-green SLOW sign, the kind that is shaped like a cartoonish pedestrian and stands upright, with a red cap and pennant flag. You see them at school crosswalks; this one had been swept off some Menlo Park or Palo Alto street into the San Francisquito. That's right, I thought to myself: it's time to give up this journey and lie down.

I sprawled out below El Palo Alto and peered up through its branches. The tree was a complex ladder that might live another thousand years. I felt the pricks of the needles beneath me through the salty long-sleeve shirt I'd worn almost every day since the San Mateo Campground beside Camp Pendleton. Each needle was like a reminder of the past pressed into my back as I stared forward, upward, into the present and future. Each year, El Palo Alto sends out tender lime-green shoots of about six inches in length and adds two rings to its heart: the pale, wide band of spring and early summer; the dark, thin band of dry fall. Now the tree's canopy, capturing sunlight and throwing shade, was healthier, more robust, than it had been in a long time. I would lie beneath El Palo Alto one more minute. Then I would get up and walk the six miles back to Portola Valley, where my mother will have set out candles, like tarmac lights, along the driveway to guide my arrival and final steps. It will have been the longest day of my expedition, twenty-five miles or so. Not quite a marathon.

"Today November 11th," Crespí wrote, "Saint Martin's Day, in the afternoon, we came head about astern, in search of the harbor of Monte Rey. May God let us find it; if not, it would a great mischance for this entire Expedition." But I was never looking for Monterey, or any harbor. There was the movement of a chestnut-backed chickadee as it climbed the tree's rungs, probing—a bird whose back seems to borrow from the *colorado* of redwood. The chickadee hung from a cone, its shoulders pointed toward me and my binoculars on the ground far below. It was searching for bugs, and perhaps extracting and eating seeds that might have become a giant redwood; alternate histories were being extinguished or promoted as I watched. Across the park's path, a handful of other adolescent redwoods lined the creek. These were El Palo Alto's progeny. Lying on my back, I spoke into my recorder: "Calls of birds in the canopy, and the whistle of the referee in the soccer game in the park across the street. Anna's hummingbird, raspy."

ACKNOWLEDGMENTS

THANKS TO JACK SHOEMAKER, JENNIFER ALTON, Jenefer Shute, Alisha Gorder, Jordan Koluch, Sarah Brody, Katie Boland, and the rest of the Counterpoint team for their belief in and care with this book. Thanks also to Colin Webber for his wonderful maps, and to Sam Stoloff for his early and important help. Many thanks to my family, especially Sarah, for their support and patience as I walked this distance, and then rewalked it many times over in the writing. Among the many sources I referenced to produce this book, I am indebted especially to the late Alan K. Brown's translation of Juan Crespí's journals, *A Description of Distant Roads* (San Diego State University Press, 2001), and his thorough introduction therein. Finally, thanks to the Californians who gave their time and spoke with me, a bearded stranger, on my journey up the coast. Your kindness and honesty eased the miles.

ADDITIONAL SOURCES FOR QUOTED MATERIAL include:

Adams, Kathleen M. "Public interest anthropology, political market squares, and re-scripting dominance: from swallows to 'race' in San Juan Capistrano, CA." *Journal of Policy Research in Tourism, Leisure, and Events* 3, no. 2 (2011): 147–169.

Castillo, Edward D., ed., trans. "The Assassination of Padres Andrés Quintana by the Indians of Mission Santa Cruz in 1812: The Narrative of Lorenzo Asisara." *California History* 68, no. 3 (1989): 120–124.

Castillo, Elias. *A Cross of Thorns: The Enslavement of California's Indians by the Spanish Missions*. Fresno, CA: Craven Street Books, 2015.

Cooper, Ellwood. *Forest Culture and Eucalyptus Trees*. San Francisco: Cubery & Co., 1876.

Costansó, Miguel. "Diary of the Portolá Expedition, 1769–70." Santa Clarita Valley Historical Society. scvhistory.com/scvhistory/costanso-diary.htm.

Engelhardt, Zephyrin. *San Luis Rey Mission*. San Francisco: James H. Barry Co., 1921.

Geiger, Maynard J., ed., trans. *Palóu's Life of Fray Junípero Serra*. Washington, D.C.: Academy of American Franciscan History, 1955.

Harrington, John P. "The Soul's Journey to Similaqsa." In *December's Child: A Book of Chumash Oral Narratives*, ed. Thomas C. Blackburn. Berkeley: University of California Press, 1975.

Heizer, Robert F., and Albert B. Elsasser, eds. "Original Accounts of the Lone Woman of San Nicolas Island." In *Aboriginal California: Three Studies in Culture History*. Berkeley: University of California Press, 1963.

Hewes, Minna and Gordon Hewes, eds., trans. "Indian Life and Customs at Mission San Luis Rey: A Record of California Life Written by Pablo Tac, an Indian Neophyte [Rome, ca. 1835]." *The Americas* 9, no. 1 (1952): 92–106.

Jeffers, Robinson. *The Selected Poetry of Robinson Jeffers*. Edited by Tim Hunt. Stanford, CA: Stanford University Press, 2001.

Palmer, Christine Savage. "New Deal Adobe: Fred Hageman's Architectural Research and Reconstruction of Mission La Purisima Concepcion." *Southern California Quarterly* 74, no. 1 (1992): 39–54.

Sal, Hermenegildo. Letter of September 25, 1791. Bancroft Manuscripts, California State Provincial Records, C-A 54, 270. The Bancroft Library, University of California, Berkeley.

Saunders, Charles Francis, and Fr. St. John O'Sullivan. *Capistrano Nights*. New York: Robert M. McBride & Co., 1930.

Sproul, Christopher A. "Public Participation in the Point Conception LNG Controversy: Energy Wasted or Energy Well-Spent?" *Ecology Law Quarterly* 13, no. 1 (1986): 73–153.

Steinbeck, John. *East of Eden*. New York: Viking Press, 1952.

Tibesar, Antonine, ed. *Writings of Junípero Serra*. 4 vols. Washington, D.C.: Academy of American Franciscan History, 1955.

Photo courtesy of the author

NICK NEELY holds an MA in literature and environment from the University of Nevada, Reno, and MFAs in nonfiction and poetry from Hunter College and Columbia University. He is a recipient of PEN Northwest's Boyden Wilderness Writing Residency, a UC Berkeley–11th Hour Food and Farming Journalism Fellowship, and an AAAS Kavli Science Journalism Award. His first book, *Coast Range*, was a finalist for the John Burroughs Medal for natural history writing. Originally from the San Francisco Bay Area, he now lives in Hailey, Idaho, with his wife, the painter Sarah Bird. Find out more at nickneely.com